THE LOST REVOLUTION

The International Socialism book series (IS Books) aims to make available books that explain the theory and historical practice of working class self-emancipation from below. In so doing, we hope to rescue the main tenets of the revolutionary socialist tradition from its detractors on both the right and left. This is an urgent challenge for the left today, as we seek to rebuild this tradition in circumstances that often downplay the importance of organized revolutionaries.

By reissuing classics of the international socialist tradition, we hope to offer accessible and unique resources for today's generation of socialists.

Other titles in the International Socialism series:

THE LOST REVOLUTION

Germany 1918 to 1923

CHRIS HARMAN

Haymarket Books
Chicago, Illinois

© 1993 and 2017 Chris Harman
First published in 1982 by Bookmarks

This edition published in 2003 and 2017 by
Haymarket Books
P.O. Box 180165
Chicago, IL 60618
773-583-7884
www.haymarketbooks.org
info@haymarketbooks.org

ISBN: 978-1-60846-539-2

Trade distribution:
In the US, Consortium Book Sales and Distribution, www.cbsd.com
In Canada, Publishers Group Canada, www.pgcbooks.ca
In the UK, Turnaround Publisher Services, www.turnaround-uk.com
All other countries, Publishers Group Worldwide, www.pgw.com

This book was published with the generous support of Lannan Foundation
and Wallace Action Fund.

Cover design by Eric Kerl.

Library of Congress Cataloging-in-Publication data is available.

Entered into digital printing November, 2022.

Contents

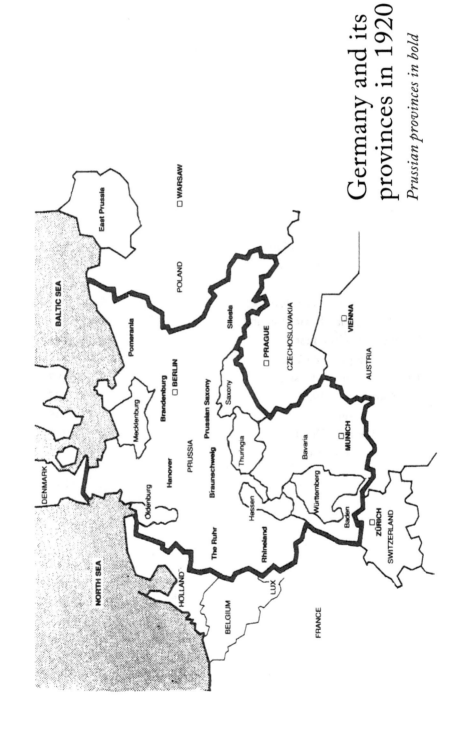

Germany and its provinces in 1920

Prussian provinces in bold

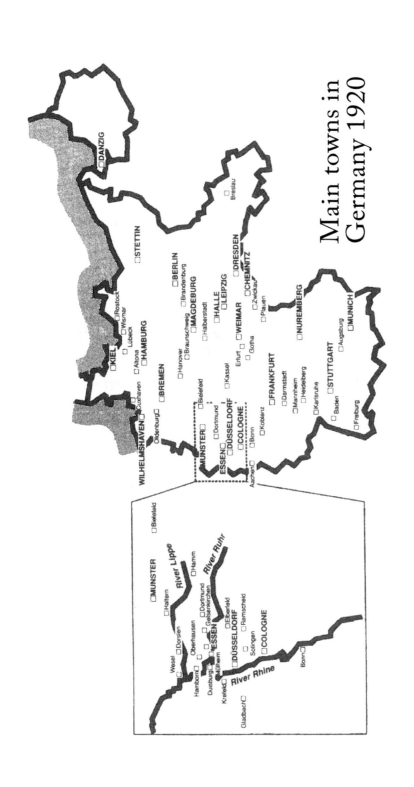

Main towns in Germany 1920

Acknowledgements

I could not have completed this book without help and encouragement from large numbers of people. In particular thanks are due to Alex Callinicos, Tony Cliff, Lindsey German, Pete Goodwin, Donny Gluckstein and Colin Sparks for comments on the manuscript, to Colin Barker for the arduous job of going over it, to Sybil Cock for helping with translations with the German and to Pete Marsden for seeing the final draft through to publication.

Chris Harman (1942–2009) was a leading member of the Socialist Workers Party (UK) and the editor of Socialist Worker newspaper. He is the author of many books, articles and pamphlets, including *A People's History of the World, Class Struggles in Eastern Europe, The Fire Last Time: 1968 and After, Economics of the Madhouse, How Marxism Works* and *Zombie Capitalism.*

Introduction

The Kaiser Alexander Regiment had gone over to the revolution; the soldiers had rushed out of the barracks gates, fraternised with the shouting crowd outside; men shook their hands with emotion, women and girls stuck flowers in their uniforms and embraced them. The officers were being stripped of their cockades and gold lace... Endless processions of workers and soldiers were passing without break along the road... Army lorries passed by with red flags; they bore soldiers and red-ribboned workers, crouching, kneeling or standing alongside the machine guns, all in some fighting attitude, all ready to fire... All the men around the machine guns on the lorries or resting their rifles on their knees in commandeered private cars were manifestly filled with iron revolutionary determination.[1]

The Hotel Escherhaus is now the headquarters of the Red Army. The hotel rooms are stuffed full of red troops... Outside there is constant movement in this disorderly collection of armed men. Sailors, civilians with hardly any sign of the military on them, armed men in uniforms or in 'civilianised' military clothing, with caps, hats or bare heads, with rifles, guns, hand grenades—everything moves around like an ant-heap. Cars constantly arrive with new loads of armed men, while from the other side red soldiers march in, singing... From the front come wounded and exhausted Red Guards.[2]

No elegant gentleman or well-to-do lady dared show themselves in the streets. It was as if the bourgeoisie had vanished from the surface of the globe. Only workers—wage slaves—were to be seen. But they were seen with arms... It was an unprecedented sight: a throng of armed proletarians in uniform or working clothes, moving in endless columns. There must have been 12,000 to 15,000 armed men... The meeting outside the palace presented a picture familiar from May Day demonstrations—yet how different the spirit...[3]

Revolutions that are defeated are soon forgotten. They become lost from view; footnotes to history, glossed over by all but a few specialist historians. The eyewitness accounts above, of events in three different German cities, bear testimony to a great revolutionary upheaval. And, despite similarities with what was happening at the same time in Russia, thousands of kilometres to the east, they show an upheaval in the heart of an advanced industrial society, in Western Europe. Sufficient to prompt the British prime minister Lloyd George to write to the French premier Clemenceau: 'The whole existing order, in its political, social and economic aspects, is questioned by the masses from one end of Europe to the other'.[4]

Without an understanding of the defeat of the revolutionary movements of Germany after the First World War, the Nazism that followed cannot be understood. The great barbarism that swept Europe in the 1930s arose out of the debris of defeated revolution. The road which led to Buchenwald and Auschwitz began with little known battles in Berlin and Bremen, Saxony and the Ruhr, Bavaria and Thuringia in 1919 and 1920. The swastika first entered modern history as the emblem worn in these battles by the counter-revolutionary troops.

Not only in Germany did the lost revolution leave its imprint. Germany was the world's second industrial power at the close of the First World War. What happened there was bound to affect decisively the whole of Europe, and in particular what happened to the revolutionary state just created in Russia, within easy marching distance of Germany's eastern boundaries.

The leaders of revolutionary Russia knew only too well that in the miserably backward conditions of Russia it was not possible to create the kingdom of plenty that Marxists had always seen as the material precondition for the ending of class society. They looked to *international* revolution to relieve Russia's backwardness.

When news reached Russia in early November 1918 of the fall of the German monarchy, one witness, Karl Radek, tells how:

> Tens of thousands of workers burst into wild cheering. Never have I seen any like it again. Until late in the evening workers and Red Army soldiers were filing past. The world revolution had come. The mass of people heard its iron tramp. Our isolation was over.[5]

The expectations of world revolution were to prove wrong. The years 1918 to 1924 saw empires fall—in Germany and Austria-Hungary as well as Russia. They saw workers' councils rule in Berlin and Vienna and Budapest as well as in Moscow and Petrograd. They saw some of the biggest strikes in British history, guerrilla war and civil war in Ireland, the first great national liberation movements in India and China, the occupation of the factories in Italy, bitter, bloody industrial struggles in Barcelona. But it was a period which ended with capitalist rule intact everywhere except Russia.

A central argument of this book will be that this was *not* inevitable. But it happened. And having happened, it undercut all the premises on which the Russian Revolution was based.

'Without the revolution in Germany, we are doomed,' Lenin declared in January 1918. Doom struck in a way that Lenin had not expected. He had thought that an isolated Soviet Russia would eventually collapse under the sheer pressure of hostile forces from outside. These it survived—but only at enormous cost, as isolation produced economic devastation and economic devastation led to the closure of all the great factories, bringing appalling hardship and starvation to cities and villages alike. Above all it led to the disintegration of the industrial working class that had made the revolution in 1917. The Bolsheviks who had led the workers in 1917 were forced to change from being the representatives of the working class to being a sort of Jacobin dictatorship acting in their place. And in a backward country pushed still further backward by long years of world war and long years of civil war, a new bureaucratic dictatorship could all too easily crystallise out of that revolutionary dictatorship.

Isolation begat devastation and devastation begat bureaucracy, bringing a new form of class rule. To tell that story would take us right away from the theme of this book.[6] But the crucial point is that the starting point for the process of degeneration of the Russian Revolution lay outside Russia. Stalinism, as much as Nazism, was a product of the lost German Revolution.

There is another reason for looking at the defeat of the revolutionary movement in Germany. Since 1968 the world has entered a new period of revolutionary explosions: France in 1968, Chile in 1972-73, Portugal in 1974-75, Iran, Nicaragua and El Salvador in 1979-80. In each of these the force which was central to the events in Germany in 1918-23, the industrial working class, played a key role.

A knowledge of what happened in Germany, of the mistakes made by the revolutionaries and of the manoeuvres made by their opponents, throws useful light on what is happening in the world today. It is no accident that so many of those who argue over the possibilities of working class revolution in the world today—whether American liberals such as Barrington Moore[7], former Communist militants such as the Spaniard Fernando Claudin[8], or the revolutionary socialists of every country—refer for evidence to the events of the lost revolution.

The aim of this book is to present the history of the period in a readily accessible form to an English speaking audience. It is for all those who are—like myself before I started work on the book—frustrated by the need to pull together a fragmentary knowledge of the German Revolution out of a plethora of different sources, some out of print and many of the best only available in German or French. This is not an 'original' work, in the sense of breaking new academic ground. I think, however, it will be useful for those who recognise that you need to understand history in order to change it.

One final point. This is not one of those works in which the author makes an unsuccessful attempt to hide his own 'prejudices'. I write from a standpoint of sympathy with those who fought desperately to make the German Revolution a success—for the very simple reason that I believe the world would be an immensely better place had they not been defeated.

1.   Theodor Wolff, *Through Two Decades* (London 1936), quoted in H C Meyer, *Germany from Empire to Ruin* (London 1973) p77.

2.   *Buersche Zeitung*, 4 March 1920, quoted in Erhard Lucas, *Märzrevolution 1920* vol 1 (Frankfurt 1973) p64.

3.   *Mitteilungsblatt*, Munich, 23 April 1919, quoted in Richard Grunberger, *Red Rising in Bavaria* (London 1973).

4.   Quoted in E H Carr, *The Bolshevik Revolution* vol 3 (London 1966) p136.

5.   Karl Radek, quoted ibid, p102.

6.   For one account, see Alan Gibbons, *Russia: How the Revolution was Lost*, Socialist Workers Party pamphlet (London 1980).

7.   See for example, J Barrington Moore, *Injustice: The Social Bases of Obedience and Revolt* (London 1978).

8.   See for example, Fernando Claudin, *Eurocommunism and Socialism* (London 1978).

CHAPTER 1

Before the storm

Social upheavals do not begin because political organisations summon them. Governments and oppositions alike usually fear the unleashing of the passions of the masses. If the state is torn asunder, it is because the very development of events confronts millions of people, peripheral to the old political institutions, with no choice but to change things.

Germany in the summer of 1914 was apparently the most stable of societies. Two forces contended for the allegiance of the population: the Prussian state and the million strong Social Democrat Party (SPD). Each regularly abused the other, and on occasions engaged in carefully restricted forms of direct action against its antagonist. Neither recognised the legitimacy of the other. Yet neither thought seriously of upsetting the stable framework within which they both operated, a framework whose main components had endured for nearly half a century without serious challenge, and which the state and social democracy alike assumed would circumscribe their actions into the indefinite future.

The German state

The German state was not a conventional bourgeois democracy. In Germany, unlike France, the middle class had not fought an all out battle to bring power into its own hands, and after its miserable failure in 1848 it had meekly subordinated itself to the Prussian monarchy. The result was a compromise in which the old monarchic structure continued, but adapted itself increasingly to serve the ends of big business. Concessions were made to the middle classes—and in a very limited form to the working class—but the state machine continued to be run by the Prussian landowning aristocracy, a governing class whose allegiance was to the emperor and not to any elected parliament.

This compromise involved a welter of hybrid political institutions. Germany was a unified empire, or *Reich*—yet in addition to the Prussian state (more than half the territory of the empire), there remained a motley patchwork of kingdoms, principalities, free states and free cities, all accepting Prussian rule, but each with its own local powers and distinct political structures. The empire had a parliament, the *Reichstag*, chosen by male suffrage—but its powers did not go beyond vetoing government bills, and the choice of the government rested with the emperor. Each local state had its own form of 'democracy', in the most important instances involving a restricted franchise based upon a three or four class system of voting; in this the upper class held most of the votes, and those for a parliament whose powers over the hereditary monarchy were severely restricted.

There was freedom of speech, but only within tight limits. The Social Democrats, despite being the largest political party, had been formally banned until the early 1890s, and the law was used with great frequency against the socialist press on one pretext or another in what one study has called 'a policy of persistent guerrilla war against the party by the authorities'.[1] The Social Democrat Max Beer described how, during a 22 month spell as an editor in Magdeburg, he spent, all told, 14 months in prison.[2] Between 1890 and 1912 Social Democrats were sentenced to a total of 1,244 years in prison, including 164 years of hard labour.[3] As late as 1910 the Bremen city senate sacked some school teachers for the heinous crime of sending a telegram congratulating the Social Democrat leader Bebel on his 70th birthday.

The use of police and troops against demonstrations and strikes was frequent—as in 1912 when cavalry used sabres and bullets against striking miners in the Ruhr.

The middle classes had originally been hostile to the Prussian state. But in the 1860s and 1870s Bismarck had used it to advance the interests of German industry and, in the process, won the collaboration of the bourgeoisie. Most of the old liberal opposition to the monarchy now swung behind the pro-monarchist National Liberal Party (later the German National People's Party) which took a position on the question of 'subversion' barely distinguishable from that of the Prussian aristocracy. Authentic 'liberal democracy' was a feeble force, and the only other 'bourgeois' opposition was a Catholic party in parts of southern Germany which distrusted the Protestantism of Prussia. By and large, the children and grandchildren of the bourgeois revolutionaries of 1848 were ardent supporters of the empire.[4] In some states, the result was that the regime became *more* illiberal as time passed.

Yet it would be wrong to imagine imperial Germany as a grim, totally oppressive despotism. German capitalism had experienced more than 40 years of sustained economic expansion, overtaking Britain in industrial capacity. A by-product of this success was the state's ability to make economic concessions to the lower classes. Large sections of the population experienced the years before the First World War as a period in which their lives had become a little less burdensome.

Real wages had risen in the 1880s and 1890s from the very low levels of the 1860s and 1870s, even if they stagnated or fell a little after 1900 when 'a minority of workers suffered an actual decrease in their living standards; the majority experienced stability or moderate wage rises.'[5]

One element in Bismarck's attempt to weaken the socialist opposition had been his provision of limited welfare benefits to the working class. There was a general reduction in working hours during the first decade of the 20th century. In many older established industries, employers had reluctantly recognised unions and allowed employees a limited degree of control over their pace of work. And if the working class movement was prevented from exercising its full political clout both nationally and in most of the states, it could still organise, still temper the wilder excesses of those who ran the empire, and thus wield a certain influence in many localities. It might not enjoy the same degree of freedom as its fellows in France or Britain, but it still operated in a markedly more favourable environment than that of the neighbouring Tsarist empire.

German social democracy

Men and women make history. But they do so in circumstances not of their own choosing, in conditions which react back upon them and shape their own behaviour and thinking. That was certainly true of the men and women who built the German working class movement in the last third of the 19th century.

The Social Democratic Party embodied the political aspirations of nearly all organised workers. Its only competitors were a handful of isolated and ineffectual anarchists on the one hand and weak, ineffectual Catholic and yellow unions on the other. The party is usually characterised by historians as being revolutionary in theory, gradualist in practice.

It had originated from two rather different movements within the young working class of the 1860s and 1870s: an openly revolutionary current inspired by Marx and a current inspired by Lassalle, who envisaged winning reforms through a compromise with the Prussian state. But the experience of organising within that state had pushed the two currents together. The Lassalleans, whatever their reformist dreams, had to face the reality that the working class movement was persecuted and its leaders denied any place in national decision making. As for the Marxists, their revolutionary aspirations were tempered by the fact that the state was too powerful to overthrow, thus forcing them to avoid policies of open confrontation.

The whole movement was driven to the expedient of acting as a castout minority within German society, laboriously using every opportunity to build up its strength through those legal means permitted to it by the state. It contested elections, held meetings, sold its newspapers, distributed its propaganda, built up trade unions. But it was never able either to infiltrate its way into the 'corridors of power' nor to storm the buildings through which they ran.

The party activists responded to state persecution by accepting the revolutionary notions argued by the Marxists. In the 1880s the party had declared itself 'revolutionary' with 'no illusions' in parliamentary methods. These notions were embodied in the general declaration of principles (the 'maximum' demands) of the programme adopted by the party at its 1891 Erfurt Congress. At the same time, however, the leeway available in society for the party's operations also influenced the views of its members. They were able to construct powerful institutions, which seemed inexorably to increase in might from year to year. Even if they could not overthrow the state, the socialists could erect their own 'state within the state'. With its million members, its 4.5 million voters, its 90 daily papers, its trade unions and its co-ops, its sports clubs and its singing clubs, its youth organisation, its women's organisation and its hundreds of full time officials, the SPD was by far the biggest working class organisation in the world.

The activists treasured this achievement, and continually searched out ways to develop it further by involving working class people in the party's organisations, even if on the basis of activities that seemed a million miles from the struggle for state power. But decades of working through legal aid schemes and insurance schemes, of intervention in the state run labour exchanges, above all of electoral activities, inevitably had an effect on the party membership: the revolutionary theory of the Erfurt programme came to seem something reserved for May Days and Sunday afternoon oratory, hardly connected with most of what the party actually did.

The scope for forms of action which involved direct clashes with the state was limited. In the 1890s strikes were few and far between, involving only half a million workers in the whole decade (fewer than those involved in strikes in the very non-revolutionary conditions of Britain in the first month of 1979). There was a certain upturn in strike activity in 1905-6, but of the three years that followed, the best historian of German social democracy concludes, 'Not even the most militant revolutionary could discover a concrete opportunity for radical action'.[6]

The Erfurt programme itself had contained a programme of minimum demands as well as the maximum principles. It was these minimum demands that became the real concern of SPD party activists on a day to day basis. The theory of the party came to reflect its practice. The party's leading theorist, Karl Kautsky, author of the Erfurt programme, defended Marxist orthodoxy and gained the title 'the Pope of Marxism'. But for him the goal of revolution was something that had shifted into the indefinite future, an inevitable occurrence to be waited for, but to which it would be quite wrong to try to find a short cut. In the meantime, party members had to commit themselves totally to the decidedly non-revolutionary round of daily party activities. Political lessons did have to be drawn from agitation, but the key lesson was the need to win a majority of votes in elections before socialist change could begin.

The transformation of socialist activity involved in all this was not something imposed on the party by treacherous leaders. It followed from the circumstances in which the membership found themselves. But it did produce within the party an increasing number of activists for whom the daily non-revolutionary routine became the be all and end all. This was especially the case with the band of full time administrators that arose around the collection of finance, the running of election campaigns, the production of newspapers. These people came very much to control the party, especially when the veteran Marxist Bebel handed over the party secretaryship to the administrator Ebert in 1906.

Yet until 1914 there was no real alternative, even for this group, to their continued exclusion from the mainstream of imperial politics, so their experience gave them little reason to jettison Marxist principles. As Schorske has noted:

> So long as the German state kept the working class in a pariah status, and so long as the working class, able to extract a share of the material blessings of a vigorous expanding capitalism, was not driven to revolt, the Erfurt synthesis could hold.[7]

There had been an attempt to revise the party's revolutionary principles at the turn of the century by Eduard Bernstein, a former disciple of Engels. This received substantial sympathy from some party functionaries, especially in southern Germany where there were more opportunities for the Social Democrats to influence local parliaments. But the national leadership soon crushed the 'revisionist' moves.

In the year 1907 the national leadership itself briefly seemed to be turning to the right. After the pro-monarchist parties had won almost all the middle class votes in an election campaign in which a key issue was the German colonisation of South West Africa, a section of the leadership, including Bebel, began to seek justifications in Marxist terminology for 'national defence' and even colonialism. But the formation of a government of all the bourgeois parties, including the 'democratic' ones, soon revealed the isolation of the Social Democrats and took away any possibility of playing parliamentary games. 'Social Democracy returned to the Erfurt policy of pure, but actionless, opposition.'[8]

The Party Centre defended this policy against the left, as well as against the right. It had supported the left in the arguments against Bernstein's 'revisionism'. But when Rosa Luxemburg, the leading figure on the left, under the influence of the strike wave of 1903-6 and the 1905 Russian Revolution, argued that the party should push for mass strikes against the state, she found the national leadership doing its utmost to stop these. And when she returned to the argument again after a new wave of strikes and clashes between the police and demonstrators for the vote in 1910-12, it was the 'Pope of Marxism' himself who took up cudgels against her.

Yet to those who were not privy to all the leadership's internal manoeuvres, the party seemed still committed to socialist revolution. Even Lenin continued to regard Kautsky as a final authority on Marxism right up to the outbreak of the war in August 1914.

The revolutionary left

There were a few individuals within the German working class movement who *were* aware of the inadequacies of the leadership. The most significant was the Polish exile Rosa Luxemburg. But to most SPD activists the left's criticisms seemed rather remote. After all, any activist spent most of his or her life engaged in exactly the routine activities that the bureaucracy extolled. There was little else to do, given the low level of industrial struggle. Even Luxemburg's main activities were not that much different—giving Marxist lectures in the party school, writing for party papers, making propaganda in election campaigns, arguing at internal party meetings and conferences.

Rosa Luxemburg herself certainly felt helpless to change things. The number of people who shared her extreme doubts about the leadership was very small, and she felt they could not get any mass following for their views. Under such circumstances, her greatest fear was that they might become cut off from the mass of workers inside the Social Democratic organisations. Such a separation, she felt, would be the greatest imaginable mistake. So she opposed any notion that the radical wing of social democracy might form an organisation of its own, inside or outside the party. That would make them too easy a target for the party leadership. As one of her biographers records:

> Not even later Communist historians, looking hard for traces of emerging left wing organisation before the war, were able to make any case for the existence of an organised radical group. By temperament as much as necessity, Rosa Luxemburg acted as an individual and on her own behalf.[9]

Instead of organising such a group, the only hope she saw was to wait until a mass, spontaneous upsurge of working class struggle smashed through the complacency of the social democratic apparatus. She wrote to her friend, Clara Zetkin, leader of the social democratic women's movement, in 1907:

> I feel the pettiness and the hesitancy of the party regime more clearly and more painfully than ever before. However, I can't get so excited about the situation as you, because I see with depressing clarity that neither things nor people can be changed until the whole situation has changed—and even then we shall have to reckon with the inevitable resistance of such people if we want to lead the masses on. Our job will take years.[10]

The left was forced to pull itself together a little in the years after 1910, when the revival in the level of working class struggle gave its arguments more significance and when the Party Centre began attacking them seriously. There began to develop in the party a loose network of people who more or less agreed, who would vote together at party meetings and conferences, and who would try to get articles by the leaders of the left into local party papers. The intensification of the debate in the party even led Rosa and her friends to form, towards the end of 1913, a weekly review in which to air their own ideas.

But this was still a long way short of anything like an organised faction. There was no disciplined body of adherents organised around the review, discussing the interrelation between their theory and their practice, establishing criteria for membership. At the first serious test the network was to prove completely inadequate. Some of its members swung immediately to the right; the majority lacked any central direction for intervention and organisation. Nor was this all. Reliance on the Social Democratic Party as the organisation of the working class meant acceptance of its disciplinary norms, to the extent that in 1912 Rosa Luxemburg was prepared to resort to the Party Centre in an effort to drive out a fellow exiled Polish revolutionary, Radek, for alleged breaches of discipline in Warsaw seven years earlier. One byproduct of this episode was to intensify mutual suspicions and hostilities among different sections of the left.

Rosa Luxemburg was a great revolutionary. But there was to be a high price to pay for this failure to draw her followers together into a minimally cohesive force before 1914.

Germany in 1914

On the one hand, the Prussian state, a capitalist state with feudal trimmings, manned by reactionary officials from the landed aristocracy; on the other, the social democratic working class movement, preaching a revolutionary doctrine, very non-revolutionary in practice, with only a small disorganised minority of radicals noticing the contradiction—these were the actors who were to fill the major roles in the great postwar upheavals. But before we see how the drama unfolded, let us briefly examine the stage on which it was played.

Germany in 1914 is usually reckoned to have been an advanced industrial country. So it was—by the standards of the time. It was the world's second industrial power, with huge electrical engineering works in Berlin, giant iron and steel plants of the Ruhr, mines in central Germany and the Ruhr, shipyards and docks at Hamburg and Bremen, and a large textile industry in Saxony. But by today's standards Germany was still relatively backward. A third of the population still lived on the land. The east, an area later mostly incorporated into the USSR and Poland, was dominated by huge landed estates and the south by medium to small, conservative minded peasant farmers. Much of the industry even was not what we would think of today as large scale. Mass production, with its assembly lines and masses of 'semiskilled' workers, was only just getting off the ground, and much production was still by local firms with only a few hundred workers.

Significantly, Germany's largest factory during the period of the revolution, the Leuna works near Halle, had not been built until 1916. Only 1,378,000 out of a total industrial workforce of 11 million worked for firms with more than 1,000 employees.[11] Most workers still lived in towns or even industrialised villages, rather than cities, and remained subject to the pressures of local middle class opinion. It was still the exception rather than the norm for working class women to work in production: in the engineering town of Remscheid a significant proportion still went 'into service'.[12]

This was not a fixed state of affairs. The small firms were being overtaken by the growth of giant cartels and trusts, which began the vertical integration of whole sections of industry. Big factories were replacing small: in Remscheid in 1890, 60 percent of workers were in factories of less than 50 workers; by 1912, 60 percent were in factories of more than 50 workers. New mammoth industrial complexes were developing in which old skills often counted for nothing: three great enterprises in the Ruhr town of Hamborn employed 10,000 workers between them in 1900, and 30,000 in 1913.[13]

All these changes had been taking place for decades without the fundamental structure of German society being threatened. The successful expansion of German capitalism enabled it to make enough concessions to the different sections of the population to ensure decades of social peace. By 1914 revolution seemed the most distant of distant prospects. But the very successes of German capitalism had the inevitable effect of destabilising the international environment in which it existed. British and French capitalism, though weaker economically, had much more powerful global presences, with empires on which 'the sun never set'. Sections of German capital wanted to expand outwards beyond their national boundaries in a similar way. The British and French ruling classes sought to protect their holdings by an alliance with Tsarist Russia against Germany and its allies, Austria-Hungary and the decaying Turkish Empire. Rival imperialisms pushed against each other's influence in Morocco, in East and Southern Africa, in the Middle East, above all in South East Europe. At some point the friction of local forces was bound to produce a spark that would light fuses which ran to the rival imperial centres.

The explosion came when a Serbian nationalist assassinated an Austrian archduke. Austria took punitive action against Serbia; Russia backed the Serbs; Germany rushed to support Austria; France backed Russia; Britain used an 80 year old treaty with Belgium as an excuse to fight alongside France and, hopefully, put Germany in its place. Forty four years of 'peaceful' capitalist expansion turned out to have been the birth period for the most horrendous war known to humanity up until that point. The stable environment which had conditioned the thinking of both the Prussian state and the German working class movement was utterly transformed.

1.   Alex Hall, *Scandal, Sensation and Social Democracy* (Cambridge 1977) p53.
2.   Max Beer, *Fifty Years of International Socialism* (London 1935) p65.
3.   Figures from A Hall, op cit.
4.   A situation well described in Heinrich Mann's novel *Man of Straw* (English translation, London 1972).
5.   G Bry, *Wages in Germany 1871-1945* (Princeton 1960) p74. Compare also A V Desai, *Real Wages in Germany* (Oxford 1968) pp15-16, 35.
6.   C E Schorske, *German Social Democracy 1905-1917* (London 1955) p53.
7.   Ibid, p6.
8.   Ibid, p6.
9.   Peter Nettl, *Rosa Luxemburg* (London 1966) p460.
10.   Paul Frölich, *Rosa Luxemburg* (London 1940) p147.
11.   J Barrington Moore, *Injustice: The Social Bases of Obedience and Revolt* (London 1978) provides a mass of figures—they are about all that is of value in the book. Compare also K H Roth, *Die 'andere' Arbeiterbewegung* (Munich 1974).
12.   Erhard Lucas, *Zwei Formen Arbeiterradikalismus in der Deutschen Arbeiterbewegung* (Frankfurt 1976) p35.
13.   Ibid, pp35-36.

CHAPTER 2

4 August 1914

The class conscious German proletariat raises a flaming protest against the machinations of the war mongers... Not a drop of any German soldier's blood must be sacrificed to the power hunger of the Austrian ruling clique, to the imperialist profiteer.[1]

For our people and its peaceful development much, if not everything, is at stake in the event of the victory of Russian despotism... Our task is to ward off this danger, to safeguard the civilisation and independence of our own country... We do not leave the fatherland in the lurch in the hour of danger.[2]

Ten days separated these two statements from the German Social Democratic Party, ten days which saw Austria's threat to crush Serbia develop into a full scale world war, ten days which began with the organisation by the Social Democrats of 27 anti-war meetings in Berlin alone, and which ended on 4 August with the party's joint president, Hugo Haase, declaring to the Reichstag that his party would be voting for the government's war credits.

Haase himself, together with 13 others out of the SPD's 92 Reichstag deputies, had been opposed in the closed caucus meeting of the party to the vote for war credits. But their belief that the SPD was *the* organisation of the working class led them to abide by its discipline—even in Haase's case to the point of reading out the majority statement. It was not until November that one solitary member, Karl Liebknecht, defied party discipline and showed in public that there was an opposition to the war by voting against the credits.

Outside parliament those who had crowded to the anti-war meetings were either carried away by a tide of wild chauvinism or swept to the margins of political life by its impact. There was frenzied excitement on the streets. Crowds sang patriotic songs. Mad rumours seized hysterical mobs, who went hunting for 'Russian spies' or 'French bomb makers'. Young men could not wait to get to the Front.

The few socialists who continued to oppose the war found themselves isolated and confused, not knowing who agreed with them, half afraid to express their views because of the lynch mob atmosphere and new decrees against 'seditious' statements. Inside the working class organisations, the most chauvinistic elements made all the running. The vote for the war by the SPD deputies was matched by the declaration of a 'social truce' by the unions. Most of those who had doubts about the war kept their heads down, or tried to mouth a distinction between a war of 'national defence' which they were supporting and any expansionist aims, which they would oppose. Those who stood out completely against the war mania among the SPD leaders—Rosa Luxemburg, Clara Zetkin, Karl Liebknecht, the aging Marxist historian Franz Mehring and a handful of others—found themselves without a following or any means of propagating their views.

> Both Rosa Luxemburg and Clara Zetkin suffered nervous prostration and were at one moment near to suicide. Together they tried on 2 and 3 August to plan an agitation against the war; they contacted 20 SPD members with known radical views, but they got the support of only Liebknecht and Mehring... Rosa sent 300 telegrams to local officials who were thought to be oppositional, asking their attitude to the vote [in the Reichstag] and inviting them to Berlin for an urgent conference. The results were pitiful. Clara Zetkin was the only one who immediately and unreservedly cabled support.[3]

They were not even to give public notice of their opposition until September—and then only in a single paragraph in a Swiss paper saying that opposition existed which could not state its views because of martial law. Inside Germany itself, not until Liebknecht voted and spoke out against the war credits in early December was the revolutionary case against the war heard in public:

> This war is not being waged for the benefit of the German or any other peoples. It is an imperialist war, a war over the capitalist domination of the world market... The slogan 'against Tsarism' is being used—just as the French and British slogan 'against militarism'—to mobilise the noble sentiments, the revolutionary traditions and the hopes of the people for the national hatred of other peoples.[4]

Liebknecht's voice was an isolated one. The editors on one or two provincial Social Democratic papers showed some opposition to the war—and were purged from their jobs. Otherwise only a handful of socialists gathered around Luxemburg and Liebknecht. And their members were further decimated by the state: Rosa was soon in prison, and Liebknecht was drafted to the Front, despite being over 40, and then jailed.

But the war itself began to change the popular mood. It dragged on month after month, year after year. Soldiers on leave brought stories of the horrors of trench warfare. The mass enthusiasm for the war began to wilt.

Already early in 1915 Rosa Luxemburg could write:

> The scene has fundamentally changed. The six week march to Paris has become a world drama. Mass murder has become a boring monotonous daily business, and yet the final solution is not one step nearer. Bourgeois rule is caught in its own trap, and cannot ban the spirits that it has invoked... Gone is the ecstasy. Gone are the patriotic street demonstrations, the chase after suspicious looking automobiles, the false telegrams, the cholera poisoned wells. Gone the excesses of a spy hunting population, the coffee shops with their deafening patriotic songs... The show is over... No more do trains filled with reservists pull out amid the joyous cries of enthusiastic maidens. We no longer see their laughing faces, smiling cheerily at the people from train windows. They trot through the streets quietly, with their sacks on their shoulders. And the public, with a disturbed face, goes about its daily tasks.[5]

More than just enthusiasm was being lost. The war was undermining the very conditions that had allowed the working class movement to adapt to the Prussian state for so long.

The economic and social impact of the war

When the war started, the politicians and military commanders on all sides thought it would be over within a matter of months. Schlieffen, the first German chief of staff, thought a long war 'inconceivable'. His successor Moltke was a little more pessimistic: he thought it just 'possible' that the war would last two years. All the government's economic calculations assumed a nine month war.[6] So no provision was made for the economic burden of a war that just dragged on and on, using up undreamt of amounts of munitions, a war in which each side resorted more and more to blockades to try to crack the other's economy.

The problems of waging economic warfare in a conflict having an 'industrial' character had not been even remotely anticipated.[7]

As the rival armies became bogged down in the fields of northern France, the whole German economy had to be raided to keep the war machine going. First to be hit were the living standards of workers. Food supplies slumped, partly because of the blockade, but more importantly because of the conscription of agricultural labour into the forces. By late 1916 the meat ration had fallen to less than a third of the prewar average, the egg ration to a fifth, the bread ration by nearly half, and milk became available only through the black market. The weekly diet of most workers was restricted to four pounds of bread, three ounces of butter, half a pound of meat. Its calorific value—1,313—was half what a normal adult needed.

Things reached an all-time low in the winter of 1916-17 when food distribution to the cities broke down. In the 'turnip winter', elements of the staple diet were replaced—with turnip bread, turnip marmalade, even turnip coffee. Hunger stalked most working class districts. In its train almost any epidemic disease took a fatal toll: the town of Hamborn alone experienced 854 cases of typhus in 1917.

In the space of a few months the German working class found life transformed. Forty years of slow improvement gave way to a nightmare deterioration.

Not only material conditions suffered. Millions of workers had, of course, been conscripted and sent to the Front. Those who remained in the cities found that the tenuous civil rights that had been extracted from the state in the previous decades were torn from them by wartime regulations against sedition. An Auxiliary Labour Law in late 1916 provided for industrial conscription of male workers, tying them to their employers and putting them under military jurisdiction. Conservative circles and industrialists welcomed the law as the first step towards a direct military dictatorship by the new heads of the armed forces, Hindenberg and Ludendorff.

The very fabric of everyday life was transformed by the war. As millions of men were drafted into the forces, they were replaced in the factories by women; until in 1916 the industrial workforce consisted of 4.3 million women and 4.7 million men.[8] The government decided there was no point in imposing industrial conscription on women, because hunger was driving them to seek work in any case. In pits and steelworks in the

Ruhr deported foreigners and prisoners of war became a fifth or even a quarter of the workforce.

The immediate effect of such changes was to increase the confusion within the working class and to weaken its inner organisation. As old activists (no less than three quarters of the male membership of the SPD) were sent to the Front and replaced by new, inexperienced workers, the membership of the social democratic and trade union organisations slumped by more than half.[9] The task of those who wanted to campaign in these organisations against the war remained very difficult, even after the fading of pro-war enthusiasm.

But the cumulative effect of the war economy was to create a greater than ever potential for working class organisation. Germany in 1914 was still, by present day standards, a country of relatively small factories and relatively undeveloped production. Now, government decrees shut down small factories and concentrated production in the largest, most efficient modern plants. In plant after plant the techniques we associate with mass production—the breaking down of individual 'skilled' tasks into a multiplicity of 'semi-skilled' ones—became the norm for the first time.

The backbone of pre-war social democracy had very much been the skilled workers in industries such as engineering, where the unions were strongest. Above all, their experience of rising real wages had provided the material base for the reformism in practice of social democracy. Now inside the factory the skilled workers were under threat from new forms of industrial discipline, even though they were most able to avoid the Front because of their importance to the war industries. What is more, they really felt the impact of the war on living standards. Until 1914, because of differentials, they had found life easier than the unskilled. Now all workers were forced down on the minimum rations needed for physical survival.[10]

The war destroyed many of the links which had bound organised workers together, but at the same time it concentrated the working class into ever larger units of production and created a new uniformity of conditions within the class. If the immediate effect was to make organisation against the war all but impossible, the long term effect was to create a new basis for revolutionary organisation, both among the sectors traditionally influenced by social democracy and among newer sectors, immune to its influence.

The first stirrings

Among a minority of workers loss of enthusiasm for the war began to give way to anger at its results.

In the year 1915 there were once again demonstrations in the streets. But they were no longer the patriotic demonstrations of August 1914. That mood had evaporated. People no longer looked for spies, but for bread. Hunger drove people, especially women, into the streets. In the course of the year there were demonstrations for peace in Berlin. At first a few hundred people took part, and then thousands. These comparatively small numbers signified a great deal at the time, when everyone stood beneath the rod of the military dictatorship.[11]

Some of the demonstrations were more or less spontaneous outbursts by unorganised groups of people, usually women: anger would flare when a shop ran out of food, or put its prices up, or when rations were suddenly cut. There was a rash of such 'demonstrations' in the winter of 1915-16 and again in the following winter, often leading to bitter clashes between 'non-political' workers and the police.

But there were more overtly political demonstrations as well. The change in the popular mood gave new heart to those within social democracy who had opposed the war. At SPD meetings people would demand that the local Reichstag deputy vote against the war credits and that the local party paper carry discussion on the war. For instance, in Bremen in 1915 the left had been only 15 strong and held only private discussions. In the winter of 1915-16 there were aggregate meetings of the local party, with an attendance of up to 1,100 (a quarter of the total membership), where views on the war were openly argued.[12] In Berlin the left was strong enough for the Internationale group of Luxemburg and Liebknecht to call a demonstration on May Day 1916. Liebknecht was arrested as he began to speak to several thousand workers and young people. On the day of his trial 55,000 workers struck in solidarity with him. By now Liebknecht's was no longer a lone voice even in the Reichstag: in December 1915, 19 other deputies had joined him in opposing war credits.

The anti-war feeling was given further impetus by the growing openness of military and industrial circles about their war aims. The preservation of Germany's old frontiers would not satisfy them. They demanded the incorporation into the Reich of Belgium and northern France, the setting up of a puppet government in Poland and 'hegemony' over the other states of Eastern and Central Europe. As Hindenberg and Ludendorff took command of the armed forces (and the war economy) in the summer of 1916, the military and the industrialists were more and more openly running things—even if the government did not itself endorse their aims for fear of upsetting its Austro-Hungarian ally (their aim was for Austria-Hungary to be 'hegemonised').

The arguments of the right Social Democrat leaders about a 'war of national self defence' sounded even more hollow after the collapse of Tsarism in Russia with the February revolution of 1917. 'Russian tyranny' could no longer be presented as a menace—to a growing minority of workers the real menace was seen as the expansionist war policy of the Prussian state and big business.

April 1917 saw a 200,000 strong strike of metal workers against a cut in the bread ration, led by opponents of the war. Spontaneous unrest over food shortages was beginning to merge with political opposition to the war. But only just beginning.

Events in the summer of 1917 and the beginning of 1918 showed both the potential impact of the spontaneously fermenting discontent—*and* the inner political limitations it had yet to overcome.

The class structure of German society found its perfect reflection in the relations of officers and men in the armed forces. The privileges of the officers stood in permanent contrast to the low rations and harsh discipline imposed on the other ranks. At the Front, the camaraderie that came from a common danger often blunted the resulting resentment. Not so in the fleet, which sheltered in the ports of the north west coast for fear of an open confrontation with the British fleet at sea.

> The men slaved and engaged in perpetual drill, but the officers sat about idle, cleaning and polishing their finger nails and combing their hair. The difference between the living conditions of the officers and the men was emphasised by their close proximity on the ships. The crew saw that their superiors ate better food, went ashore whenever they pleased, had special clubs for their entertainment...[13]

Resentment gave way to organisation as food rations were cut to a minimum in the aftermath of the 'turnip winter'. A movement to elect 'food committees' started. The sailors felt they could build something akin to a trade union organisation, and there were hunger strikes and work stoppages in June and July 1917 demanding recognition for such committees. But at the beginning of August the authorities arrested a number of sailors. The crew of one ship took protest action, only to abandon it almost immediately. Their passive trade union notions of action were impotent against the armed might of the state and its military justice. The movement collapsed. Two of its leaders were executed; the others received between them 360 years of hard labour.

The sailors had learnt a bitter lesson the hard way: you cannot take on a military machine with peaceful, 'non-political' protests. They were to remember that lesson 14 months later. But first it had to be learnt by the workers of Berlin.

The January strikes

The growing discontent with the war received a political focus in November 1917. The Bolsheviks established a new power in Russia, based on soviets—councils of workers and soldiers. They offered an immediate armistice to the powers that had been at war with Russia, pending a permanent peace on the basis of 'no annexations and indemnities', exposed the secret treaties that had led to the war, and renounced Tsarist Russia's colonial possessions.

The new government in Russia desperately needed peace. But it did not believe that the rulers of imperial Germany or imperial Austria-Hungary could accept on such terms—they had entered the war because they were economically driven to seize ever greater chunks of the world. What the Bolsheviks did believe, however, was that the appeal for peace would turn people throughout the world—especially in Germany—against their old capitalist governments. Revolution abroad would produce the peace and international assistance needed to secure the rule of the soviets in backward Russia.

Hardly had the revolution been completed in Russia than the Bolsheviks took the first steps towards spreading it abroad. They began producing *The Torch*, a paper for distribution to German soldiers in the trenches on the Eastern Front. Half a million copies of each issue were printed.

The German military establishment saw the Russian offer of peace as a chance to expand the German Empire still further. They sent representatives to negotiate with the Bolsheviks at the town of Brest-Litovsk—and there demanded that a huge area of the former Tsarist empire be converted into nominally independent states which would, in effect, be German 'protectorates'.

But the Russian negotiators were appealing as much to the German workers as the High Command. When Trotsky arrived at Brest-Litovsk in late December 1917 he was accompanied by a Polish-Austrian who had been an active revolutionary in Germany before the war—Karl Radek. 'Radek, before the eyes of the diplomats and officials assembled on the platform to greet them, began to distribute pamphlets among the German soldiers'.[14]

The negotiations at Brest-Litovsk broke down in face of the German demands for annexations and revolutionary Russia had to sit back helpless as German troops advanced. But news of the Bolshevik declarations began to filter through to those discontented with the war in Germany and Austria-Hungary. Karl Liebknecht wrote from his prison cell, 'Thanks to the Russian delegates, Brest has become a revolutionary tribune. It has denounced the Central European powers, the brigandage, the lies and the hypocrisy of Germany'.[15]

In the first fortnight of January the members of a small revolutionary group in Germany, the Spartakus League (formerly the Internationale group), issued leaflets calling for a general strike over the question of peace. More 'moderate' opponents of the war, such as the dissident Social Democrat leader Haase, called for a three day strike.

But just as these preparations were under way, news came of momentous events in the neighbouring Austro-Hungarian Empire. On 14 January the workers at the Daimler works in the Austrian town of Wiener Neustadt struck against a cut in the food ration. At about the same time the workers in the Csepsel munitions works in Budapest walked out. Within two days factories throughout both cities were paralysed. The Austrian social democrats estimated that a quarter of a million workers were on strike in the Vienna region alone.[16]

Nor was that all. In Vienna workers' councils were elected which demanded the abolition of censorship, the end of martial law, the eight hour working day and the release of the imprisoned anti-war socialist Friedrich Adler.

The strike petered out within a week. But it was the biggest protest anywhere yet against the effects of the war. It did not take long for what had happened in German speaking Austria to find an echo in Berlin.

The Spartakus League there put out a leaflet telling how 'the Viennese workers elected councils on the Russian model' and proclaiming 'Monday 28 January the beginning of the general strike'.[17] This call was taken up by an assembly of members of the turners' branch of the metal workers' union. One of the branch officials was the anti-war socialist Richard Müller and, on his proposal, they voted to strike on the Monday and to run the strike through delegates elected at mass meetings.

The German strike had a resoundingly successful beginning. 400,000 workers struck on the first day and were joined the next day by 100,000 more. The movement stretched well beyond the confines of the capital and involved Kiel, Hamburg, Danzig (now Gdańsk), Magdeburg, Nuremberg, the Ruhr, Munich, Cologne, Mannheim and Kassel.[18] At first too the organisation of the strike seemed perfect. 414 factory delegates met in Berlin and appointed an action committee of 11.

But the authorities did not sit back. They broke up the next meeting of the delegates, forbade mass meetings in the factories and occupied trade union buildings. By the Thursday Berlin was plastered with official posters reinforcing the state of siege and announcing extraordinary military courts. There were clashes between strikers and the police, who were joined by 5,000 reinforcements from outside the city. Even the official, pro-war, Social Democrat paper *Vorwärts* was banned by the authorities for 'spreading false information'—they printed the number of strikers.

The clashes left the workers bitter. One of the Spartakist leaders, Jogiches, described how 'after each clash with the police you heard: "Comrades, tomorrow it will be a matter of arms".'[19]

But there were basic weaknesses within the strike movement. The militants leading it had not given much thought as to what to do once it was successful. As Jogiches wrote shortly afterwards, they 'did not know what to do with the revolutionary energy'.[20]

In order to establish the unity of the whole working class in the strike, the action committee had insisted, against some opposition, on three representatives of the pro-war Social Democratic Party joining the committee. But these leaders were only prepared to join for one reason, as they explained several years later. Ebert insisted, 'I joined the strike leadership with the clear intention of bringing the strike to a speedy end to prevent damage to the country'.[21] His colleague Scheidemann added, 'If we had not joined the strike committee, law and order would not now exist here'.[22]

Ebert and Scheidemann went out of their way to introduce confusion into the strike. Ebert, for instance, even defied the law by speaking at a banned meeting—but only to damage the movement in a way the military authorities could never have done themselves by saying, 'It is the duty of workers to back up their brothers and fathers at the Front and to manufacture the best arms... Victory is the dearest goal of all Germans'.[23]

For speaking at this meeting the left socialist Dittmann received a four year prison sentence. Ebert, of course, was not touched.

The Social Democrat leaders took confusion into the heart of the action committee itself. They offered to mediate with the government over the strikers' purely *economic* demands—as if the strikers did not have political motives, however confused these might be. The strike leadership were unhappy with this Social Democrat suggestion, but had no clear alternative. They recognised the war as the crucial issue, even though they had used economic questions to mobilise workers. Yet to end the war they needed revolutionary action as well as strikes—and they had not prepared themselves for this. In the end they found themselves with little choice but to recommend a return to work, despite the massive numbers who had joined the strike.

The government seized the opportunity presented by the resulting demoralisation to decapitate the working class movement. Many strike leaders were arrested, and in Berlin one worker in every ten was sent to the Front. The vanguard of the anti-war movement was physically removed from Berlin's factories.

Like the Kiel sailors the previous summer, the strike was smashed because it attempted to use purely trade union tactics to deal with a question of political and military power. As Jogiches summed it up, 'Because they could not imagine the strike wave as more than a simple protest movement, the committee, under the influence of the Reichstag deputies, tried to enter into negotiations with the government, instead of refusing all negotiations and directing the energy of the masses'.[24]

The left

None of these movements had been directed by a revolutionary organisation. Individual revolutionaries played a key role at certain points. They gave expression to the anger of much larger numbers of workers against the hunger, the low wages and the futile bloodshed of the war. But these workers were not themselves revolutionary socialists nor were they following the discipline of a revolutionary organisation. Most simply wanted a return to pre-war conditions. They still retained a certain faith in the Social Democrat leaders, even while striking against the war that those leaders backed.

The growing discontent had a significant impact on the Social Democratic organisation itself. Even the extreme right wing leaders of the party, such as Ebert, could not stand completely apart from the great strike movements. They knew that to do so would mean losing their influence over the masses—the sole influence which, they thought, could prevent a breakdown of 'law and order'.

The change in the popular mood had an even greater impact on thousands of lower Social Democrat functionaries. Many had not been exactly enthusiastic about the war in 1914. But they were members of a party with millions of pounds of funds, hundreds of union and co-op buildings, dozens of daily papers, hundreds of employees. All, they feared, would be destroyed by repression if the party opposed the widespread pro-war hysteria. It was much easier, as they saw it, to be 'realistic', to go along with the pro-war mood while resisting its worst excesses. So they supported the war, but opposed the demands of the general staff and big business for the annexation of huge tracts of foreign territory.

Trotsky, who was in Vienna when the war broke out, described attitudes within the Social Democratic Party there. What he wrote applied equally in Germany:

> What attitude toward the war did I find in the leading circles of Austrian Social Democrats? Some were quite obviously pleased with it... These were really nationalists, barely disguised under the veneer of a socialist culture which was now melting away as fast as it could... Others, with Victor Adler at their head, regarded the war as an external catastrophe which they had to put up with. Their passive waiting, however, only served as a cover for the active nationalist wing.[25]

This was very much the situation inside the German party. 'Reluctant acquiescence' was rife.

But now that anti-war sentiments were again popular, these people felt it expedient to voice their previously secret doubts. They could do so now without breaking with the mixture of cowardice and careerism that had kept them silent in 1914.

So it was that in 1916 a current developed within the Social Democratic Party in opposition to the pro-war leadership. The mood of rank and file workers who had had enough of the war but did not yet want revolution was matched by many party functionaries who did not like the war either and were as hostile to revolution as they had ever been.

This current became known as the 'centre' or the 'centrists', because of its midway position between the leadership of the party and the revolutionary element around Rosa Luxemburg and Karl Liebknecht. The centre's leaders wanted an end to the war—but they did not want any great social upheaval. They saw peace as coming through 'good faith' within the contending powers, and tended, as the war proceeded, to place their hopes in the policy of the American president, Woodrow Wilson. They were careful to keep their distance from the slogans of the Spartakists: 'The enemy is at home. Peace through socialist revolution'. They insisted they did not believe in 'seditious' acts, such as advising the sailors to mutiny. The most they were prepared to do was to operate as a parliamentary group distinct from the right within the SPD.

But the bureaucratic leadership of the SPD was not prepared to tolerate any opposition to its pro-war policies, even this half-hearted opposition. It seized from the oppositionists newspapers under their influence—most importantly the Berlin daily, *Vorwärts*—and then expelled the minority en bloc early in 1917, forcing them to form a party of their own, whether they wanted to or not. The Independent Social Democratic Party (USP or simply the 'Independents') was born.

This was by no means a revolutionary party. Its leaders were united by only one thing—their desire for an end of the majority Social Democratic Party's support for the war. Over most other things there was the same range of differences that had existed inside the SPD. Some were for revolution, others for reform, most preferring to speak in revolutionary language and to act in a reformist manner. Some wanted a negotiated end to the war, others spoke of turning the war into a civil war.

Characteristically, the party was joined by the main theoretician of pre-war social democracy, the 'Pope of Marxism' Karl Kautsky, and by the theoretician of pre-war reformism, the 'revisionist' Eduard Bernstein.

But the development of the new party was of tremendous importance. It carried with it a good part of the old SPD apparatus—dozens of full time functionaries, Reichstag and state deputies, daily papers, trade union officials, offices and meeting halls. Above all it was a legal party, able to hold open meetings, even if these were constrained by the laws of sedition and by censorship. The USP provided a mass focus for the aspirations of tens of thousands of people who were, however hesitantly, beginning to question the war. Six months after the split it could claim 120,000 members as against 150,000 in the SPD.[26] Many of the strike leaders of April 1917 and January 1918 were in its ranks; and the restive sailors of August 1917 began to identify with it and made contact with its local and national leaders.

The real revolutionaries were further to the left. In place of the vague demand for 'peace' voiced by the Independents, these demanded *revolution* as the only way to end the capitalist war. But around them were still little more than small, isolated groups of activists.

True, Liebknecht was nationally known, and widely admired as the Reichstag deputy who had first spoken out against the war and as the victim of government persecution since. But repression made it virtually impossible for his colleagues to explain to more than relatively restricted circles of workers what he stood for in detail. Liebknecht himself was conscripted to the Front, despite his age (he was well over 40) and then imprisoned. Rosa Luxemburg too was imprisoned. Their contacts in the factories were the first to be victimised and conscripted after the strike of January 1918.

One recent estimate of the strength (or weakness!) of the revolutionary left tells:

> The revolutionary left in Bremen no longer had a single militant in the shipyards or in the factories... In Berlin the Spartakist grouping in the south district, which included Charlottenburg, Berlin-Moabit and Spandau, only contained seven members... The Spartakist leadership had been broken by arrests.[27]

The numerical weakness of the revolutionary left was made worse by the fact that it lacked a single national organisation. Instead it was divided into three separate and at times antagonistic groupings.

The Spartakist leaders—Rosa Luxemburg, Leo Jogiches, Franz Mehring, Clara Zetkin and Karl Liebknecht—still adhered to the pre-war belief that small groups of revolutionaries could maintain a living contact with the majority of workers only if they were part of a wider organisation. So the Spartakists remained within the USP, although their politics were quite different from those of the party's leadership. They argued that workers who turned against the war would not at first be able to distinguish between the vaguely anti-war sounds emitted by the Independent leadership and the stand made by Liebknecht. They would turn to the biggest opposition force, the Independents. The revolutionaries could establish contact with these workers by being within the USP, where they would be able to maintain their own organisation, their own press and their own discipline as a faction. Jogiches wrote:

> We must fight for the unclear or still wavering masses who today follow the AG [the independent parliamentary group]. And we can only do that if we lead the fight inside the party and do not have a completely separate organisation outside...[28]

Another section of the left rejected this perspective. Based mainly in Bremen, they had relations with the Russian Bolsheviks through one of their pre-war associates, the Polish exile Radek who was now working with Lenin. This group was known as the 'Left Radicals' (later the International Communists of Germany). By remaining within the USP, they argued, the Spartakists were making it more difficult for workers to distinguish between the real left and the half hearted pacifists who led the USP.

The best known figures in this group were Johann Knief, the inspirer of its Bremen group, the worker turned journalist Paul Frölich, and the Hamburg intellectual Laufenberg. Despite their criticisms of the Spartakists, these leaders were themselves to prove a far from cohesive or politically homogenous group.

Finally, there was effectively a third revolutionary grouping, although this time not a fully organised tendency, made up of a number of influential working class militants within the Berlin Metal Workers Union. These led the great strikes of 1917 and 1918 and saw themselves as revolutionaries, organised into a grouping known as the 'revolutionary shop stewards'. Yet they did not completely break their links with the USP leadership, being particularly close to the veteran Reichstag deputy Georg Ledebour. His advice was often decisive in moments of crisis.[29]

Altogether in the summer of 1918 there were probably three or four thousand revolutionary socialists in the whole of Germany. They had no united organisation, no tradition of working within a common discipline, no way at arriving at an agreed strategy or tactics, no mechanism for selecting from among themselves leaders who were reliable and had cool heads. Yet these revolutionaries were about to enter one of the most intense periods of class struggle in the history of capitalism.

In the summer of 1918 the German army launched a massive offensive on the Western Front. This stretched the resources at the disposal of the generals beyond breaking point. As the initial gains were rolled back by a counter-offensive by the Allied forces, it became apparent to the German High Command that defeat was staring them in the face. They were stunned. Only a few weeks earlier they had been talking confidently of victory. The withdrawal of Russia from the war had left their eastern flank free and enabled them to move everything to the Western Front. The anti-war agitation of January had subsided, seemingly for good: it was possible for one contemporary writer on the split inside the SPD to claim in May that the effect of peace in the east had been to 'draw the masses to the side of the government'.[30]

The argument in ruling class circles had not been over the advisability of war or peace, but over exactly what was to be annexed after a German victory. Now the generals saw that the whole Front would collapse unless the country could be extricated from the war with maximum speed. They stopped boasting of victory and started to look for ways to avoid personal responsibility for defeat.

Hindenberg and Ludendorff, for the general staff, had an audience with the Kaiser on 29 September. They revealed that 'the war was lost' and the situation desperate. Immediate negotiation of a compromise peace was the only alternative to shattering defeat. The only way to guarantee social stability was to replace their own absolute power by that of a new, liberalised government including Social Democratic ministers.

The Kaiser was astounded. The representatives of the Prussian military elite were suggesting that its traditional enemy be brought into the government. They insisted there was no choice. As the secretary of state, Hintze, put it, 'It is necessary to prevent an upheaval from below by a revolution from above'.[31]

So, with the blessing of the most illiberal sector of German society, a new 'liberal' coalition government was formed. The Chancellor was the Kaiser's cousin, Prince Max of Baden. Its programme—concession, both to the German workers and to the Allied powers. Its aim—to preserve the monarchy.

One of the basic principles of the SPD had always been republicanism. Now, however, the party's leaders agreed to join a government whose reason for existence was to preserve the monarchy. The party secretary, Ebert, told a meeting of its leadership:

> If we don't come to some understanding with the bourgeois parties and the government, then we will have to let events take their own course. Then we will be resorting to revolutionary tactics... A similar development would take place to that experienced in Russia.[32]

That was enough to convince Ebert's colleagues that he was right to support the efforts of Prince Max—but it was too late for such support to lay the spectre of revolution.

The talk of an armistice had an immense impact within the army. Rank and file soldiers saw little point in fighting any more. As one historian of the German army has noted, already in the spring of 1918 many 'new, young recruits' were 'infected with leftist, anti-war propaganda'. The mood was less prevalent at the Front than in the 'home' army. Nevertheless, there were more than 4,000 desertions to the enemy in 1918. Now the soldiers had been told that all their previous efforts had achieved nothing... 'Desertions among the ranks grew after Ludendorff's hasty request to the Allies for a compromise'.[33]

The turn in the political situation opened new opportunities to the forces of the far left. The feeling that the old order was in crisis grew among a significant layer of workers and found expression on the streets. 'The month of October was a time of the awakening of wide sections of workers, of stormy mass meetings and spontaneous demonstrations'.[34] The impression that the government was unsure of itself was increased when, on 23 October, Liebknecht was released from jail—a concession made under Social Democrat pressure in an attempt to take from him the martyr's halo.

But the concession was not enough to stop the growing unrest. People were only too aware that the old repressive machine and the old laws remained intact: sentences were still being handed out to those involved in the January strikes. Above all, the war was not over. The German High Command had hoped for an easy compromise peace. But the Allied powers, especially France, were determined to treat Germany as the Germans had treated Soviet Russia earlier in the year—to smash its power, to grab for themselves areas of its territory, to take over its colonies, to loot its economy.

Rather than accept these terms, the High Command preferred to send out its troops to fight lost battles. Finally, in a desperate attempt to change the odds, they ordered to sea the very fleet which they had kept hidden from the risks of battle through most of the war.

The mood among the rank and file sailors was more bitter, if anything, than the year before. They knew that if they allowed the fleet to challenge the British fleet they would face defeat and certain death. When sailors in Wilhelmshaven were ordered to move their ships at the end of October, they responded by putting out the boilers. As one sailor wrote to his father, 'We all felt this would be our last voyage, and so we instinctively refused to follow orders'.[35] They were immediately arrested.

But the movement was not crushed by the repression as it had been the year before. Too much was now at stake. Five days later thousands of sailors marched through the streets of Kiel to protest at the arrests. They were joined by the port's workers. Clashes with patrols loyal to the government left nine dead on the streets. But the patrols were met with counter-fire and forced to retreat from the town. The German revolution had begun.

1.   *Quoted by Edwyn Bevan, German Social Democracy During the War* (London 1918) p6.

2.   Quoted ibid, p21.

3.   Peter Nettl, *Rosa Luxemburg* (London 1966) p610.

4.   Quoted in Paul Frölich and others, *Illustrierte Geschichte der Deutschen Revolution* (Berlin 1929, reprinted Frankfurt 1970) p116.

5.   Rosa Luxemburg, *The Junius Pamphlet* (reprinted in English, London 1967).

6.   Hardach, *The First World War* (London 1977) p56.

7.   Ibid.

8.   K H Roth, *Die 'andere' Arbeiterbewegung* (Munich 1974) p40.

9.   E Bevan, op cit, p229.

10.   For figures, see G Bry, *Wages in Germany 1871-1945* (Princeton 1960) pp83-84.

11.   P Frölich et al, op cit, p134.

12.   E Lucas, *Die Sozialdemocratie in Bremen während des Ersten Weltkrieges* (Bremen 1969) p45.

13.   Daniel Horn, *Mutiny on the High Seas* (London 1973) p33. For a different account, see P Frölich et al, op cit, pp157-160.

14.   Isaac Deutscher, *The Prophet Armed* (London 1954) p360.

15.   Quoted in Pierre Broué, *Révolution en Allemagne* (Paris 1971) p109.

16. There are various accounts of the Austrian strikes which differ somewhat in detail. See, for example, ibid, p111.

17. In *Dokumenten und Materialen zur Geschichte der Deutschen Arbeiterbewegung, Ruhe 11 (1914-45)* vol 2 (East Berlin 1957).

18. For an account of the Berlin strike by one of its leaders, see Richard Müller, *Vom Kaiserreich zur Republik* vol 1 (Berlin 1924) pp100-110.

19. Reprinted in *Dokumenten und Materialen* vol 2, op cit.

20. Ibid.

21. Quotes in P Frölich et al, op cit, p152. Also R Müller, op cit, p110.

22. P Frölich et al, op cit, p162.

23. Ibid.

24. *Dokumenten und Materialen* vol 2, op cit.

25. Leon Trotsky, *My Life* (New York 1960) p235.

26. E Bevan, op cit, p232.

27. P Broué, op cit, p133.

28. Quoted in P Frölich et al, op cit, pp147-148.

29. For a full account of the revolutionary shop stewards, see R Müller, op cit, p115 onwards.

30. E Bevan, op cit, pxv.

31. Quoted in P Broué, op cit, p137; and more fully in P Frölich et al, op cit, p169.

32. Quoted in P Frölich et al, op cit, p170.

33. H J Gordon, *The Reichswehr and the German Republic 1919-26* (Princeton 1957) pp3-5.

34. P Frölich et al, op cit, p181.

35. Ibid, p185.

CHAPTER 3

The November Revolution

The Prussian monarchy had reigned for hundreds of years. It had ruled the whole of Germany for half a century. Now it collapsed in a few short days. And hardly a shot was fired in its defence.

Events in Kiel laid a pattern that was followed in virtually every town in Germany. The evening after the first demonstrations in the streets, a mass meeting of 20,000 men elected a sailors' council. At its head was a stoker, Karl Artelt, who had been sentenced to five years in prison for his part in the previous, unsuccessful mutiny. By the next morning this council was the authority in the town.

News of the events in Kiel soon travelled to other nearby ports. In the next 48 hours there were demonstrations and general strikes in Cuxhaven and Wilhelmshaven. Workers' and sailors' councils were elected and held effective power.

In the biggest city in the region, Hamburg, it looked at first as if the revolutionary movement might stall. A meeting of the Independent Socialists on 5 November called for the liberation of the imprisoned sailors, but rejected a call for the election of a workers' council. One of the sailors, Friedrich Zeiler, then took things into his own hands. He collected 20 others and went along the harbour seeking support. By midnight they were a hundred strong, had taken over the union headquarters to call for a demonstration the next day and had sent delegations off to all the barracks.

The mood in the city was such that 40,000 joined this improvised, 'unofficial' demonstration and voted for a 'republic of workers' councils'. That evening a workers' and soldiers' council was formed, headed by the revolutionary, Laufenberg. Meanwhile a group of armed soldiers, headed by another revolutionary, Paul Frölich, took over the printing works of the daily paper, the *Hamburger Echo*, and produced a paper for the workers' and soldiers' council titled *Rote Fahne (Red Flag)*.

'This is the beginning of the German revolution, of the world revolution,' it proclaimed. 'Hail the most powerful action of the world revolution. Long live socialism. Long live the German workers' republic. Long live world Bolshevism'.[1]

The first great city in Germany had fallen to the revolution. Now nothing could stop its spread. Already there had been demonstrations in the southern cities of Munich and Stuttgart. Now sailors from the northern ports acted as a bacillus carrying the revolutionary infection from town to town. Once the Baltic fleet had risen, many of the sailors wanted to return to their homes. There was no longer any authority to stop them beginning their homeward journeys—but when they arrived, they found that the local military authorities still regarded them as deserters. The sailors faced the choice: spread the revolution in their home towns, or face arrest and imprisonment.

On 6 November the revolution was successful throughout the north west. Councils took power in Bremen, Altona, Rendsburg and Lockstedt. On the 7th it was the turn of Cologne, Munich, Braunschweig and Hanover. The remaining large towns fell to the revolution on the 8th: Oldenburg, Rostock, Magdeburg, Halle, Leipzig, Dresden, Chemnitz, Düsseldorf, Frankfurt, Stuttgart, Darmstadt and Nuremberg. Berlin remained as an isolated centre of imperial power, where, as one newspaperman described it:

> News is coming in from all over the country of the progress of the revolution. All the people who made such a show of their loyalty to the Kaiser are lying low. Not one is moving a finger in defence of the monarchy. Everywhere soldiers are quitting the barracks.[2]

Yet the authorities still seemed to hold the capital. The soldiers remained in their barracks, dutifully saluting their officers. The workers clocked on and off at the factories as if nothing was changing. Only a narrow stratum of their leaders were involved in frenetic activity. The Social Democrats had been doing their best to head off the revolution by pressing for the Kaiser to abdicate voluntarily in favour of some other member of the royal house. As their leader Ebert told the prime minister, Prince Max, 'Unless the Kaiser abdicates, a revolution is inevitable. But I will have none of it. I hate it like sin'.[3]

Meanwhile the Spartakists, the revolutionary shop stewards and the Independent Social Democrats had been arguing about when to unleash the revolutionary movement in Berlin. Already, several days earlier, there had been a meeting of the leaders of these three groups. The revolutionaries had proposed a mass strike and a demonstration to be led by units of sympathetic troops. The meeting turned it down.

The main opposition to action came from the Independent Social Democrat leader Haase, who feared anything which might upset his desire for unity with the Majority Social Democrats. He called the Kiel uprising an 'impulsive explosion' and said that he had promised the SPD leader Noske to do nothing that might make unity between the two parties more difficult.

So, while revolution swept from one end of the empire to the other, the question of action in Berlin was left in the air. What is more, in the capital the machinery of repression remained intact. The police moved to nip any rising in the bud. On 6 November they prevented a meeting of the revolutionary shop stewards, then arrested one of their leaders, Däumig. Effectively they prevented coordination between the various groups that wanted action. They broke up a meeting to celebrate the anniversary of the Russian Revolution on 7 November. The next day armed police patrolled the streets and guarded all public buildings.

A meeting of Majority Social Democrat activists in the factories on the evening of 8 November told their leaders that the workers could no longer be held back, that they wanted action the next day.

Liebknecht, for his part, was desperate. It seemed impossible to get the revolutionary shop stewards to move in solidarity with the other German cities—they were still influenced by the Independent Social Democrat leaders who claimed an armed uprising was not technically possible yet. Liebknecht's great fear was that the SPD leaders, although in the government, would call for action so as to put into power a new, revamped anti-revolutionary government. Finally, on 8 November, Liebknecht issued a leaflet calling for revolution, with just two names on it, his own and that of another member of the Spartakist League, Ernst Meyer. It appeared in the streets just as the revolutionary shop stewards and a number of Independent Social Democrats had also decided not to wait any longer and had issued a leaflet of their own.

The military High Command were still of the belief that any 'disturbances in Berlin' could be crushed by using front line troops. Their confidence was short lived. The scene at the barracks of one of the 'reliable' regiments the next morning was described by the editor of Berlin's leading news agency:

> The Kaiser Alexander regiment has gone over to the revolution; the soldiers had rushed out of the barracks gates and fraternised with the shouting crowd outside; men shook their hands with emotion and girls stuck flowers in their uniforms and embraced them. Members of my staff told me that officers are being stripped of their cockades and gold lace.[4]

The call for the general strike was followed in all the factories. Those who had hungered and bled for four years of war now poured from the suburbs into the centre of the city, led by groups of armed soldiers and red flags.

> Endless processions of workers and soldiers were passing without a break along the road... Most of the workers were of middle age, with grey bearded faces... They had the trade unionists' corporate spirit and marched conscientiously, in order. Some of them were shouldering rifles... Everyone in the procession had a red badge in the button hole or on the breast; the marshals of the procession, marching alongside with rifles slung over their shoulders, were distinguished by red armbands. In the midst of this slow marching throng, great red flags were carried.[5]

The initiative in directing this vast marching horde was taken by the persecuted minority of the day before, the Spartakists, and the revolutionary shop stewards. The words they had been scratching out on rough leaflets for four years were now taken up by hundreds of thousands of voices. Now they could call for action and tens of thousands would hear the call. Liebknecht led one column of soldiers and workers to seize the imperial palace, the Schloss; Eichhorn, a left independent, led another to take over the police headquarters, where he was installed as the new, revolutionary police chief. Power seemed to be passing straight from the Kaiser's officials to proponents of revolutionary socialism.

While the masses were taking over the city, the Majority Social Democrat leaders were conferring with the rulers of the old regime. In a desperate attempt to keep the situation under some sort of control, Prince Max had handed the premiership to the SPD leader Ebert. But the Social Democrats had to give the impression that they were with the workers in the streets as well. They told a meeting of Independent deputies, 'We have been holding our people back till 12 o'clock.' Then, at 1pm, a special edition of their paper *Vorwärts* called for the general strike that had been already under way for five hours!

When one of the huge columns of workers and soldiers marched up outside the Reichstag, deputies rushed to one of Ebert's colleagues, Scheidemann, who was taking a meal in the Reichstag restaurant, and begged him to speak to the crowd and calm them down. Reluctantly, he left his soup and went to one of the balconies. Below he saw a mass of hungry faces, red flags, clenched fists, many of them grasping rifles. He told them that everything had changed, that the socialist Ebert was now premier. But that did not stop the clamour of the crowd. So he added, 'Long live the German Republic.' A roar of applause shook the building.

Scheidemann's colleagues were not exactly happy with his efforts. Ebert screamed at him afterwards, 'You have no right to proclaim the republic'.[6]

But Scheidemann had, in fact, only just been in time. A few hundred yards away Liebknecht was climbing to a window in the imperial palace—the very window from which the Kaiser used to address patriotic throngs. Liebknecht's message was rather different from the Kaiser's: 'The day of Liberty has dawned. I proclaim the free socialist republic of all Germans. We extend our hand to them and ask them to complete the world revolution. Those of you who want the world revolution, raise your hands'.[7] Thousands of hands rose up.

The Social Democrats take control

The German Empire had collapsed. The monarchy was no more. There was not even a parliament with any authority. In the days that followed the only bodies with any semblance of power were the workers' and soldiers' councils. No wonder many workers regarded the revolution as over, with a government that called itself 'socialist' in power.

But toppling the old order was not the same thing as beginning the new. To destroy the German Empire, spontaneous strikes and street fights were enough. But to build a new socialist order, the majority of the working class had to be conscious of what they were building. This was far from so.

An event at the beginning of the revolutionary upheaval provided living proof of its limitations. As soon as the uprising in Kiel began, the naval command requested that the government send a Social Democrat leader to the port 'to prevent the rising spreading through the fleet'.[8] The government persuaded the right wing Social Democrat Noske to take the job. Noske had orders to offer the sailors an amnesty if they returned to their ships and handed over their arms. Noske was appaled at the sight of 20,000 armed sailors refusing to accept the authority of their officers, and found he had no forces to persuade them to return to their ships. Instead he searched out the Independent Social Democrats and members of the elected sailors' committee—and found they were quite prepared to hand command of the revolution in Kiel over to Noske himself.

Artelt (the leading mutineer) and the trade union leader Garbe suggested that Noske assume the chairmanship of the sailors' council. Noske mounted the hood of a car and announced to the crowd that he was taking charge. The crowd cheered; the revolt had found its master.[9]

Noske emerged as the representative of the government charged with putting down the revolution in Kiel *and* as the representative the sailors and workers expected to carry the revolution forward. In the days that followed he used his position to prevent a destruction of German capitalism or of the structures—the hierarchies in the army, the police, the civil service—that had protected it for so many years.

Noske's success in Kiel was repeated when the monarchy collapsed in Berlin. The Social Democrats had not initiated the revolution. But in Berlin as in Kiel the vast mass of workers—and even more the vast mass of soldiers—were entering into political action for the first time in their lives. Many had previously been supporters of the openly capitalist parties and regarded the Social Democrats as the extreme left. They did not yet differentiate between one 'socialist' party and another. The mass of workers and soldiers did not know of the Social Democrats' support for the monarchy. They did not know that Scheidemann had proclaimed the 'republic' only to pre-empt Liebknecht's proclamation of the 'socialist republic'.

The leaders of the Independent Social Democrats increased the confusion over what the Majority Social Democrats aimed to do. Haase, the most prominent of the Independent leaders, had readily agreed, in Kiel, to Noske taking the chairmanship of the sailors' council. Now in Berlin the trick was repeated. A joint 'revolutionary government' was formed of three members from each of the two Social Democrat parties, but with the Majority Social Democrats clearly in control. The government was given a revolutionary veneer—it was entitled, Russian fashion, the 'council of people's commissars'.

In fact it was far from revolutionary. The three Majority Social Democrat members (Ebert, Scheidemann and Landsberg) had, a mere 24 hours earlier, been frantically trying to stop the revolution. Two of the Independents, Haase and Dittmann, were on the right wing of their party, whose aim was not revolution, but the 'reuniting of Social Democracy'—as if the war had never taken place. Only one of the so-called people's commissars, Emil Barth, came from the left wing associated with the revolutionary shop stewards.

Liebknecht had been offered a place in this 'revolutionary government', but refused, seeing that he would be a prisoner of the non-revolutionary majority. Unfortunately Barth was neither as principled nor as perceptive.

The new government claimed to be 'purely socialist'. But linked to each 'people's commissar' were 'expert advisers', acting as secretaries of state. These were generally members of the various bourgeois parties, who ensured that the 'commissars' left intact the ranks of bureaucratic officialdom which had administered the old empire. What this continuity with the old order meant was shown within days when the 'revolutionary' government endorsed the decision of the Kaiser's government to expel the embassy of revolutionary Russia.

But the revolutionary veneer was good enough to fool the workers and soldiers—at least for a few vital weeks.

The 'revolutionary government' was formed on 10 November, the second day of the revolution in Berlin. The left Independents and the Spartakists had made their own preparations for solving the question of power that day. They called for an assembly of workers' and soldiers' delegates—one delegate for each 1,000 workers and for each battalion of soldiers. But when the assembly convened in the Circus Busch the revolutionaries found matters rather different from what they had expected.

The Social Democrat leaders had put their whole party machine to work to ensure their dominance at the assembly. The previous day, while the revolution was raging on the streets, they had set up their own 'soldiers' and workers' council', made up of a dozen hand picked Social Democrat workers and three of the party leaders. This had then rushed thousands of leaflets to the barracks demanding 'no fratricidal strife'. The politically raw soldiers were given the impression that anyone who questioned the need for unthinking unity between the different 'socialist' parties was a splitter, wrecker and saboteur.

More than 1,500 delegates packed out the meeting hall. The Social Democrats had managed to get the soldiers there early, so that they took up almost all the space on the floor, forcing the more politically experienced workers' delegates into the balconies. The soldiers were not interested in the niceties of debate. Many waved fists and guns. There were frequent interruptions of speakers—especially anyone who seemed to question the slogan of unity at any price. In this atmosphere it was difficult for left wing workers' delegates to object when Social Democrat notables took charge of the platform.

Ebert spoke for them. He announced the formation of the 'pure socialist' joint government with the Independents. Haase then went to the platform and repeated the same message. To the masses in the hall it seemed that the revolution was over. Their best known leaders were united. The last thing anyone wanted was talk of further bloodshed.

The resolution moved at the assembly sounded revolutionary enough. It proclaimed that Germany was a 'socialist republic': 'All power lies with workers' and soldiers' councils... Peace is the watchword of the revolution... Brotherly greetings to the Russian workers' and soldiers' government.'

The soldiers were not happy when Liebknecht put a question mark over the revolutionary euphoria. 'He was calm and incisive. But he did not have an easy time. The vast majority of the soldiers were against him. They interrupted his speech, they even threatened him with their guns, shouting 'Unity', 'Unity' in the face of each of his attacks against the Majority Social Democrats'.[10]

Nevertheless he persevered, warning the delegates that the Social Democrats 'are going along with the revolution today, but were its enemies the day before yesterday. The counter-revolution is already underway. It is already in action. It is already among us'.[11]

Liebknecht's warnings had no effect on the soldiers. They insisted on putting 12 Majority Social Democrat soldiers on an Executive for the Workers' and Soldiers' Council of Berlin, alongside 12 workers—of whom six came from each of the Social Democrat parties.

The newly elected Berlin Executive of the Councils claimed the right to control the government. It was, for the time being, the sovereign power. But it was controlled by supporters of the Social Democrat

Party. The organ of revolution was controlled by those who feared the revolution.[12]

In mid-December the Berlin Executive handed its sovereignty to a Congress of workers' and solders' delegates from the whole of Germany. But the Social Democrats' efforts were crowned with still further success. The delegates voted to relinquish this sovereignty to the Reichstag to be elected within four weeks—to a parliament for which the classes that had opposed the revolution had the same vote as those that had made it.

In the first weeks of the revolution there had been real fear among the old bourgeois politicians that they would be excluded by the councils from political power for ever after. Now they were reassured. They could with confidence face elections in which big business control of the press and finance would give them a head start over the socialists. The elections could be used to destroy the revolutionary power that had called for them.

The manoeuvres of the Social Democrats played into the hands of the old possessing class. But these manoeuvres were only possible because of the contradiction that always appears at the beginning of any great revolution. Revolutions throw into political life people who have previously sat in their homes, on the margins of history, ignoring the great questions of society. When they move they often identify with those who the old society itself allows to be prominent, the 'official opposition'. The ex-minister is likely to be much better known than the ex-political prisoner. His vague mumblings of opposition are likely to connect at first with those who have not yet learnt why they are fighting. Only bitter experiences can bring millions of people to turn from the official opposition and move further to the left.

Of course, in the heat of an insurrection against an oppressive system it is those who are most outspoken and most courageous—the Rosa Luxemburgs and the Karl Liebknechts—who call hundreds of thousands on to the streets. But when the dust settles a little, it is those still half connected with the old order who command mass support—for the masses do not abandon overnight the prejudices hammered into them over a lifetime. There is no easy path by which the hard lessons of experience, that alone will change their views, can be evaded.

That is why the first successful, spontaneous upsurge against the old order is almost invariably followed by a period of exhilaration, when the underlying tensions in society are forgotten. Journalists seize on poetic epithets to describe such times—the 'revolution of the flowers', the 'Spring in October', 'the revolution of fraternity'.

So it was in Berlin in November 1918. As a number of participants recalled ten years later:

> Within a week the revolution had broken out all over Germany. Demonstrations and meetings of workers were held. But there was no longer any threat. They were festivals of friendship. Red flags flew, red ribbons flaunted in buttonholes, and faces laughed. It was as if the dim, rainy November days had turned into spring. Everyone bathed in mutual trust. The revolution had begun, and it had begun with a universal fraternisation of the classes.[13]

Things were not to last like that for long.

1.   Paul Frölich and others, *Illustrierte Geschichte der Deutschen Revolution* (Berlin 1929, reprinted Frankfurt 1970) pp189, 192. Where no sources are given for events described in this chapter, the material is usually based on this *Illustrierte Geschichte*, or on Pierre Broué, *Révolution en Allemagne* (Paris 1971).
2.   Theodor Wolff, *Through Two Decades* (London 1936).
3.   Quoted, for instance, in R M Watt, *The Kings Depart* (London 1973) p206.
4.   T Wolff, op cit.
5.   Ibid.
6.   There are numerous accounts of this. See for example, P Broué, op cit, p154; and R M Watt, op cit, p221.
7.   P Frölich et al, op cit, pp209-210; and P Broué, op cit, pp154-155.
8.   Daniel Horn, *Mutiny on the High Seas* (London 1973) p248.
9.   Ibid, p251.
10.   P Broué, op cit, p159.
11.   Ibid.
12.   For a history of the executive by its chairman, see Richard Müller, *Der Burgerkrieg in Deutschland* (West Berlin 1974) pp15-98.
13.   P Frölich et al, op cit, p215.

CHAPTER 4

Days of workers' power

The symbols of the first days of the revolution were those of revolutionary socialism—red flags, singing of the Internationale, formation of workers' and soldiers' councils throughout the country. The old political structure had disintegrated—and its symbols disappeared for a time. The bourgeois political parties were in deep crisis, their leaders wondering how they were going to save anything. They knew that their only salvation lay with the Social Democrats that they had so despised in the past.

The Social Democrats held half the seats in the government. But to get these they had had to voice slogans of the extreme left. Two days after the revolution Scheidemann was despondent. 'Yes, the Independents now have the power,' he told the Berlin newspaper editor Theodor Wolff. 'I have no soldiers.' Scheidemann's fellow 'commissar', Landsberg, added, 'We are in an impossible situation. Haase is much stronger than we are. If things go on like this, we will have no choice but to resign'.[1]

Government office meant little if it could not command those who had armed power. In the past this had meant the officers of the armed forces. But now the authority of these officers was fast disintegrating. On the first day of the revolution in Berlin the symbols of authority within the army were torn up:

Across the compact mass of the moving crowd big military lorries urged their way, full to overflowing with soldiers and sailors who waved red flags and uttered ferocious cries... These cars, crowded with young fellows in uniform or in mufti, carrying loaded rifles or little red flags, seemed to me characteristic. These young men constantly left their places to force officers or soldiers to tear off their badges of rank...[2]

The mosaic of workers' power

The rank and file soldiers were fed up with war, hardship, military discipline, with eating miserable rations while their officers feasted in luxury. They insisted that the officers listen to the men for a change. Everywhere they set up soldiers' councils.

> In the days of November, soldiers' councils sprang up spontaneously not only in all major German towns, but also in the field armies in Belgium and France, as well as in Russia.[3]
>
> In Brussels, a communications centre of vital importance for the retreat from occupied France and Belgium, a soldiers' council was formed on 10 November and took over control of all military and civil authority in place of the government... In Malines on the same day a soldiers' council of 20 was elected for the Fourth Army, among them two lieutenants. It issued a proclamation which abolished the separate officers' messes and the duty to salute when off-duty... In occupied Poland the soldiers' council elected at Grodno proclaimed on 12 November that it was taking the power of command within the government of South Lithuania.[4]

The army in Germany itself tended to be much more radical than that at the Front. It had had much closer contact with the organised working class and much more opportunity to discuss politics. In one industrial centre after another the soldiers' councils joined with the workers' councils in putting their elected leaders in charge of state and city governments.

In Cologne, for instance, a council made up of equal numbers of workers' and soldiers' delegates established subcommittees for security, food and accommodation, demobilisation, the press, sanitation and transport. Members of the council were appointed as supervisors over the mayor (who was later to become premier of West Germany, Konrad Adenauer), the railways, the post and telegraph, the police, the courts, the national bank and the army command.[5]

In a number of places the new workers' council which took over local government hardly recognised the Ebert government in Berlin. In Saxony the workers' and soldiers' councils from Dresden, Leipzig and Chemnitz met together and announced that the revolutionary proletariat was taking power in order to abolish capitalist exploitation. The old government of Saxony was replaced by a joint socialist one, with most of the main posts in the hands of Independents. In the small state of Braunschweig a radical socialist government was similarly formed.

The most significant 'autonomous' council government was in Germany's second largest state, Bavaria. The new premier, the Independent Social Democrat Eisner, even negotiated with foreign powers independently of Berlin. Bavaria had long had aspirations towards separatism.

In the army things were even more accidental. Until 9 November discussion in the barracks or the trenches had to be secret. Lacking experience, soldiers could not know who could provide trustworthy leadership to their fellows, and who was merely on the make or even a raving lunatic. The soldiers tended to turn to those who were most outspoken and most articulate, providing they promised peace, a quick return home, better food and an end to military discipline. So in one key military centre the leaders of the councils would be Majority Social Democrats, in another Spartakists, in a third demagogues and adventurers, in yet another the most sympathetic of the officers. There were even cases of soldiers electing their commanding officers to the councils, and of soldiers' councils appointing old bourgeois politicians to run towns.

In Berlin itself the workers of the largest factories tended to align with the Independents, as even the pro Social Democrat historian Landauer admits.[6] But this was compensated for by the balance of power in the army. The majority of soldiers returning from the Front sympathised initially with the Majority Social Democrats—as shown in the Circus Busch assembly of delegates.

> The old Social Democrat Party had shrunk numerically in the big cities, and the Independent Social Democrats had the upper hand. But the Social Democrat activists could use the promises of the government to grab hold of the unpolitical, inactive and slow thinking masses and get their votes. Above all, the soldiers' councils came to their help. Out of the heterogeneous, confused mass of soldiers, the most valuable elements of the middle class came to the fore—clerks, intellectuals, NCOs and even officers, to the greater part fresh baked 'November socialists', who spoke political gibberish and who always worked for their middle class interests.[7]

But an army in decomposition does not remain frozen in its attitudes. Soldiers who were breaking with the old discipline soon began to break with the old views as well. A rapid political polarisation began to take place. The Social Democrat dominated soldiers' councils did not for long command allegiance in the barracks of the great cities. And large numbers of soldiers had abandoned the barracks, taking their guns with them. These soon discovered they could not find work. Hunger and anger radicalised them, and in Berlin they swarmed behind demonstrations led by Karl Liebknecht and the Red Soldiers' League.

To the question, 'Who rules Germany?' there was only one possible answer: the councils did. But they only half reflected the confused, half thought out and rapidly shifting aspirations of the armed masses who controlled the barracks and the streets. And they were certainly not organised into any ordered system for running the country on a new basis. Instead there was a patchwork of different councils, possessing different powers, pursuing different goals, owing varying degrees of allegiance to the Ebert government—which was itself half appointed by the old imperial order, half subject to the Executive of the revolution in Berlin.

The Social Democrats could not ignore the power that lay with this mosaic of councils. They attempted to win control of the movement in order to destroy its power. Partly this meant using the soldiers' councils against the workers' councils—even to the extent of armed clashes between the retreating army and the local workers. Partly it meant preventing the changing mood of the masses from finding a reflection in the councils. Social Democrat functionaries thrust into the councils in the euphoric mood of 9 November refused to allow fresh elections in December and January. The workers' attitudes could not be frozen in a period of revolutionary upheaval. But the attitudes of the councils could be.

The National Congress of Workers' and Soldiers' Councils, held in mid-December, was an assembly of those who exercised revolutionary power locally throughout the country. But it was also an assembly mainly of those whose preoccupation was to destroy the revolutionary basis of power. Of 499 delegates, only 179 were manual or white collar workers; 71 were intellectuals; while no fewer than 164 were journalists, deputies, trade union and Social Democratic officials or professional men. Not surprisingly an overwhelming majority of 288 supported the Social Democrats, compared to 90 for the Independents and 21 for the revolutionary left. Those who called most loudly for the establishment of workers' power, Rosa Luxemburg and Karl Liebknecht, were not even allowed into the hall.

The other power

The Majority Social Democrat leaders were perceptive enough to see that with time the rank and file of the army would grow more radical and their power base in it would disintegrate. From the first day of the revolution they began to look for a different sort of support. They made sure that 'responsible', conservative 'experts' were appointed as assistants to the 'people's commissars'. They used these to prevent any dismantling of the administrative machine that had run Germany for the Kaiser.

As a far from revolutionary historian of the council movement wrote:

> What changed least was the bureaucratic apparatus which had governed Prussia for centuries. This machine was created by the Hohenzollerns [the Kaiser's dynasty] and served them loyally and devotedly. The large majority of the higher civil servants who administered the country, as well as the judges, police officers and the secondary school teachers (all of whom were state officials) were firmly conservative and monarchist, as all dissidents had been carefully weeded out... Their emotional ties linked them to the old order and not to the new government and republic.

There was a famous scene at a cabinet meeting when Dr Solf, who remained under-secretary of state at the foreign office, refused to shake hands with Haase because Haase had allegedly taken Russian gold for his party before the revolution. Not only Solf remained in office, but equally the secretaries in the ministries of justice, finance, labour, posts and telegraphs, the secretary of the navy and the Prussian minister of war, General Scheuch, although the social democrats had at first thought it essential to remove Scheuch.[8]

The bureaucratic machine could not get its way, however, unless in the last resort there was armed force to back it up. Its counterpart under the empire had been the High Command of the Imperial Armed Forces. The social democrats looked to this to do for them what it had done for the Kaiser.

On the second day of the revolution in Berlin, 10 November, Ebert had been confirmed in power by the stormy meeting of workers' and soldiers' delegates in the Circus Busch. Shortly afterwards he was confirmed in power in a quite different way. He received a phone call from

General Groener, who told him that the Imperial High Command would recognise the government.

> 'What do you expect of us?' Ebert asked.
> 'Field Marshal Hindenberg expects the government to support the officer corps in maintaining strict discipline and strict order in the army.' 'What else?'
> 'The officer corps expects that the government will fight against Bolshevism and places itself at the disposal of the government for such a purpose.'
> Ebert asked Groener to pass on 'the government's thanks to the Field Marshal'.[9]

Hindenberg had exercised a virtual military dictatorship in the last two years of the war. Now Ebert was pledging to maintain control over the armed forces for him and the rest of the old officer caste. Fourteen years later they were to use this control to install Hitler in power.

Ebert was helped by the willingness of the Independent Social Democrats to go along with this policy. One of them, Dittmann, later wrote, 'My consent to the leading back of the army by the old command was a foregone conclusion'.[10] Even the most left wing of the Independent 'commissars', Barth, allowed his name to go on an order putting the troops under the command of the officers and restricting the soldiers' councils to a merely advisory role.

Thus left and right Social Democrats concurred in placing a monopoly of armed power at the disposal of men who hated not merely 'Bolshevism', but any party, however 'moderate', that threatened their centuries old privileges. Such men would use this force to reverse the changes of 9 November and eventually to bring to power a dictator determined to destroy social democracy.

The army at the Front

So far, however, the agreement the High Command had obtained from the two wings of social democracy was merely a piece of paper. It had to be translated into action. The High Command had to find fighting men prepared to implement it.

At first they thought they could rely upon the old field army. The troops in retreat from the Front seemed much more disciplined than those in the cities, and their councils were much more right wing. It seemed only too easy to use them against the armed workers of the cities.

In later telephone conversations with Groener, Ebert fully approved of this aim. 'A scheme was planned,' Groener told a court eight years later:

> Ten divisions were to march into Berlin, to take power from the workers' and soldiers' councils. Ebert was in agreement with this... The Independents had asked that the troops retreat without ammunition. Ebert insisted that they retreat with plentiful ammunition. We worked out a programme for the cleaning up of Berlin and the disarming of the Spartakists... These agreements were made against the danger of the Bolsheviks and against the council system.[11]

But Ebert and Groener were to be disappointed. The 'discipline' of the field army lasted only until it had retreated back across the border into Germany. Then it began to fall to pieces. Even the divisions of professional soldiers would not stick together. They had accepted discipline because they wanted to get home as soon as possible. Now they were home they began to listen to the 'Bolshevik' agitators. The 'reliable' troops were soon abandoning the barracks, refusing to salute their officers and joining the demonstrations called by the League of Red Soldiers.

But the plan misfired. The only left Independent in the government, Barth, managed to get to the platform. He seems to have had second thoughts about his acquiescence in the government's call for 'discipline'. He told the soldiers that they were being duped by the officers. The soldiers listened to him. They were prepared to accept the propaganda against 'Bolshevik subversives' in general terms—and voted for the calling of elections to the National Assembly and for a ban on strikes in 'essential services'—but they were not prepared to go back to the old system of blind obedience to a privileged officer caste inside the army. They voted to abolish all external marks of rank and to reelect the soldiers' councils.

The rank and file soldiers had had enough of military discipline. For many the main thing was to get back to civilian life as soon as possible. Every attempt by the officers or the Social Democrat leaders to subject them to discipline only radicalised them further. The march of the army from the Front into Berlin was more like a sugar lump going into hot water than a knife going into butter. The disciplined units simply dissolved into the vast mass of hungry, cold, bewildered, grey uniformed figures that crowded the streets.

In the first week of December, there was a full blooded attempt to use the army against the revolution. The bourgeois press began a hysterical campaign against the left, claiming that the Allied powers had told the German government no food could be supplied to their starving country until the workers' and soldiers' councils were dissolved. Thousands of 'anti-Bolshevik' posters began to appear—with messages such as 'Kill Liebknecht'.[12]

On 5 December a mass meeting of NCOs was led in a demonstration to the Chancellor's office, where they told Ebert they were ready for the word 'to deal with a coup from Liebknecht or his comrades'.

The next day troops from various barracks in Berlin marched on the Reichstag building. They had been told that the Executive of the Berlin Councils had embezzled 2.5 million marks, and they arrested its members. Other troops marched to the Chancellory where they called for the dissolution of the Executive Committee and the declaration of Ebert as president with full power.

Ebert did not say yes and he did not say no. He merely said that he would have to consult his 'colleagues'. He was not prepared to throw his weight behind a military movement whose outcome was uncertain; but he was not prepared to disavow it either.[13]

The coup collapsed. The troops involved were not clear what they were fighting for, and their leaders had not prepared any detailed plans for the seizure of power. They had assumed that if the troops moved, everything else would simply fall into place. But Ebert's hesitation stopped that happening. So after controlling the centre of Berlin, the troops simply returned to their barracks. Not, however, before 200 of them had opened up with machine guns against a Spartakist demonstration, killing 18.

The immediate aftermath of this attempted coup was to radicalise Berlin even more. The most reactionary agitators in the garrison were compromised. The soldiers who had followed their lead on 6 December now began to ask what it was all about. One of the units involved in the action—the Marine Division—was at the centre of disaffection from the government by the end of the month.

The new defence forces

The army was visibly disintegrating. Whoever wanted to control Berlin had to look elsewhere.

The revolutionary left had called at the beginning of the revolution for the formation of a 'Red Guard' to keep order and to deal with any attempts at counter-revolution. This had even been passed by the Executive of the Berlin Councils on 12 November, but they dropped the plan under pressure from the right wing within the government. The revolutionary left did, however, retain control of one force—the Security Force which the left Independent Eichhorn had built up within the police headquarters. Two thirds of its members were revolutionary volunteers, a third the remnants of the police.

The Majority Social Democrats set out to counter this force—and to sidetrack any further call for Red Guards. They began recruiting their own Republican Soldiers Corps from their sympathisers within the disintegrating army. The first moves were made by Noske when in charge of Kiel. He had picked out 3,000 of the sailors who were loyal to him and dispatched them to Berlin. He thought this 'People's Marine Division' would give the Social Democrat government the armed backing it needed. Ensconced in the imperial palace, the Schloss, under the command of an old monarchist, Wolff Metternich, they seemed to guarantee protection for the government against any renewed revolutionary disturbances.

But after their involvement in the abortive coup of 6 December the arguments of the left wing Berlin workers began to influence them. A large number deserted, to return to their homes. And the remainder followed the lead of a revolutionary, the former lieutenant Dorrenbach.

The Prussian Social Democrat Minister of the Interior, Wels, and his military governor of Berlin, Anton Fischer, raised the Republican Soldiers Corps as a second force, financed by donations from big business, in the hope that it would supplant their first, now unreliable, instrument. As Fischer later wrote, 'Already on 17 November Wels and I had taken the steps to get together an armed force which would be to some extent reliable.' The problem was finance. But this was solved by 'a certain foreigner' who said:

> He thought all Berlin was interested in the re-establishment of order and offered financial assistance to Wels... When the money was forthcoming,

Wels, Colin Ross (later a supporter of Hitler), Striemer and I went to the barracks to recruit from the best elements among the soldiers.[14]

The Republican Soldiers Corps was soon involved in street clashes with the revolutionary left, often leaving dead in the streets. But in the long run it was itself to cause headaches for the Majority Social Democrat ministers. Its members were, by and large, fairly conservative minded Social Democrats. They did not like the apparently 'wild' and 'undisciplined' behaviour of the Spartakists. They tended in the first months of the revolution to believe government promises that 'socialism' would come through 'order' and 'discipline'. But they did not want capitalism. They had suffered under the old order and did not want its return.

The Social Democrat leaders, by contrast, had made an agreement with the military High Command and the old imperial bureaucrats—men to whom the old order was sancrosanct and to be restored as soon as possible. This agreement demanded of the government things which were incompatible with any notion of 'moving towards socialism'. As the Republican Soldiers Corps had to enforce obedience to such policies, the first grumblings began within its ranks. As its commander, Fischer, later put it, it became 'a daily more unreliable factor'.[15]

No force drawn from the rank and file of the old army could be relied on by the High Command, Ebert, Noske and their friends. They had instead to create what became known as the Freikorps or the Noske Guards.

The Freikorps

There were layers in the army who were not drawn in any way to the revolution. There were the tens of thousands of officers who identified with the upper class and had nothing to gain from demobilisation. Alongside them were a number of privileged and highly trained troops—called the stormtroopers—who had not suffered from the same rigours of discipline, hardship and bad food as the mass of the army. They were bound together by an array of privileges on the one hand, and a fighting camaraderie on the other. They stood to lose all this if demobilised—and leapt at the chance to gain a living by fighting 'the reds'.

On 22 December the Social Democrat government agreed that one of the imperial generals, Märcher, should organise these officers and stormtroopers into a highly paid mercenary force, the Freikorps.

'Most of the leaders were monarchist in spirit. Conspicuously lacking were the moderate, organised workers'.[16] After seeing the Freikorps on the march, the conservative historian Meinecke commented, 'It was as if the old order rose again.'

Yet when he first saw these troops on parade on 4 January, the Majority Social Democrat Noske turned to Ebert and said, 'Just be calm. Everything is going to be all right again.'

The first clashes

In Berlin the months of November and December were marked by a growing radicalisation, especially among sections of the soldiers and the vast numbers of unemployed ex-soldiers. The daily demonstrations of the Red Soldiers League drew increasing support. As a hostile witness tells:

> The Spartakist movement, which also influenced a section of the Independents, succeeded in attracting a fraction of the workers and soldiers, and keeping them in a state of constant excitement, but it remained without a hold on the great mass of the German proletariat. The daily meetings, processions, and demonstrations which Berlin witnessed in November and December 1918 deceived the public and the Spartakist leaders into believing in a following for this revolutionary section which did not exist.[17]

We have seen how the right reacted to this—the officers tried to turn the garrison against the left on 6 December—and the Social Democratic press added to the hysteria by accusing the Spartakists of 'planning a coup'. The aim was to isolate and smash the revolutionary left, before the majority of less militant workers realised that the government was out to destroy the gains of 9 November. But things did not develop according to plan.

The idea spread among the masses of the workers that the Right Socialists had delivered up the revolution to the reaction, that the Independent members of the government feebly allowed themselves to be kept in tow, and that the revolutionary workers would be obliged to take up the defence. These sentiments found a strong expression in the protest meeting of 8 December. The Spartakist demonstration was attended by a vast crowd. Thirty thousand workers and soldiers marched through the town on this day, under the leadership of Liebknecht. Several motor loads of soldiers were disarmed by demonstrators.[18]

The Spartakist paper, *Rote Fahne*, claimed 150,000 people joined this demonstration—and a quarter of a million for another a week later when the National Congress of the Councils gathered in Berlin. The Congress ignored the demands of the demonstration, and, as we have seen, agreed to hand its power over to a parliamentary assembly, but it was not able to dismiss so easily pressures from within the Berlin garrison against any resurrection of an army of the old sort. After hearing a report from Dorrenbach on behalf of the units of the garrison, it adopted a resolution from Hamburg that called for abolition of external signs of rank, for the election of officers, for discipline to be under the control of soldiers' councils and the rapid replacement of the regular army by a militia-based 'people's army'.

But the biggest rebuff for the government came over Christmas. The People's Marine Division was still stationed in the imperial palace, right at the heart of Berlin's government buildings. The government, fearing that this force, designed to protect it from the revolution, would now overturn it on behalf of the revolution, attempted to get the sailors to disperse by withholding their pay. The angry sailors responded by seizing the Prussian Social Democrat leader Wels on 23 December. He would not be released, they insisted, until they got their pay.

The government seized upon this action as an excuse to destroy the division. They sent into action the next day the apparently reliable Horse Guards, commanded by General Lequis and based outside Berlin and away from its subversive atmosphere. An officer gave the sailors an ultimatum: if they had not laid down their weapons and surrendered within two hours, he would open fire with artillery. In fact, the bombardment began even before the time limit was up.

> Meanwhile groups of civilians had joined in the fighting, members of the Spartakist League and other organisations—as well as sections of Eichhorn's Security Force and the Republican Soldiers Corps who also backed up the sailors. Above all, working class women, ignoring danger, had infiltrated the ranks of the Guards and made clear to them the outrage that was taking place. That broke the cohesion of the besiegers. The Guards threw their guns down and arrested their officers. By midday the sailors had won an all-out victory. The struggle had cost 11 dead on the side of the sailors and 56 on the side of the Guards.[19]

The Majority Social Democrats' grip on Berlin was fast slipping. The special detachments they had built up in the city had sided with the sailors against the government. The Social Democrat dominated Berlin Executive of the Councils condemned the attack on the Marine Division. The Social Democrats did not even have the forces to prevent several thousand revolutionaries seizing the premises of the Social Democrat paper *Vorwärts* that night.

Their isolation was accentuated in the following days when the Independent ministers resigned from the government. They had stood by helplessly during the Christmas fighting, while Ebert colluded with Lequis. They could not afford to be compromised any more, for fear of losing their support in Berlin.

Among a growing layer of workers, soldiers and unemployed in the capital there was the feeling that the government was helpless, that with a little effort they could re-ignite a movement like that of 9 November and replace it with a government of their own choosing. But the government was already reaching for another weapon, the Freikorps detachments gathering outside Berlin. And its opponents had one great weakness it could take advantage of—extreme disorganisation.

The founding of the Communist Party

In the rapidly developing revolutionary situation, the left suffered from one great lack—there was no powerful revolutionary party capable of binding the revolutionary soldiers and the armed workers into a force based on voluntary acceptance of a common discipline. Both the Spartakist League with its 3,000 or so members and the smaller left radical group, the International Communists, were lost among vast numbers of workers and soldiers who believed that their own enthusiasm could act as a substitute for strategy and tactics.

Pierre Broué, the French historian of the revolution, may paint an exaggerated picture, but his account contains a very important element of truth:

> Liebknecht, an untiring agitator, spoke everywhere where revolutionary ideas could find an echo. Entire columns of *Rote Fahne* were devoted to the appeals, meetings, demonstrations of soldiers, unemployed workers and deserters... These demonstrations, which the Spartakists had neither the force nor the desire to control, were often the occasion for violent, useless or even harmful incidents caused by the doubtful elements who

became involved in them... Liebknecht could have the impression that he was master of the streets because of the crowds which acclaimed him, while without an authentic organisation he was not even the master of his own troops... To these hard and impatient men who had just returned from the war it was not a question of having conferences or courses in 'theory': there had to be action.[20]

Indeed, the Spartakus League itself was hardly a coherent force, despite its small size. As Paul Frölich has described it: 'The Spartakus League was still rudimentary, and consisted chiefly of innumerable small and autonomous groups scattered all over the country.' It was 'a loose organisation of a few thousand members only.'

A later biographer of Rosa Luxemburg tells how:

Organisationally Spartakus was slow to develop... In the most important cities it evolved an organised centre only in the course of December and in many cases not until February or March 1919... Attempts to arrange caucus meetings of Spartakist sympathisers within the Berlin Workers' and Soldiers' Council did not produce satisfactory results and an independent Communist caucus within the Berlin council was only formed on 20 February 1919.[21]

Such an organisation was neither powerful nor cohesive enough to provide a disciplined core to the rapidly growing ranks of revolutionary soldiers and workers.

Four days after the Christmas fighting 112 delegates from different parts of Germany came together in an attempt to deal with this deficiency by turning the Spartakus League into a fully independent Communist Party, the KPD. Rosa Luxemburg had decided on this course of action after her call to the Independent Social Democrats for a special party conference had been rejected.

Most of the delegates were from the old Spartakus League, but a minority were from the Bremen based Left Radicals who decided to join the new party—despite the forebodings of their ablest leader, Knief.[22] Also present as a representative of the Russian Communist Party was the pre-war Polish-Austrian associate of the Bremen group, Karl Radek.

From the beginning there was a marked contrast between the appreciation of events by the older revolutionary leaders and the majority of the delegates. Rosa Luxemburg, Leo Jogiches, Paul Levi, Karl Radek, all recognised that a successful revolution depended on more than temporary support for certain slogans by a disorganised mass of workers and soldiers. Luxemburg insisted when she introduced the party's programme on the third day of the conference that the revolution was still in its early stages:

> What general tactical consideration must we deduce in order to deal with the situation which we will be confronted with in the immediate future? Your first conclusion will no doubt be a hope that the fall of the Ebert-Scheidemann government is at hand, and that it will be replaced by a declared socialist-proletarian-revolutionary government. For my part, I ask you to direct your attention not to the leadership, not above, but to the base. We must not nourish and repeat the illusion of the first phase of the revolution, that of 9 November, thinking that it is sufficient to overthrow the capitalist government and set up another to bring about the socialist revolution.[23]

Only the struggle in the factories could begin to overturn social relationships and establish the basis for a real socialist revolution. She continued:

> It was characteristic of the first stage of the revolution, until 24 December we might say, that the revolution remained exclusively political. This explains the uncertain character, the inadequacy, the half-heartedness, the aimlessness of the revolution. It was the first stage of a revolution whose main tasks lie in the economic field: to make a fundamental conversion of economic conditions.
>
> It is the very essence of this revolution that strikes become more and more the central focus, the key aspect of the revolution. It then becomes an economic revolution and therefore a socialist revolution. The struggle for socialism has to be fought out by the masses, by the masses alone, breast to breast against capitalism, in every factory, by every proletarian against his employer. Only then will it be a socialist revolution...
>
> Socialism will not and cannot be created by decrees; nor can it be established by any government, however socialist. Socialism must be created by the masses themselves, by every proletarian. Where the chains of capitalism are forged, there must they be broken.

The need was to 'undermine the Ebert-Scheidemann government step by step', not to attempt to seize power before conditions were ripe.

> There is an extensive field to till. We must prepare from the base up; we must give the workers' and soldiers' councils so much strength that the

overthrow of the Ebert-Scheidemann government or any similar government will be merely the final act of the drama. The conquest of power will
not be effected with one blow. It will be a progression; we shall progres-
sively occupy all the positions of the capitalist state...

The economic struggles of workers were not something separate from
this political task, she said, but central to it.

In my view, and that of my most intimate associates in the party,
the economic struggles will be carried on by the workers' councils. The
direction of the economic struggles and the continued expansion of the
area of this struggle must be in the hands of the workers' councils. It is
a question of fighting step by step, hand to hand in every province, in
every city, in every village, in every municipality in order to transfer all
the power of the state bit by bit from the bourgeoisie to the workers' and
soldiers' councils...

History is not going to make our revolution an easy matter like bourgeois revolutions in which it suffices to overthrow the official power at
the centre and to replace a dozen or so persons in authority. We have to
work from beneath... There at the base, where the individual employer
confronts his wage slaves, where all the executive organs of political class
rule confront the object of this rule, the masses; there, step by step, must
we seize the means of power from the rulers and take them into our own
hands.[24]

Rosa Luxemburg was received with rapturous applause. Yet the
majority of the delegates did not understand fully the key point of her
analysis—that the decisive conflict for national state power was still a
considerable distance away, that there could not be a successful taking of power in Berlin until the workers' councils were really strug-
gling for control of society in each locality, drawing the broad masses
into the struggle and not only the most advanced section in the capital.
Nonetheless, they voted for the party programme, which insisted:

The Spartakus League will never take over governmental power except
in response to the clear, unambiguous will of the great majority of the
proletarian mass of all Germany, never except by the proletariat's conscious affirmation of the views, aims and methods of struggle of the
Spartakus League... The Spartakus League will never enter the government just because Ebert and Scheidemann are going bankrupt and the
Independents, by collaborating with them, are in a blind alley.

But the majority of the delegates were far from accepting Rosa's patience with the revolutionary process, her conviction that it was necessary to win the masses for an all out seizure of power before trying to take over the government. This had been shown in the previous discussions of the Congress, over participation in elections for the National Assembly and on the economic struggle. On these, most *rejected* Rosa's caution.

The whole Congress accepted that the elections were part of the overall plot against the revolution. As Rosa Luxemburg had put it a week before:

> We are now in the midst of a revolution, and the National Assembly is a counter-revolutionary fortress erected against the revolutionary proletariat. Our task is to take this fortress by storm and raze it to the ground.[25]

The leaders of the Spartakists were certainly not partisans of the nonsense preached by the Independents and the Social Democrats—and by present day Communist Parties—to the effect that somehow socialism can be introduced by parliamentary means. But they did believe that revolutionaries could use the elections as a tactic in the struggle to destroy workers' illusions in parliament.

In order to mobilise the masses against the National Assembly and lead them in a decisive struggle against it, wrote Rosa:

> ...we must utilise the elections and the platform of the National Assembly itself... Our aim in participating in the National Assembly must be to expose and roundly denounce all the tricks and machinations of this fine assembly, to reveal its counter-revolutionary activities step by step to the masses, and to appeal to them to intervene and force a decision.[26]

The point was hammered home at the Congress by Paul Levi, who argued that the Communists could only ignore the elections if they felt powerful enough to overthrow the Assembly. But although they might be that strong in Berlin, the Ruhr and Upper Silesia, in the rest of Germany conditions were very different.

> We regard the question as very serious. The decision on this question can determine for months the destiny of our revolution. Think of the situation as it is. The National Assembly is going to meet. You cannot stop it. For months it will dominate the whole of German political life.

You will not be able to stop all eyes being fixed on it... It will be in the consciousness of the German workers, yet you want to stay outside it, to work from the outside.[27]

But the delegates were unmoved. They had seen only a few days earlier the humiliation of the Ebert government as it failed in its attempt to crush the Marine Division. They did not believe that it could divert attention, even temporarily, along parliamentary channels.

Paul Levi himself later described the mood:

> The air of Berlin was filled with revolutionary tension. There was nobody who was not convinced that in the immediate future there would be new mass demonstrations and new actions. The delegates, who represented the unorganised masses who had just come to us through action alone, by action and for action, could not understand that a new action, easily forseeable, could end not in victory but in a setback. They could not even dream of following a tactic that would leave room for manoeuvre, just in case there was a setback.[28]

The mood of the majority was expressed by the former Social Democratic deputy Otto Rühle, who insisted there was no need to use the Assembly as a tribune: 'We have other tribunes. The street is the great tribune that we have conquered and that we will not abandon, even if they shoot at us.'

The revolutionaries did not need a 'new corpse', he said. They had finished with 'compromises and opportunism'. There was no need to worry. Perhaps the Assembly would flee to some provincial town to escape the revolutionary atmosphere of the capital. 'We will be able to establish a new government in Berlin.' In any case, there were a full 14 days before the elections were due.[29]

Not all the delegates who opposed taking part in the elections expected a battle for power in so short a time. But many did. Their support for Rosa Luxemburg's programme two days later did not constitute any real agreement with the perspective contained in it.

The same impatience was displayed in the discussion on the economic struggle. Lange, who introduced the session for the leadership, did not take a position on whether revolutionaries should remain inside the unions. But many other delegates had no doubts that Communists should break with such 'reformist' institutions. Paul Frölich raised the slogan 'Out of the unions', calling instead for 'workers' unions' which would end for once and for all the distinction between the party and the trade unions. He was attacked by Rosa Luxemburg—but for not putting the emphasis on the workers' councils. She was not happy with the slogan 'Out of the unions', but still suggested that the 'liquidation' of the unions was the order of the day. Only Heckert pointed out that the unions were far from finished, that they still embraced vast numbers of workers and that the slogan 'Out of the unions' was extremely dangerous.

The impatience with trade union organisations dominated by right wing bureaucrats was natural for a conference taking place in the midst of repeated strikes and street demonstrations. But there was little doubt that it was mistaken. The militant workers in the big Berlin factories might not look to the national union organisations before moving into action, but for workers in many smaller factories with less experience of struggle, the unions were more important than ever. Even while the Spartakists were discussing how quickly to write off the unions, workers were joining unions as never before: union membership grew by 50 percent in the first month of the revolution alone, and trebled in the next 12 months. As Radek insisted some months later:

> The masses who are developing through the revolution go as a determined force into the unions to abuse their leaders. About four million new trade unionists since the revolution. That is the answer for the masses on the question of the need for unions, which no revolutionary can overlook.[30]

There was an important contrast between the attitude of the majority of the Spartakists and the attitude of the Bolsheviks in Russia. The Bolsheviks found it necessary to put an effort into trade union work even after the October Revolution: it was a way to bring to political activity whole new layers of workers. The discussions at the Spartakist Congress all revealed the same impatience, the same inability to take seriously the task of winning the broadest layers of workers to the revolution.

Many of the most experienced leaders of the new party were dismayed. The veteran revolutionary organiser and lifelong colleague of Rosa Luxemburg, Leo Jogiches, saw the Congress decisions as proof that it had been called prematurely, in isolation from the masses who still trusted the Independents. He was deeply pessimistic about the future, despite the rising tide of struggle outside the conference hall. He voted, alone, against the founding of the party. That did not, however, stop him becoming its key organiser.

His doubts were shared by Radek, who wrote in his memoirs, 'The Congress showed in an acute way the youth and inexperience of the party... I did not feel I was in the presence of a party'.[31]

Rosa Luxemburg was less pessimistic, although she did not doubt that her opponents at the Congress had been wrong. 'Our defeat', she wrote to her old friend Clara Zetkin:

> was merely the triumph of a somewhat childish, half baked, narrow minded radicalism. In any case that happened at the beginning of the conference. Later, contact between us [the leadership] and the delegates was established... The Spartakists are a fresh generation, free from the cretinous traditions of the 'good old party' [the SPD]... We decided unanimously not to make the matter [of the boycott] into a cardinal question and not to take it too seriously.[32]

What mattered most for Rosa was that the newly founded Communist Party was attracting the best of the younger generation to its ranks. Their inexperience and their 'ultra-leftism' was the other side of their youth and fighting spirit. But she underestimated the impact of this inexperience in a party that lacked a reliable and experienced cadre. This was to prove fatal in the days that followed, even though the old leadership was re-elected in its entirety at the end of the Congress. As Radek noted eight months later:

> In the Communist leadership, only a minority correctly understood this problem... That is why the struggle in the Communist Party against the putschist ideology was so weak.[33]

The lack of cohesion of the revolutionary left was made worse by another consequence of the ultra-left policies adopted by the Congress. The most experienced group of worker militants in Berlin itself, the revolutionary shop stewards, had been expected to join the party at its foundation. But discussions between their leaders and a delegation from the new party, headed by Liebknecht, soon ran into difficulties. They demanded a number of policy changes—including the dropping of any reference to Spartakus in the name of the new party.

What they really wanted were guarantees that the new party would have nothing to do with the unruly armed mobs that many identified with Spartakism. Richard Müller spelt this out when he insisted that joint activity depended on the abandonment by the Communist Party of what he called 'putschism'. Liebknecht replied that Müller was speaking the language of the Social Democrat paper *Vorwärts*. On that acrimonious note the negotiations collapsed.[34] Yet eventually two of the three delegates for the shop stewards, Müller and Däumig, were to prove their revolutionary sincerity by joining the Communists in 1920.

The immediate outcome was disastrous. The Communist Party was to be faced with massive struggles without some of the best and most influential workers' leaders in Berlin in its ranks. The shop stewards, on the other hand, were to be plunged into a complex and rapidly changing situation without the immediate guidance that figures such as Rosa Luxemburg, Jogiches and Radek could have given them. The result, paradoxically, was that many of them were to fall into the very putschism they so denounced among the Spartakists.

1.   Theodor Wolff, *Through Two Decades* (London 1936) p131.

2.   Quoted in R M Watt, *The Kings Depart* (London 1973) p122.

3.   F M Carsten, *Revolution in Central Europe* (London 1972) p56.

4.   Ibid, pp26-27.

5.   Details ibid, p36.

6.   Landauer, *European Socialism* (Berkeley 1959) p986.

7.   Paul Frölich and others, *Illustrierte Geschichte der Deutschen Revolution* (Berlin 1929, reprinted Frankfurt 1970) p217.

8.   F M Carsten, op cit, p45.

9.   The transcript of the discussion between Ebert and Groener came to light at a libel trial in late 1925; see P Frölich et al, op cit, p233.

10. Quoted in F M Carsten, op cit, p59.

11. Quoted in P Frölich et al, op cit, p233.

12. For examples, see ibid, pp238, 241.

13. Quoted ibid, p243

14. Quoted in M Phillips Price, *Germany in Transition* (London 1923) p88.

15. Quoted in H J Gordon, *The Reichswehr and the German Republic 1919-26* (Princeton 1957) p20.

16. Ibid, p23.

17. Heinrich Ströbel, *The German Revolution and After* (London 1923) p88.

18. Ibid.

19. P Frölich et al, op cit, p257.

20. Pierre Broué, *Révolution en Allemagne* (Paris 1971) pp207-208.

21. Peter Nettl, *Rosa Luxemburg* (London 1966) p725.

22. See Karl Radek's memoirs of Berlin, in Schudenkopf, *Archiv fur Sozialgeschichte II* (1962) p132 onwards.

23. Rosa Luxemburg, 'What Does the Spartakus League Want?' in *Selected Political Writings*, edited by Dick Howard (New York 1971) p366 onwards.

24. Ibid.
25. *Rote Fahne*, 23 December 1918.
26. Hermann Weber (ed), *Der Gründungsparteitag der KPD* (Frankfurt 1969).
27. Ibid.
28. Paul Levi in *Rote Fahne*, 5 September 1920, quoted in P Broué, op cit, pp239, 241; and in R M Watt, op cit, pp294-295.
29. *Der Gründungsparteitag der KPD*, op cit.
30. Karl Radek (writing under the pseudonym Arnold Struthörn), *Die Entwicklung der Deutschen Revolution und die Aufgaben der Kommunistischen Partei*, September 1919.
31. Radek's memoirs of Berlin, in Schudenkopf, op cit.
32. Quoted in P Nettl, op cit, p758.
33. Karl Radek (aka Arnold Struthörn), op cit, p8.
34. For an account of the negotiations between the Spartakists and the revolutionary shop stewards, see Richard Müller, *Der Burgerkrieg in Deutschland* (West Berlin 1974) pp88-89.

CHAPTER 5

The Spartakus days

Berlin in the first few days of 1919 seemed a city in which nothing could stop the growing influence of the revolutionary left. The Ebert government was becoming more and more precarious. The Independent Social Democrats had abandoned it. The army was falling apart. A strike wave was bringing more and more workers into opposition and the government had to sit back helpless while its own party newspaper was seized. Above all the revolutionary left had influence over two of the most important armed forces in the city—the Marine Division and Eichhorn's Security Force.

Ebert seriously considered abandoning Berlin. 'We shall go away,' he told General Groener. 'If the Liebknecht crowd take this opportunity to seize power, there will be nobody here... And we shall set up a new government somewhere else in a few days'.[1]

But the generals persuaded him to hold out. On 4 January the government made its first counter-move. It announced that Eichhorn had been dismissed from his position as police chief.

This was a deliberately provocative manoeuvre. The government knew that the longer it waited, the more it would lose popularity in the capital. But it also believed that the Freikorps had gathered sufficient forces outside Berlin to crush any coup from the left. It aimed now to provoke premature action by the Berlin masses, and then to retake the city forcibly, claiming that it was merely restoring order and preventing chaos.

General Groener told a libel court in 1925 that as early as 29 December, 'Ebert ordered Noske to lead troops against the Spartakists. The Volunteer corps assembled that day and everything was ready for the opening of hostilities'.[2]

Noske readily took on the job of defence minister. And he was quite candid as to what it entailed. 'Somebody must be the bloodhound,' he declared.

On the day that Eichhorn's dismissal was announced, Noske and Ebert inspected six Volunteer corps of handpicked right wing officers outside Berlin. General Märcher tells how:

> In the first days of January a meeting at which Noske was present took place at General Staff Headquarters with the leaders of the Volunteer corps, and the details of the march on Berlin were settled.[3]

None of this was in response to any 'Spartakist uprising' in Berlin. Rather, it was part of a carefully worked out plan to provoke action that could be depicted as a rising and then to crush it. As the Social Democrat Ernst, who was nominated to replace Eichhorn as police chief, told journalists a fortnight later, 'We, through our preparations, forced the Spartakists to strike prematurely'.[4]

The Berlin workers greeted the news that Eichhorn had been dismissed with a huge wave of anger. They felt he was being dismissed for siding with them against the attacks of right wing officers and employers. Eichhorn responded by refusing to vacate police headquarters. He insisted that he had been appointed by the Berlin working class and could only be removed by them. He would accept a decision of the Berlin Executive of the Workers' and Soldiers' Councils, but no other.

If the government had been concerned only with Eichhorn's post they would have taken up this offer—since the Berlin Executive contained a Social Democrat majority. But something else was at stake—a battle to the death with the revolution and with its organisations, even if these were temporarily under Social Democratic control. Such a battle could not be carried through by acknowledging the power of one such organisation to appoint the Berlin police chief.

The Independent Social Democrat leaders met representatives of the revolutionary shop stewards and the newly formed Communist Party to discuss how they should react to the sacking of one of their members from such a key post. It was agreed that it should be resisted with a *peaceful* demonstration the next day, a Sunday. A leaflet was distributed which spelt out what was at stake:

The Ebert-Scheidemann government intends, not only to get rid of the last representative of the revolutionary Berlin workers, but to establish a regime of coercion against the revolutionary workers. The blow which is aimed at the Berlin police chief will affect the whole German proletariat and the revolution.[5]

The response of the workers was greater than anyone expected. 'A huge mass of hundreds of thousands responded on the Sunday to the call of the organisers to show that the spirit of November is not yet beaten'.[6] The workers, many armed, responded enthusiastically to militant speeches from Liebknecht, from Däumig of the revolutionary shop stewards, and from Ledebour for the Independent leadership.

The organisers had intended this to be a peaceful protest. But the angry crowd were not willing merely to demonstrate and then return home. With a little encouragement (it was claimed later that this came from paid right wing provocateurs out to provoke a premature rising[7]) they rushed off to seize control of the newspaper buildings and an entire issue of the Social Democrat paper *Vorwärts* was dumped in the river. Other groups began to seize the railway stations.

'The meeting of the organisers', Eichhorn later told, 'was not over-joyed at the news of this occupation of the newspaper offices, which they had not contemplated'.[8] The Spartakist leadership had in fact met the previous day and had been unanimous that an uprising must be avoided at all costs. Paul Levi wrote:

> The members of the leadership were unanimous: a government of the proletariat would not last more than a fortnight... It was necessary to avoid all slogans that might lead to the overthrow of the government at this point.
>
> Our slogan had to be precise in the following sense: lifting of the dismissal of Eichhorn, disarming of the counter-revolutionary troops, arming of the proletariat. None of these slogans implied an overthrow of the government: not even the arming of the workers in a situation where the government had the support of a sizeable part of the workers.[9]

Rosa Luxemburg's attitude was that the demand for the overthrow of the Ebert-Scheidemann government was:

> ...a propaganda slogan to rally the revolutionary proletariat rather than a tangible object of revolutionary action. Under the given conditions, such an action, confined chiefly to Berlin, could at best become no more than a

'Berlin commune' and probably on a smaller historical scale. Her only immediate aim therefore was the vigorous repulse of all counter-revolutionary attacks.[10]

In any battle a leader needs a cool head and an ability to see through the hourly fluctuations in fortunes to the real, developing balance of forces. Rosa Luxemburg and Leo Jogiches had this. But they did not have a powerful party capable of communicating their tactics to the workers. Instead they had a small number of individuals, some well enough known for the workers to follow on occasion. But the best known of these, Liebknecht, certainly did not have a clear head. He was easily carried away by events and only too ready to forget leadership decisions. He admitted at the time of the party conference debate over elections that he went to bed with one attitude and awoke with another.

Now Liebknecht voted at the meeting of the leadership against any attempt to seize power. But he privately admitted to having reservations. 'Our government is impossible yet it is true. But a government of Ledebour supported by the revolutionary shop stewards is possible'.[11]

Yet it was Liebknecht who, with Wilhelm Pieck, represented the Spartakists in the crucial discussions with the Independents and the revolutionary shop stewards on the tactics in the aftermath of the Sunday demonstration.

The leaders of the Berlin Independents were not, by and large, revolutionaries. Their local conference of only a fortnight before, on 15 December, had voted against the revolutionary point of view by 485 votes to 185. They had not yet understood that in order to make a revolution and to begin building socialism it was necessary to transform society from below, through the conscious action of the working class. They were the sort of people Rosa Luxemburg was talking about when she spoke of 'the illusion of the first phase of the revolution, that it is sufficient to overthrow the capitalist government and set up another in its place in order to bring about the socialist revolution'.[12]

On 9 November such people had put their faith in a joint USP-SPD government acting *for* the workers, but over their heads. Now they felt more and more the pressure, the anger, of the Berlin masses. They felt that somehow they had to respond. They did so without changing their fundamental view that they had to act *for* the masses. On 9 November the masses had been used as a lever to replace the Kaiser by Ebert and

Haase. Now they were to be used as a lever to replace Ebert by Ledebour and Liebknecht. The names were to be different, the mechanism the same.

When Lenin and Trotsky denounced such people as 'centrists' and 'reformists' they usually meant that they would rely on parliamentary means above all others. But that did not mean that reformists always ruled out the use of force. There were situations where violence seems the best means to *reform* the existing structure of society: witness today the succession of left wing military coups in the Third World, where one may speak of military as well as parliamentary 'reformism'.

The one thing the reformists and centrists will not do is place their trust in the self activity of the workers. The masses are for them an army to be wheeled on to the stage of history, just long enough for themselves to be hoisted into prominence. Once a real struggle develops, however, they attempt to wheel the army off again, even if the result is a defeat of immense proportions. Hence reformism does not just mean timidity—it also means occasional acts of suicidal adventurism.

Ledebour was a former Social Democrat deputy, a man who was soon to be very hostile to Bolshevism, who was always to refuse to join a thoroughgoing revolutionary organisation. But on 5 January he felt that the pressure of the masses was such that it only required a minimal effort to make Ebert hand over power to a government in which he, Ledebour, would be a central figure, a government capable of introducing socialism 'by decree'.

'It was reported', he told later of the meeting held that evening:

> that in addition to the working class, the Berlin garrisons were also on our side. Not only the Marine Division, but practically all the regiments were ready to take up arms and place themselves at the head of the Berlin working class to overthrow the Ebert-Scheidemann government. We received further the news that in Spandau great masses were ready to rush to our help in case of need, with 2,000 machine guns and 20 cannons. We received similar news from Frankfurt-on-Oder.[13]

In a frenzy of enthusiasm the Berlin organisation of the Independents set up a 'Joint Revolutionary Committee' together with the revolutionary shop stewards and Liebknecht and Pieck, who claimed to speak for the Spartakists. They issued a leaflet which called for a general strike and mass demonstrations the next day, concluding, 'Throw yourselves into the struggle for the power of the revolutionary proletariat. Down with the Ebert-Scheidemann government'.[14]

A second leaflet, which never seems to have been distributed, made the committee's intentions even clearer:

> The Ebert-Scheidemann government has become intolerable. The undersigned revolutionary committee, representing the revolutionary workers and soldiers (Independent Social Democratic Party and Communist Party), proclaims its removal.
>
> The undersigned revolutionary committee assumes provisionally the functions of government.
>
> Comrades, workers—form ranks around the decisions of the revolutionary committee.
>
> Signed: Liebknecht, Ledebour, Scholze.[15]

At first everything seemed to go perfectly for the revolutionaries. The general strike was a massive success. Even the right wing Independent Heinrich Ströbel had to admit, 'The general strike made a good start'.[16] Rosa Leviné-Meyer, who was in Berlin at the time, writes, 'The response of the workers, right down to those in the SPD, was overwhelming and the government was utterly helpless'.[17]

Another massive demonstration paraded through the streets. Revolutionary workers seized all the bourgeois papers, as well as *Vorwärts*. The government printing offices had been taken over, as were the railway stations. Snipers on the Brandenburg Gate dominated the whole centre of the city. 'Only a few strong points in the government quarter remained in government hands'.[18]

At a meeting in the Chancellory Landsberg reported, 'The Spartakists have taken over the Railway Administration Building, the Ministry of War is next, and then it is our turn.' Out of fear of the masses swarming in the streets, even 'the bloodhound' Gustav Noske, the newly appointed minister of defence, fled from inner Berlin to set up his headquarters in the suburb of Dahlem.

But the revolution was not as strong as it seemed, nor the government as powerless. Even while the revolutionary workers seemed to be in control of inner Berlin, the revolutionary committee was showing its weakness.

To begin with, it was not really representative of the three bodies that had constituted it. Liebknecht and Pieck had joined it for the

Spartakists. But the Spartakist leadership had not been consulted and in fact strongly disapproved. Pieck later admitted:

> The leadership of the Communist Party could not be kept informed about these decisions, nor was it possible to inform them of what was decided. Only at a later meeting of the party leadership it appeared they were in agreement with the struggle against the government's measures, but not with the aim of fighting for governmental power.[19]

According to Radek, it was not until a week later that Rosa Luxemburg learnt that Liebknecht had signed the call with Ledebour for the establishment of the 'provisional government'. 'Rosa said nothing more all evening. It was clear that Liebknecht had allowed himself to be carried away with the idea of a Left Independent government and had kept this from the knowledge of the *Zentrale* [the day to day party leadership or Party Centre]'.[20] Rumours circulating in the German Communist Party afterwards had it that she said to Liebknecht, 'Karl, how could you—and what about our programme?'[21]

The January fighting went down in history as the 'Spartakist Uprising'. But the Spartakist leadership of the Communist Party were opposed to the project! Such is the fate of revolutionaries who have the right policy, but don't have a powerful disciplined party to put it into effect. They get the blame for actions they do not initiate and cannot control.

The revolutionary shop stewards were no more united behind the attempted seizure of power than the Spartakists. Their two most influential members in the Berlin factories, Richard Müller and Däumig, both argued strongly against the action—yet both were revolutionaries and were later to join the Communist Party.

The Independent Social Democrats were, by their very nature, riven with internal divisions over this matter as over every other. They were soon to prove themselves the most dangerous and most unreliable of allies in any bid for power.

The revolutionary committee was not only unrepresentative—it was also too large and unwieldy to direct any action, let alone a seizure of power. With 52 members it was a mini-parliament, not an executive capable of coordinating the movements of revolutionary troops and armed workers. Instead of acting, it debated endlessly what to do.

The effect on the morale of those fighting on the streets was catastrophic. As one of the Spartakist leaders, Paul Levi, later wrote:

What was seen on Monday in Berlin was probably the greatest proletarian demonstration in history... From the statue of Roland (in front of the city hall) to the statue of Victory (in the Königsplatz) proletarians were standing shoulder to shoulder... They had brought along their weapons and their red flags. They were ready to do anything, to give everything, even their lives. There was an army of 200,000 such as Ludendorff had never seen.

Then the inconceivable happened... The masses were standing from nine in the morning in the fog and the cold. Somewhere their leaders were sitting and conferring. The fog lifted and the masses were still standing. Their leaders conferred. Noon came and in addition to the cold, hunger came. And the leaders conferred... The masses were feverish with excitement. They wanted one deed, even one word to calm their excitement. But nobody knew what to do, because the leaders were conferring.

The fog came again, and with it the dusk. The masses went home sadly. They had wanted great things, but they had done nothing. Because their leaders conferred. They sat the entire evening and the entire night and conferred. When dawn came they were still conferring or were conferring again.[22]

Paul Frölich, who also witnessed the events, tells how:

The 'Revolutionary Committee' which had so valiantly proclaimed armed resistance and the overthrow of the government showed itself completely incapable of leadership. It issued an appeal, it distributed a certain number of rifles and it made a feeble attempt to seize the war ministry. That was all. It did not bother its head about the armed workers in the newspaper offices; it neither took over command itself nor gave any instructions on what they should do, but left them in useless occupation of points of no strategic significance. The only measures of any military value on the side of the revolution throughout the whole fighting were taken by the workers themselves at their own initiative when they occupied the railway stations.[23]

The Revolutionary Committee had been formed on the basis of an over-favourable evaluation of the feeling of the workers and soldiers in Berlin. They were prepared to demonstrate, they were prepared to strike, they were prepared to strip the insignia of rank from the officers. But they were not yet prepared to take power into their own hands.

Many of the workers and soldiers who had resented the dismissal of Eichhorn had done so out of the feeling that the Majority Social

Democrats were disrupting 'socialist unity'. But now the government could present the left offensive in the same light. Typical of its arguments was a leaflet to 'workers, citizens and soldiers' distributed on the evening of 6 January:

> For the second time armed bandits of the Spartakus League have physically seized *Vorwärts*. The leaders of these bands today openly proclaimed in speeches the overthrow of the government, bloody civil war and the setting up of the Spartakist dictatorship. The German people and the German working class face the gravest danger. Anarchy and hunger will be the result of Spartakist rule.[24]

The blame for unrest was shifted from the government to the left. There were still considerable numbers of workers and soldiers prepared to accept this claim. The Berlin Executive of the Councils denounced the Spartakists—even though barely a week earlier it had criticised the government's attack on the Marine Division. The following day a demonstration of several thousand Social Democrats around the government buildings impeded the operations of the revolutionary forces inside. Sections of the Berlin garrison thought by the government to be 'unreliable'—such as the Republican Soldiers Corps—fought for it nonetheless.

More significant, perhaps, was the opposition of many workers and soldiers to *both* sides. Key groups of soldiers, such as the Marine Division, refused to support the armed action of the left and declared their neutrality. On 9 January a joint meeting of workers from two of the great factories, Schwartzkopf and AEG, voted for 'workers to unite over the heads of your chiefs'. This was echoed by a 40,000 strong meeting of workers from these and other factories which called for a government made up of all three 'workers' parties'.[25]

The Communist leaders were aware that the mass of workers were still prevaricating; Müller and Däumig of the revolutionary shop stewards were aware of it; but the Revolutionary Committee from Liebknecht to Ledebour were not. They ignored the neutrality of the key sections of workers and soldiers. They refused to see that despite the general strike and the huge demonstrations, the number of soldiers and workers prepared to fight was a few thousand only.

Yet, even when the decision to fight was taken, all was not lost. The balance of forces in Berlin itself was not on the government's side. 'A tremendous material advantage was on the side of the rebels', is the judgement of one historian of the German army.[26] With determined action, the revolutionary forces could quickly have overpowered the concentrations of government troops in the city. This would have forced the government onto the defensive. To keep their ministerial positions, Ebert and Scheidemann may well, under those circumstances, have agreed to a formula that left them in power, but the workers armed (as had happened after the clashes at the beginning and end of December). The revolutionary left would have secured positions from which it could advance with much greater working class support in the not-too-distant future.

But the Revolutionary Committee provided no coordination. They allowed the government to retain a hold on buildings that it would not have been able to defend for an hour given a determined assault. From these buildings it was able to plan its counter-attack with impunity.

Worst of all, the Revolutionary Committee compounded one error with another. The moment it was clear that the government was not going to collapse immediately into their arms, the Independent leaders asked for negotiations with the government—even though they had declared it overthrown only a day or two before!

The French Jacobins pointed out that 'those who half make a revolution dig their own graves', and Karl Marx reiterated the point when he argued that 'the defensive is the death of any insurrection'.[27] An uprising can only succeed if the masses feel they have a chance of success. They are not drilled military formations, trained to maintain their ranks in retreat as in advance. They are men and women who will give their all if they believe they are going to achieve liberation, but who will quickly disperse and drift back to their normal, hum-drum lives in the factory, the tenement, the pub, if they feel that that objective has been abandoned. A revolutionary movement that is sure of victory will forget everything else. But the moment the leaders acknowledge that the old order is to continue, by negotiating with it, the rank and file will begin to worry about their jobs, their homes, the attitude of the foreman and the local policeman. Even under the best conditions, negotiations with the enemy mean that support begins to crumble. This was what happened now. A bad situation for the revolutionaries was turned into an appaling one.

Rosa Luxemburg recognised the danger. Although she had opposed any attempt at a rising, she was adamant that once it was under way there was no choice but to carry it forward energetically. As Clara Zetkin later told, Rosa was not for a taking of power but for 'a vigorous repulse of all the counter-revolutionary attacks... But at least these demands were to be won by action, not by negotiation'.[28] That was why in *Rote Fahne* on 7 January Rosa stressed the difference between the fighting mood of the masses and the fatal indecision of the leaders:

> Anyone who witnessed yesterday's mass demonstration in the Siegesallee, who felt the magnificent mood, the energy that the masses exude, must conclude that politically the proletariat has grown enormously through the experiences of recent weeks. They have become aware of their power, and all that remains is for them to avail themselves of this power.
>
> The masses must learn to fight, to act in the struggle itself. And today one can sense that the workers of Berlin have learned to act; they thirst for resolute deeds, for sweeping measures.
>
> However, are their leaders, the executive organs of their will, well informed? Have the revolutionary shop stewards, have the energy and resolve of the radical elements in the USPD, grown in the meanwhile? Has their capacity for action kept pace with the growing energy of the masses?
>
> We are afraid we cannot answer these questions with a straightforward Yes...
>
> What have the leaders done? What have they decided? Which measures have they taken to safeguard victory in this tense situation in which the fate of the revolution can be decided? We have seen and heard nothing. Perhaps they are discussing their tasks very thoroughly. But now is the time to act.
>
> The Ebert-Scheidemann clique are not wasting their time in endless discussion. Behind the scenes they are preparing to act with the usual cunning and energy of counter-revolutionaries; they are loading their weapons for the final surprise attack to destroy the revolution.
>
> There is no time to be lost. Energetic measures must be taken at once. The vacillating element among the troops can be won for the cause of the proletariat only by vigorous and determined action on the part of the revolutionary bodies.
>
> Act! Act! Courageously, consistently—that is the 'accursed' duty and obligation of the revolutionary shop stewards and the sincere leaders of the USPD. Disarm the counter-revolution. Arm the masses. Occupy all positions of power. Act quickly![29]

But the Spartakists were not capable of giving the movement the determination, organisation and direction it needed—any more than they had been capable previously of restricting it to defensive demands. They were just too small to wield the necessary influence.

Individual Spartakist militants could make an impact. Leviné, for instance, who only a few days before had been sent by the leadership to stop a premature uprising in Upper Silesia, now took charge of the military operations in and around the *Vorwärts* building. But that was not at all the same thing as being able to impose some overall strategic and tactical organisation on the revolutionary forces.

The government was only too ready to take advantage of the disorganisation and indecision of its opponents.

Already on 6 January Noske had delegated his police powers to General Lüttwitz in preparation for the use of the Freikorps from outside Berlin. But the disorganisation of the revolutionaries allowed the creation of a pro-government force in the heart of Berlin itself. On 8 January two regiments of Social Democrat soldiers had been organised in the Reichstag building. Their total strength of about 5,000 was rather less than the numbers on the revolutionary side, which could easily have dispersed them. But there was no overall command on the revolutionary side to ensure that such things were done. Instead, by engaging in negotiations, the Independents gave the government time to collect these forces until it felt strong enough to throw them into a battle to dislodge the revolutionaries.

The determined leadership of the government forces enabled them to drive the revolutionaries from their positions very quickly. The commander of the pro-government Republican Soldiers Corps tells that by 13 January:

> I was in a position to report to Noske that there was nothing more to be done, except to maintain the order that had been restored and to continue the process of disarming. The Berlin troops of the Republican Soldiers Corps and the Volunteers [the Social Democrat soldiers] under Kuttner and Baumeister, who captured the Brandenburg Gate and defended the Reichstag, had re-established the reign of order in Berlin.[30]

But this order was not good enough for the Social Democrat leaders, especially Ebert and Noske, since it depended on armed Social Democrat workers and soldiers. They preferred to control Berlin with more 'reliable' troops—the thousands of pro-monarchist Freikorps who were assembling outside the capital while the rebellion was crushed. These began to march into Berlin on 11 January, but it was another 36 hours before the main force entered.

When they entered the city they had nothing better to do than to tear the republican armbands off members of the Republican Soldiers Corps and insult them on every possible occasion.[31]

This seems to be a slight exaggeration: there were still left wing snipers in a number of buildings. The Freikorps soon flushed these out, stationing machine guns and armoured cars in the main squares. Any resistance was dealt with in the most peremptory manner. When a group of seven delegates were sent out to discuss the peaceful surrender of the *Vorwärts* building they were murdered. Artillery was used to blow the front off the police headquarters before Eichhorn's men abandoned resistance. 'Little quarter was given to its defenders, who were shot down where they were found. Only a few managed to escape across the roofs'.[32] The head office of the Communist Party was seized and demolished.

The old police force, from under the monarchy, were recalled to duty and given the job of helping the Freikorps hunt out the 'Spartakists'. The daily press praised the Freikorps for the 'delivery of Berlin' from 'anarchy and dictatorship'.

> The armed mercenaries of the counter-revolution were savagely slaughtering their prisoners and the press sang hymns in praise of the 'deliverers'. It described with gusto the blood and brain splattered walls against which batches of workers were being mown down. The unscrupulous campaign of the press turned the middle and lower middle class into a bloodthirsty mob eager to drive men and women before the rifles of the execution squads on the slightest suspicion.[33]

'The bloodshed was naturally attributed to the Spartakists, and a wild hue and cry after their leaders swept the town...' relates Rosa Leviné-Meyer. 'My hospital shared the general excitement. The nurses were running to and fro like a disturbed flock of sheep, telling gruesome stories about the bloodthirsty Spartakists'.[34]

The Social Democrat paper *Vorwärts* gave every encouragement to the murderous hysteria, calling openly for slaughter of the Spartakist leaders:

Many hundred corpses in a row
Proletarians.
Karl, Rosa, Radek and company
Not one of them lies there—
Proletarians.[35]

The white terror reached its crescendo two days later. Rosa Luxemburg and Karl Liebknecht had refused to flee from the city—indeed, although living in hiding, Rosa continued to edit *Rote Fahne*. On 15 January they were arrested at their hiding place, together with Wilhelm Pieck, and dragged off separately to one of the Freikorps headquarters, the Eden Hotel. Here a Captain Pabst had already made arrangements for their murder. After questioning, Liebknecht was taken from the building, knocked half conscious with a rifle butt and then driven to the Tiergarten where he was killed. Rosa was taken out shortly afterwards, her skull smashed in and then she too was driven off, shot through the head and thrown into the canal.

> *Vorwärts* had the honour of announcing in advance of all other papers on Thursday 16 January that Liebknecht had been 'shot while trying to escape' and Luxemburg 'killed by the people'.[36]

The news caused immense joy among the middle classes. In Rosa Leviné-Meyer's hospital 'the special edition went from hand to hand; everyone was screaming and jumping for joy'.[37]

The German Revolution was still far from over. There were many bitter battles still to come. Even in Berlin there was to be renewed fighting within two months, and it was to be all of five years before German capitalism achieved anything like full stability. But success in the January fighting gave the bourgeoisie an important victory on which to build.

They had emerged from the November revolution with the state machine in tatters. They had lost their monopoly of armed force: the army was torn between the pressures of the rank and file and the orders of the generals. At the time of the January fighting the generals had under their immediate control at most 10,000 men—hardly enough to control one city, let alone a modern state. Their victory gave them a monopoly of armed force again and the chance to expand the reliable units at great speed.

What is more, the murder of Rosa Luxemburg had taken from the revolutionaries their most able and experienced leader. Her successors were able and courageous—but they lacked her experience and her ability to cut through immediate impressions and grasp a situation in its totality. The German working class was to pay an enormous price for this loss. The best summary of what the government had succeeded in doing was given some months later by the deposed revolutionary police chief, Eichhorn:

> The Berlin proletariat was sacrificed to the carefully calculated and artfully executed provocation of the government of the day. The government sought the opportunity to deal the revolution its death blow; the January movement offered this opportunity.
>
> Although to some extent armed, the proletariat was in no way equipped for serious fighting; it fell into the trap of the pacification negotiations and allowed its strength, time and revolutionary fervour to be destroyed. In the meantime, the government, having at its disposal all the resources of the state, could prepare for its final subjugation.[38]

The lessons of January

In the last article that Rosa Luxemburg wrote before she was murdered, she blamed the defeat on 'the contradiction between the powerful, resolute and offensive appearance of the Berlin masses on the one hand, and the irresoluteness, timidity and indecision of the Berlin leadership on the other'.[39]

There is little doubt that she was right. With a powerful revolutionary party, the Berlin working class would probably not have walked into the trap laid by Ebert, Noske and the generals. With a powerful revolutionary party there would have been the overall leadership necessary to coordinate the revolutionary forces if a rising had begun despite its advice.

But there was not such a party. This was ensured by the history of the previous years: the growth and stability of pre-war German capitalism; Rosa Luxemburg's own failure at that time to give a practical organisational form to her principled opposition to the politics of Kautsky and the SPD leadership; the friction between the Spartakists and the Bremen revolutionaries in 1916; the predominance of impatient, ultra-left elements in the Communist Party when it was eventually formed a bare week before the fighting began.

There were, of course, objective differences between Germany at the beginning of 1919 and Russia in 1917. But these were not the decisive explanation for the January defeat: in Russia in 1917 there were often situations in which the workers in particular industrial centres wanted to go into battle unprepared and isolated from the workers elsewhere. Luxemburg was as capable as Lenin and Trotsky of seeing the immense dangers of such premature action. What was lacking was the sort of party that Lenin had been able to build over the previous 20 years. And without such a party Rosa's own ideas were reduced to the level of commentary on the revolutionary events, instead of providing them with direction.

But that does not necessarily mean there was no way the Spartakist leaders could have acted to avoid the worst aspects of the defeat.

The debate over the Spartakist tactics began even as events unfolded. And it began within the leadership of the recently formed Communist Party, as a disagreement between Rosa Luxemburg and Karl Radek.

Rosa's position was formulated in the last articles she wrote—'What Are the Leaders Doing?', 'The House of Cards,' and 'Order Reigns in Berlin'[40]—and in an account of her views given some years later by her friend and comrade Clara Zetkin. The key point for her was that 'the revolution is making its way, step by step, through all the apparent zig-zag movements and is marching forward irresistibly. The masses must learn to fight, to act in the struggle itself.'

Action would distinguish in the eyes of the masses those who were revolutionaries from those who were not. 'Act! Act! Courageously, resolutely, consistently—that is the accursed duty and obligation of the revolutionaries,' she wrote.[41]

> In this struggle could we have expected a definitive victory of the revolutionary proletariat, the overthrow of Ebert and Scheidemann and the establishment of the socialist dictatorship? Certainly not, when one considers all the factors which crucially affect the question... Was the struggle of the last week then a mistake? Yes, if it was a general question of a so-called 'forward thrust', a so-called 'putsch'. But what was the starting point of the last week of battle? A brutal provocation by the government...
>
> The revolution does not operate of its own accord, in an open field of battle, according to some plan concocted slyly by 'strategists'. Its opponents also have the initiative and indeed ordinarily make far greater use of it than does the revolution itself.
>
> Confronted with the fact of the insolent provocation on the part of Ebert and Scheidemann, the revolutionary workers were compelled to take to their arms. Indeed, it was a matter of honour for the revolution

to repel the attack immediately and with all its energy if the counter-revolution was not to be encouraged to press even further forward.

The vital inner law of the revolution is never to remain inactively, passively at the level it has attained. The best parry is a vigorous thrust. This elementary rule of any fight prevails especially at all stages of the revolution.

The contradiction between the demands of the task and the inadequacies of the pre-conditions for its fulfilment in the initial phase of the revolutionary development results in the individual struggles ending formally in defeat. But revolution is the sole form of war in which the final victory can be prepared by a series of 'defeats'.[42]

For Rosa, the outbreak of the fighting was inevitable. Once it had begun, the Spartakists had to win the confidence of the masses, to remove them from the influence of the waverers and opportunists within the Independent Social Democracy, by showing themselves to be the best, most courageous and best directed fighters. Hopefully, this would allow the government attack to be warded off. If the worst came to the worst, there would be a defeat—but it would only be a partial defeat. It would strengthen the support for the revolutionaries within the working class, and it would leave the class with the strength to fight another day.

Scarcely will the ruins and the corpses of this latest episode be cleared away than the revolution will take up anew its daily, untiring work. The 'Spartakists' will continue to go their own way with unshakeable purpose. The number of their slain comrades is mounting weekly, but the number of their supporters is growing a hundred times as fast.[43]

As Clara Zetkin explained Rosa's attitude:

The young Communist Party was therefore faced with a very difficult task involving many conflicts. It could not accept the object of the movement—the overthrow of the government—as its own. But at the same time it could not let itself be separated from the masses who had joined the movement.

Despite the difference of opinion, the party had to remain with the masses in order to strengthen them in their struggles against the counter-revolution, and further the process of revolutionary maturity by making the circumstances and significance of their action abundantly clear to them. The Communist Party therefore had to show its own face and make its own position crystal clear, but without breaking the revolutionary solidarity with the fighting workers. Its role in the action had to be negative and critical on the one hand, and positive and encouraging on the other.[44]

Rosa Luxemburg's own articles of these days contain none of her own misgivings about the fighting in the streets. The tenor of her writing was to urge the masses forward, not to hold them back. The 'negative and critical' side lay in her bitter criticism of the wavering by the leaders, the left USP and the revolutionary shop stewards. Radek said the tone of *Rote Fahne* was 'as if the final battle' was taking place.[45]

Radek himself had a markedly different approach to Rosa's. He started from the same evaluation of the balance of forces—that the workers could not take power. But he translated this assessment into a quite different set of tactics. He thought the party had to tell the masses, quite crudely, to end the struggle. On the third day of the fighting, he wrote in a letter to the Spartakus *Zentrale* (the nine-strong central leadership body):

In your party programme 'What Does the Spartakus League Want?' you declare that you would not take power unless you had the masses behind you. This completely correct standpoint has its basis in the fact that the workers' government is inconceivable without existing mass proletarian organisation.

At present the only mass organisations to be considered, the workers' and soldiers' councils, are only of nominal strength. Consequently, they are not dominated by the combat party, the Communist Party, but by the social patriots and the Independents. In such a situation there can be no question of thinking of a taking of power by the working class. If the government fell into your hands after a putsch, you would be cut off from the provinces and strangled within a few hours.

In such a situation the action decided by the revolutionary delegates in reply to the attack of the social patriot government against the head of police should have simply had the character of a protest action. The proletarian vanguard, exasperated by the politics of the government, and badly led by the revolutionary delegates whose political inexperience made them incapable of weighing up the balance of forces throughout the country, in their enthusiasm transformed the movement of protest into a fight for power. It is this which is allowing Ebert and Scheidemann to give a blow to the Berlin movement that can completely weaken the movement.

The only force capable of restraint and of preventing this disaster is you, the Communist Party. You have enough clarity to know this is a battle without hope. You know it, your comrades Levi and Duncker told me. Nothing can prevent those who are too feeble to fight from retreating in the face of a superior force. In July 1917, when we were infinitely stronger than you are today, we restrained the masses with all our force and when we did not succeed in that, we led them to retreat from a battle without hope.[46]

Radek was calling on the Spartakist leaders to tell their followers to abandon the battle. His arguments were defended within that leadership by Paul Levi and Leo Jogiches. But although Rosa Luxemburg had said (according to Levi) that it would no longer be possible to work with Liebknecht, after his call for the fight for power, she was not prepared to give the order for the retreat. She knew that the Independents were negotiating for a retreat of their own, and did not want the Spartakists to provide an excuse for them. She felt that only by standing firm while the Independents led the retreat could the necessary polarisation within the masses take place, with the most militant being drawn to the Communist Party. The danger with Radek's formulation was that it would involve the Spartakus League members fleeing for cover, while the most radical workers and soldiers kept fighting by themselves. This would only strengthen ultra-left, anarchistic anti-party attitudes, rather than build the party.

January 1919 and July 1917

Radek compared the January fighting with the July days in Russia in 1917. There were close similarities. In Petrograd in July 1917, as in Berlin in January 1919, the workers and soldiers felt very powerful; the government staged a provocation (ordering the machine gun regiment to the Front), and the workers reacted by pressing for a seizure of power. And just as Liebknecht and Pieck took part in the insurrectionary call in January 1919, notwithstanding party discipline, so in July 1917: 'The leaders of the Bolshevik military organisation were instrumental in fanning the flames of revolt. The soldiers I M Golovin, K Kazakov, K N Romanov and L Linsky (all members of the Bolshevik military organisation collective) spoke out in favour of an immediate coup d'etat'.[47] The Bolshevik military paper, *Soldatskaya Pravda*, called openly for the workers to 'remove from power the bourgeoisie'.[48]

But Lenin held firmly to the view that the movement was premature and extremely dangerous:

> We must be especially attentive and careful, so as not to be drawn into a provocation...one wrong move on our part can wreck everything... If we were now able to seize power...we would not be able to hold it.[49]

The attitude of the Bolshevik leaders was expressed clearly in a speech given by Tomsky when the Petrograd conference of the party heard of moves by the machine gun regiment, 'The regiments that have come out', he declared, 'have acted in an uncomradely manner, not having invited the Central Committee of our party to consider the question of a manifestation... It is impossible to talk of a manifestion at this moment unless we want a new revolution'.[50]

The Bolshevik leaders were not able to hold the masses back. The demonstrations took place despite them. Should they have simply ordered their own party members not to take part in the demonstrations? To have done so would have been fatal. It would have confused and demoralised vast numbers of workers who only the day before had broken with the Mensheviks and identified revolutionary militancy with taking part in the demonstrations. They would not in the future have looked upon the Bolsheviks as their party if Lenin had given orders to withdraw from battle without the masses.

Party members had to be with the masses on the streets, raising slogans which would hold the masses together and express their combative spirit, while avoiding anything that could be construed as a bid to seize power. As Kamenev, for the Bolsheviks, told the workers' section of the Petrograd Soviet at the height of the demonstrations:

> We did not summon the manifestation. The popular masses themselves came into the street... But once the masses have come out, our place is among them... Our present task is to give the movement an organised character.[51]

Lenin was adamant that the party could not simply leave the masses to fight it out:

> Had our party refused to support the 3-4 July mass movement, which burst out spontaneously despite our attempts to prevent it, we should have actually completely betrayed the proletariat, since the people were moved into action by their well-founded and just anger.[52]

As he wrote two years after the event:

Mistakes are inevitable when the masses are fighting, but the Communists must *remain with the masses*, see their mistakes, explain them to the masses, try to get them rectified, and strive perseveringly for the victory of class consciousness over spontaneity.[53]

In practice, when the Bolsheviks saw that any attempt to argue against an action by the workers would be useless, they issued their own call for armed demonstrations, but for 'peaceful and organised demonstrations'. Trotsky tells how:

Under the walls of the Tauride Palace during the July days, Zinoviev was extraordinarily active, ingenious and strong. He raised the excitement of the masses to its highest note—not in order to summon them to decisive action, but, on the contrary, in order to restrain them.[54]

After three days of such demonstrations, the enthusiasm of the masses exhausted itself. It was at that point that the Bolsheviks were able to call for the masses to withdraw, knowing that vastly greater numbers than merely their own members would obey the call. They could get a hearing because the Bolsheviks themselves had shared all the risks of the struggle on the previous days, while the Mensheviks had not.

Looked at in this light, it is possible to see more clearly the mistake made by the Spartakists in January 1919. It was not that they took part in the movement—they were far, far weaker than the Bolsheviks had been during the July days, and the Bolsheviks had not been able to stand aside. Nor was it even that they did not issue the call for retreat—the Bolsheviks had not been able to do so until they felt the masses would follow, and the weakness of the Spartakists made them less able to do this.

The real mistake was that the Spartakist leaders did not make sufficiently clear—in their paper and in their speeches—that they regarded the movement as having strictly limited objectives.

It was not the case that while Liebknecht was issuing wild statements and making wild speeches, Rosa Luxemburg was speaking in very careful tones, publicly warning the revolutionary workers about proceeding too quickly. In fact, Rosa Luxemburg's articles in *Rote Fahne* had a very strident tone. When Radek reproached her with this, she insisted that she had to match the mood of the masses: 'When a healthy child is born, it struggles and yells, it does not simply bleat'.[55]

But this meant there was no way for the masses to hear Rosa's realistic assessment of the movement. She issued the call for the overthrow of the government as a 'propaganda slogan', aimed at educating the masses, not at moving them straight into action; but the strident tone in which she issued it must have given a very different impression to many newly militant, inexperienced workers.

Here was the real contrast with Lenin in 1917. He insisted that a slogan should not be raised if there was the danger that the workers would not understand what it was possible to achieve immediately:

> The slogan 'Down with the Provisional Government' is an incorrect one at the present moment because in the absence of a solid majority of the people on the side of the revolutionary proletariat, such a slogan is either an empty phrase or objectively amounts to attempts at adventurism.[56]

Such a mistake by a great Marxist and revolutionary such as Rosa Luxemburg cannot be explained by saying she had a 'different temperament' to Lenin. Her real problem was that she was afraid to be too hard in her criticism of the actions of the recently radicalised groups of workers, because she was trying to build a party from these groups. By contrast Lenin had already built a party. Its militants were already so widely respected within the class that they could afford to risk temporary unpopularity among the newly radicalised workers—provided that they participated in mass actions alongside them.

Anyone who ends up in Rosa Luxemburg's position of trying to build a revolutionary party out of next to nothing in the course of the revolution itself will face extreme difficulties. This is shown by the fact that those who were most critical of Rosa's attitude in January—Paul Levi and Karl Radek—disagreed with each other on how Communists should intervene in a number of major struggles after Rosa's death: Levi criticised Hungarian and Bavarian Communists for 'prematurely' taking power, while Radek defended them; Radek encouraged the 'March Action' of 1921—an adventure if there ever was one.[57]

Rosa Luxemburg made a tactical mistake in the first week of January 1919 by adopting too strident a tone in her writings. Yet her overall assessment of the situation was correct. Her tactical error is not to be explained by anything that happened in December or January, but by a much earlier error—when in 1912 and 1916 she underrated the importance of building an independent revolutionary socialist party. She had written in March 1917:

> The Spartakus League is only another historical tendency in the whole movement of the German proletariat. It is characterised by a different attitude on all questions of tactics and organisation. But the view that therefore it is necessary to form two carefully divided parties, corresponding with these two aspects of the socialist opposition [Independents and Spartakists] rests on a purely dogmatic interpretation of the function of parties.[58]

The contrast with Lenin's repeated insistence on the political *and* organisational independence of revolutionaries from 'centrists' could not have been sharper, and helped prepare the ground for the tragic quandary faced by Rosa Luxemburg and the German Revolution in January 1919.

1. Groener, quoted in Paul Frölich and others, *Illustrierte Geschichte der Deutschen Revolution* (Berlin 1929, reprinted Frankfurt 1970) p272.

2. Quoted in Paul Frölich, *Rosa Luxemburg* (London 1940) pp316-317.

3. Ibid.

4. Quoted in M Phillips Price, *Germany in Transition* (London 1923) p30.

5. Quoted in Heinrich Ströbel, *The German Revolution and After* (London 1923).

6. P Frölich et al, op cit, p274.

7. This is particularly stressed in the *Illustrierte Geschichte* account, pp280-281.

8. *Meine Tätigkeit im Berliner Polizeipräsidium und mein Anteil an den January-Ereignissen* (Berlin 1919).

9. In *Rote Fahne*, 5 September 1920.

10. Clara Zetkin, quoted in P Frölich, *Rosa Luxemburg*, op cit, p323.

11. Quoted in Pierre Broué, *Révolution en Allemagne* (Paris 1971) p239.

12. Her speech at the KPD founding conference, 'What Does the Spartakus League Want?', in *Selected Political Writings*, edited by Dick Howard (New York 1971).

13. Quoted in H Ströbel, op cit, p117.

14. *Dokumenten und Materialen zur Geschichte der Deutschen Arbeiterbewegung, Ruhe 11 (1914-45)* vol 3 (East Berlin 1957) p11.

15. Quoted in P Broué, op cit, p244.

16. H Ströbel, op cit, p118.

17. Rosa Leviné-Meyer, *Leviné* (London 1973) p80.

18. H J Gordon, *The Reichswehr and the German Republic 1919-26* (Princeton 1957) p28.

19. Quoted in Peter Nettl, *Rosa Luxemburg* (London 1966) p766.

20. Radek's memoirs of Berlin, in Schudenkopf, *Archiv fur Sozialgeschichte II* (1962) p138.
21. According to Rosi Wolfstein, quoted in P Nettl, op cit, p767.
22. Paul Levi in *Rote Fahne*, 5 September 1920.
23. P Frölich, *Rosa Luxemburg*, op cit, p321.
24. Examples reproduced in P Frölich et al, op cit, pp276-277.
25. P Broué, op cit, p247.
26. H J Gordon, op cit, p28.
27. Quoted in V I Lenin, 'Can the Bolsheviks Retain State Power?', *Collected Works* vol 26, pp131-132.
28. Quoted in P Frölich, *Rosa Luxemburg*, op cit, pp323-324.
29. Rosa Luxemburg, 'What Are the Leaders Doing?', *Rote Fahne*, 7 January 1919, translated in *Selected Political Writings*, edited by R Looker (London 1972) p293.
30. Quoted in M Phillips Price, op cit.
31. Fischer, quoted ibid.
32. R M Watt, *The Kings Depart* (London 1973) p299.
33. P Frölich, *Rosa Luxemburg*, op cit, p331.
34. R Leviné-Meyer, op cit, p80.
35. *Vorwärts*, 13 January 1919, reprinted in P Frölich et al, op cit, p293.
36. P Frölich, *Rosa Luxemburg*, op cit, p332.
37. R Leviné-Meyer, op cit, p80.
38. Quoted in H Ströbel, op cit, p123.
39. Rosa Luxemburg, 'Order Reigns in Berlin', *Rote Fahne*, 14 January 1919, translated in *Selected Political Writings*, op cit, pp300-306.
40. All translated in *Selected Political Writings*, op cit.
41. Rosa Luxemburg, 'What Are the Leaders Doing?', op cit.
42. Rosa Luxemburg, 'Order Reigns in Berlin', op cit.
43. Ibid.
44. Quoted in P Frölich, *Rosa Luxemburg*, op cit, p324.
45. Radek's memoirs of Berlin, in Schudenkopf, op cit, p133.
46. P Frölich et al, *Illustrierte Geschichte*, op cit, p282.
47. Rabinowitch, quoted in Tony Cliff, *Lenin* vol 2 (London 1976) p259.
48. Quoted ibid, p263.
49. Quoted ibid, p261.
50. Leon Trotsky, *History of the Russian Revolution* (London 1965) p532.
51. Quoted ibid, p536.
52. Quoted in T Cliff, op cit, p268.
53. Ibid.
54. L Trotsky, op cit, p558.
55. Quoted in Radek's memoirs of Berlin, in Schudenkopf, op cit.
56. Bolshevik resolution of 22 April 1917, quoted in T Cliff, op cit, p174.
57. See Chapter 10 below.
58. *Der Kampf*, 31 March 1917.

CHAPTER 6

The months of civil war

The military and the bourgeoisie who are today helping Ebert and Scheidemann out of the mire, want to enjoy the fruits of the bloody harvest themselves. These elements support the 'socialist' government only so long as they believe they can keep a tight rein on the proletarian masses by waving the false banner of socialism. But now the spell has been broken. The past week has torn open the abyss that yawns between the Ebert government and the revolution. Today it is obvious that Ebert and Scheidemann can only rule by the bayonet. If this is the case, however, then the bayonet will rule *without* Ebert and Scheidemann. Thus the counter-revolutionary officers' corps is rebelling against Ebert's government.

Whatever may come about tomorrow or the day after as a result of and solution to the crisis, it will be a provisional arrangement, a house of cards...

In the shortest time the primeval force of the revolution, namely the economic struggle, will put an end to all these games... Scarcely will the ruins and corpses of this latest episode be cleared away than the revolution will take up anew its untiring daily work.[1]

Thus Rosa Luxemburg, only a couple of days before she was murdered, pointed to the problems facing the victors of January 1919. It was not long before her predictions were proved correct.

The crushing of the revolutionary left in Berlin had enabled the Social Democrat leaders and the military High Command to achieve their first goals. They had created conditions in which the January elections to the National Assembly could safely take place; they ensured that the elections were dominated by the old established SPD party machine on the one hand and the massive funds given by big business to the bourgeois parties for propaganda on the other; and they left intact the old structures of power in the press, the civil service, the army and the judiciary.

But their victory over the revolution was precarious. Much of Germany was still under the influence of the workers' and soldiers' councils. The civil service still depended on their good will to get things done. The only effective police forces in many localities were the 'security detachments' or 'people's armies' operated by these councils.

In the early days of the revolution the Social Democrats had usually been able to dominate these councils, because many of the workers and soldiers were completely new to politics and believed that the Social Democrats were following a 'realistic' socialist strategy. But the Social Democrats could hold on to this support only if they made verbal concessions to the workers. They did not sail into battle under the banner of counter-revolution. Quite the opposite. They made promises that in normal times would have sounded revolutionary.

The first proclamations of the government stressed 'its purely socialist composition' and that 'it set itself the task of carrying out the socialist programme', as a historian sympathetic to the SPD leaders noted.[2] Above all this was true in the economic sphere, where there was continual talk of 'socialisation'. The same National Congress of the councils that voted to hand power to the National Assembly also voted for 'the socialisation of industry, especially the mines'. And the Congress was dominated by the Social Democrats.

The Social Democrats also had to make verbal concessions over the workers' councils themselves. The councils were extremely popular among wide sections of workers, including those who backed the government: again, the National Congress of the councils had voted for the Hamburg resolution giving great powers to the soldiers' councils.

One reason why the government had found it so easy to suppress the January movement in Berlin was that a sizeable section of the city's workers were still prepared to help actively put down the revolution. The biggest factories and some of the key regiments remained neutral, urging 'peace' between the two sides. The executive of the Berlin councils denounced the rising. But this meant that the smashing of the left forces did not destroy the power of the working class as a whole, but only of its most revolutionary elements. A complete decimation of the workers would have meant not merely the smashing of the Spartakists and left Independents, but also of some of the very Social Democratic forces that had fought against the revolutionaries. There were tens of thousands of workers and soldiers prepared to countenance the disarming, even the shooting, of 'reds', yet who were far from ready to accede to the other demands of the counter-revolution—the restoration of the essentials of the pre-November regime, the destruction of the power of the unions, the return of old-style military discipline, and for wage rises to be less than the rise in the cost of living.

Hence it was possible for the Social Democrats to take by far the majority of working class votes in the elections to the National Assembly, held less than a week after that first bloodbath in Berlin. They got 11.5 million votes, against the Independents' 2.3 million, out of a total electorate of 30 million. Only one voter in 13 showed any sign of sympathy with revolutionary socialism. Most workers wanted socialism—but they still thought they could get it through non-revolutionary means.

However, once Berlin had been crushed and the Assembly elections safely held, the Social Democrat leaders began to make it obvious that they were moving away from rather than towards socialism. They formed a coalition government with the bourgeois parties, and then, on 19 January, Noske issued a decree destroying the power of the soldiers' councils and reinvesting the officers with all their old authority.

'The feeble policy of the Right Socialists, and the subsequent policy of the coalition government, excited resentment in the degree that the conditions of the labouring masses worsened,' wrote one contemporary observer.

> In addition to the number of unemployed which assumed powerful proportions with the demobilisation of millions of soldiers and the cessation of the war industries, the employed section of the proletariat suffered more and more from the unceasing rise in prices. The efforts of workers to compensate themselves by wage increases were unavailing.[3]

In November and December, while the Independents were still in the government, they had denounced strikes which aimed to maintain living standards—in much the same way that some would-be Marxists denounce 'economism' today; the left wing Independent Emil Barth, for instance, attacked the attempt 'to degrade the revolution into a great wages struggle'. Rosa Luxemburg, by contrast, had insisted that it was only through economic struggles that the political struggle would be raised to a higher level. She was now vindicated. In one part of Germany after another the struggle for a livelihood led workers to turn to the institutions thrown up by the revolution of November—above all the councils—against the government that most workers had voted for.

The Social Democrat leaders responded by turning to their military friends to destroy the power of the councils and the local worker-based security forces. The Freikorps were now sent on a march through Germany to 'clean up', just as they had 'cleaned up' the left in Berlin. It took them from Berlin to Bremen, from Bremen to the Ruhr, from the Ruhr to central Germany, from central Germany back to Berlin, from Berlin once more to the Ruhr and yet again to central Germany, from there to Munich, from Munich to Chemnitz and Hamburg. The Freikorps were increasingly directed against any working class organisation, not just the revolutionary minority. Thousands of workers were killed, and by the end much of Germany's working class felt as if they were living under military occupation.

Bremen

The revolutionary left had achieved an influence in Bremen unmatched anywhere else. The city, on Germany's northwest coast, had been a centre of opposition within the SPD even before 1914, its local party publishing articles by Luxemburg, Mehring and Radek. The split inside the SPD in 1917 was on terms much more favourable to the opposition in Bremen than elsewhere, leaving the 'old party' with only 'a few hundred' members.[4] Meanwhile the revolutionary left, under the very able leadership of Johann Knief, had succeeded in producing a weekly paper from the city, *Arbeiterpolitik*. They countered the repression of the imperial state by building up an illegal organisation rooted in the workplaces.

In the first week after the revolution, the Social Democrats were able to gain control: in the general euphoria many people felt that the councils were quite compatible with the old Senate that had run Bremen as a city state within the empire. But attitudes soon began to change, especially after Knief arrived in the city on 16 November with a detachment of revolutionary sailors, determined to build 'a kernel of armed workers' power'.[5]

By 24 November the revolutionaries were leading mass demonstrations outside the town hall, and the city workers' and soldiers' council was voting for the dictatorship of the proletariat and against the convening of the National Assembly. The Communists had 'a majority of the industrial workers behind them',[6] although the Social Democrats retained some base in the garrison. In a re-election of the workers' councils on 6 January the SPD received fewer than half the votes—113 against 64 for the Independents and 62 for the Communists.

Fighting was still going on in Berlin when the new council met in Bremen Town Hall on 10 January. The streets around had been taken over by a huge Communist-led demonstration of armed workers. The Independent Social Democrat members of the council responded to the mood. They voted with the Communists to declare Bremen 'an independent socialist republic'. A 'council of people's commissars' (five Independents and four Communists) was elected, and a number of revolutionary measures taken: martial law to be enforced by the 'proletarian people's army'; the surrender of all arms by the bourgeoisie and by officers within 24 hours; censorship of the bourgeois press.

At this point the revolutionary movement in Bremen suffered a completely unexpected and unavoidable setback; Johann Knief, by far its ablest leader, was taken fatally ill. His last political act had been to warn against any attempt at military support for Berlin or at a local insurrection. His advice was ignored.

The correctness of Knief's warning was proved only three days later, as most of the Independents began to turn their backs on the struggle. The workers' and soldiers' council voted narrowly to allow the election for the National Assembly to go ahead in the city. The Communists found they had not support enough among the workers to maintain the 'republic'. By 21 January the council was voting to set up a new authority in the city through 'citizens' elections' to be held in March. The 'independent socialist republic' was forgotten by its initiators—but it continued to provide an excuse for military intervention.

For the time being the workers' council remained the power in Bremen, and the workers remained armed. This in itself was an affront to the government in Berlin. The moment the National Assembly elections were over, the campaign against Bremen began.

A press campaign claimed that the radical regime in Bremen was holding up the delivery of US food supplies to the rest of Germany. Once 'public opinion' had been inflamed in this way, military action began. On 28 January the Freikorps commander and future Nazi, Erhardt, led the troops against the naval base of Wilhelmshaven. Machine guns, artillery and grenades were used to smash the power of the sailors' council. There were eight dead. On 30 January orders were given for troops to move on Bremen.

In some ways the situation was like that in Berlin at the beginning of the month. The extreme left had blundered into an attempt to seize power. They could be presented to workers in the rest of the country as 'fanatics' and 'putschists', intent on disrupting the 'orderly progress towards socialisation' of the Berlin government.

But there was one important difference. In Berlin the Executive of the Workers' Councils, the body with legitimacy from the November revolution, had supported the government. In Bremen it was the power of the workers' council itself that was under attack.

The result was support for the stand of the Bremen left from a wide range of working class opinion, both inside and outside the city. 'The working class of the whole Wasserkante [the northwest coast] found the action against Bremen to be a threat'.[7] The Social Democrat paper in the other big city of the region, Hamburg, the *Hamburger Echo*, asked, 'Must we strangle the revolution through militarism?'

The region had been the cradle of the council movement that had overthrown the empire only three months earlier. Now it seemed that all its councils would present a united front for the defence of Bremen.

The soldiers' council of the 11th Army Corps, based in Hamburg, promised support. The workers' council in Hamburg voted by 232 votes to 206 for the 11th Army to obstruct any march against Bremen, for the 'arming of the workers of Hamburg within 48 hours', for the occupation of the wharves to take control of all the means of livelihood, and for support for Bremen 'by all military means'.

In Bremen itself the people's commissars and the workers' and soldiers' councils offered the government a compromise. The Bremen workers would not give their guns up to the Freikorps, but would do so to troops from units stationed in Hamburg and Bremen, and the council of commissars itself would be reconstructed to give the Social Democrats half the seats.

The Bremen Social Democrats were enthusiastic for this scheme. But Noske was not interested. The Freikorps leaders Lüttwitz and Erhardt had told him that 'the prestige of the army was at stake'.[8] To compromise with Bremen would be to accept the right of soldiers' councils to determine the movements of the army.

On 3 February the Freikorps moved into the city. Bitter fighting followed:

> The workers had not, as so often in this revolution, allowed security to slacken off because of negotiations. Since the arrival of a warning telegram from Berlin on 30 January had set off the factory sirens, the arming of the working class had been set in motion.[9]

The Freikorps had to drive the workers back street by street. The workers holding the bridges withstood attack after attack from armoured cars: only the use of bombs finally dislodged them. In the fighting itself 46 Freikorps were killed, almost twice as many as the 28 workers who died.[10]

But the workers had been relying on support from Hamburg—and that support never came. The Social Democrats in Hamburg had verbally denounced the government's threats against Bremen. But they were not prepared to turn their bluster into action. They sat back and allowed Bremen to be smashed.

The 'clean up' in Bremen cost about a hundred lives, as random arrests were followed by random killings and the ransacking of workers' homes for guns. The same Bremen Social Democrats who had 'negotiated' to stop the onslaught now worked with the Freikorps to form a provisional state government.

The revolutionary mood of the workers was not, however, completely broken. The city was paralysed by a general strike in April for the release of the prisoners taken in February. Further military intervention was necessary to smash it, with shooting in the streets, mass arrests, military trials and sentences for 'looting' of up to 15 years.

The Ruhr

In revolution, as in war, timing can be all important. A few days, or even a few hours, can spell the difference between victory and defeat. Had the Social Democrats and the High Command faced a simultaneous revolt against their policies in all parts of the country, they could not have survived. But their centralised organisation enabled them to keep the initiative. That could not prevent the revolt—but it could ensure that workers in different towns and regions rebelled separately, and were defeated separately.

This was particularly important in February. For just as the Freikorps were moving from Berlin to Bremen, the Ruhr began to erupt. Ebert and Noske were threatened with a battle on two fronts, which might easily engulf them. It took all their skill at verbal concessions to postpone confrontation in the Ruhr until Bremen had been smashed.

The Ruhr was the industrial heartland of German capitalism. Its mines and steelworks were the launching ground for the great trusts run by Krupps, Thyssen and Stinnes which had been the driving force behind the war, which were to dominate the economic life of the republic, and which eventually were to pay for Hitler's accession to power.

The workers of the region were already in a bitter mood when the empire collapsed on 9 November. Six years earlier a miners' strike had been smashed by the use of police and troops and the miners ended up with worse wages and longer hours than before. During the war the miners had been subject to military regulations and even longer hours. Their union organisation had not traditionally been strong—it was split four ways, with a Social Democratic 'free' union, a Christian union that was fairly strong in the Essen area, a liberal, 'non-political' union and a special union for Polish immigrant workers. In the war union organisation was further weakened by the use of war prisoners as workers without rights. Nonetheless, there were growing strikes in 1916, 1917 and 1918.

The November revolution itself was peaceful in the Ruhr: there was virtually no opposition for it to overcome. And the Social Democrats tended to dominate the newly elected workers' councils. But it was not long before the workers began to use their newfound freedom to push the economic claims that had been suppressed in the past.

Already, in October, the employers had rushed to recognise the unions for the first time. They had agreed to an eight hour day in an attempt to calm the miners down. But the miners were already demanding more than this—they wanted the six hour day, pointing out that malnutrition made eight hours work impossible. The number of strikes multiplied. On top of hunger there was bitter anger at the employers, who raised the price of coal by 50 percent in December.

The unions warned against unofficial strikes, and the workers began to turn against the union leaders, first the Christian union and then the 'Old League', the Social Democrat union.[11] Inevitably they also became disenchanted with the mentors of the unions, the Social Democrat officials who dominated the workers' councils.

The workers' councils ran improvised 'security forces' or 'people's armies' in most towns, and had purged the revolutionary elements from them back in November. Now they were used against strikers: in Gladbach the security force shot dead three demonstrators on 17 December and another two on 13 January.

Such incidents caused growing numbers of workers to demand the re-election of the councils—these were effectively the first elections in many places, for the Social Democrats had simply nominated their officials as 'workers' councils' in the early days of the revolution. In Gladbach the Social Democrats were forced to appease the anger over the shootings by admitting three Communists to the workers' and soldiers' council. In Oberhausen a 'council' appointed by representatives from the Majority Social Democrat and bourgeois parties was forced to give way to one made up of Communists and Independents, under pressure from radical elements in the local security force. Similar developments led to changes in the councils in Hamborn, Duisburg, Ickern and Hervest-Dorstein. In Buer, after new elections, a state bureaucrat who had been a member of the old workers' council persuaded disgruntled soldiers to surround the town hall and open fire on a meeting of the new council, killing five people.

The growing bitterness of the miners found its expression in the political demand for 'socialisation' of the mining industry. This had always been in the programme of the Social Democrat parties and gained widespread popularity after the collapse of the empire. It seemed only a matter of time. But the miners did not just wait for Berlin to act. On 10 January—just as the left was being smashed in Berlin and just as the 'socialist republic' was being proclaimed in Bremen—a conference of workers' and soldiers' councils in Essen voted for a nine man Commission of Control to occupy the offices of the mining syndicates and trusts. Their aim was 'preparation for the socialisation of the mines' in collaboration with the Berlin minister for socialisation.

The decision was endorsed by the local Social Democrats as well as by the Independents and the Communists, and all three parties were equally represented on the nine man commission. As one of the leaders of the movement said later, 'While in Berlin, Bremen and other places bloody street battles were taking place between the troops of the Social Democrat 'people's commissars' and the revolutionary workers, in Essen the leaders of the Social Democrats, the Independents and the Spartakus League sat peacefully together and took votes through the pit councils'.[12]

A joint statement from the three parties declared that the conference had decided 'to take in hand the socialisation of the mines' and that 'with this the revolution moves from a political to a social revolution'.

But the attempts to supervise the mining offices ran into sabotage from all sides. The companies and the state bureaucracy made the task of the nine man commission as hard as possible, while the union leaders thought up all sorts of reasons for not cooperating with it.

The government seemed at first to go along with the socialisation movement. It appointed its own commission of experts to produce a scheme for socialisation, which commission of course took many weeks to report. This was enough to prevent an eruption in the Ruhr in the crucial weeks in which Berlin and Bremen were crushed.

But by early February even the government's own supporters in the coalfield were beginning to think it was a bit slow over socialisation. A new conference of the workers' and soldiers' councils appointed the Communist Karski as 'economic and journalist adviser' to the nine man commission, and gave the government a week's ultimatum: if the nine man commission was not given full powers to carry through the socialisation there would be a general strike.

The following day the miners' position was strengthened by a decision of the soldiers' council of the 7th Army Corps based on Munster, just north of the Ruhr, to ignore the government regulation of 19 January restricting their power and to retain a veto over all military orders in the region. It seemed that any refusal by the government to proceed with socialisation would meet solid opposition from all the councils and all the workers' parties in the Ruhr.

But the government, while pretending to draw up its own plans for socialisation, had been making careful preparations with the military High Command. Freikorps units began to move from Bremen towards the Ruhr and General Watter used them to disarm the local security force in Munster and arrest the soldiers' council. From Munster the units crossed into the Ruhr itself, entering the mining village of Hervest-Dorstein. Their entry was resisted by a group of about a hundred armed miners. But Freikorps artillery soon smashed such resistance and the mining villages of the area were occupied, with the usual mass arrests.

At the end of the day 40 miners were dead, including Fest, the leader of the workers' council, who was battered to death while hiding in a church.

Such brutal actions aroused bitter anger even where Social Democrat influence still prevailed. A hastily convened—but unrepresentative—workers' council conference called for immediate general strike. As work began to stop, a more representative meeting endorsed the decision—but not before the majority of the local Social Democrat leaders had walked out, denouncing a movement they had previously claimed they supported. Large numbers of Social Democrats joined the strike, but others were still sufficiently influenced by their leaders to aid them in trying to 'restore order' in opposition to those the Social Democrat press referred to as 'bandits'. The Social Democrat security detachments attacked workers in a number of places: in Elberfeld, railway patrols fired on workers; in Dortmund the security force arrested workers calling for the general strike; in Essen a company of sailors shot dead two workers; in Barbeck the local 'people's army' killed another two and further clashes in Elberfeld left 12 dead.

But not everything went the authorities' way. In Bottrop armed workers seized the town hall and took the members of the security force prisoner after a pitched battle in which 72 workers died.

What has sometimes been called the 'first Ruhr Red Army' came into being for a few days, as armed workers acting for the various workers' councils fought the advance of the Freikorps into the Western Ruhr coal and steel towns. As one detailed study has recently concluded:

> On 19 February the forces of the left were at their strongest. They controlled the whole western region with the exception of Duisburg. In addition to Düsseldorf, Remscheid, Mülheim and Hamborn, radical workers' and soldiers' councils controlled Obershausen, the Wupper cities, Dinslaken and Sterkrade. Their military power was sufficient to halt the Freikorps troops at the river Boye between Gladbach and Bottrop.[13]

Participation in the strike was massive. On 20 February 183,000 workers were out. But the combination of military repression and Social Democratic betrayal began to have its effect; the next day the numbers had fallen to 154,000. On the same day Freikorps reinforcements from Bremen began to take over Hamborn.

At this point the Independent Social Democrat leaders decided that the strike had failed. But instead of organising an orderly retreat, they made the same mistake as in Berlin and tried to negotiate with their enemies. The core of the workers' armed strength lay at Bottrop. But the very successes of the workers were too much for some of the Independent leaders.

They may have used radical language, but when suddenly faced with the reality of bloodshed they lost heart. The violent turn the strike took was too much for Baade, the pacifist and Essen USP leader; the distorted newspaper reports about the battle of Bottrop must have disheartened Wills (USP Mülheim) too. The two men began to negotiate with the army authorities at Munster.[14]

Watter, still waiting for all of his reinforcements from Bremen, was only too happy to oblige—but went back on the deal two days later and recommenced his march from town to town, entering Bottrop on 23 February to the usual accompaniment of mass arrests and summary executions.

The first stirrings in the Ruhr had been crushed—but at the cost of radicalising a wide layer of workers, as both the government and the High Command were to discover to their cost on two later occasions. Before the struggle the Central and Eastern Ruhr coalfields were still a Social Democrat stronghold; afterwards they were no longer so.

Central Germany

Within days of the defeat of the general strike in the Ruhr, central Germany was aflame. The region was one of the main mining areas and stood, geographically, in an important strategic position, separating Berlin from the south and southwest of the country—from Munich, Frankfurt, Stuttgart and the Ruhr.

Its governmental structure under the empire had been complex—and this continued in the early years of the Weimar Republic. The empire had been made up from a multitude of petty principalities, kingdoms, and 'free states'. In central Germany there was the kingdom of Saxony, which included Leipzig, Dresden and Chemnitz, a plethora of free states that made up Thuringia, which included Weimar, Gotha and Erfurt, and the Prussian province of Saxony, with Halle and Madgeburg—itself often confusingly referred to as 'Mid-Germany'.

Early in 1919 this fractured geography was matched by wide political variation. In Halle, Leipzig, Magdeburg and the towns and industrial villages of Thuringia, the Independent Social Democrats had been strong even before the revolution. By contrast in Dresden and Chemnitz the Majority Social Democrats initially had the main support within the working class.

Where there was a predominant Independent influence, the machinery of local government, including the police power of the security detachments, remained in the hands of the workers' councils even after the elections to the National Assembly. The Berlin government set out to end this, but in such a way as not to take on the central German councils at the same time as Berlin or Bremen or the Ruhr. The first problem was Thuringia, for the simple reason that the National Assembly had fled there, to Weimar, to escape the pressures of the Berlin workers.

Noske sent a section of the Freikorps to Weimar 'to protect the National Assembly'. The Thuringian soldiers' council objected, saying that it was quite adequate to do the job itself and resented 'alien troops': General Märcher duly dissolved the council at the beginning of February and sealed off an area 10 kilometres around Weimar. Then he directed his attention to the other towns, starting with Gotha, where he occupied the government building and the Freikorps fired on protesting demonstrators.

Meanwhile workers elsewhere in central Germany were moving into action over a quite different issue. There had been a growing agitation, especially in the coalfields, over the power of factory and pit councils, which the Independent Social Democrat leaders presented as 'the first step towards socialisation'. The government was doing its utmost to delay things through negotiations: it was the third week of February and with the agitation in the Ruhr it did not want a war on two fronts.

By 23 February the issue could be deferred no longer, especially after Märcher had dissolved the council-based government in Gotha. A conference of delegates from the Erfurt and Merseberg workers' and soldiers' councils, from the pits, from electrical workers, chemical workers and railway workers voted for all out strike action. Half the delegates were Independent Social Democrats and a quarter Communists. But— an important point—the rest were SPD. The call for strike action was a call from the leadership of the whole working class in the area.

The strike was tremendously effective. Not only did it shut down the region's industry, it also stopped power supplies to Berlin and cut the rail link between the capital and the south. The deputies of the National Assembly, in Weimar, were cut off from the ministries in Berlin. 'The

National Assembly that had fled to Weimar to get away from 'the influence of the streets' now sat besieged by a strike'.[15]

The Freikorps could not by itself deal with this crisis. Only the 'socialist credentials' of the SPD ministers could calm the workers. The government resorted to a manoeuvre designed to split the strikers. It issued a leaflet full of 'left wing' phraseology: 'We are going to create a statute book of industrial democracy. We will rebuild on the basis of industrial democracy and factory councils.' A headline proclaimed, 'Socialisation is under way, especially in the mines.' But, the government leaflet warned, all this was being put in danger by 'terrorists who have besieged the National Assembly and who would destroy the country through political and economic anarchy'.[16]

While this leaflet was having its effect on those workers who still believed in the socialist intentions of the government, Noske ordered the Freikorps to move on from Gotha to Halle. This town—close to the Leuna works, the biggest factory in Germany—was run by a workers' council of left Independents, with a security detachment under Communist influence. Faced with attempts by the local middle class to starve the workers through a 'counter-strike', the workers' council had censored and then banned the bourgeois press.

The workers' council decided that the odds were against effective resistance when the Freikorps entered the town on 1 March, but the outrageous behaviour of the troops soon led to bitter fighting in which 27 workers and seven Freikorps were killed. Märcher then set up a local version of the Freikorps, a 'Watch Regiment' of the middle class and students, to keep down the workers when his own troops had left.

Yet the government was still trying to present a 'left' face to the strikers. In negotiations it agreed to legislation for the 'anchoring' of factory councils in the constitution. Although the agreement carefully restricted the powers of the factory councils, reducing them to harmless bodies for 'participating' with the employers, the workers' delegates, influenced by the Independents, felt that enough concessions had been made. They called off the general strike on 6 March—at the very moment when the Freikorps were returning to Berlin to deal with a movement that had begun in part with a call for solidarity with the workers of central Germany.

Berlin again

The January rising in Berlin had been crushed because its supporters were a minority within the working class. They were mostly disarmed by soldiers under the influence of the Social Democrats before the Freikorps entered the city. But the aims of the Freikorps and of the soldiers who wanted 'orderly progress to socialism' were diametrically opposed. There was very soon open antagonism between the two armed groups who had crushed 'the Spartakists'. According to the commander of the Social Democratic Republican Soldiers Corps:

> Among the Noske troops a persistent propaganda was carried out against 'rebellious Berlin' and its socialist defenders... When they entered Berlin they had nothing better to do than to tear the republican armbands off the members of the Republican Soldiers Corps and to insult them on every possible occasion.[17]

The behaviour of the Freikorps worried even one of their own generals. Märcher wrote to his superior Lüttwitz on 25 January:

> In actual fact the population of Berlin were kept for ten days in terror of their lives by irresponsible elements of the Freikorps. The latter are becoming a danger to the capital and I consider it quite probable that before long fighting will take place between the various korps.[18]

One historian has claimed, on the other hand, that sections of the Freikorps began to hesitate in the execution of their duties:

> The experience of firing on German workers, of searching their flats for arms and facing the hate-filled glances of the workers in the streets, was too much even for the Freikorps. Their officers became alarmed at the change in the attitude of the troops and abruptly pulled them out of the capital.[19]

There was, however, an added reason for the removal of most of the Freikorps from Berlin after a fortnight—they were needed to put down workers elsewhere in Germany. But among the workers who had kept apart from the January fighting there was certainly growing hostility to Noske's troops. The Independents gave some expression to this, calling for a protest strike after the murder of Luxemburg and Liebknecht, addressing 'every working man and woman, even if they did not agree with Rosa Luxemburg and Karl Liebknecht'.[20] According to one of the right Independent leaders, 'The funerals were the most impressive mass demonstrations that Berlin had ever seen'.[21]

The large, bitter strikes in the Ruhr and central Germany in February aroused the sympathy of the Berlin workers. Six weeks of military occupation had not destroyed their spirit, and a movement developed that was to revive the armed confrontation.

On 27 February the workers in the state enterprises at Spandau called for a strike in solidarity with central Germany, and for a list of demands of their own, ranging from pay increases to the election of factory councils and the setting up of revolutionary tribunals to try the old military chiefs. The next day the matter was discussed at a general assembly of the Berlin councils. Fifteen hundred delegates were present, each representing 1,000 workers. The re-election of the Executive of the Berlin Councils revealed a political shift in the working class: the Independents got 205 votes, the old Social Democrats 271, the Communists 99 and the Democrats (the most 'left wing' of the bourgeois parties) 95. The new executive included seven members from the SPD, seven from the USP, two Communists and one Independent; for the first time the 'organ of the revolution' in Berlin could be dominated by the left if the Communists and Independents voted together.

The general assembly reconvened on 4 March and this time, after vigorous lobbying by workers from Spandau, Siemens and Schwartzkopff, called for a general strike by a large majority, including the votes of almost all the delegates who supported the SPD. The demands included recognition of the councils, freeing of political prisoners, the organisation of a workers' guard and the dissolution of the Freikorps.

The Spartakists refused to sit on the strike committee because it included members of the SPD: they said this was in contradiction with the strike demands, which were in opposition to the policy of the Social Democrat government.

The strike was much more effective than that in January had been. All industrial activity in Berlin ground to a halt, the electricity supply was cut off, and the buses, trams and trains stopped. This was no action by an impatient minority of the working class, wanting immediate socialist revolution. It was a strike that included large numbers of workers who still considered themselves loyal Social Democrats but were confused by the election results (which had given a majority to the bourgeois parties), workers who were afraid that their virtual control of the factories was going to be ended, who were protesting at the repression by the Freikorps and who wanted to protect their living standards.

There was also a marked difference to the approach of the Communist Party now to that in January. As we have seen, in January the leadership had been for a *defensive* action—but the public tone of the party's publications had been 'offensive' and did little to counter the insurrectionist agitation by Liebknecht. Now the Communist Party daily, *Rote Fahne*, insisted loud and clear that the strike was not an insurrection. It began by calling for massive strike action:

> Workers! Proletarians! The dead arise once more. Again the downtrodden ride through the land... The 'socialist' government of Ebert-Scheidemann-Noske has become the executioner of the German proletariat. Now they are only waiting for the chance to 'defend order'. Wherever the proletariat rules, Noske sends his bloodhounds. Berlin, Bremen, Wilhelmshaven, Cuxhaven, Rhineland-Westphalia, Gotha, Erfurt, Halle, Düsseldorf: these are the bloody stopping places of Noske's crusade against the German proletariat.

But then it went on to warn against provocation:

> Workers! Party comrades! Let all work cease. Remain quietly in the factories. Don't let them take the factories from you. Gather in the factories. Explain things to those who want to hesitate and hang back. Don't let yourself be drawn into pointless shooting. Noske is only waiting for you to do that as an excuse to spill more blood.
>
> The greatest discipline. The greatest care. Perfect order. But also an iron will! You have the fate of the world in your hands.[22]

Unfortunately, however, the party was still too small to be able to control events in the way it hoped. Its leading members had learnt the lessons of January. But vast numbers of workers and soldiers who had been passive or even on the government's side before were now being drawn into battle. Many had suffered bitter disappointments in the weeks since January. They hated the government and the Freikorps, but did not see the small Communist Party as the natural leader of their struggles.

The government prepared to repeat its provocative tactics of January. Despite the massive support for the strike within the ranks of Social Democrat workers, the Social Democrat Prussian government proclaimed a state of siege 'to protect Greater Berlin from the terrorist activities of a minority'. Noske moved units of the Freikorps back into the city. By the second day of the strike, despite the calls for a peaceful action, 'Berlin was quivering with the thunder of artillery, shells crashed into the houses of working class quarters, and machine guns rattled'.[23]

There are various accounts of how the fighting broke out—given the massive numbers of workers involved in the strike, it is not surprising that it is difficult to pinpoint the exact sequence of events. The French Marxist historian Broué, for instance, describes how:

> On the night of 3-4 March there were incidents in several parts of Berlin between workers and police. There were several cases of looting of shops, which revolutionaries and workers blamed on provocateurs. On 4 March, using this as a pretext, Noske ordered the Freikorps to march on Berlin.
>
> On the fourth a huge crowd had assembled before midday near the prefecture of police; anger rose rapidly when news came of incidents in Spandau, where the Freikorps had disarmed soldiers guarding the machine gun depot and there had been shooting. A detachment of Lüttwitz's Freikorps had tried to penetrate the crowd. The officer in charge was attacked, and armoured cars intervened, firing on the crowd: 'butchery' resulted.
>
> The next day the Freikorps moved against a detachment of the People's Marine Division—who had remained neutral in January. The incident was decisive: the sailors in their majority turned against the Freikorps, distributing to the crowd the arms stocks at their disposal.[24]

The American historian R M Watt, by contrast, blames the outbreak of fighting on concerted action by a section of the revolutionaries:

> No sooner had the strike been proclaimed than armed revolutionaries attacked and captured 32 Berlin police stations. The sailors of the People's Marine Division marched into the streets and laid siege to the main police headquarters.[25]

Both M Phillips Price and Heinrich Ströbel—who were in Germany at the time—give accounts that are closer to Broué than to Watt. Phillips Price writes:

> It soon turned out that the fighting was going on not between the Volunteer corps of the old army and the armed Spartakist forces, but between the former on the one hand, and the People's Marine Division

and the Republican Soldiers Corps, which had always been regarded as a loyal force to the government.[26]

And Ströbel writes:

The March struggle in Berlin originated in the petty jealousies and the mistrust between the Noske troops in Berlin, the Marine Division and the Republican Guard. These troops were a thorn in the side of the generals who were at the head of the Noske Volunteers, and they had to be dispersed at all costs. These struggles arose out of conflicts between these two bodies of troops. The Communists had as little to do with it as the Independents.[27]

On 5 March a crowd collected in the Alexanderplatz, in front of the police headquarters, and some of its disorderly members began to plunder a warehouse. The Marine Division sent 800 men and two motor lorries in answer to a telephone request to re-establish order. This detachment caught 20 plunderers and placed a guard on the warehouse.

As a deputation of the Marine Division was leaving the police headquarters [run by the right since January] the leader of the deputation was wounded by a shot... In a twinkling of an eye shots were exchanged between the Marine Division and the police headquarters. And now the events of Spartakus week were repeated with slight variations. A section of the Marine Division and the Republican Guards, reinforced by armed bodies of civilians, entrenched themselves in the eastern quarter of Berlin, while the Noske troops occupied the centre and the other parts of the town.[28]

The Republican Soldiers Corps commander Fischer gave a more or less identical account.[29]

The Communist Party continued to dissociate itself completely from the fighting. It issued a leaflet which stressed that the fighting was by sections of the People's Marine Division and the Republican Soldiers Corps who had been against the workers in January:

We are fighting for socialism and against capitalism, whereas their chiefs are fighting for their military posts against employers who they've fallen out with. It is that, and much more besides, that separates us... Between us and them, there is no solidarity.[30]

If anything, the Communist leaders were abstaining too much from the struggle. The fact that the sailors and the rank and file Social Democrats of the Republican Corps had taken the wrong side in January did not mean that they could not learn the errors of their ways through hard experience.

But the statements of the Communist Party made little difference anyway. The Social Democrat union leaders in Berlin, who had felt compelled to support the strike because of the pressure of their own rank and file, now seized on the fighting as an excuse for changing sides. On 6 March they called for an end to the strike. When they found themselves a minority in the assembly of workers' councils, they simply withdrew from it and issued their own leaflets and posters calling for a return to work.

The Freikorps immediately took advantage of this betrayal and the splits within the workers' ranks. They began to break the strike, ensuring the distribution of supplies to the bourgeois part of the city. Within two days the strike was no longer effective, and the strike committee felt compelled to call for an unconditional return to work. By 9 March the strike and the fighting were over.

But Noske and his friends were not satisfied. They were out to win a war, not merely a battle. And they felt that neither the revolutionary left nor the working class movement were now in a position to defend themselves. The attack which followed:

> ...far exceeded in frightfulness that which Berlin had experienced in January... For days the government soldiery conducted a campaign in the eastern quarters of Berlin with all the resources of modern warfare—with cannons, bombs and aeroplanes. Innumerable houses were damaged, and some were completely demolished by grenades and explosive bombs... In many cases workers in whose homes rifles were found, were shot dead.[31]

The death toll has been estimated at between 1,500 and 2,000, with 20,000 wounded. The number of those killed on the left was ten times the number on the government side.

Noske resorted to downright lies—uncritically repeated by the Social Democrat and bourgeois press—in order to justify such bloodletting. It was claimed that Spartakists were behind the fighting and that they had massacred 70 policemen in the Lichtenberg police station. 'This report was not true and Noske knew it,' one recent non left wing historian has concluded, 'but it was convenient that there should be an "atrocity" to avenge: it provided an excuse for reprisals'.[32]

Noske issued a decree that anyone found to have taken up arms against the government would face summary execution. *Vorwärts*, the Social Democrat daily, declared this to be 'the only possible response to the atrocities of Lichtenberg'. Many loyal Social Democrat workers and soldiers were among those who were murdered as a result. Typical of the murders was the fate of some members of the People's Marine Division who had played *no part* in the fighting. They were lured to a building where it was promised they would be paid off. When they arrived, 29 were ordered to report behind the building, where they were shot out of hand.

Throughout the working class districts hundreds of people shared a similar fate—among them Leo Jogiches, Rosa Luxemburg's lifelong colleague and the most experienced remaining leader of the Communist Party.

The Ruhr again

The early Freikorps expeditions of January and February were rarely enough to put a complete end to armed working class resistance. Max Hoelz—who rose to national prominence as a sort of Communist Robin Hood or Che Guevara figure—has described in his memoirs the situation in the Vogtland, the area close to the Czech border. The Freikorps would enter a town in the morning; the armed workers would hide in the nearby forests; the Freikorps would leave at midday; the armed workers would re-enter the town and hold a public meeting for the thousands of unemployed.[33]

That must have been the situation in many of the smaller industrial towns where the Freikorps did not have sufficient troops to leave a permanent garrison—even if it did not always take on such a dramatic form. Armed force could crush an isolated minority of the workers, such as the revolutionaries in Berlin in January; it could prevent the working class as a whole seizing power in a particular locality; but it could not yet crush all resistance.

This was shown starkly in the Ruhr. In late March a new movement began there with far fewer illusions in the government. The workers were now fed up with vague talk of 'socialisation'. Instead they returned to something that tied in with the very fabric of their lives—the call for the six hour day. As Rosa Luxemburg had predicted in December, the revolution was deepening through the struggle in the workplace.

Support for the demand for the six hour day grew throughout March. Even the bureaucrats who ran the mining unions had to voice support—although they spoke of implementing it over two years. The miners were not prepared to wait. On 27 March 32 pits imposed the six hour day by the simple device of leaving work two hours early. A conference on the issue at the end of the month attracted 475 delegates from 195 pits. An attempt by the Social Democrat led union to stop the struggle only served to anger the delegates: they voted for the formation of a break-away revolutionary 'General Mineworkers Union' with a joint KPD-USP leadership—a move which the Communist leader Karski warned against.

The struggle which followed was bitter. Eight workers were shot by the forces of 'law and order' at Castrop on 32 March. On 1 April the movement spread from the pits to heavy industry when the Krupp Hammer Works struck. On 4 April delegates from 211 pits called for a joint strike with central Germany and Upper Silesia—Germany's two other mining areas. The government then cut off food supplies to the strikebound areas and sent the Freikorps to occupy the main cities.

The troops resorted to the crudest means in an endeavour to crush the strike. It was no longer just demonstrators and picketers who were attacked: soldiers opened fire on a syndicalist meeting, killing four, and again a few days later on a meeting of several hundred strike delegates. Four hundred were marched away to prison.

The strike grew from strength to strength in the face of such provocation: 160,000 strikers on 1 April; 300,000 on the 10th; according to one historical study the total figure may have reached as high as 800,000.[34] The number of miners on strike was surpassed by the number of other workers striking in solidarity, with sympathy strikes in other parts of Germany as well—in Württemburg, in Berlin, in Frankfurt, in Danzig.

The government found things more and more beyond its control. The union leaders told them that only one thing would end the strike: 'Only the implementation of the six hour day can bring the miners back into the hands of our organisation.'

Noske had appointed the Social Democrat politician Severing as special commissar for the Ruhr, with near dictatorial powers. It was Severing who oversaw most of the repressive measures. But it soon became clear that only concessions would end the strike. The miners were eventually offered the seven hour day—provided they would do any 'essential' extra work. With the offer went further threats—new decrees providing for 500 mark fines or 12 month prison sentences for anyone who continued on strike. This combination—together with the very real hunger from which most mining families were now suffering—began to have an effect. The number of strikers was down to 130,000 by 24 April. As the strike wilted, the repression was intensified further, until the majority of the workers' elected leaders in the region were the prisoners of the government and its military bloodhounds.[35]

The return of the old order

The march of the Freikorps through Germany destroyed the once powerful workers' and soldiers' councils. The power of the councils—especially of the armed soldiers' councils and the left wing sections of the security detachments—was replaced by the old state structure of Germany under the Kaiser, manned by bureaucrats, officers, judges and police chiefs. By and large they had the same political views as the members of the Freikorps who had reinstated their power—they supported the more right wing of the bourgeois parties. Like the personnel of the Freikorps they were eventually to become enthusiastic supporters of the Nazi Third Reich. But for the time being the bourgeoisie still did not feel secure enough to allow the far right to push itself to the centre of the political stage: the Social Democrat leaders were still needed.

As Stresemann, leader of the right wing party of big business, the German National People's Party, put it:

> A government without the Social Democrats during the next two to three years seems to me quite impossible, since otherwise we shall stagger from general strike to general strike.[36]

A sign that the workers' movement was still far from smashed was the way in which the most backward section of the class entered into struggle in the summer of 1919. Hundreds of thousands of agricultural workers joined a union for the first time in the summer of 1919 (*after* the march of the Freikorps through Germany) bringing its membership to 700,000. They challenged the formerly all-powerful agrarian magnates, the Junkers, demanding increased wages and freedom from restrictions over their personal lives.

Against such a background the Social Democrats themselves could not survive if they allowed themselves to seem only a front for the Freikorps. They still had to parrot phrases about 'socialisation' and 'industrial democracy', although with lessening conviction. And they still felt the need to pretend that the workers' councils existed. They called a Second National Congress of Workers' Councils in mid-April. This was a case, if ever there was one, of history repeating itself, the first time as tragedy, the second as farce.

The delegates to the First Congress had enjoyed power and had tragically abandoned it. The Second Congress met after the power of the councils had been destroyed nearly everywhere. Its 219 delegates were no longer elected from local councils based in the factories and barracks, but from district elections open to everyone with an income of less than 10,000 marks. This ensured a three to one majority for the SPD. The Communists boycotted the Congress as a 'poor version of the National Assembly'. After the Congress had consecrated the reconstitution of bourgeois power, no more was heard of it.

For the government, however, the 'clean up' had not yet finished. Not only was there the formerly autonomous kingdom of Bavaria, where the council movement rose to its highest peak at precisely the time when the Second Congress was burying the movement elsewhere, but there were other districts where power still lay in the hands of working class bodies.

The final crushing of central Germany had been delayed by the preoccupation of the Freikorps with events in Berlin and then by a renewal of the struggle in the Ruhr.

Magdeburg was still run by an Independent-led workers' and soldiers' council. The area had been quiet since the revolution and had not joined in the February strike. But that did not stop Noske giving a local liquor manufacturer (and later Nazi) full power to build a middle class 'Home Guard' to 'restore order'. Nor did it stop him dragging three of the leaders of the workers' council (including a Social Democrat) off to Berlin under arrest. On 9 April the Freikorps entered the town, fired into a crowd of demonstrators, killing seven, arrested the workers' council and set up armed middle class forces, the 'Home Guard' and a 'Magdeburg Regiment'.

Next it was the turn of the town of Braunschweig, where the workers had joined an all-German general strike in support of the Ruhr in April. The strike leaders were effectively the power in the town for several days, controlling food distribution and enforcing a curfew. On 11 April 10,000 Freikorps moved on the town. At first they met armed resistance, with 11 workers killed in clashes. Then the strike leaders decided all further resistance was useless—though that did not stop the Freikorps behaving in their usual murderous way.

Finally, moves were made against Leipzig—a sore spot not only for the central German authorities, but for the national government as well. While the rest of Saxony—especially Chemnitz—was still an SPD stronghold, Leipzig was very much under the influence of workers' and soldiers' councils with Independent majorities. Its workers took part in the February general strike, and the Communist paper, *Rote Fahne*, fled to Leipzig after being banned in Berlin. On 11 May 20,000 Freikorps occupied the city without resistance, dissolved the councils, banned the left wing press and established a middle class 'Home Guard' to keep order.[37]

Hamburg was Germany's second biggest city and a traditional bastion of social democracy. The party there had 40,000 members in 1913 and the 'free unions' 140,000, out of a total population of a million. It controlled all the city's seats in the national parliament, although the undemocratic 'three class' system of voting kept it a minority in the Senate and Burgerschaft that governed the city itself.

Before the First World War, Hamburg had also been one of the handful of industrial centres where trade union militancy had tended to escape from the control of the 'official' labour movement. There had been bitter strikes in 1896-97, in 1906 and in 1912. 'There was…an element in the Hamburg labour movement that was rapidly growing… A rather large group of workers, at first in the harbour but in other areas as well, which was not adequately represented in the trade unions, cooperatives or party organisations'. In the years immediately before the First World War, 'unauthorised strikes followed closely behind one another.'[38]

The city should have been ideally placed to become a centre of the extreme left in 1918-19, and at first that was how things seemed to develop. It was, as we have seen, the first major city to follow Kiel's lead and overthrow the old order, on 5 November. The local Majority Social Democrats were completely bypassed by events. The workers' councils, elected from delegates from the factories in the first days of the revolution, had a clear majority to the left of the SPD, and elected as their president and effective ruler of the city the Left Radical Dr Heinrich Laufenberg.

Laufenberg was a former right wing Social Democrat who had swung over to the left in reaction against the war and had established relations with the Bremen 'Left Radicals'. He had gained enormous popularity among wide sections of workers as war weariness grew. This now enabled him to dominate the workers' council, although most of the 'left majority' were Independents.

But the Social Democrats and the bankers and merchants who had previously dominated the city were soon fighting back. The Social Democrats quickly organised for themselves a majority in the soldiers' councils, while the bankers threatened to cut off all credits to the city government.

Laufenberg later gained a certain reputation as an 'ultra-left'. In this period, however, his behaviour was of the sort normally associated with the USP. He subordinated everything to manoeuvres designed to keep himself in control of the councils and his 'left government' in office. He accepted the Social Democrat argument that elections to the National Assembly were necessary[39] and, after dissolving the City Senate on 10 November, reinstated it on the 18th so as to get credits from the banks.

> Laufenberg continued to make use of the established ministries and their bureaucratic staffs... Much of the real power in Hamburg resided exactly where it had always resided—in the hands of the leaders of business, finance and the state bureaucracy.[40]

Laufenberg did not even ensure the existence of an independent revolutionary press—instead he negotiated with the Social Democrats for joint control of a paper printed on their presses.

A government based on conciliation with the bankers and the Social Democrats could take no real action to deal with unemployment and food shortages. It was easy for the Social Democrats to blame all the problems of the working class on the left figurehead of Laufenberg. By the beginning of January they were able to counter large pro-Laufenberg demonstrations with even larger demonstrations of their own. One sign of the lack of real support for Laufenberg's policies among the majority of workers came in the elections to the National Assembly in mid-January: the SPD got 51 percent of the Hamburg vote, the USP only 7 percent. Another sign was that the workers' council could exercise no control over troops who had been formed into a 'people's army': on one occasion these actually arrested Laufenberg.

Finally, on 19 January, Laufenberg was forced to recognise that political manoeuvring was no substitute for organisation on the ground. He resigned as president of the councils and allowed a re-election of the councils that produced an SPD majority. That majority soon handed over power to a new Senate jointly run by the old oligarchs of the city and the SPD electoral majority.

The Social Democrats still had one major crisis to surmount, however. The invasion of neighbouring Bremen by the Freikorps at the end of January produced deep anger in Hamburg, and Laufenberg found it easy to push a resolution through the workers' council for armed assistance to be sent to Bremen.

But Laufenberg still had not learnt that support for his speeches and resolutions was not the same as action. The lack of an organisation of the revolutionary left, which he had refused to build, was now a key weakness. Armed workers assembled to set off for Bremen—only to find that railway officials and Social Democratic trade union bureaucrats had sabotaged transport arrangements.[41] Violent demonstrations followed, but the Social Democrats in Hamburg showed that they could keep control there with their own armed force, the people's army, and did not need the Freikorps from Bremen—who were, in any case, desperately needed in the Ruhr.

However, once the Social Democrats were visibly the dominant political force in Hamburg, they could no longer blame anyone else for the continuing hardship and began to lose much of their popularity with the workers. There were violent demonstrations against unemployment in mid-April, and—a serious omen—the people's army displayed considerable sympathy with the demonstrators.

Hostility to the new power came to a head at the end of June. In an apparently spontaneous demonstration, workers, soldiers and sailors led a procession of barrows from a local meatpacking factory where *Sülze*—jellied meat—was made. The front barrow carried the factory owner, followed by barrows with factory girls waving dogs' heads and dead rats which, apparently, went into his jellied meat. The good humoured demonstration ended with the ducking of the factory owner into the waters of the Alster.

The authorities were deeply disturbed by these happenings. For, once again, the people's army sided with the demonstrators. The city commandant decided that the time had come to show where the real power lay—he sent 300 men from the Bahrenfelder, a locally raised body modelled on the Freikorps, to seize control of the City Hall. But he underestimated the fighting qualities of Hamburg's workers. A virtual civil war raged that night and, when morning came, the Bahrenfelder had been evicted from the City Hall and disarmed. Nineteen of the right wing troops were killed in the fighting while the left lost 16 men—six Social Democrats, five Independents and five Communists.

Peace was soon restored. The left had learnt the bitter lesson of Berlin and Bremen and made no attempt to seize power. Once the Bahrenfelder were disarmed, they urged workers to keep off the streets. But such 'order' was not good enough for Noske in Berlin. The Hamburg people's army had shown that it could not protect profiteers from humiliation—so it had to be replaced by a 'reliable' force. On 30 June 10,000 Freikorps soldiers entered the city with armoured cars, torpedo boats and artillery. A military occupation followed that lasted until December.

Events in Chemnitz, on the other side of Germany, in August were very similar to those in Hamburg in June. This city too had long been a Social Democratic stronghold. The revolutionary left had played an important role in the November events, but had not made the mistake of trying to cling on to power without majority working class support. The city was run by the Social Democrats, using their own security forces to keep order.

The Social Democrats in power rapidly lost their popular support. By August there was growing unrest—particularly over food shortages. The beginning of the month saw a week of peaceful demonstrations. The military then set out to provoke disturbances. Anti-Semitic leaflets attempted to incite crowds to violence. Then, on 7 August, locally-based troops fired into a crowd. The whole working class of the city rose up against the military provocation. While the Social Democrats in the Saxon government were decreeing that any worker who fought against the troops would be shot, local Social Democrats were compelled to join the protests against the troops.

It was not long before this first military attack was crushed—with 14 troops killed and 15 workers—but Noske now had the excuse he needed.

Ten days later a large contingent of troops moved into the city, banned the Communist press, and began to build up a 'reliable' police force.[42]

Hamburg and Chemnitz proved conclusively that the march of the Freikorps was not just directed against the left, but against any independent armed force based upon the working class movement. The armed intervention in both cases was followed by increased bitterness against the Social Democrats, but there were differences—differences of vital importance to the subsequent course of the revolution.

In Hamburg there was no one to form any substantial revolutionary organisation to the left of the Independents. This was the inevitable consequence of Laufenberg's playing with power and his reliance on resolutions. It was the USP that grew as the workers became discontented, not the Communist Party. But the USP was incapable of giving a clear lead at decisive moments. When the next great crisis of the revolution came the following March the USP was a confused mishmash of rival tendencies incapable of giving any direction to the workers' movement.

Later there was much talk about 'Red Hamburg'. Yet the fact is that the organisational failures of 1919 were to haunt the city throughout the history of the Weimar Republic: the Social Democrats remained a much more powerful force inside the city's labour movement than the Communists.

By contrast, in Chemnitz the revolutionary left had begun, after the November revolution, with an honest assessment of its forces. Under the leadership of building worker Heinrich Brandler it had avoided any premature insurrectionism or any attempt to hang on to power by subterfuge. Instead, it carefully built up its forces, served as a focus for all those who lost their illusions in the SPD, and prevented the USP growing deep roots. By the spring of 1920 it was in a position to lead the whole labour movement of the city into battle.

1.   Rosa Luxemburg, 'The House of Cards', *Rote Fahne*, 13 January 1919.
2.   Landauer, *European Socialism* (Berkeley 1959) p814.
3.   Heinrich Ströbel, *The German Revolution and After* (London 1923) p134.
4.   Paul Frölich and others, *Illustrierte Geschichte der Deutschen Revolution* (Berlin 1929, reprinted Frankfurt 1970) p334.
5.   Ibid, p335.
6.   Ibid.
7.   Ibid, p342.
8.   Ibid, p344.

9.   Ibid.
10. Ibid, p345.
11. Ibid, p314.
12. Heinrich Teuber, *Für die Sozialisierung des Ruhrberghaus* (Frankfurt 1973) p55.
13. Jurgen Tampke, *Ruhr and Revolution* (Canberra 1978) p135.
14. Ibid, p136
15. P Frölich et al, op cit, p374.
16. Ibid.
17. Quoted in M Phillips Price, *Germany in Transition* (London 1923) p32.
18. Quoted ibid, p33.
19. R M Watt, *The Kings Depart* (London 1973) p331.
20. *Freiheit*, 17 January 1919.
21. H Ströbel, op cit, p127.
22. *Rote Fahne*, 3 March 1919, reprinted in *Dokumenten und Materialen zur Geschichte der Deutschen Arbeiterbewegung, Ruhe 11 (1914-45)* vol 3 (East Berlin 1957) pp282-286.
23. M Phillips Price, op cit, p34.
24. Pierre Broué, *Révolution en Allemagne* (Paris 1971) p271.
25. R M Watt, op cit, p340.
26. M Phillips Price, op cit, p34.
27. H Ströbel, op cit, p146.
28. Ibid, p148.
29. P Frölich et al, op cit, p362.
30. Quoted in P Broué, op cit, p272.
31. H Ströbel, op cit, p43.
32. R M Watt, op cit, p342.
33. See his memoirs, *From White Cross to Red Flag* (London 1930).
34. J Tampke, op cit, p164.
35. For details of the strike, see Beuer, pp63-65, and Temple, pp153-158.
36. Quoted in H A Turner, *Stresemann and the Politics of the Weimar Republic* (Princeton 1963) p44.
37. The details of the struggle in central Germany come from P Frölich et al, op cit, pp377-384.
38. R A Comfort, *Revolution in Hamburg* (London 1970) p28.
39. P Frölich et al, op cit, pp351-352.
40. R A Comfort, op cit, p48-49.
41. P Frölich et al, op cit, p354. For a slightly different version, see R A Comfort, op cit, p71.
42. P Frölich et al, op cit, p384.

CHAPTER 7

The Bavarian Soviet Republic

The Bavarian Council Republic began as a farce. It ended as a tragedy. Its beginning was frankly laughable. But despite that it has historical significance. It was the close of a stage in the German Revolution, a stage which had already been reached in Berlin in January.[1]

The November revolution had handed power to those who were most vocal and most prepared to take it: in Bavaria's case the Independent Social Democrat literateur, Kurt Eisner. Before the war Eisner had been a Social Democrat journalist and a well known follower of the 'revisionist' Bernstein. In this capacity he had been appointed political editor of the Social Democrat daily paper in Munich, Bavaria's capital. At the outbreak of hostilities he supported the war as a 'war of national defence', but soon revised his opinion and moved to extreme pacifism, holding strong views on Germany's 'war guilt'.

He received eight and a half months in prison as a result of his activities during the January 1918 strikes and on his release in October 1918 was the closest Munich had to a socialist martyr. But his own political views were 'moderate': he wrote that 'there exists between Kautsky and me full agreement on almost all questions'—and Kautsky was the most vocal opponent of Bolshevism within the Independent Social Democrats.

However, by the end of October 1918 the vibrations of the revolution in neighbouring German-speaking Austria were being felt in Munich. Eisner resumed the campaign for peace—and put himself into political prominence—by standing in a by-election against the Social Democrat leader Auer. Then, early in November, news filtered through of the rising in Kiel—just as some hundreds of German sailors stopped off in Munich on their way home from their base in now-revolutionary Austria.

121

A new mood began to grip Munich's workers. Hundreds turned up to meetings for 'peace' at which only dozens had been expected. Eisner, with virtually no organisation to back him, became virtually a political force in himself—to such an extent that Auer, for all his powerful Social Democratic Party apparatus, could not refuse to sign with Eisner a joint call for a general strike.

On 7 November the city was paralysed by the strike. Auer turned up to address what he expected to be a peaceful demonstration, to find the most militant section of it composed of armed soldiers and sailors, gathered behind the bearded Bohemian figure of Eisner and a huge banner reading 'Long Live the Revolution'. While the Social Democrat leaders stood aghast, wondering what to do, Eisner led his group off, drawing much of the crowd behind it, and made a tour of the barracks. Soldiers rushed to the windows at the sound of the approaching turmoil, exchanged quick words with the demonstrators, picked up their guns and flocked in behind. Now Eisner led them straight into the local parliament building, proclaimed the 'Bavarian Free State', the overthrow of the monarchy, and the end of the war. That evening the king and his old ministers fled the city.

By taking the initiative at the right moment, Eisner had effectively seized state power. The Social Democrat leaders had little choice but to throw their lot in with him, at least for the time being, if they were not to lose all control over events.

To most historians the new regime had seemed an anomaly. It gave the appearance of being among the most radical state governments to emerge from the November revolution. Yet Bavaria was among the most conservative, clerically dominated parts of Germany, with its eight million population made up chiefly of deeply Catholic peasants. 'Not one of the towns of Bavaria', a Communist leader noted a few months later, 'is characterised by big industry, least of all Munich'.[2] This was reflected in the right wing character of Social Democrat organisation there before the war.

The 'anomaly' was the result of the shaking that the war had given to the whole social structure. By November 1918 everyone wanted change. Even those who had supported the monarchy, and who were later to flock to the banners of Nazism, felt that things could not go on in the old way. Among the peasantry, resentment at the war economy and rationing had encouraged the growth of a radical Peasant League. Although only a minority of peasants ever joined it, the League did challenge the age-old conservatism of the countryside. In Munich itself a new working class had been created. Krupp had built a new munitions factory employing 6,000 workers (a large number in a city of 600,000). Some of these workers were brought from northern Germany, and came with much more radical traditions than those of Bavaria. The Krupp workers had been in the forefront of the January 1918 strike and were now an important political force.

What was more, Munich was a staging post for troops withdrawing from the Front. By mid-December there were 50,000 of them lodged in temporary accommodation—equivalent to a fifth of the city's adult population. The resulting concentration of industrial workers and soldiers undergoing rapid radicalisation more than compensated for the political weight of rural Bavaria.

One further factor enabled Eisner to play a role apparently independent of the balance of social forces: the Bavarian middle class and peasantry had a strong separatist tradition. Bavaria had been an autonomous kingdom within the German Empire, even maintaining the fiction that it had its own army and conducted its own foreign policy. The overwhelmingly Catholic population was distrustful of Protestant Prussia and felt considerable affinity with neighbouring German-speaking Austria—a feeling strengthened now that Austria had lost its empire and was looking towards unity with other German-speaking peoples.

Eisner was able to play on this to maintain his position as head of the government, backing the separatist claims in a way that divided the separatist middle class from the centralist Social Democrat leaders. And Eisner's own politics were by no means extreme left wing. His first declarations called for the early convening of a Bavarian parliament, and he opposed socialisation as 'premature', putting a laissez-faire economist in charge of the commission to investigate the matter.

But Eisner could not balance indefinitely between the various different elements at work in Bavarian politics. His own Independent Social Democratic Party was weak. It had grown out of a tavern discussion circle of a handful of dissident Social Democrats and intellectuals, such as the anarcho-Communist poet Mühsam and the expressionist playwright Toller. During 1918 its opposition to the war had won it considerable support from the shop stewards in the big factories, especially Krupps. But in electoral terms it had nothing like the roots and organisation of the Majority Social Democrats nor could it match the influence of the bourgeois parties among the peasantry.

There cannot have been many occasions in history like that of 12 January 1919 in Bavaria, when the head of the government's party received only 2.5 percent of the total vote—yet he continued in office.

It wasn't even that Eisner could claim an alternative base of support through the backing of a system of workers' councils. Six thousand different councils were said to have been formed in Bavaria in the November days,[3] but their strength varied enormously. They virtually ran the textile centre of Augsburg, and in other places took over the powers of the old municipal authorities. But most seem to have represented little apart from a vague aspiration for change after the jubilation of the first days of revolution. The soldiers' council in Munich, for example, still left the Social Democrat war minister in real control of the army.

Above all, there was little in the way of council organisation to coordinate the different forces that had brought about the revolution. The various executive bodies for the councils formed in November had usually been self-appointed, with little base in the factories and barracks. Then the Social Democrats had set up an allegedly unified council for Munich. Their own supporters had a 50 to one majority and its statutes declared that it had 'no executive power'.

Already in December Eisner's position was weak. He could hang on to power only by making concessions to his Social Democrat coalition partners—for instance by agreeing to the establishment of some sort of regular security force 'to keep order'. The election result pushed him more into their hands.

While Eisner was moving to the right, the living conditions of the Munich workers and soldiers were rapidly deteriorating. The municipal council announced that it could procure no more vegetables for sale; the number of unemployed grew; inflation destroyed the value of wages.

There had already been rioting in mid-December: in protest at a public meeting by the sociologist Max Weber in favour of elections to the National Assembly. By the beginning of January the mood of many workers, unemployed workers and soldiers was bitter: they had just heard about the Christmas bloodshed in Berlin. It was not long before blood flowed into the gutters of Munich as well—three workers were shot dead after a militant unemployed demonstration.

The response of the Social Democrats to this growing bitterness was to press still harder for the establishment of a 'reliable' police force. They gave this task to Rudolf Buttman, who had earlier expressed himself for 'counter-revolution'. But the main effect of the proposal was to antagonise the soldiers' council and push it to the left.

Eisner himself seems not to have known what to do. He tried to conciliate both the Social Democrats in his cabinet and the increasingly disaffected workers and soldiers. In mid-February he voted at a cabinet meeting for the new force to keep order—and then went to speak at a huge workers' demonstration which carried banners reading 'All Power to the Councils', 'Remember Liebknecht and Luxemburg', 'Long Live Lenin and Trotsky'. In office without any power base of his own, he was forced to behave in an increasingly arbitrary and apparently irrational manner.

That such behaviour was not just a result of Eisner's personality is shown by the way it was matched by the Social Democrat leaders. They too realised that for the time being they had somehow to placate the only organised military force in Munich—the radicalised soldiers; yet to do so was anathema to everything they stood for. So one day the Social Democrat minister of defence could concede the right of the soldiers' council to countersign his orders; the next day an SPD conference could vote this to be 'impossible'.

Weeks of non-government

Eisner himself finally decided to resign in an effort to allow the Social Democrats to form a stable government. But he did not tell anyone. He set off to give his resignation speech to the first meeting of the new Bavarian parliament on 21 February—and a right wing count shot him dead on the way.

For the working class throughout Bavaria Eisner's murder was a symbol of everything they feared. In Munich and Nuremberg there were general strikes. Armed groups of workers and soldiers took over the streets of Munich. One armed worker simply walked into the assembled parliament and shot down the right wing Social Democrat, Auer, who many thought was behind Eisner's murder. The deputies fled in terror from the city.

Now the only power in the state was the armed workers and soldiers of Munich—and whatever bodies could hold their allegiance. Effectively decisions were taken by a newly formed central executive for the Bavarian councils, headed by the 'left' Social Democrat Niekisch and including the Communist Levien. This imposed martial law and a loose censorship of the bourgeois press. But its predominantly Social Democrat membership refused to accept that it was a power in its own right. The day after Eisner's assassination they agreed with the unions, the SPD and the USP 'to recall the parliament as soon as conditions permit'.

For some weeks, however, conditions did not permit, and 'the Central Council of the Workers' and Soldiers' Councils alone had a semblance of power. But it was not a government.'[4]

A congress of the Bavarian councils met—and kept talking for two weeks without coming to any conclusion, except to vote by 23 votes to 70 against the establishment of a workers' council government. It was mid-March before a proper government was formed, led by the Social Democrat Hoffmann and including USP ministers and the left Social Democrat workers' council chairman, Niekisch. The state parliament was reconvened for one day to give the government emergency powers, then prorogued indefinitely.

But the new government was powerless. Its SPD ministers wanted to 'restore order' but had little influence over the troops. 'The mass movement was already so powerful that the government apparatus could not function in an organised fashion'.[5] Hoffmann himself later explained, 'As I took over government on 17 March there was organised against the government in Munich an army of 30,000 unemployed'.[6]

The government was also paralysed by its own internal disagreements. The USP ministers pushed for socialisation of industry—but this was blocked by Hoffmann. The SPD ministers wanted a rapid restoration of 'order'—but could not go too far for fear of upsetting the USP, in whom the soldiers had some faith. The biggest party outside the government—the Bavarian People's Party—was demanding a declaration of independence from Berlin. Hoffmann said this was 'impossible'. But the pressure for independence was strong enough to stop him turning to the Berlin-run Freikorps to suppress the left.

Meanwhile, conditions for the mass of the population were getting worse daily. There were now some 40,000 unemployed in the city. A bitterly cold March had depleted coal stocks and caused a cancellation of all fuel rations. The city municipality was bankrupt, with its own employees refusing to accept its paper currency.

If domestic conditions were driving workers to despair, external events soon turned them to revolutionary hope. On 22 March a workers' republic took over in Hungary. The workers' councils remained an important force in Austria, where the dominant politics remained a left wing version of social democracy. To many workers it seemed that Bavaria could provide one pole in a line of workers' republics stretching through Austria into Hungary and on to Moscow. Such visions seemed still more possible in the last days of March as the Ruhr moved into general strike, a state of emergency was proclaimed in Stuttgart and there were riots in Frankfurt.

Things finally erupted at the beginning of April. There were rumours that parliament was to be reconvened with its bourgeois majority. The soldiers were saying they would not oppose the workers if there was a general strike. Nightly meetings of thousands of unemployed warned Hoffmann that they would 'help themselves' unless he cancelled increases in the gas and electricity charges and tram fares. Then a meeting of workers' councils in Augsburg addressed by the left Social Democrat minister Niekisch voted overwhelmingly for the foundation of a Council Republic. It was a motion that enjoyed the support of the rank and file Social Democrats of southern Bavaria, as expressed at an SPD conference two days earlier.

The Pseudo-Soviet Republic

The most amazing scene followed. A meeting was organised to discuss the formation of a Council Republic—by the right wing Social Democrat war minister, Schneppenhorst, in his own office.

A hundred people were present, from the workers' and soldiers' councils, from the SPD, from the Independents and from anarchist-influenced Bohemian circles. All seemed most enthusiastic for a scheme by which the government crisis would be solved by forming a council-based government of the three workers' parties, the SPD, USP and KPD. But then the Communist Leviné, recently arrived from Berlin, turned up at the meeting. He rejected the scheme and warned perceptively:

> I have just learned of your plans. We Communists harbour profound suspicion of a soviet republic initiated by the Social Democrat minister Schneppenhorst and men like Durr, who up to now have combated the soviet system with all their power. At best we can interpret their attitude as the attempt of bankrupt leaders to ingratiate themselves with

the masses by seemingly revolutionary action, or worse, as a deliberate provocation.

We know from our experience in northern Germany that the Social Democrats often attempted to provoke premature actions which are the easiest to crush.

A soviet republic cannot be proclaimed at a conference table. It is founded after a struggle by a victorious proletariat. The proletariat of Munich has not yet entered the struggle for power.

After the first intoxication the Social Democrats will seize upon the first pretext to withdraw and thus deliberately betray the workers. The Independents will collaborate, then falter, then begin to waver, to negotiate with the enemy and turn unwittingly into traitors. And we as Communists will have to pay for your undertaking with blood.[7]

The speech provoked an explosion of anger. Schneppenhorst screamed, 'Punch the Jew on the nose!' But it was not enough to stop the dangerous games. On 7 April the citizens of Munich were amazed when they went onto the streets to discover that the Bavarian Soviet Republic had been proclaimed.

The Communists referred to this as the 'Pseudo-Soviet Republic'. It was a caricature of the real thing, 'one of those comedies whose collapse was required in the interest of the progress of the revolution'.[8]

The Soviet Republic did not arise from the immediate needs of the working class... The establishment of a Soviet Republic was to the Independents and anarchists a reshuffling of political offices... For this handful of people the Soviet Republic was established when their bargaining at the green table had been closed... The masses outside were to them little more than believers about to receive the gift of salvation from the hands of these little gods. The thought that the Soviet Republic could only arise out of the mass movement was far removed from them. While they achieved the Soviet Republic they lacked the most important component, the councils.[9]

But without any structure linking the 'Soviet' ministers to the masses, they could achieve nothing. As an American historian of the Bavarian revolution has put it, 'The First Soviet Republic lasted for six days—a week of raucous and at times ridiculous confusion'.[10]

Decrees were issued for the socialisation of the press and the mines, for the reorganisation of the banks, for special revolutionary tribunals to replace the courts, for the confiscation of food stocks and for the creation of a Red Army. But 'the measures signed in the name of the Revolutionary Central Council existed only on placards'.[11] The Communist leader Leviné summed it up:

> The third day of the Soviet Republic... In the factories the workers toil and drudge as ever before for the capitalists. In the offices sit the same royal functionaries. In the streets the old armed guardians of the capitalist world keep order. The scissors of the war profiteers and the dividend hunters still snip away.
>
> The rotary presses of the capitalist press still rattle on, spewing out poison and gall, lies and calumnies to the people craving for revolutionary enlightenment... Not a single bourgeois has been disarmed, not a single worker has been armed.[12]

The government itself was as much a farce as its measures were ineffectual. The man who had presided over its formation, Schneppenhorst, had decamped to Nuremberg. Allegedly this was to get support for the council government. But once there he attended an SPD meeting that voted unanimously against the council government and began gathering troops with which to attack it. The first head of the council government, the 'left' Social Democrat Niekisch, stayed around a day longer—then he too disappeared.

The Communists later claimed that the role of the Social Democrats was 'a treacherous act of demagogy'.[13] The more recent argument of the American historian Mitchell is not much different: 'Schneppenhorst did not have a clear idea of what he was doing... By inviting the KPD into a coalition government he hoped to commit its leaders to official responsibility for their words and deeds which could then—by some means or other—be vigorously opposed'.[14] He failed to get the KPD into the government. But he could still go to get an army to 'vigorously oppose' it.

The desertion by the Social Democrats left, as the predominant influence within the 'revolutionary' committee, the 25-year-old Independent Social Democrat and expressionist poet Ernst Toller. Communist critics claimed that Toller's main concern was to play a role, as if in one of his own historical dramas. 'Toller was intoxicated with the prospect of playing the Bavarian Lenin,' wrote Rosa Leviné-Meyer.[15]

The rest of the 'revolutionary council' was made up of old habitués of Eisner's bohemian discussion circle such as the anarchists Mühsam and Landauer. The Commissar of Finance was a local currency freak, Dr

Gesell. Toller produced an 'old friend' of his, a Dr Lipp, and persuaded the others to accept him as Commissar for Foreign Affairs. According to most reports, Lipp was a complete lunatic: he said he had 'declared war on Switzerland and Württemburg because these dogs have not at once lent me 60 locomotives', and he wrote to Lenin, 'The proletariat of Upper Bavaria is happily victorious... But the fugitive Hoffmann has taken with him the key to my ministry toilet.'

But Hoffmann was to do more dangerous things than stealing toilet keys. He reformed his government outside Munich, in the northern town of Bamberg. Without any resistance from the comic opera soviet in Munich he was soon able to secure control of the other main Bavarian towns—apart from Augsburg. He then blocked food supplies to the Munich area and began looking for troops to attack it. By the end of a week he had gathered 8,000 armed men. But it was thought there were 25,000 troops inside the city—and it was still out of the question for him to call on the Freikorps, because of the vexed question of Bavarian autonomy.

Nevertheless, a first attempt was made to seize the city when the would-be Council Republic was six days old. A middle class detachment based in Munich, the Republican Security Force, seized a few buildings on Sunday 13 April and put up posters proclaiming 'the overthrow of the revolutionary council'.

Hoffmann, however, was perceptive enough to keep his main forces out of the city. It was just as well for him. Soldiers from one of the Munich barracks attacked the right wing force, driving it back to the railway station. They were joined by several thousand armed workers and soldiers and after several hours fighting smashed the attempted coup at the cost of 20 dead. By luck rather than judgement, the would-be soviet remained intact. But the manner by which it remained intact threw its leaders into complete crisis.

The Second Soviet Republic

Members and supporters of the Communist Party had played the key role in the rapidly improvised defence of Munich. All week workers had been urging them to do something to overcome the bungling of the Bohemian 'Revolutionary Committee'. Now the urging became almost irresistible. If something was not done, there would be not 20 dead but hundreds.

Yet the general strategy of the Communist Party throughout the country was to avoid any repetition of the January events in Berlin. The national leadership believed that armed struggle could not be victorious until there was a powerful party with the support of the majority of the workers and capable of coordinating action in all parts of the country.

Eugen Leviné had been sent to take control of affairs in Munich with the instruction that 'any occasion for military action by government troops must be strictly avoided.' He had immediately set about reorganising the party to separate it off clearly from the anarchist-inclined Bohemian elements. He insisted on calling in all party cards, and only re-registered as members those he thought reliable. This still left the party a fairly substantial force for a city of Munich's size, with 3,000 members compared with the hundred or so who had made up the USP-inspired left in the city 12 months before.

In line with his general instruction (and his own instincts) Leviné kept well clear of the Pseudo-Soviet Republic. Each day it existed, the local *Rote Fahne* hammered home the point that it was not a real council republic. This was something that could be built only by people who had broken completely with social democracy; and that included breaking with the USP, whose leaders had compromised with the Social Democrats. Even the 'councils' at the base of the 'Council Republic' were not adequate: they had been elected for a quite different purpose than the holding of political power. The workers elected to these councils were expected to have knowledge of the national insurance system, of the laws governing the auxiliary labour service, of health and safety in the factory:

> Quite different qualities are expected of members of a revolutionary workers' council: those necessary for a stubborn struggle against the citadels of the bourgeoisie and capitalism and their pseudo-socialist accomplices.[16]

There was, however, a problem that could not be avoided. A wide section of the Munich working class identified with the call for soviets, even if not with the Pseudo-Soviet Republic. And they saw the manoeuvres of Hoffmann as a threat to the existence of any sort of soviets. As they grew fed up with the comic opera, they demanded that the Communists take the lead in establishing the real thing. According to Leviné's widow, 'At many meetings resolutions were accepted to hand over "power" to the Communists'.[17]

At first the Communists restricted themselves to saying that they opposed the proclamation of the Soviet Republic, but that they would be in 'the forefront of the fight' against any counter-revolutionary attempt. Leviné urged the workers to elect 'revolutionary shop stewards' in order to defend the revolution. 'Elect men consumed with the fire of revolution, filled with energy and pugnacity, capable of rapid decision-making, while at the same time possessed of a clear view of the real power relations, thus able to choose soberly and cautiously the moment for action,' he wrote.[18]

Only out of such forces could a real workers' republic be formed. But for the moment that was quite hypothetical, since it was patently obvious that the Pseudo-Soviet Republic would soon collapse and the whole half-baked soviet experiment would be at an end. Talk of how the revolutionary delegates could form the basis of a *real* soviet republic seemed like simple educational propaganda. 'It will all be resolved amicably,' Leviné told his wife on 12 April. 'In a few days the adventure will be liquidated.'

But when the counter-revolutionary coup came the very next day, it collapsed miserably. What is more, it transformed the previously passive mood of the mass of workers:

> When the news of the putsch spread, the workers were roused to a pitch. The indignation against Hoffmann's government was universal. The Social Democrat executive did not dare appear at meetings for fear of its own rank and file. The appeal of the Revolutionary Council for protest demonstrations only evoked scorn and contempt. The unity was born in one single movement out of the will: to conquer or to die![19]

The workers now had the energy to create the real workers' councils that Leviné had been telling them about. They urged him and the Communist Party to take the lead of a second, genuine, Council Republic. He agreed. The Communists threw all their energy into creating a real council system and a real government out of the shambles of the previous week.

The Second Soviet Republic was everything its predecessor had not been. It was based upon newly-elected councils in the factories. These enabled it to implement its decisions with ease. It decreed the arming of the workers: 10,000 to 20,000 rifles were distributed. It ordered the disarming of the bourgeoisie:

The Ministry of War was positively besieged and swarms of people kept thronging towards it. There were people who had come to surrender their arms... They were pressing forward to get rid quickly of the dangerous objects concealed under their coats. 'This is the vote of confidence of the bourgeoisie in the new government,' remarked Leviné.[20]

The executive of the new workers' councils ordered a general strike: not a wheel turned in the city.

Armed workers' patrols began to search bourgeois houses for hidden food supplies for the hungry population, to confiscate motor cars (at that time, of course, an upper class luxury), to install revolutionary delegates charged with supervising the banks.

> From 14 to 22 April there was a general strike, with the workers in the factories ready for any alarm. The Communists sent their feeble forces to the most important points. On their proposal a military commission, a commission for the disarming of the counter-revolution, a propaganda committee, an economic commission, and a transport commission were appointed. The sailor Rudolf Egelhofer, who had led the fighting on 13 April, carried through as Kommandant of the city and commander of the Red Army in the disarming of the bourgeoisie... The administration of the city was carried on by the factory councils... The banks were blocked, each withdrawal being carefully controlled. Socialisation was not only decreed, but carried through from below in the enterprises... The bourgeois press was banned. The telephone and telegraph services were carefully supervised.[21]

The efficiency of the new Council Republic even won the respect of sections of the middle class. White collar workers and petty functionaries who were far from Communism joined in the general strike.

As an official report to the Hoffmann government told on 23 April:

> Time and again one could hear in the discussions in the streets that Bavaria was called upon to promote the world revolution, that the whole world now looked to Bavaria, etc. The speakers were often quite reasonable people. Time and again it was also emphasised that Bavaria should have nothing to do with the Reich government.
>
> It would be a fateful error if it were assumed that in Munich the same clear division between Spartakists and other socialists exists as for example in Berlin. For the present policy of the Communists aims constantly

at uniting the whole working class against capitalism and in favour of world revolution.[22]

In an impressive show of strength, 'the last day of the general strike saw an armed demonstration of the Munich proletariat. 12,000 to 15,000 marched with arms through the streets'.[23] Egelhofer had built up a veritable Red Army, even if it was still only half trained. The army had enjoyed a real, if small, success in battle when a section, commanded by Toller, had succeeded in driving back Hoffmann's forces from the Dachau area three days earlier.

But in all this success there was one thing amiss. Munich was an isolated city. Its rule did not extend even over the other major cities of Bavaria. Elsewhere the bourgeois and Social Democrat press was portraying the city as subject to a Communist-anarchist tyranny, with wholesale murder in the streets. All over 'free' Bavaria placards proclaimed:

> The Russian terror rages in Munich unleashed by alien elements. This shame must not endure for another day, another hour... Men of the Bavarian mountains, plateaux and woods, rise like one man... Head for the recruiting depots. Signed Hoffmann, Schneppenhorst.[24]

It could be only a matter of time before the isolated revolutionary citadel was taken.

A few weeks later the Communist Paul Frölich wrote an article defending the decision to proclaim the Second Soviet Republic. He described the proclamation of the First Republic as 'an absurdity':

> Bavaria is not economically self-sufficient. Its industries are extremely backward and the predominant agrarian population, while a factor in favour of the counter-revolution, cannot at all be viewed as prorevolutionary.
>
> A Soviet Republic without areas of large scale industry and coalfields is impossible in Germany. Moreover the Bavarian proletariat is only in a few giant industrial plants genuinely disposed towards revolution and unhampered by petty bourgeois traditions, illusions and weaknesses.[25]

But all these deficiencies were still there during the Second Soviet Republic. The only change was that growing numbers of workers had seen through the Social Democrats and the anarcho-Independent *poseurs*. The objective, material conditions had actually gotten worse, as food and fuel supplies began to run out.

It did not take much effort by the Hoffmann government to put the economic squeeze on the city. Without food, without coal, it was bound to be only a matter of weeks before the Council Republic collapsed. For all the marvellous efficiency of the Second Republic could not create food and fuel out of nothing. The food patrols did manage to grab a certain amount from the rich—but that was hardly enough to feed the Red Army, let alone the mass of workers. Efforts to get more food for the poorest could lead only to clashes with the lower middle classes, which the counter-revolution was only too happy to exploit. By the end of the second week resentment began to build up even among the most radical sections of workers. They were suffering acute privation and felt the end of the Soviet Republic was near.

The ousted leaders of the First Soviet Republic were only too eager to take advantage of the developing defeatist mood. Toller spoke at a vital meeting of the assembly of factory councils on 26 April. Only a fortnight earlier he had urged the Communists to take over to repair the disaster of his own days in power. Now he denounced them bitterly: 'I consider the present government a disaster for the Bavarian toiling masses. To support them would in my view compromise the revolution and the Soviet Republic.'

His friend, the Independent Social Democrat Klingelhofer, claimed, 'The Communists are whimsical terrorists. Their immediate policy, with its provocative demands, is bound to have dangerous consequences.'

'Rumours were circulated,' one witness reports:

> The Communist leaders had secured for themselves 50 faked passports together with a large sum of money and an aeroplane, ready to flee. The speeches, even of Toller and his friends, bristled with suggestive terms, 'alien elements', 'Prussians', 'Russians'—even the inevitable epithet 'Jews' could be heard.[26]

It was clear that the Communists had lost the confidence of a now demoralised and defeatist working class. Leviné insisted on the factory councils accepting the resignation of his government and immediately tried to initiate negotiations to end the Council Republic.

This might have been possible three weeks before. But not now. For, after the failure of his first attempts at armed action against Munich, Hoffmann had dropped his 'Bavarian' scruples and turned to Noske for help. Now 30,000 Freikorps were heading for Munich under the leadership of General Oven. And he was in no mood for compromise. The Independents' attempts at compromise did not hold off the onslaught of the Freikorps. Instead they ensured a further collapse of morale in the city, with continual bickering between Toller's supporters and the Communists, with a flood of rumours against the people who had held the Council Republic together for the previous fortnight (including the claim that Levien and Leviné had embezzled war cripples' funds) and with a relaxation of controls over the bourgeoisie and their press that enabled the counter-revolution to organise openly within the city once more.

When the Freikorps eventually moved into Munich on 1 May there was little remaining of the Council Republic. But already the Freikorps had murdered 20 unarmed medical orderlies at Starnberg and the members of the Red Army knew that the choice was armed resistance or being shot out of hand. They could not but agree with a final Communist declaration:

> The White Guards have not yet conquered and are already heaping atrocity upon atrocity. They torture and execute prisoners. They kill the wounded. Don't make the hangmen's task easy. Sell your lives dearly.[27]

Despite the prior collapse of all government in the city, it took the Freikorps two days of fighting to smash resistance completely. There were more than 600 dead. The most vicious repression followed, as the most thorough academic history of the revolution in Bavaria tells:

> Resistance was quickly and ruthlessly broken. Men found carrying guns were shot without trial and often without question. The irresponsible brutality of the Freikorps continued sporadically over the next few days as political prisoners were taken, beaten and sometimes executed.[28]

To justify wholesale slaughter, the Freikorps used the execution by revolutionary soldiers of ten hostages, chiefly members of the anti-Semitic precursor of Nazism, the Thule Society. (It was pure bad luck that one of its leaders, Rudolf Hess, was not among them). 'People were dragged from their beds, shot, knifed, beaten to a pulp'.[29] Twenty one Catholic journeymen were at their regular meeting when the troops grabbed them: 'The unfortunate lads were beaten, kicked, pierced with bayonets, stamped upon', before being killed. 'Broken sticks and bent sabres were exhibited at the subsequent trial'.[30] The horror at this particular incident brought the reign of murder to a close—but not before there had been 186 military executions.

For the Hoffmann government one grisly incident only was now needed to close the chapter on the Bavarian Council Republic that its own minister of war had inaugurated: the trial and execution of Eugen Leviné. Yet even that rebounded against the Social Democrats. For although Leviné was judicially murdered in the end, he first made a brilliant speech justifying his actions—a speech that must have led many German workers to break with social democracy once and for all. One phrase from the speech has entered into revolutionary mythology—perhaps because it seems to have an almost existentialist tone if taken by itself. But it is worth quoting in context. For it sums up not only the Munich experience, but the whole course of the German Revolution in the first half of 1919:

> The Social Democrats start, then run away and betray us; the Independents fall for the bait, join us and then let us down, and we Communists are stood up against the wall. We Communists are all dead men on leave. Of this I am fully aware.[31]

A correct choice?

But had the Communists been right to proclaim the Second Council Republic?

Leviné thought they had no choice. They had ruthlessly criticised the Pseudo-Soviet Republic and they had told the masses to elect real, revolutionary delegates to defend themselves. The masses had done so—and then turned to the Communists. Leviné felt that for the Communists not to take power would be to let the masses down.

His widow, Rosa Leviné-Meyer, asserts that he took on the responsibility of power knowing that defeat was inevitable. But, he estimated, this physical defeat with the Communists at the head of the movement would be better than a moral defeat, with the Communists leading the rout.

Leviné himself seems to have developed illusions in the possibility of a victorious way out. He told a meeting of the workers' councils:

> The danger is not passed. The White Guards might assail us. Hunger might knock at the gates of Munich. But Ebert, Noske and Scheidemann can only hold out for a matter of weeks. Saxony is in ferment; in

Braunschweig a Soviet Republic has been proclaimed. Abroad the news of the establishment of the First Soviet Republic has been greeted with jubilation. Hungary is a Soviet Republic. Italy looks with joy and hope to Bavaria... We are holding an advanced post. The Russian proletariat also held a front line position. They persevered and proved right.[32]

If the proclamation of the Second Soviet Republic rested on reasoning like that, there was no doubt it was based on an illusion. Not that revolutions never spread. But by mid-April the movement in the rest of Germany was in decline; the Hungarian Soviet Republic was fighting a desperate action against foreign invasion; the Social Democrats were firmly in control in Austria. Bavaria could not in such circumstances survive for more than a few weeks at most.

In fact, it seems that Leviné only came to accept this over-optimistic evaluation some time after taking power (see his speech from the dock).[33] His own motive seems to have been closer to the argument put by his widow—that he could not let the class down. Paul Frölich wrote shortly afterwards in justification of his actions, that the defeat of the right wing putsch of 13 April:

...resulted in a victory, and that victory had to be carried to its logical conclusion. There was no longer any turning back. The most essential prerequisite existed: the victorious action of the masses. The Soviet Republic had become the only alternative. We placed ourselves without reservation at the disposal of the working class.[34]

This defence of Leviné's decision drew a powerful rebuff from the then most eminent leader of the KPD, Paul Levi. He distinguished three phases in the struggle. 'In the first there was the Pseudo-Soviet Republic,' he said. The Munich Communists 'quite rightly' denounced it. Then there was the attack by Hoffmann. The Communists were again right in opposing this—not because they were fighting for the Pseudo-Soviet Republic ('The Toller-Mühsam Soviet Republic was a nothing; one does not defend a nothing') but because 'it was a defensive action on behalf of certain real positions of power attained by the proletariat during the months of revolution.'

The peculiarities of Bavaria meant that even armed defence—ruled out elsewhere in Germany—was possible. The situation in Munich was such that the proletariat did not have to stand by while its rights were being wrested away from its hands.

The Hoffmann government was without strength, yet was reluctant to call in Noske. Therefore, 'the Hoffmann government might well have been obliged to come to terms with the Munich proletariat.' But, Levi judged, it was a fundamental mistake to declare the Second Council Republic.

> If the masses proceed with actions which are only pseudo-revolutionary and in reality can only lead to setbacks, it is our duty to step forward with warnings and criticisms [even though] it is particularly hard for us, when the masses proceed with an action while we have to tell them the action is useless.[35]

There can be little doubt that Levi's criticisms were essentially correct—even though he underestimated the importance of the Communists showing solidarity with the impatient elements who wanted to fight, while making the necessary criticisms of their action (a fault of Levi's that we will return to in later chapters).

Leviné showed how Communist leadership can transform the capacity of the masses to act. The Second Bavarian Council Republic was a shining example of how workers can organise the life of modern cities— in that respect it was like the Commune of Paris. But shining examples do not ensure the victory of the new society. In Munich the outcome was a disastrous defeat for the whole working class. From that point on the Freikorps and the extreme right had a free reign in Bavaria—ten months later they removed the Hoffmann government that had led them into Munich.

There was, of course, no guarantee that a different decision by Leviné would have avoided defeat: in this respect his decision was hard to take and not at all in the same class as Liebknecht's folly in January. Hoffmann might have turned to the Freikorps in any case, and the Freikorps might have wreaked a vicious revenge without any need for excuses. But those were not certainties. What was certain was that once proclaimed, the Second Bavarian Council Republic was bound for defeat and with it the Bavarian working class.

1. Paul Frölich, *Die Bayrische Räterepublik* (Leipzig 1920) p71. Originally published under the pseudonym Paul Werner.
2. Ibid, p9.
3. Allen Mitchell, *Revolution in Bavaria* (Princeton 1965) p146.
4. P Frölich, op cit, p11.
5. Ibid.
6. Quoted ibid, p11.
7. Quoted in Rosa Leviné-Meyer, *Leviné* (London 1973) p89-90.
8. Paul Levi, in *Die Internationale* 9/10 (1919).
9. P Frölich, op cit.
10. A Mitchell, op cit, p310.
11. Ibid, p311.
12. R Leviné-Meyer, op cit, p95.
13. P Frölich, op cit.
14. A Mitchell, op cit, p305.
15. R Leviné-Meyer, op cit, p94.
16. *Münchner Rote Fahne*, 11 April 1919, reprinted in P Frölich, op cit.
17. R Leviné-Meyer, op cit, p96.
18. *Münchner Rote Fahne*, 11 April 1919.
19. R Leviné-Meyer, op cit, p103.
20. Ibid, p105.
21. Paul Frölich and others, *Illustrierte Geschichte der Deutschen Revolution* (Berlin 1929, reprinted Frankfurt 1970) p394.
22. Quoted in F M Carsten, *Revolution in Central Europe* (London 1972) p221.
23. P Frölich et al, op cit, p395.
24. Quoted in Richard Grunberger, *Red Rising in Bavaria* (London 1973) p24.
25. Paul Frölich, in *Die Internationale* 9/10 (1919).
26. R Leviné-Meyer, op cit, p114.
27. Quoted ibid, p119.
28. A Mitchell, op cit, p329.
29. R Leviné-Meyer, op cit, p133.
30. Ibid.
31. The full speech is given ibid.
32. Quoted ibid, pp110-111.
33. Ibid, p212.
34. Paul Frölich in *Die Internationale*.
35. All quotes from *Die Internationale*.

CHAPTER 8

Balance of the first year

The new bourgeois republic seemed to have stabilised by the late summer of 1919. The workers' councils had been eliminated, the armed groups of workers disarmed, the talk of 'socialisation' had receded. The red flags and the mutinous soldiers seemed to the middle classes just a distant nightmare.

Things were not so comfortable, however, for the Social Democrats in the government. They had been able to put down the various risings and general strikes because their influence had been sufficient to keep the majority of workers passive while the Freikorps took on the different areas one by one. But as the year proceeded, the SPD's hold over the majority of workers began to weaken. Partly this was because more and more began to see with their own eyes that the Freikorps, not the 'Spartakists' and 'Bolsheviks', were the creators of disorder.

More important, however, was that more and more workers were being driven into wages struggles by the economic situation. And the government could only handle this by directing against the mass of workers the repression previously reserved for the 'Spartakists'.

The First World War had devastated the German economy. The country had been cut off from the world market and run as a war economy for four years, kept going only by cutting workers' living standards below a long term subsistence level. When the war ended, Germany's old markets had been taken over by the victorious powers. Industrial production in 1920 was half the pre-war level. Germany also found itself forced under the Treaty of Versailles to hand over a quarter of its coal supplies as 'reparation' to France, Belgium and Italy.

This meant that for German workers wartime living standards continued, with acute shortages of food and heating fuel. Meat consumption was only 37 percent of the pre-war level; flour consumption 56 percent;

coffee consumption 28 percent. And prices rose tenfold between 1913 and 1920. On top of that, unemployment was rising rapidly as the army was demobilised.

Yet workers emerged from the November revolution with the conviction that at last their traditional economic demands would be granted. They flooded into the unions. Before the revolution there had been 1.5 million trade unionists; by the beginning of December 1918 there were 2.2 million; by December 1919 7.3 million.

Strike figures shot up as well:[1]

	No. of struggles	Factories affected	Strike days
1918	773	7,397	5,219,290
1919	4,970	51,804	48,067,180
1920	8,800	197,823	54,206,942

Most of the strikes were over wages. But they rapidly involved political, or at least semi-political, issues: the right of civil servants and railway workers to organise, the powers of the factory councils, the question of socialisation. Above all, a government committed to the restoration of the fortunes of German capitalism soon took political action *against* the strikes. We have seen how troops occupied the pitheads during the Ruhr six hour strike. They were again in action during a national railway strike, arresting pickets and during a long strike by 150,000 Berlin metal workers, that lasted from August to November.

In the summer of 1919, Noske created a special force of strike breakers, the Technical Help Force. In January 1920 his colleague Heine, the Prussian interior minister, went a stage further. Faced with a huge demonstration called outside the Reichstag by the Independents over the terms of a new law controlling the factory councils, he concentrated armed military forces in the centre of the capital. After some jostling with the hundreds of thousands of demonstrators, the troops went wild. There was 'a furious machine gun fire that lasted several minutes, before which the crowd dispersed in a wild panic'.[2] They left 42 dead and 105 wounded. In the aftermath:

> ...the Social Democrat ministers Heine and Bauer insisted that the troops had behaved correctly. They shifted the ultimate responsibility on to the Independents and the Communists. The blood of the slain, said Bauer, is on the hands of the Independents.[3]

A number of revolutionary leaders, including the left Independent Däumig, were arrested and kept in prison for months. Thirty Independent and Communist papers were banned. A new government edict decreed prison sentences against any strikers in 'essential services' such as the pits, the railways, electricity and gas. When the Junkers set about smashing the agricultural workers in East Prussia, Noske sent troops to help.

Workers had flocked to the Social Democratic Party in the first thrill of the revolution. Its membership, down to 243,000 after the 1917 split, zoomed up to 1,012,800 in 1919. Many were workers who 'during the war had been conservative, liberal or pan-German,' as Wels told the 1919 SPD Congress. The same flood of support was shown in the election of January 1919. The SPD emerged as the biggest single party with 11.5 million votes, compared with a mere 2.5 million for the USP. The SPD's progress was most remarkable in the less industrialised parts of the country: in East Prussia it got 50.1 percent of the vote compared with 14.8 percent in 1912; in Pomerania 41 percent against 24 percent.

But disillusion was soon to set in. Even in the January elections, the Majority Social Democrats did not by any means hold the allegiance of the workers in the bigger cities. In Halle-Merseberg the SPD got only 16.3 percent of the votes, the Independents 44.1; in Leipzig the SPD 20.7, the Independents 38.6. Elsewhere the SPD was in the majority but only just: by 34.6 percent to 22.5 in Düsseldorf; by 34.6 to 22.5 in Thuringia; by 36.7 percent to 27.6 in Berlin.

Clearly a section of its old working class support was already leaving the SPD and moving to the left, and being replaced by lower middle class votes that had previously gone to the bourgeois parties.

In the next national elections, 18 months later, the impact of the SPD's policies in government in 1919 was shown: some votes were lost to the right, and many more to the left. The party's total vote was *halved*.

	January 1919	June 1920
SPD	11.5 million	5.5 million
USP	2.3 million	4.9 million

Taking into account the continued support of some middle class voters for the SPD, there is little doubt that for a time the Independents were the majority party within the industrial working class. The disillusion with the old-style social democracy was rapidly reflected within the unions: the 1920 congress of the main union federation, the ADGB, voted for 'neutrality' between the two main working class parties. The German working class was being radicalised—even if only *after* the first great wave of armed struggle and defeats.

Was the working class revolutionary?

But how radical did the class become? Some historians have concluded from the defeats of the first year of the revolution that the German working class was simply not revolutionary. Thus, for instance, Barrington Moore writes:

> Without the combination of material deprivation and moral grievances, it seems most unlikely that this mass political movement [for factory councils] could have gained any footing. Even with these grievances, the workers were essentially non-revolutionary and paid very little attention to putschist agitators... It took disappointment and the threat of force to drive workers to the barricades.[4]

Claudin argues in similar terms:

> Revolution seemed once more on the agenda in 1917-21. But the great majority of the workers' movement in the West, educated in the ideology and practice of Social Democracy, was in no condition to take advantage of the crisis... Under Social Democratic hegemony, the German Revolution stopped short with the overthrow of the monarchy and the installation of the new republic. The majority of the working class saw in this limited result a great victory.[5]

A more sophisticated version of the same account has been put forward by the German historian of the factory councils (and left Social Democrat politician) Peter Oertzen. Elaborating a notion of the early historian of the Weimar Republic, Rosenberg, he argues that the mass support for the movement against governments led by the Social Democrats in 1918 and 1919 came from 'a middle tendency in the socialist workers' movement, that did not want socialist revolution, but which was also not happy with the conservative bourgeois republic'.[6]

> Out of certain conditions a rising people's movement under the leadership of the workers' organisations gained the bourgeois democratic republic. Out of this movement grew a strong socialist workers' tendency which wanted to develop this further into a democratic socialist republic. This tendency was crushed between the forces of radical socialist revolution

on the one side and conservative bourgeois democracy on the other. The single real alternative to bourgeois democracy was not 'Bolshevism' but a social democracy supported by the councils.[7]

All these views have the same basic fault. They see consciousness as a fixed property of individuals. They ask what workers believed at a certain point in time, then go on to argue that these beliefs established limits beyond which the revolution could not go. But consciousness is never a fixed property of individuals or classes. It is rather one aspect of their dynamic, ever-changing, interaction with each other and with the world.

As the Italian revolutionary, Antonio Gramsci, pointed out, there is usually a split within people's consciousness of the world. We can hold different, often quite contradictory, notions at the same time. Some ideas are the result of what we have been brought up to believe in existing, capitalist, society; others the result of the struggles, however limited, which we became involved in against aspects of that society:

> The active man-in-the-masses has a practical activity but has no clear theoretical consciousness of his practical activity, which nonetheless involves understanding the world in so far as it transforms it. His theoretical consciousness can be historically in opposition to his activity. One might almost say that he has two theoretical consciousnesses (or one contradictory consciousness): one which is implicit in his activity and which in reality unites him with his fellow workers in the practical transformation of the real world, and one, superficially explicit or verbal, which he has inherited from the past and uncritically absorbed.[8]

The German working class entered the revolutionary period with a range of 'explicit', 'verbal' political theories—the social democracy of the SPD and the USP right wing, the Christian democracy of the Catholic Centre Party, the liberal democratic notions of the Democratic Party. Each told workers that the discrepancy between their desires and the harsh, war-devastated world of the German Empire would be overcome in a full-blown bourgeois democracy. In addition the Social Democratic ideology indicated that through bourgeois democracy something even better could be achieved—the 'social democracy' for which Oertzen speaks. 'Democracy' and 'social democracy' were ideologies, and like all ideologies, they did not exist in a vacuum, but made sense to millions of people because, for a period, they seemed to provide a mechanism for adjusting an unpleasant reality to the needs of those living within it.

The harsh realities of Germany in 1918-19 were, however, not to be changed merely by fulfilling the demands of democratic ideology. Workers' living conditions did not improve under the democratic republic. They tended if anything to get worse. And when workers did attempt to bridge the gaps between the 'new' reality and their desires by moving forward from 'democracy' to 'social democracy'—for instance with the socialisation movement in the Ruhr, or with the council movement in central Germany or Bavaria—they soon found all the old forces of Germany still in existence and arrayed against them.

When old beliefs no longer fit circumstances, the result is always ideological turmoil. That does not mean that workers *automatically* abandon their old beliefs. They try to cope by using the old ways of thinking. They attempt to explain away the wrecking of their expectations as an 'accident', which won't last long. They adjust their old ideas as little as possible, in an attempt to reassure themselves that nothing important has happened. But eventually these adjustments no longer make any sense of events, and a complete revolutionising of ideas becomes necessary.

This is certainly what happened all over Germany in 1918 and 1919. There is no other way to explain how the once solidly Social Democratic metal workers of Berlin took up arms against a Social Democrat led government in March 1919; how the attitude of Social Democrat workers was such in Munich in April that their political leaders played with the 'Pseudo-Soviet Republic'; how the workers of the western Ruhr moved from being 'non-political', through social democratic politics, to syndicalist or left Communist notions in a matter of months so that an observer of the eastern Ruhr could write in the summer of 1919:

> When I left Hamborn in the later summer of 1918, the workers almost to a man were Majority Social Democrats... When I went there recently the workers to a man were Communists.[9]

The process of movement from 'democratic' and 'social democratic' ideologies to revolutionary socialism was by no means as complete everywhere as in Hamborn. Different traditions and different struggles interacted in different parts of Germany to produce differing degrees of radicalisation.

There is always a relation between the readiness of people to envisage social change and the possibilities of success in the struggle for it. An experience of successful struggle opens the minds of large numbers of workers to the notion that their class can go further and revolutionise society. By contrast, struggles that end in defeat can all too easily rob such ideas of any credibility. People feel that if they cannot act together to change small things, then they certainly cannot change big ones. Even people who previously believed in a total transformation of society can retreat. As a defeated, demoralised class fights among itself for day-to-day survival, former revolutionaries can all too easily come to think that the best that can be done is to cling to what is rather than fight for what might be.

Hence it is that after any great revolutionary period, only a minority of the participants continue to adhere to explicit, thought out revolutionary theories. The rest will be won back to such ideas only when they gain new credibility from fresh achievements of collective struggle.

Thus the question of whether the working class was revolutionary in Germany in 1918-19 has, then, to be posed in a way quite different from that of Barrington Moore, Claudin or even Oertzen. The key question is: was there a momentum to the workers' struggles of the period that led workers who initially were far from revolutionary to make revolutionary challenges to existing society?

The answer is clearly yes. In town after town the majority of workers came to make such challenges, even if only for a short period. In Bremen, in the Ruhr, in central Germany, in Munich, in Berlin, such struggles were fought. But they could not survive, because they were uncoordinated and isolated from one another. And as each local experiment died, the workers involved began again to lose faith in their power to reshape society.

That does not mean that in any one of these local struggles the revolutionising of consciousness had gone all the way. The contradiction between the ideas that workers held and their actual challenge to bourgeois society remained; but their ideas were in flux as they began to comprehend new possibilities—and a further forward march of the revolutionary process would have transformed their ideas still more.

The argument about the revolutionary consciousness of German workers in 1918-19 is really an argument about revolutionary potential. Those who claim that the workers 'were not' revolutionary, are saying, in effect, that ideas must always be fixed, frozen into the pattern engraved on people's minds by existing society. In fact the whole experience of

Germany in 1918-19 brings out the phenomenal fluctuations in consciousness that take place at a time of great social struggles.

The growth of the USP

The beneficiaries of this radicalisation were not the Communists, but the Independents. In the eyes of most workers who left the SPD, 'the USP was *the* revolutionary party'.[10] Yet its leaders were still very unrevolutionary figures, such as Haase, Hilferding, Dittmann. So why did the newly revolutionary workers go to the USP?

Part of the reason was the illegal conditions under which the Communist Party had to operate after the first weeks of January. Its press was banned in much of the country. Its meetings and conferences were broken up by the police. Many of its ablest national and local leaders had been murdered; many others were in prison.

The USP by contrast was a well organised, legal party, with a powerful press and an efficient apparatus. It was the *only* party to the left of the SPD that most workers came across. And they joined it in droves.

But there was another reason as well. The KPD's initial supporters had not, by and large, been factory workers with established trade union traditions. They had been young people radicalised by the war and the bitter armed struggles that had followed. Many had moved straight from school to the Front and from the Front to the dole queue. As the organisation report to the Second Congress of the KPD noted, they had come to the party in the height of the struggle, expecting imminent revolution. They saw little point in the regular day-to-day activity in the factories and the unions, in the apparently tedious round of meetings and education circles, in the systematic labour of enrolling party members and building organisational structures. The sheer excitement of the revolution attracted them much more than the effort needed to bring it about. They wanted street fighting, not boring meetings.

But in action on the streets, it was not always possible to tell who were impatient, but serious revolutionaries, and who were unstable, over-excitable and completely unreliable. The organisation report noted, 'As in any organisation of the extreme left, we found many doubtful elements, political eccentrics, adventurers, riff raff'.[11]

In the early months of 1919 the membership of the party was prone to ignore instructions from the leadership against armed actions, petty putsches, food riots and looting. By early summer these activities were glaringly futile. As Radek noted in a pamphlet written in prison in September:

> It was necessary that Bremen, the March disturbances in Berlin and the Munich catastrophe happened in order to make an end to the impatience in the vanguard of the proletariat.[12]

But often the impatience continued. Now it found its expression in an attitude to the economic struggle: if the union leaders were selling out strikes, then break from them and form new unions free of their influence. Just as the proponents of immediate street fighting had forgotten that the majority of workers still at least half-supported the Social Democrats, the proponents of breakaway unions forgot that most workers still half-agreed with the reformist approach of the trade union bureaucracy. They looked at the minority of revolutionary workers and forgot the millions who were just joining the unions for the first time.

The Hamburg district of the Communist Party went as far as to *order* its members to leave the old unions and to form a new organisation, the Allgemeine Arbeiter Union (AAU), based on the pattern of the American Industrial Workers of the World (IWW). Its actions ensured that for many years the Communists remained a minority within the Hamburg working class—much weaker, for instance, than they were in Chemnitz, which had initially been a Social Democratic fortress.

Splitting from the unions was not likely to appeal to the mass of workers who were gradually losing their faith in social democracy, but who still had to be convinced that a revolutionary alternative was possible and quite different from the popular image of bomb-throwing anarchists.

So although the Communist Party grew many times over, from 3,000 or 4,000 members at its foundation to a claimed membership of 106,656 in the late summer of 1919, its influence where it mattered, in the factories and mines, was very small. The majority of workers who broke from the SPD were attracted by the apparently 'sane' and 'realistic' politics of the USP rather than to a KPD that they thought of as 'putschist' and in favour of breakaway unions. The USP had majority working class support, with many tens of thousands of activists, in industrial centres like Berlin, Leipzig, the southern Ruhr, Hamburg. The Communist Party was usually a small minority, with only hundreds or even dozens of activists.

The Communist Party leadership made a desperate bid to remedy this fault in October 1919. They called a party congress, ensured by a bit of rigging of delegations that they had a narrow majority, and then voted through a list of political points that defined conditions for continued membership of the party: especially recognition of the need to work inside the established unions, acceptance of participation in parliamentary elections as a means of making Communist propaganda, and support for the building of a democratic centralist party. Nearly half the delegates—and more than half the local organisations—objected to these points. By doing so they automatically disqualified themselves from membership of the party. Many of these later joined together to form a rival 'ultra-left' party, the Communist Workers Party (KAPD).

The conditions themselves were undoubtedly correct. The party could not develop meaningful influence outside a narrow circle of highly radicalised young workers without them. But the immediate result was to split away from the KPD most of the important local groups—in Hamburg, Bremen, Berlin, the Rhine and the Ruhr. The party was left with a fragment of its former membership—50,000 at most. The party leadership would have done better to have pushed through its own policies at the congress and then taken on and removed the most irreconcilable opposition figures in the localities one at a time—especially since in the months that followed it became clear that different forms of impatience were driving the different oppositionists in completely different directions. As it was, the cure was worse than the disease: the KPD was a very small, very ineffective party when the next great crisis wracked German society six months later.

Versailles

'The position of Ebert and Scheidemann is shaky. They are living off the grace of the bourgeoisie, which cannot last long,' the Spartakist leader Levi wrote to Lenin in March 1919.[13] The more they lost their working class base to the left, the more their own future depended on the good will of the High Command and the bourgeois parties. But if they could no longer control the workers, why should they be granted that good will?

The first major issue to split the counter-revolutionary Allies was external: the Treaty of Versailles which formally ended the First World War. In this the Allied powers demanded the secession of sizeable chunks of German territory, the payment of huge sums in reparations and a signed statement recognising Germany's 'war guilt'.

The initial reaction of the Social Democrats was incredulity. They had assumed that once the war was over, it was over. They could not at all understand why the good liberal democrats of the Allied powers would want to impose punitive measures on the good liberal democrats of Germany.

This has also tended to be the reaction of many who have written on German history since. They present the Versailles Treaty, the great bug-bear of the whole Weimar period, as a sort of historical mishap, due to 'French obstinacy' and not to be comprehended as part-and-parcel of the development of capitalist society. It was no more a simple 'mishap' than the war of which it was a logical continuation.

The First World War had broken out because it was no longer pos-sible for the different capitalist powers to reconcile their opposed inter-ests by peaceful means. As Lenin and Bukharin described it, writing on imperialism in the middle of the war, a point had been reached where the rival capitalist states resorted to armed force to decide the outcome of their antagonistic economic interests. 'Peaceful' competition for mar-kets became military conflict over the boundaries of states and empires. The great powers were driven by the dynamic of competitive capitalist accumulation to 'partition and repartition' the world between them.

The war had temporarily resolved the issue in favour of the Allied capitalisms. But a Germany which was allowed to continue to develop its industry would be a Germany in rivalry with the other powers over the control of resources for economic expansion. It would also be a Germany with the potential for rearmament and for renewed military conflict to get those resources. It would inevitably seek to 'repartition' the world in *its* interests (as it did, in fact, from the mid-1930s onwards). The only question for the Allied powers was whether like France and Belgium they preferred to loot and cripple Germany, or whether like Britain they favoured redirecting German capitalism's partitionist aspirations against Soviet Russia.

In neither case was there any future for the Social Democratic dream of a reborn 19th century capitalism not wracked by external power struggles. The Versailles demands of 1919—and the occupation of the Ruhr by French troops four years later—were the price Germany paid for remaining part of the capitalist world.

Even after the first announcement of the Versailles terms the Social Democrats tried to stick by their illusions in the Allies' benevolence. They believed that a show of token resistance would obtain a mitigation of the Allied demands. So they joined the right wing parties in a nationalist campaign of opposition to the treaty terms, calling massive SPD meetings on nationalist slogans.

But the Allies would not give an inch. The Social Democrats faced an acute dilemma. German capitalism, having just lost the war, had no means to resist the Allies. Any attempt at resistance would have plunged Germany back into chaos—and probably revolution. In desperation the SPD did a complete 180 degree turn, adopted the position previously held by the Independents, and voted *for* the treaty.

The representatives of the bourgeoisie within the government—the leaders of the Centre and Democratic Parties—adopted essentially the same position. They knew that German capitalism had no option but to give in. But that did not mean that the German bourgeoisie wanted to bear the responsibility for this capitulation. The non-government parties could make great headway by nationalist agitation against the treaty, financed by the great industrial and agrarian interests. It was so easy to blame the misery of the workers and a growing section of the middle class on 'foreign exploitation', and to blame this in turn on the 'November traitors' whose peace agitation had 'stabbed the army in the back' and 'led to defeat'. Hunger, misery, poverty, unemployment, inflation, all could be blamed on the 'Marxist' SPD and USP. By voting for the treaty, these parties 'proved' the point.

The impact of this argument cannot be overestimated. In November 1918 there had been widespread support for massive social change, even within the middle classes. Now these classes were convinced that it was the attempt to change things that had created all their problems. From acquiescing in revolution, they became the fodder of counter-revolution. As Rosenberg put it in his early history of the Weimar Republic:

It was the hesitancy of the republican leaders that alienated the middle classes. If a great and decisive action had been taken, for instance the expropriation of the great landowners and the nationalisation of the mines, if the government had shown the people that a new era had actually dawned, the government would have carried the middle classes along with it. Since, however, everything remained unchanged, enthusiasm for the revolution evaporated and the republic and democracy were blamed for all the trials of everyday life.[14]

Students, for instance, became the vanguard force of the counter-revolution:

The great majority of the students were bitterly disappointed by events after 9 November. They saw the economic misery and the national humiliation, and laid the blame for existing conditions upon the governing republican parties and upon the events of 9 November.[15]

But the greatest resentment against the Versailles Treaty came from the one social group whose interests were directly hit by its terms— the professional soldiers of the army that was being rebuilt around the Freikorps. The Freikorps had grown rapidly in the first half of 1919 until it was some 400,000 strong. Now the treaty terms stipulated that Germany's armed forces had to be cut to 200,000 by April 1920 and 100,000 by July. Three of every four soldiers had to be dismissed. Hundreds of thousands of those who had waged the war against the workers' councils suddenly faced a threatened loss of livelihood. 'The wave of nationalism was a wave of battles for their existence by 100,000 soldiers, NCOs and officers'.[16]

Resentment was particularly strong in the 40,000 strong Baltic Corps, who had been waging a vicious war on the eastern borders partly against the Poles but especially against the Bolshevik Revolution in the Baltic states and the Ukraine. They were withdrawn to Germany in the second half of 1919 to find that the 'Marxist' government was preparing to sack them at the request of the Allies.

The resentment provided a focus to draw together all those who wanted to eradicate the last vestiges of the November changes. The ground was prepared for a great new upheaval that was to shake the November republic to its foundations and raise again the spectre of an armed, revolutionary working class—and this time a class with few illusions in the Majority Social Democrats.

1.   Figures given in Paul Frölich and others, *Illustrierte Geschichte der Deutschen Revolution* (Berlin 1929, reprinted Frankfurt 1970) p412.
2.   Heinrich Ströbel, *The German Revolution and After* (London 1923) p221.
3.   Ibid.

4. J Barrington Moore, *Injustice: The Social Bases of Obedience and Revolt* (London 1978) p327.
5. Fernando Claudin, *Eurocommunism and Socialism* (London 1978) pp74-75.
6. Peter von Oertzen, *Betriebsräte in der Novemberrevolution* (Bonn/Bad Godesberg 1976) p60.
7. Ibid, p67.
8. Antonio Gramsci, *Selections from the Prison Notebooks* (London 1971) p333.
9. Quoted in Jurgen Tampke, *Ruhr and Revolution* (Canberra 1978) p140.
10. P Frölich et al, op cit, p438.
11. Figures given in *Bericht über der II Parteitag der KPD* (20-24 October 1919)
12. Karl Radek (writing under the pseudonym Arnold Struthörn), *Die Entwicklung der Deutschen Revolution und die Aufgaben der Kommunistischen Partei*, September 1919.
13. Paul Levi, *Zwischen Spartakus und Sozialdemokratie* (Frankfurt 1972) p21.
14. Arthur Rosenberg, *A History of the German Republic* (London 1936) p127.
15. Ibid, p159.
16. P Frölich et al, op cit, p453.

CHAPTER 9

The Kapp putsch 1920

On 13 March 1920, at four o'clock in the morning, a column of heavily armed troops marched into Berlin and declared the government overthrown. Not a shot was fired against them. Most of the army and police units 'guarding' the city greeted them with enthusiasm.

Noske, the minister of war and nominally in charge of the armies of the republic, had tried desperately to stop the marching column. He had sent senior officers to order the troops to halt: the officers had had amicable discussions with the rebellious troop commanders—then allowed them to continue on their way towards the capital. Noske had ordered the police to make arrests: they had simply warned the conspirators that moves were being directed against them. He had asked his top generals for troops to fight against the coup: the head of the army, Seeckt, replied that 'Reichswehr will not fire on Reichswehr'. He contacted the police and security police officers in Berlin: they had joined the coup themselves.

The 'Noske Guards' had turned against Noske. 'Everyone has deserted me,' declared the dauntless bloodhound of a year before, 'Nothing remains but suicide'.[1]

But Noske's skin was worth more to him than any remaining principles. Instead of suicide he and the rest of the government chose abject flight, even before the rebellious troops had entered the city. The troops, a brigade commanded by Captain Erhardt, met no resistance as they took over the ministries and proclaimed a new government headed by the conservative bureaucrat Kapp.

Berlin had been seized from the Social Democrat led government by the very military figures that the Social Democrats had brought to the fore in the previous year—Erhardt, to whom they had entrusted the fight against the Russian Revolution; Lüttwitz, who had directed the

155

actions against the workers of Berlin in January and March 1919; Pabst, who had played an organising role in the murder of Rosa Luxemburg; and Oven, who had led the Freikorps in crushing Soviet Bavaria.

A number of generals did not join the coup. But they refused to take any action against it. Seeckt's refusal to aid the 'legitimate' government was matched by many others. When Ebert and Noske and their government arrived in Dresden seeking protection, General Märcher, commander of the region, refused to let them stay, forcing them to continue to Stuttgart. He was going to see who won before declaring for one side or the other.

The coup should not have been a surprise to anyone. There had been rumours since the previous summer that some such enterprise was afoot. Lüttwitz had begun by suggesting to Noske himself the establishment of a dictatorship as early as June 1919. Pabst had been ready to make a military assault on the government in late July, but had been persuaded to call it off by a group of generals. Lüttwitz had contacted General Märcher about a coup at about the same time; Märcher had refused to collaborate—but, significantly, had taken no steps to expose Lüttwitz's mutinous efforts to the government. 'By October 1919 rumours of an impending rightist revolt were widespread,' writes Gordon.[2]

Noske simply refused to take any notice of these reports. For him the officer corps had a sacred, constitutional right to do whatever they wished. To interfere would be to infringe the honour of the army. So he allowed the other generals to persuade him not to touch Lüttwitz. Instead he worked *with* Lüttwitz to push through the measures of January 1920 suppressing the USP and KPD press and banning strikes.

Only hours before the coup, Noske told a Social Democrat colleague, Kuttner, that he had every confidence that the generals would continue to support the legal government.[3] It is hardly surprising that there was a widespread belief among the military conspirators that once the coup was successful Noske and Ebert would support—or even join—a new government.

Though they would not go so far as to join the coup, they were powerless to stop it. They had spent 14 months reinstating the state apparatus as a mechanism beyond popular control. Now they found they could not control it themselves. They had helped ensure that 'almost the entire officer corps adhered to monarchistic principles and conservative social ideas'.[4] They could hardly rely upon it now to stop a right wing coup.

The right wing bourgeois parties too were wary about throwing their full support behind a coup that might not work. But neither were they going to condemn it or do anything to prevent its success. The biographer of the leader of the main party of big business, the German People's Party, tells:

> As for Stresemann himself, there can be little question that he was unwilling to associate himself or his party actively with an assault on the republican government. But an apparently successful rebellion carried through by others was an entirely different matter.[5]

The general strike

Yet, despite its *military* success, the coup failed. There was one force which the might of the German army was still unable to crush—a united working class.

Ebert and Noske had fled Berlin. But not all the Social Democrat leaders had the same complacent attitude. Their own reputation with the workers was at stake—and something they valued even more, their skins. It was one thing to work with generals to murder revolutionaries. It was another to bow down before a coup d'état that threatened the functioning of their party.

The initiative in calling for a general strike in Berlin and organising resistance was taken by, of all people, the right wing trade union leader Legien, the bureaucrat who for years had been the scourge of the left inside the unions and the Social Democratic Party. He refused to flee, attacked the attitude of the Social Democrat leaders and threw all his weight behind the organising of a general strike.

A hasty meeting was organised between the unions and the USP and SPD leaders who remained in Berlin. A leaflet was quickly produced proclaiming a 'general strike all along the line'. Underneath were the signatures of the SPD members of the government. Characteristically though, Noske, in a telegram to General Watter, denied signing it.

The appeal had an immediate impact. It went out at 11am on the day of the coup, Saturday 13 March. By midday the strike had already started. Its effects could be felt everywhere in the capital within 24 hours, despite it being a Sunday. There were no trains running, no electricity and no gas. Kapp issued a decree threatening to shoot strikers. It had no effect. By the Monday the strike was spreading throughout the country—the Ruhr, Saxony, Hamburg, Bremen, Bavaria, the industrial villages of Thuringia, even to the landed estates of rural Prussia.

And it was not a movement only of industrial workers. Although the middle class was already swinging to the right, the determined response of the industrial workers pulled many of the traditionally conservative white collar workers with it. As the Communist Party congress was told a month later, 'The middle ranking railway, post, prison and judicial employees are not Communist and will not quickly become so. But for the first time they fought on the side of the working class'.[6]

Kapp and his supporters found, according to the Belgian socialist de Bruckere, 'the general strike now bound them with a terrible, silent power'. From this has developed a myth that the putsch was defeated by a peaceful strike alone. For instance Richard Watt, in his otherwise useful popular history of the revolutionary period, writes:

> The Kapp putsch was brought to an end by a combination of the 'Chancellor's' [Kapp's] total incompetence and the astonishing effectiveness of a general strike which the socialists called.[7]

But the putsch was, in fact, confronted by something far more threatening. In place after place workers turned the strike into an armed assault on the power behind the putsch—the structure of armed power built up so laboriously by Noske and the High Command in the previous 14 months. How could it be otherwise, since the Kapp government had ordered the army to shoot at 'peaceful' strikers? Either the workers disarmed the troops, or the troops would kill the strikers.

In three parts of Germany—the industrial heartland of the Ruhr, the mining and industrial areas of central Germany, and the northern region between Lübeck and Wismar—the armed working class effectively took power into its own hands.

The Red Armies of the Ruhr

The workers of the Ruhr had already experienced the full brutality of military occupation by the Freikorps and army. The savage 'restoration' of order in February and April 1919 was followed by a further period of military rule at the beginning of 1920. In response to a railway strike and renewed agitation for the six hour shift in the pits, the Social Democrat minister Severing had given General Watter full power to break up mass meetings, dissolve strike committees and arrest pickets. The Communist and Independent presses were banned and hundreds of left wingers thrown into prison. Workers knew what it would mean if the generals were to be able to rule without even the *pretence* of democratic forms.

As news of events in Berlin came through, meetings were called of representatives of the working class parties and the unions to take up the call for the strike. Already at these meetings, many talked of action that went far beyond simply beating off the coup and returning to the situation as before. At a meeting of delegates from the Lower Rhine (the Southern Ruhr) region, in Elberfeld, the left Independent Otto Brass moved a resolution calling for the disarming of the middle classes and the establishment of a proletarian dictatorship based upon workers' councils. The local Social Democrat leaders were at a loss for words, in face of the collapse of all their arguments about trusting in the military authorities. To everyone's amazement, they voted *for* the resolution.[8]

But even now, some workers were still under Social Democrat or right Independent influence. In Essen, when Communists and left Independents called for the dictatorship of the proletariat, the Social Democrat leaders walked out and formed their own strike action committee with members of the 'democratic' bourgeois parties.[9] This did not happen at Hagen, an Independent stronghold—but only because the demands of the action committee were restricted to a call to 'defeat the putsch', secure the republic, restore rights to workers.[10]

Under such circumstances, the call for the general strike went out, and the industry of the Ruhr ground to a halt on the Monday morning. Armed action against the military authorities was slower in developing. In Dortmund, the Social Democrats managed to fob off such demands by saying that the local Home Guard was 90 percent Social Democratic and could be relied on. In Hagen the Independent leadership agreed to the arming of the workers—but set about doing so slowly, in a typical bureaucratic way.

What changed such attitudes rapidly was the behaviour of the authorities. In Hagen the slow moves to arm the workers were replaced by spontaneous mass action when a local right wing paper appeared supporting Kapp. Within hours crowds of workers had taken over the centre of the town, seizing arms from the police and imposing a workers' censorship on the press.

But it was the action of the army command which most radicalised workers. The Freikorps' general, Watter, was stationed outside the Ruhr proper, in Munster. He was wise enough not to commit himself either to Kapp or the government until he could see who was going to win. He stood on the sidelines, even getting the agreement of the Social Democrat leader Severing to issue joint calls for 'peace and order'. But for Watter, 'peace and order' meant a continuation of the military repression of the local working class movement, while taking no action against his own subordinate officers who were openly for Kapp: part of the national plan for the coup was for the Lutzow Corps, based in Remscheid, to march on Berlin, and the monarchist flag flew over the Mülheim barracks.

As part of his efforts to keep 'peace and order', Watter sent two brigades under a Captain Hasenclaver to take the guns away from the Hagen workers. A leader of the 'Red Armies' later described what happened:

> The battery of Captain Hasenclaver arrived at the station of Wetter-on-Ruhr at ten in the morning of the Monday. The local action committee— made up of Independents and Social Democrats—shouted to the captain, 'Which side are the military on?' And then came the portentious words, on which the whole development of the armed action in the Ruhr coalfield hung: 'We come on the orders of General Watter and stand on the side of General Lüttwitz.'
>
> Then began a struggle that has never been surpassed in the history of the German workers' movement. The workers attacked with their few guns. The mountainous terrain was favourable to them. From behind every rock and tree, from out of every bush and hiding place cracked Red death. Fellow workers came to join in from Bommern, Volmarstein, Wengern, Hagen, Witten, in their hands captured weapons.
>
> By the time the murderous battle was over, the hopes of Kapp, Lüttwitz and Watter lay slain on the station—slain by the blazing spirit of the workers—64 dead, among them four officers including Captain Hasenclaver, a hundred prisoners; the workers lost seven.[11]

Meanwhile in Dortmund the '90 percent Social Democratic' Home Guard opened fire on a workers' mass meeting killing six people. Antagonism to the Social Democrat leaders grew. It became even more powerful the next day, when two local Social Democrat leaders joined the Freikorps Lichtschlag in a march in the direction of Hagen. 'This was the break between the Social Democrat masses and their leadership.'[12]

Now there was no holding back a more or less spontaneous rising, a movement that was to develop into coordinated frontal attacks that drove the army right out of the Ruhr.

In Hagen a central military leadership for the area was set up under the Independent Joseph Ernst. While electric trains were used to send armed worker reinforcements to help out in Wetter, all other transport was stopped to prevent the troops getting any reinforcements. Dortmund, a few miles to the north, was still in military hands. When Watter tried to send reinforcements to the garrison, they faced first a sabotaged railway system, then attacks by armed workers at Berghofen and Aplerbeck. Meanwhile, armed workers marched on Dortmund itself, where an action committee of Independents, Communists and Syndicalists (the Social Democrats refused to join in) was directing the attack on the troops. After a bitter battle, the army was forced to abandon its positions and retreat back to its base at Remscheid—only to be attacked on all sides.

Workers who had only 50 guns between them when they began the attack on the Tuesday had, by Thursday, forced the troops to withdraw—until, attacked again by workers in Morsbachtal, many surrendered and were disarmed. Thirty three workers were killed in these battles.

The workers now held the whole of the eastern part of the Ruhr, with a front facing Munster to the north and Essen to the west. In Essen the 'Green' security police and the Home Guard had imposed tight military control, banning the strike action committee and shooting at demonstrators in the streets. But, as one eyewitness related:

By 18 March the Red front had already reached the boundaries of the town of Essen. The 'Greens' defended with tenacity every building. Especially bitter was the fight for control of Stoppenberg. In the night of 18-19 March the Red Army crossed the northeast boundary of the town. The occupying forces hastily made preparations to halt the Red Army. In the early hours of the morning there was a bitter battle for the slaughter house. There were many losses on both sides.

Between 9 and 10am the first Red Guards appeared in the Beustrasse. They were received with jubilation. The slaughterhouse was now under fire from two sides. Now the 'Green' occupants of the slaughterhouse knew that further resistance was useless. They poured back into the city in a rout, leaving huge supplies of weapons and munitions to the workers.

The Essen workers could now join in the battle for the first time. Thousands armed themselves and joined the Red front. But it was a long time yet until the town of Essen was in the hands of the workers. The Greens put up considerable resistance... It was midday when the Red flag was raised over the town hall... And big battles were still raging around the station and the post office.[13]

With the loss of Essen, Watter saw that his other garrisons in the area were not going to last long. He ordered his troops to withdraw from Düsseldorf, Mülheim, Duisburg and Hamborn.

As he explained to his officers in an order on 22 March, seven days after the attempted putsch:

> The present battle in the industrial belt is different from the previous struggles to put down disorder, in that on the other side now we are faced with well-organised, well-armed and well-led troops that have a single tactical plan... We are dealing with a purely military operation, the battle of government troops against the revolutionary Red Army.[14]

What had begun as a series of isolated uprisings had developed in less than five days into a frontal confrontation between two armies—the Reichswehr and the 'Red Army', 50,000 strong according to some estimates[15] and equipped with the most modern weapons, including artillery. And the Reichswehr had been defeated. As it fled the only power now within the industrial region of the Ruhr was the power of the Red Army.

Yet, in one sense, the words 'Red Army' are mistaken. This was workers' power, but there was no single command structure to unite it. The workers' uprisings had started in response to attacks from the right in various areas.

> The workers got their first arms from the police, the bourgeois members of the Home Guard, etc, as a defensive response in the local cities... Often they were taken by surprise by the military... The more the troops moved into towns, the more the workers began to coordinate with each other, with the big towns becoming the coordinating centres.[16]

The workers who began the struggle, 'spontaneously' chasing the Reichswehr and the police from place to place, did so in more or less organised groups—perhaps from one factory, from a union branch or workers' party branch. Soon these began to be organised by local centres under the control of the action committees. One bourgeois observer described a 'recruitment office' for the workers' army:

In front of the recruitment office people gather in exemplary silence. The handing out of weapons takes place in another spot, where captured weapons appear. The first payment for each volunteer is counted out... the roll calls, the dividing up of the troops, the distribution of weapons, the checking of them by the weapon master, the distribution of bread, the marching off of units. It looks the same as the mobilisation of 1914. Ordered troops, in columns, with a leader at the front of them, march in the greatest discipline through the streets.[17]

Minimum qualifications began to be laid down for membership of the Red Army; usually 12 months membership of a workers' party or trade union and six months fighting experience at the Front during the war.

But the growing organisation locally was not matched by any centralisation. In each town the action committees tended to transform themselves into executive workers' councils as the police and Reichswehr were driven out; but only in Dortmund and Mülheim were these subordinated to delegate bodies elected from the factories; elsewhere they remained coalitions of party nominees. The battle had been raging for ten days before any serious attempt was made to coordinate the action committees of the whole Ruhr.

What is more, the organisation of the armed struggle tended to separate itself off from these bodies. The bigger the workers' army was, the less were the executive councils in charge of it and the more did the organisation of the Red Army come from itself'.[18] Leaders emerged who commanded the units in each section of the front. But, as a leading member of the Dortmund Executive Council pointed out:

The leading men had only a more or less local impact. No better placed were the parties, the USPD, the Spartakusbund, and the Syndicalists... Around Dortmund the USPD 'ruled'; from Dortmund the organisationally weak Spartakusbund sought with clear, historically grounded slogans—for a central council, for a council dictatorship—to organise and solidify the power of the workers; around Mülheim flourished an anti-centralist, anti-leader syndicalism.[19]

In both Mülheim and Hagen attempts were made to establish a centralised military leadership for the whole of the Ruhr. The Mülheim leaders formed a 'Headquarters of the Red Army', declaring the dictatorship of the proletariat. But the influence of neither extended beyond a few towns in its own area, and between the two there was little communication.

In the initial reaction to the Kapp putsch these deficiencies did not matter much. Despite them, the armed workers chased out the police and troops, seized their arms—including heavy artillery and even a couple of planes—and established what was effectively workers' power. The Red Armies controlled the front, while the executive councils organised local policing by armed workers, censored the bourgeois press, tried to negotiate for food supplies to prevent starvation, released political prisoners and supervised the activities of the local authorities. But the lack of central coordination was to become all important once the first stage of the struggle was over and the question arose, what to do next? To see why, we have first to look at what was happening elsewhere in Germany.

Central Germany

In 1919 the miners' struggles in the Ruhr had been followed quickly by similar struggles by miners and industrial workers in central Germany. Now, a year later, the effect of the Kapp putsch was to cause the central German workers to respond at the same time, in much the same way as the Ruhr workers. In almost all the industrial centres of central Germany there was an immediate general strike which soon gave birth to armed struggle.

In the western part of central Germany, the seven statelets of Thuringia contained more residues of the November Revolution than anywhere else in Germany. The USP was the biggest workers' party, controlling many of the local state governments and influencing the composition of the police and security detachments. The Kapp government declared these state governments removed from power; they responded by giving official backing to the general strike and by taking measures for armed self-defence.

In Gotha, after the state government had called for the formation of workers' defence committees based on the factories, the building of workers' councils and the formation of a 'people's army', workers and sympathetic police seized control of the town's major buildings. They were soon driven out by army reinforcements. But workers from outlying towns and industrial villages, who had disarmed local right wingers, marched on Gotha and defeated the army after a battle costing 46 lives.

Developments were similar in Weimar. Workers in the nearby town of Jena disarmed the local reactionary 'Farmer Guard' and marched to relieve the state capital.

In Gera workers armed themselves and stormed the town hall, government buildings and the barracks. In Sömmerda, 25 kilometres from Erfurt, workers disarmed the reactionary Home Guard, captured 2,000 weapons and built a workers' army. The fact that there were a number of arms factories in Thuringia came in very useful to the workers. They had soon taken armed power into their own hands in every major centre apart from Erfurt.

The picture was very similar in the Prussian province of Saxony, which lay to the north of Thuringia. Here too the outlying towns and villages were soon under the control of armed workers. In Burg the officers of the garrison were arrested, while the town council donated 30,000 marks to strengthen the Home Guard with workers. In Neuhaldensleben there were armed confrontations between the workers and the reactionary Volunteer force. In Stassfurt the workers took over the town completely. The workers of Aschersleben took up arms and marched to Quedlinburg, where, after fighting that cost a hundred lives, 'the agricultural workers ran the place'.[20]

The largest town in the area, Halle, continued to be dominated by right wing Volunteer forces. Mass meetings of workers voted to build a military command and to enlarge the Home Guard with workers, but could not break the stranglehold of the military on the town until armed workers from the nearby region surrounded the town with what was effectively a military front.[21] A regular battle followed, in which the workers had overwhelming numbers, but lacked weapons and ammunition. 106 people died in the fighting, which lasted a week.

Finally there was the state of Saxony (not to be confused with the Prussian province of the same name), with industrial concentrations around the three cities of Chemnitz, Leipzig and Dresden.

In Chemnitz the workers immediately enjoyed great success. One of Germany's main news agencies reported:

> The workers dominate in Chemnitz. On Saturday an action committee was built from three members each of the Social Democrats, the Independents and the Communist Party. It disarmed the Volunteer forces, drove the middle class elements from the Home Guard and armed 3,000 revolutionary workers. The post office, the railway station and the

town hall were occupied by armed workers. The bourgeois newspapers were suppressed... In the neighbouring towns the workers also had power in their hands.[22]

Workers' power soon spread out from the city, as the bourgeois military forces were disarmed for an area of 50 kilometres around. Elections were held in the Chemnitz factories for a workers' council to replace the action committee of the parties. The 1,500 delegates (one for each 50 workers) appointed an executive of ten Communists, nine Social Democrats, one Independent and one Democrat. A workers' army was set up, made up of roughly the same number from the two main parties, the Communists and Social Democrats. The Chemnitz council soon became the hub for a structure of workers' power right across the region, calling a conference of workers' council delegates from the rest of Saxony and neighbouring parts of Thuringia and Bavaria. Indeed, the actual *organisation* of workers' power was at a higher level than in the Ruhr, where little such centralisation took place.[23]

The reason for such success lay partly in the relative weakness of the reactionary armed forces in the city at the time of the coup. Disarming the enemy was not the major problem that it was, for example, in Halle. But probably more important was the political leadership within the working class movement. Chemnitz had the most powerful Communist Party in Germany, as a result of the activities of Heinrich Brandler and Fritz Heckert, activists in the local socialist and trade union movement since before the war. They had built up the local Spartakus League, even during the grimmest days of the war, and had not made the mistake of launching a premature bid for power in 1918-19. They took seriously Rosa Luxemburg's insistence that the Communists could not take power until they had majority working class support, and had set out to build that support by working politically to break the workers' illusions in social democracy.

In terms of the response to the Kapp putsch, that meant that they did not attempt to seize power themselves, or to insist that the Social Democrats fight around a programme for the dictatorship of the proletariat. Instead they proposed joint action to the Social Democrat leaders around a list of demands which these leaders could hardly refuse if they were serious about resisting the putsch: purging of the middle class from the Home Guard; the transformation of the rest of the Home Guard into a workers' army; a takeover of Freikorps barracks and dissolution of the Freikorps; a takeover of all official buildings; and the election of delegates to a workers' council from all the factories.[24]

The Social Democrat leaders were forced to agree to these demands by pressure from their own supporters, yet, as the best fighters, the Communists were bound to get most of the prestige from joint action. The implementation of the demands meant the erection of a *de facto* structure of workers' power involving Social Democrat as well as Communist workers—and opened up the prospect of persuading workers influenced by the Social Democrats that this was how society should be run in future.

Unfortunately the development of the Chemnitz region as a nucleus of workers' power was not matched by developments in the two other cities of Saxony, Dresden and Leipzig.

Dresden was the military centre of the state, and its commander, General Märcher, had, like Watter in the Ruhr, declared himself 'neutral' between the government and the supporters of the putsch. The local working class movement did not know how to respond to this politically. The USP was almost as influential as the Social Democrats—but also almost as bureaucratic. So all that took place was a one day general strike, which in itself led to no conflict with Märcher's forces—though 50 people were killed after troops fired on a small group of workers who had tried to seize the postal building. The Communist group in the city was incapable of a realistic intervention, since its leading figure, Otto Rühle, refused on principle to call for joint action with the SPD or USP.[25]

Leipzig was a stronghold of the USP. It was also the base of 4,000 pro-Kapp troops. On the second day of the putsch these fired on a workers' demonstration, killing 15 people. Workers seized arms from wherever they could—getting hundreds from Chemnitz and the arms factories of Thuringia—and besieged the troops in the inner city. Bitter fighting raged for three days, until a Social Democrat minister from the state government in Dresden arranged a ceasefire with the agreement of the Independent leaders. As so often in the history of the German Revolution, negotiations were used by the military as a cloak to strengthen its positions. As the vigilance of the workers on the barricades relaxed, the troops moved in to attack, smashed their way through and took control of the city.

North Germany and elsewhere

In one other area the tempo of struggle had reached that of the Ruhr and central Germany: the northern coast—an area not known in the past for any great tradition of revolutionary struggle. Yet in Wismar the council republic was declared and in Rostock 1,000 right wingers were disarmed and their weapons used to create a workers' army.

The same militancy—although not always the same success—was found in the agricultural areas east of the Elbe. The Kapp supporters had expected to find their strongest base here. Yet in many areas agricultural workers not only joined the strike, but also disarmed the troops supporting the putsch. They seized guns from isolated police units, from members of the Home Guard and from railway transports, and used them to take control of villages and towns.

The significance of these actions was that Social Democrat workers (the Communists hardly existed in such areas) were behaving in ways previously characteristic of the Communists and left Independents only. They had been called on to strike by their Social Democrat trade union leaders—yet in rural areas military repression made a strike impossible unless it involved armed resistance. Everything Social Democrat workers had been told by their leaders about the need to 'respect the forces of law and order' had to be forgotten if the general strike called by those same leaders was to take place.

This was true through much of Germany. In place after place, the strike inevitably led to armed clashes with the military, even if these did not reach the scale of central Germany and the Ruhr. In Nuremberg, for instance, 22 demonstrating workers were shot down by the army, and infuriated workers attempted to storm police stations. In Stuttgart 47 factories elected workers' councils. In Hanau workers tried to turn round troop transports heading for the Ruhr. In Kiel workers fought with guns against supporters of the putsch—and in doing so won the support of the lower ranks in the navy, who mutinied against their officers.

The picture was not uniform. In two of the storm centres of 1918-19, Hamburg and Bremen, very little happened. In Hamburg the ruling Social Democrat state government merely incorporated an extra 1,000 workers into the Home Guard. In Bremen only the railways joined the general strike. Surprisingly Berlin too was relatively quiet. The strike was absolutely solid there, but it was not until the fourth or the fifth day that armed risings began in the working class suburbs, and none reached the level of the Ruhr or central Germany.

Yet overall, the right wing generals had prompted the beginnings of a new revolution in their efforts to bury the last remnants of the old. The situation was rather similar to that in Spain in July 1936, after Franco's military uprising. The right wing army coup provoked a counter-rising of the workers. But this could not content itself with merely attacking the open supporters of the coup. The workers understood that if Kapp and Lüttwitz were successful, the rest of the military would soon swing behind them. The whole officer corps yearned for the days before the November Revolution, not just a few backwoodsmen.

Many workers had opposed the Spartakists in January 1919, had stood back when the Freikorps marched into Berlin and Bremen, had considered the Ruhr strikers extremists, and had accepted the Social Democrats' reasons for crushing the Bavarian Soviet Republic. Now they could see that not only the 'extremists', but they themselves were under attack, and they followed the call of local left Independents and Communists to destroy the power structure that had made the Kapp putsch possible. In doing so they began to create new alternative power structures—structures of workers' power—alongside the old.

Within three or four days of the coup, the authority of the state no longer held sway in some of the main industrial centres of Germany. The military forces that had lorded over the country as they marched from one end to the other in 1919, had suffered defeat in battle. They began to lose all confidence once they faced, not one section of workers fighting while another section a few miles away stood back, but simultaneous risings in many different places. What is more, the railway strike prevented them from moving fresh troops to aid besieged local garrisons.

Kapp backs out

In Berlin Kapp's supporters found themselves in a bewildering position. They had carried through a highly effective military coup: in military terms it was not a putsch, a failure, but a very successful operation. Half the army was supporting them and the other half was merely waiting to make sure the coup was a success before doing so. The right wing parties recognised their rule.

Yet they could not cope with the general strike and the local insurrections—because the whole power of the army could not cope with a united, determined working class. In a desperate attempt to smash the strike, Kapp issued a leaflet on the third day decreeing the execution of strikers—and, unable to implement the measure, withdrew it only a few hours later. The 'strong state' built up by Noske had feet of clay which were fast crumbling. Kapp and Lüttwitz had proclaimed a 'government of action'—but could not put into action the simplest measure.

Kapp and his supporters had hoped to get the allegiance of a section of workers through the collaboration of the extreme right wing Social Democrats. 'Severing, Heine and Sudekum were trusted by the Kappists'.[26] But the strength of feeling within the SPD prevented the Social Democrat leaders from responding to that trust—with the exception of Winnig, the Social Democrat who presided over East Prussia. The Kappists were left isolated, unable to act, in a deteriorating military situation.

The right wing bourgeois parties that had recognised the Kapp government began to have second thoughts. Stresemann's biographer tells how, 'The spokesmen [of the bourgeois parties] became alarmed at rumours of a Communist rising in Berlin'.[27] They pressed the insurgent generals to come to a settlement with the Social Democrat government before it was too late.

Lüttwitz was the military head of the coup—but similar fears had taken hold of many of his officers by the end of the third day. That evening the Guards Engineering Battalion in Berlin mutinied, arrested its officers and declared for the Ebert government. The security police began to switch sides. Lüttwitz was warned by his officers that 'other troops were on the verge of mutiny' and that he ought to resign.[28] Then Kapp himself lost his nerve and fled, leaving Lüttwitz to hold the dying baby.

What then followed was of decisive importance for the whole subsequent history of the Weimar Republic. The government parties, headed by the Social Democrats, had an opportunity to smash for once and for all the hold of the far right over the armed forces. They did not take it. Instead they proceeded to bail out most of the figures who had made the coup possible. Ebert, Noske and their friends, even as they fled in terror from Berlin, had not completely abandoned faith in the generals who headed this right wing coup. They had issued a call to the workers that 'there should be no bloodshed' (after themselves presiding over government policies that had led to an estimated 20,000 dead at the hands of the Freikorps in 14 months). And they had left behind in Berlin as intermediary between the rival governments the Democrat vice-premier Schiffer.

Severing, the Social Democrat minister-of-the-interior-in-exile, actually issued an instruction on 16 March to workers of the Ruhr not to obstruct the movements of the troops trying to take over the region: 'In the interests of the old government, troop movements must not be interfered with'.[29]

Why? Because the head of the Ruhr army, Watter, had not declared himself for Kapp. But he did not declare himself for the government either—until it was clear that Kapp was doomed to failure. And his subordinate officers had been enthusiasts for the coup. Together they had given orders to their troops to harrass and repress the general strike called by the 'legitimate' government. If Severing's order had been obeyed, it would have decisively shifted the balance of forces in favour of the coup.

The leaders of the bourgeois parties (including those in the government) had remained in Berlin throughout the coup. At the first opportunity they opened negotiations with Lüttwitz for a 'peaceful' solution of the conflict. They soon came to a verbal agreement with him that some of the putschists' demands be granted—new elections, which the right expected to win (even though there had been elections only 13 months earlier, the right wing parties saw new elections as 'a constitutional right') and an amnesty for the officers who had supported the putsch.

But the popular movement was now too far advanced for the government itself formally to concede these demands. Lüttwitz himself seems to have grasped at this point that if he stayed in power, he would be overthrown within hours by a repeat performance of November 1918. He relied on the vague promises of the bourgeois parties and fled.

The Social Democrat led government had survived its most difficult moment. But its first thought was not how to prevent a repetition of that moment by purging the army of the putschists, but how to bring the strike and the uprisings against the putsch to an end. It placed in full charge of the army the man that the putschists themselves had nominated in the dying moments of their adventure—Seeckt. Only four days earlier, it will be recalled, he had refused Noske's order to move against the coup.

Now he and Schiffer, for the government, produced a leaflet which was dropped by plane over the length and breadth of the country: 'Against Bolshevism—End the General Strike Together'.[30] The Social Democrat parliamentary group used a very similar tone when they warned that 'Junkers and syndicalist insurgents still threaten the German People's State... The general strike no longer hits the traitors, but our single Republican Front'.[31]

Seeckt himself 'protected' many of the putschists,[32] allowing those senior officers most deeply involved to escape, taking no action against the secret Kapp supporters who had kept their sympathies quiet and letting off scot-free all the junior officers.

The Social Democrats, however, faced a problem in all this. Their ability to play a political role rested, in the last resort, on their influence over broad layers of workers. And that influence was threatened. Everyone could see that all they had said for the past year about the 'loyalty' of officers such as Lüttwitz and Erhardt had been proved wrong. Rank and file Social Democrats throughout the country had struck and fought alongside those they had previously been taught to revile, the left Independents and the Communists. They had been shot at by troops still widely referred to as the 'Noske Guards'. They were not going to take kindly now to a simple reversion to the state of affairs before the putsch.

Those in the leadership of the party felt compelled to express some token of regret (however insincere) for what had come to pass. Even Scheidemann made speeches bitterly denouncing Noske. The first issue of the Social Democrat paper *Vorwärts* to appear after the collapse of the coup demanded:

> The government must be restructured. Not to the right, but to the left. We need a government committed without reservation to fight the nationalist, militarist reaction, and which does its utmost to get the confidence of the left wing workers.[33]

A fortnight later the Social Democrat minister Wels described his party's problem as 'How to get the party out of the confusion it had fallen into with the common struggle against reaction'[34]—in other words, how to get the members to identify with their national leaders and not with the left wing elements alongside whom they had just been fighting.

The 'problem' was most acute in the first few days after the collapse of the putsch. The flight of Kapp and Lüttwitz did not bring an automatic end to the general strike in much of Germany, including Berlin. And in the Ruhr the fighting continued. By and large, the workers wanted to win some concrete guarantee against another right wing attack. The climate was such that trade union leaders did not feel they could yet give the order for a return to work. Instead, Legien suggested to the Social Democrats, the Independents and the Communists that the precondition for a return to work should be a complete break with the past pattern of government, with a new 'workers' government' made up of all three parties and the unions.

Legien may or may not have been sincere in this suggestion. He was certainly distressed at the trouble caused to himself personally by the gallivanting of the Social Democrat ministers with the right wing generals. But probably he also felt, as the Bavarian Social Democrat leaders had felt the previous April, that the easiest way to stop the continual criticisms from the extreme left was to put them in government, so as either to temper their actions or to put them in a position where it would be easy to develop 'moderate' opposition to them. The 'workers' government' offer was both a way out of a difficult situation for Legien and his friends *and* a possible trap for the left. But it could also be an opening towards something far more radical, despite Legien, since such a government would be responsible to the working class organisation and *not* to the bourgeois majority in parliament.

Which combination of possibilities resulted depended on the response made by the left, and the clarity with which they explained it to the mass of workers. Fortunately for German capitalism, the left made no clear response at all.

The Communist Party did eventually make a coherent reply—but only after disagreement within the leadership had led to the position adopted at a meeting of the Party Centre being rejected by another meeting the next day, and that position in turn being reversed a couple of days later. The final position was that, as a Communist Party, it could not join such a government, since the majority of workers were not yet convinced of the Communist viewpoint. But it would view a government of the two Social Democrat parties and the unions in a different light from an Ebert-Noske government. As *Rote Fahne* said on 26 March:

> At the present stage there does not yet exist a solid base for the dictatorship of the proletariat. The proletariat does not dispose of sufficient military force, the Majority Social Democrats still have a big influence over the civil servants, the white collar workers and other sections of workers, the Independents still influence the majority of the urban workers. In order that the great mass of the proletariat can come to accept

the Communist doctrine, it is necessary to create a situation of almost complete political freedom and to prevent the bourgeoisie exercising its capitalist dictatorship.

The KPD estimates that the setting up of a socialist government, without the least bourgeois element in it, will create extremely favourable conditions for the energetic action of the proletarian masses and allow them to reach the maturity they need to establish their political and social dictatorship.

The party went on to declare that it would act as 'a legal opposition to that government', provided that government did not 'break its guarantees to the working class and fought by all means the bourgeois reaction and did not prevent the strengthening of the social organisation of the working class.' To be a 'loyal opposition', it said, meant 'not to prepare coup d'états,' while retaining 'complete freedom of action as regards political propaganda for its ideas.'

The formulation was well designed. It provided a basis for joint action with Social Democrat workers against the right wing ministers, without making the Communists responsible for the actions of a 'left government' that still acted within the confines of capitalism.

This was very similar to Lenin's offer in August-September 1917 to support the Menshevik-Social Revolutionary majority in the Russian soviets if they replaced the coalition government with the bourgeois parties with an all-socialist government responsible to the soviets. As Lenin explained it to his fellow party members:

> We may offer a voluntary compromise...to our nearest adversaries, the 'ruling' petty bourgeois democratic parties, the Social Revolutionaries and the Mensheviks... We may offer a compromise only by way of exception and only by virtue of the particular situation which will obviously last only a very short time... The Bolsheviks, without making any claim to participate in the government (which is impossible for internationalists unless a dictatorship of the proletariat and the poor peasants has been realised) would refrain from demanding the immediate transfer of power to the proletariat and the poor peasants and from employing revolutionary methods of fighting for this demand... The Mensheviks and the Social Revolutionaries would then agree to form a government wholly and exclusively responsible to the soviets, the latter taking over power locally as well.[35]

Unfortunately, the Central Committee of the KPD did not finally agree to its version of the 'compromise' until the negotiations over the form of government following the Kapp putsch were completed.

The Independents were even more confused. Both their right and left wings were split by Legien's offer. One part of the right wing, led by Hilferding, wanted to accept—they saw the chance of ministerial office and of stopping new attacks by the military right. The other section, led by Crispien, protested that they would not even 'sit at the same table as the murderers of workers'. Crispien seems to have been motivated by fear of upsetting his supporters rather than by principle, since only two and a half years later he rejoined the party of the 'murderers of workers' and shook the bloodstained hand of Otto Wels.[36]

On the *left* of the Independents there were those, like Koenen, who opposed simply rejecting the notion of an all-socialist government, fearing that this would not be understood by Social Democrat workers fed up with Ebert, Noske, Wels and company. By contrast, most of the left Independents agreed with Däumig when he said that an USP-SPD-trade union government would be a 'simple repetition' of the November-December 1918 government.[37]

There was, of course, that danger—Hilferding was to join a government just as bad as that in 1923—but when the question was raised in March 1920 such a government would have been judged by the mass of Social Democrat workers, many of them armed, according to a simple criterion: would it use the strength gained in the past few days to smash the officer corps and the armed forces of the right? If it had manoeuvred in the same way as the SPD-USP government of November-December 1918 had, there was a strong chance that the Social Democrat workers would have joined forces with the revolutionaries against the government and the right. They would have been prepared to follow the lead of the left and take into their own hands the task of disarming the counter-revolution, and the working class would have remained united in defence of the positions gained in the fight against Kapp.

But none of this could even be put to the test. The Independents failed to make any positive response to Legien's offer. Even if they were not themselves prepared to join the government, they could have pressed for a left Majority Social Democrat government with a clearly laid down and timetabled commitment to disarm the reactionaries, dissolve the reactionary units, the Freikorps, the Volunteers and the right wing

Home Guards, and to build up the strength of the armed working class organisations. That at least would have made it clear to every worker involved in the strike and uprisings what the Social Democrats were up to. If the SPD had accepted such demands, they would themselves have given the go-ahead to the workers to keep up the struggle to disarm the right. If they had rejected them, their own members would have seen that nothing was offered in return for the end of the strike and the laying down of arms.

But the Independent Social Democratic Party, uniting within its midst those with completely different conceptions of the struggle for socialism, was incapable of any such clarity. Its leaders simply refused Legien's proposition and left him to negotiate as he wished with the government.

The result was a shambles. Whatever Legien's motives, he was too long a right wing bureaucrat to enforce on his old friends inside the SPD a clear timetabled agreement for disarming the right, specifying the units to be disarmed, the names to be purged and *how* this was to be done. Instead what he produced were a number of vague commitments: 'recognition by a future government of the role of trade unions in economic and social reconstruction'; 'immediate disarmament of the rebels' (without specifying who the rebels were); a 'democratic reform of the state' (whatever that meant); 'no touching of units of the Reichswehr and police that have been loyal in the putsch'[38] (again no specification—were Watter and Märcher loyal, when they had refused to aid the government?)

On this basis the union federations called for a return to work. But the USP and the Berlin strike committee rejected this. In Berlin the strike continued. But it had no clear goals, and in other parts of the country, where the left wing organisations were weaker, workers saw no point in staying out on strike unless they could see something to be achieved. They began to drift back to work.

In Berlin itself further negotiations followed. But again the outcome was unsatisfactory. And the government knew that with every day that passed its hand was strengthened as the strike grew weaker.

Bauer, the Social Democrat premier, promised a withdrawal of troops from Berlin, 'no offensive action against the armed workers', especially in the Ruhr, and the enrollment in Prussia of workers into 'security detachments' controlled by the unions. The offer was still vague—there was no mention of the various Volunteer corps, no specification of the army units that had been 'disloyal', of what would happen to the police units that had fought, at some point or other, for the putsch. It gave no power to the action committees and workers' councils to deal with such matters. But the Independents finally accepted the proposals—the right Independents talking of an 'end' to the strike, and the left, under Däumig, of an 'interruption' conditional upon government behaviour.

But strikes are not mechanical appliances that can be switched on and off at will. Their success depends on the determination of the strikers, a certain momentum in the struggle, which brings the expectation of victory. A halt in the struggle—or sometimes the mere talk of such a halt—can destroy that momentum, breaking unity and sending workers back into their separate lives. That is why strikes are nearly always easier to keep going, despite the hardship, than to resume after 'interruption'.

By this time the Berlin strike had been going ten days. The confused negotiations had left many workers unclear about its objectives. Many of the provincial centres had already withdrawn from the movement. The call for the return to work meant the effective end of the united struggle that had stopped the putsch, *without* any radical transformation in the structures of military power that had made the putsch possible.

Meanwhile, the ministries had returned to work, the orders of the old bureaucrats began to be obeyed again, and the chain of command was re-established in the army under Seeckt. While the workers' leaders dithered, the bourgeoisie was recovering from its fright and reasserting itself.

Its hand strengthened, it could begin to answer back to the working class movement. The press began to complain about the 'counter-government' of the unions. Legien was told that any government would have to get a majority in the Assembly—which meant it had to get support from at least one of the bourgeois parties. Finally a new coalition government was formed, very much like the one that had allowed the Kapp putsch to develop. Noske was too compromised to play a role but he was replaced by a politician even more pliable to the demands of the High Command (if that was possible!), the bourgeois politician Gessler who allowed Seeckt a free hand.

Return of the Freikorps

The extent of the missed opportunity was soon felt. 'The government did not take the slightest step to break the power of reaction and to safeguard democracy from fresh attacks,' a right Independent complained shortly afterwards:

> Not a single workers' battalion was formed: instead the Chancellor, Bauer, invested Seeckt with full powers to set up a militarist reign of terror. Once more martial law reigned throughout the country, as under Noske. In Kopenik—to mention one of the many incidents which occurred in the environs of Berlin—the Independent, Futran, and three companions were arrested and shot. He was well known as a moderate politician, guiltless of the slightest misdemeanour.
>
> On 19 March the government decree was published which conferred upon Seeckt full power to set up extraordinary court martials and to proclaim martial law... The workers who...had armed themselves and risen in defence of democracy and to disarm the rebels, now became the prey of the reactionary citizens' guard, the Volunteer corps, and those bodies of troops which had tolerated the rebels with unmistakable benevolence.
>
> The workers on strike, or those who had risen for armed resistance, suddenly became 'Spartakists' and 'Communists' who aimed at a Bolshevist dictatorship and consequently had to be suppressed with utmost ruthlessness. What had taken place at Köpenik was now repeated on a large scale elsewhere. An incident in Thuringia may be mentioned as an example. On 24 March Bad Thal in Thuringia was occupied by Volunteer students from Marburg, and the mayor of the district was summoned to indicate the residences of 15 citizens, who were thereupon arrested and removed. On the following morning the corpses of the prisoners, in a fearfully mutilated condition, were found at a street corner. The unarmed men had been handled with appaling callousness by the nationalistic students corps, amid cries of 'shoot them' and 'we want some corpses for our anatomy'.[39]

Against this background, even Kapp's supporters were not denied one significant victory. In Bavaria at the height of the coup the local military command had 'persuaded' the Social Democrat government under Hoffmann to resign. Power passed into the hands of a right wing Bavarian People's Party government headed by Kahr—which was to provide protection for the next three years for fascist and nationalist elements from the whole of Germany. The local Social Democrats actually issued a joint call against the general strike with General Mohl, who leaned towards supporting Kapp. When Kapp disappeared, his Bavarian protégés remained in power.

But the most significant developments were in the area of the heaviest fighting during the coup itself, the Ruhr.

While the negotiations were going on in Berlin, Watter's army in the Ruhr remained under pressure from the Ruhr Red Army. The left's resolve to keep up the fight was increased when they discovered military supplies which Berlin had sent for Watter to use against them.

But although supplying arms to Watter, the first concern of the Berlin government had to be to bring the fighting in the Ruhr to an end. In the south of Germany the railways had returned to work, which made it much easier for the Reichswehr to concentrate its troops around the Ruhr. But in Berlin not until 22 March did the factories under Independent influence agree to end the general strike. Any upsurge in the fighting in the Ruhr could easily prevent the reconsolidation of government power in the capital. So, on the very day that the strike ended in Berlin, Severing—who had overseen the repression in the Ruhr the year before—began negotiations in Bielefeld to bring hostilities in the Ruhr to a halt, at least temporarily, and buy time for the government. He later explained:

> I could only allow a new march of troops into the Ruhr when it was guaranteed that these troops had overwhelming power, so that any resistance to them would seem useless. But for that it was necessary to draw away from the movement the part of the working class that had only fought to defend the constitution... Such a strength the authorities could not achieve in a few days. The troops were at their weakest in the area.[40]

The negotiations involved not merely the government and those who had been fighting the military, but also the leaders of all the unions and 'democratic' parties in the region and the mayors (usually belonging to these same parties) of the big towns. The workers' forces were represented by the Hagen workers' council leadership. But significantly, there were no representatives there from Essen and the areas where fighting was still going on.

The agreement that emerged—the 'Bielefeld Accords'—laid down the basis for a ceasefire. Watter's troops were to stay outside the Ruhr; a section of the Red Army was to be allowed to retain its weapons through incorporation into the police or the local authorities; the rest of the Red Army was to give up its weapons. Like the agreement reached for ending the general strike in Berlin, the Accords were characterised chiefly by their vagueness. They left Watter's forces intact and enabled them to continue to reinforce themselves.

The Accords certainly bought the government the time it needed. They threw the workers' movement into complete confusion.

The section of the Red Army that had been represented at the negotiations, from the eastern front around Hagen, saw the Accords as a victory and laid down their arms. The workers on the western front, however, who had not been represented at Bielefeld, felt they had been on the verge of driving Watter's troops out of their last foothold, the barracks in Wesel, and from there could move to take Watter's HQ in Munster. They denounced as traitors the signatories to the Accords—including two Hagen Communists who had been at Bielefeld—and kept up the fighting.

It is clear that both positions were mistaken. To give up one's arms and withdraw from the front on the basis of a piece of paper was folly, given the Social Democrats' record of betrayal since November 1918. To maintain the fighting was also folly, given that the strike elsewhere in Germany was over and that with each day that passed the military was reinforcing. The tactically most sensible position was that advised by a representative from the Communist Party in Berlin, Pieck, who arrived in the Ruhr the day after the Accords: for the Red Army to keep its guns and to maintain its front, but to avoid battle, throwing the blame for any renewed fighting clearly on to Watter and Severing. The significance of any further bloodshed would then have been obvious to workers elsewhere in Germany, who might be persuaded to move in support of the Ruhr.

However, had the whole Red Army supported either mistaken position it would have been better than what did happen, with one half going one way and one half the other. The government had the excuse to march the troops back into the Ruhr—and faced diminished resistance when it did so. The Ruhr workers ended up with the worst of all possible options. That was the price they had to pay for the failure to build a centralised command, based upon the workers' councils, during the euphoric days when the Red Armies were beating back Watter's troops.

Some sort of central structure did come into existence the day after the signing of the Accords. Delegates from 70 councils met in Essen with the main leaders of the Red Army and elected a central leadership. But it was another two days before it could agree to the policy of holding on to the guns but avoiding armed clashes. And it could not enforce this policy on the front at Wesel.

By now it was too late. The balance of forces had shifted towards the government, and the government knew it. Its own forces were growing stronger by the hour, and it was able to present the continued fighting to workers elsewhere in Germany as nothing but a rerun of the 'Spartakist putschism' of 1919. The Chancellor, Müller, informed the Essen central council that there could be no negotiations until the workers had laid down their arms, and that the Bielefeld Accords no longer held, since the Red Army had 'broken them'.

The class war is like any other war in one respect: the outcome is decided not merely by the absolute balance of forces at a single point in time, but also by whether the leaders are able to direct their forces according to the strengths and weaknesses of the enemy. In a war between more or less evenly matched armies, a single misjudgement can lead from the verge of victory to disorder and disintegration. This is even more the case in the class war, where the forces of the working class are not soldiers trained to blind obedience, but volunteers whose commitment to the fight comes very much from the belief that their liberation is at hand; they are quickly thrown into disarray when the forward momentum of the struggle is lost. It may be just a single mistake that opens the road to defeat—but once made, the result can be more devastating than if battle had not been engaged in the first place.

In the Ruhr, one of the greatest victories of the German working class now turned into one of its greatest defeats. By the beginning of April what had been a massive, disciplined workers' action had fallen apart, with demoralisation and passivity on the one hand, and isolated guerrilla attacks and acts of sabotage on the other. When Watter began his new march into the Ruhr on 4 April, no one felt that armed struggle could hold him back and he met no resistance. But that did not prevent his forces taking the most vicious reprisals.

Ernst, the Red Army commander on the Hagen front, describes how:

> During the march into Hamm, workers were shot without any judicial proceedings. There was a method to the behaviour of the troops. On the first day when they occupied places everything was peaceful. The military authorities themselves allowed musical performances in the market places. On the second day they suddenly began the arrests and the shooting. The murder of workers was carefully planned. The cowardly middle classes

also played a part in these proceedings. Workers were pulled from their homes and shot. How the beasts behaved can be seen by the way 65 canal workers were shot. They were engaged in building a bridge at Haltern and had taken no part in the fighting. As the Reichswehr advanced it opened fire on them with machine guns and then threw grenades.[41]

The methods that were later to be identified with Nazism were tried out here for the first time, against German workers and with the consent of Social Democrat ministers: in Pelkum 90 victims of the advancing army were buried in a mass grave; among the victims were women and girls dressed as nurses.

> The national army restored order quite in the old way by mass shootings. Many thousands of the workers fled before this White terror, in which numerous Kapp officers took part, into the [French] occupied areas. Upon being assured by the government that they had no cause to fear reprisals, they returned, only to fall victims of extraordinary court martials, which pronounced hundreds of death sentences.
>
> Among the population of the districts of Düsseldorf, Munster and Augsburg, tremendous excitement prevailed in consequence of the wholesale sentences.[42]

There was no equivalent action against the reactionary forces involved in the initial putsch. None were executed—such punishment was restricted to those who had fought for the 'legal government'. Proceedings were begun against 540 officers for their part in the putsch—but never completed. The leading conspirators were allowed to escape abroad for a couple of years before returning home. Lüttwitz even received a state pension of 18,000 marks until his death. The Erhardt brigade were 'punished' by being sent to help crush the workers of the Ruhr. In fact, only one prison sentence was ever handed out—Jugow got five years.

The outcome of the putsch

The Kapp putsch began as an offensive by the extreme right. Within two days it had given way to a huge counter-offensive of the left, which threatened to undermine the whole structure built up by the old ruling class in the previous 14 months. Yet within a few weeks the counter-offensive too was on the ebb. The government was reconstructed—but not to the left. The army and the Freikorps resumed their march through Germany. And the Social Democrat led government gave in to the demands of the right for new elections, in which the right gained heavily. (The Independents too gained, picking up nearly as many votes as the Social Democrats—but that was not sufficient in parliamentary terms to make up for the votes gained by the parties of the right.)

The Social Democrat leaders had united with the right against the armed workers after the Kapp days. Now the right turned against them. Within months of the putsch they were ousted from office by a new government under the 'moderate republican' Fehrenbach. Not surprisingly, people began to regard the frenetic days of the Kapp putsch as of minor importance, as a footnote to history.

Yet those days could have been much more. Lenin once compared them to the time of the Kornilov offensive against Russia's Kerensky government in August 1917. The Bolsheviks had been able to emerge from that struggle as the most powerful party of the working class, which had half taken state power in the process of fighting the extreme right. From the Kornilov struggle to October 1917 was a short journey. But in Germany things did not turn out like that. Why?

The simplest explanation would be to invoke 'objective circumstances' or the 'non-revolutionary consciousness of Western workers'. But that would be to beg the question.

In places such as Chemnitz, Halle, the Ruhr, even in rural Meklenberg and in Vogtland on the Czech border, the consequences of the putsch *were* like those in Russia in August-September 1917. The old military structure was defeated, the workers were armed, in many cases workers' councils did emerge as the effective power. And, a marked difference from the November days of 1918, these were workers' councils with revolutionary majorities. It hardly makes sense to say that the *objective* circumstances were different in these places from the rest of Germany. How 'objectively' did Chemnitz differ from Bremen, or the Ruhr from Berlin, so as to produce a revolutionary outcome in one but not in the other?

Yet a challenge to the old state structure did not develop in all the industrial centres. In some of the large towns the strike did not turn into an armed rising; in one or two places even the strike was not solid. And in many places it was run, not by workers' councils, but by action committees dominated by leaders—often the bureaucrats—of the 'workers' parties' and the unions.

Talk of 'working class consciousness' in the abstract cannot explain these discrepancies. The places where the struggle did *not* rise to the level of all out armed confrontation included cities such as Hamburg, Bremen, Leipzig and above all Berlin—cities generally regarded as strongholds of the extreme left in these years; and mostly cities where the supposedly revolutionary party of the Independents had enjoyed a majority of working class support for 12 months and more.

What *was* lacking was solid organisation and leadership within the working class capable of measuring up to the consciousness engendered by the putsch. The majority of industrial workers looked to the Independents for leadership. But the right wing Independents, for all their talk of 'revolution', longed above all for unity with their old colleagues within the Majority Social Democrat leadership. And the left Independents did not have a structure capable of implementing decisions independently of the right.

The result was that the way in which the newly militant consciousness of the majority of workers was translated into action depended upon relatively accidental things. The 'subjective' factor was decisive: whether there were in a particular district or big factory revolutionaries capable of taking the initiative in calling for the election of councils to lead the armed struggle—and with sufficient influence to get such a call accepted.

Objectively, for instance, the working class in Chemnitz was not 'more revolutionary' than that in nearby Leipzig. Indeed, in the early part of 1919 it seemed the other way round—Leipzig was a bastion of Independent support, while Chemnitz was still dominated by the SPD. The difference was that the Chemnitz Communists had in the course of 1919 been able to build up their influence in the local working class movement through participation in and leadership of 'partial', 'economic' struggles until they put the Independents in the shade and directly challenged the influence of the SPD. Hence they were able to take the lead on the first day of the putsch in calling for the general strike, and to extend it into a call for the election of political workers' councils, the disarming of the middle class and the building of armed workers' detachments.

By contrast, in Leipzig, as the Chemnitz Communist Brandler told a congress of his party a month later:

> The left wing Independents allowed Lipinski [a right Independent] to take over the leadership and negotiate with the government. They

sabotaged the voting-in of workers' councils on the grounds of pure party egoism. The working class was split, allowing the Kapp forces to enjoy success.[43]

The result of this one 'accident of influence' was of major national importance. Brandler pointed out that Leipzig and Chemnitz together would have controlled much of central Germany: 'Together we would have been able to put pressure on Dresden' (where the government had first fled and where the key 'wait and see' general, Märcher, was based). 'We would not only have demanded the unmaking of the old government, but would have carried it through.'

As it was, the Leipzig Independents called with the local Social Democrats for a return to work and an end to 'confrontation with the troops' the moment that Kapp himself had decamped. They gave no thought to the need for guarantees that action would be taken against the old military structures.

The picture in Hamburg and Bremen seems to have been even more dismal. In Hamburg 1,500 Social Democrat and USP workers were armed—but they were kept under the tight control of the Social Democrat state government through incorporation in the Home Guards and the police. The strike there had lacked any real enthusiasm. In Bremen an 'Action Committee' set up by the three 'workers' parties' seems to have done next to nothing.

In Berlin, as we have seen, the left Independents led a massive strike that began to show signs of turning into a rising—but then did not know how to translate its success into permanent gains.

The Communist Party and the Kapp days

The Communist Party had been formed precisely because of the gyrations of the Independents in such situations. But it was in no position to counter them on a national scale in the spring of 1920. It was an extraordinarily weak organisation. Although it had grown from a membership of three or four thousand at its inception to 110,000 in the summer of 1919, it had then split. The fragment that remained with the party leadership had very little strength indeed outside Chemnitz and Stuttgart. It had virtually no membership in key cities such as Hamburg, Bremen, Hanover, Dresden and Magdeburg. In Berlin it had only 'a few hundred members' (according to speakers at its Fourth Congress) compared to '100,000' held by the Independents.[44]

Brandler told the party's Third Congress, a bare month before the putsch:

> In general we have no party yet. I say this after visiting the Ruhr, where there is no Communist movement. It won't be possible to put one together in the near future. The things that have happened have discredited our party... When the miners' and the railway workers' strikes broke out we had no influence on the workers.[45]

In the few places where the party did exist, it did usually give some sort of lead which workers followed during the days of the putsch. We have seen how it put itself at the head of the movement in Chemnitz; in Stuttgart the party called for the general strike and the arming of the workers within half an hour of hearing the news of the putsch from Berlin; even in the Ruhr the isolated party members were able to exercise some influence over the course of events.

The weakest spot was Berlin. A depleted meeting of the Party Centre—Levi, for instance, was in prison; Brandler was in Chemnitz—took place on the day of the putsch. It made a catastrophic error. It issued a statement *opposing* the general strike. It defined the struggle as a fight 'between two counter-revolutionary wings', and went on:

> Ebert-Bauer-Noske are dead and helpless in their graves... Just as it is foundering this society of bankrupts calls on the working class for a general strike to 'save the republic'... The revolutionary proletariat will not lift a finger for the government that murdered Rosa Luxemburg and Karl Liebknecht. It will not raise a finger for the democratic republic, which is only a mask for the dictatorship of the bourgeoisie.[46]

Rote Fahne the next day explained that the workers were not powerful enough for a general strike!

> Must the workers in this situation go into a general strike ? The working class, which was still being attacked by Ebert and Noske yesterday, is disarmed, in the worst condition and not ready for action. It is our duty to speak clearly. The working class movement will take up the struggle against the military dictatorship at the time and with the means that appear right to it. This moment has not yet come.[47]

On 14 and 15 March the Party Centre swung over to supporting the strike: it could hardly do otherwise, since the strike was now a growing success. But it still did not call for the *arming* of the working class—even though the best Communist militants in the provinces were not merely calling for this, but putting it into practice. Even on the Monday, the third day of the putsch, when the first armed battles were breaking out in central Germany and the Ruhr, the party did not go beyond calling for the general strike and the election of workers' councils. Instead of calling for the workers to take up arms, it warned, 'Workers, do not go into the street. Meet daily in the factories. Do not be provoked by the White guards.'

The main way in which the party centrally tried to distinguish itself from the Social Democrats, the Independents and the union leaders was through verbal attacks on Ebert and Noske:

> For the general strike. Down with the military dictatorship. Down with bourgeois democracy. The Communists are against the Ebert-Noske government, against the re-establishment of a government with a bourgeois basis, with parliament and the state bureaucracy.[48]

The best comment on these statements came in a letter to the Centre from one of its members, Paul Levi, who was temporarily imprisoned:

> I have read the leaflets this minute. My judgement, the KPD is threatened with moral and political bankruptcy. It is incomprehensible that anyone can write sentences such as, 'The working class is not ready for action at present'... After you had said on the first day that the workers were not ready for action, on the next day your leaflet says, 'Now, at last, must the German proletariat open the struggle for the proletarian dictatorship and the Council Republic'... I always thought we were clear and agreed on the following: when an action comes—although for nonsensical aims, we join the action, so that our slogans can lead it beyond the nonsensical aims... and do not scream, 'Do not move a finger,' if the aim is not agreeable to us.
>
> We have to give concrete slogans, to tell the masses what must be done immediately... The Council Republic comes last and not first. It seems to me that no one is thinking now of elections to factory councils. The only slogan at the present moment should be: 'Arming of the proletariat'.

A strike needs demands. You have to know what the strike can obtain. With such slogans the KPD must give a complexion to the strike, a complexion that the strike has not had so far... Then and only then, when the masses have taken up our demands and the 'leaders' refuse them, then there arises from the action other demands, for example about councils, a council congress, a Council Republic, 'Down with the democratic republic' etc; all these demands arise if the strike demands are fulfilled. Once the strike demands are met, the force holding up the republic is the proletariat, and its government, whatever it calls itself, is a child of these completely changed social forces. From there to the Council Republic is a span of only six months of normal development.[49]

Levi's judgement on the inanity of the Centre's leaflets was without doubt correct. But how did the Centre come to make such mistakes?

Afterwards it was said, within the party, that the leadership had been 'slow' and 'out of touch', located in Berlin where the party membership was small and not rooted among the mass of workers. On top of that there was the memory of the oft-repeated sequence of events in 1919, when the Social Democrats enticed the Communists to put their heads on the chopping block. A leadership that lacked immediate access to the class through a network of experienced militants could not sense that this time millions of previously passive workers would respond to the call of the union leaders and not leave the Communist to act—and die—alone.

We must not forget that only 12 months earlier in March 1919 what had begun as a united movement of the whole Berlin working class had ended in a bloody massacre, with Communists and left Independents being slaughtered wholesale. To this extent the mistake of the Centre was a mistake that repeatedly plagued the German Revolution—overcompensation for past errors. Instead of learning enough from the past to be able to cope in the present, the revolutionary leaders seemed doomed to endure a vicious circle, by which one defeat created the confusion that made the next defeat inevitable.

But timidity cannot be the only explanation for the statements issued. For that does not explain the equation of Social Democratic government, however miserable and murderous, with an all out right wing dictatorship.

The explanation lies in the still strong temptation to 'ultra-leftism' within the party leadership, which the split from half the party had not eliminated. This was expecially true in the weak Berlin district, led by Ernst Friesland. The declarations about the Kapp putsch expressed this 'ultra-leftism' in a form that at the same time permitted abstention from mass struggle—a favourite combination for small ultra-left sects that want to retain their purity of principles without taking the risk of action.

At the party conference a month later there was much discussion over the party's response to the Kapp putsch. Most of it was about whether it had been right to join in the call for a SPD-USP-union 'workers' government'. Paul Levi, however, made the point that by the time the party was asked its opinion on this subject, it had very little pulling power. It had not had anything to say at the beginning of the struggle; why should anyone listen to it now?

'Did the KPD', he asked, 'give slogans that created for it political and moral credit, so as to allow it to lead when other factors prevented it?'

The failure to take the lead on the Saturday of the putsch meant that:

> ...by Sunday 14 March the leadership was in the hands of the five union federations and the USP right wing. The masses were not going to be won to another leadership. And now, after five days of strikes in which the entire city was shut down, with not a single wheel turning, with no movement of food or fuel, with no light, no gas, a completely dead city, after five days, could the Party Centre that had not played a predominant role, now move the strongest forces in the struggle? If we had taken the leadership in the beginning, then all sorts of things might have been possible when the unions called for the end of the strike.[50]

The dissident Communists

Those who had broken with the Communist Party because it was 'too right wing', were themselves incapable of giving any national leadership. In Hamburg the breakaway Communist district under Laufenberg and Wolffheim put out a leaflet saying, 'The general strike is general nonsense,' and never reversed its position. The result was no Communist presence in the city to counter the passive response of the Social Democrats.[51]

In Mannheim the syndicalist influenced workers' council told the workers to keep off the streets and to 'take power at the point of production', by running the factories under workers' control. Effectively this meant refusing to challenge the power of Kapp's supporters, the troops, the Volunteers and the police.[52]

In the Ruhr many of the breakaway Communists played a very positive and courageous role in organising the fighting detachments and building them into the Red Army. What they lacked was any notion that each military battle had to be part of a unified struggle, taking into account strategic and political considerations. At the end of the day they cut themselves off from the workers' councils and engaged in isolated, guerrilla-type actions that played into the hands of Watter and Severing. Paul Levi claimed that by threatening to blow up the pits they turned many of the miners against them to the point that some of these were prepared to regard Watter's troops as 'liberators'—you could not expect the miners to welcome the destruction of the only jobs in villages where they worked like their fathers and grandfathers before them.[53]

'In Rhineland-Westphalia [in other words the Ruhr] a fully developed council system was built that fully reflected the will of the workers...' Levi argued. 'But against the will of the councils, some comrades thought they could make a revolution over the heads of the working class'.[54]

What can be said with certainty is that if the Communist Party did not rise to the moment on 13 March, those who had split from it 'to the left' failed to provide any clear strategy and tactics at all.

A missed opportunity

The struggle against the Kapp putsch joined the long list of 'might have beens' in the history of the German Revolution—a list which ends in 1933 with the greatest tragedy of the 20th century. And the basic reason was the failure of revolutionary organisation and leadership to measure up to the sudden leap forward in working class consciousness.

As an account written by some of the leading revolutionaries concluded, eight years later:

> In the ranks of the Spartakus League, and above all in the leadership around the Kapp putsch, was reflected all the organisational and ideological weakness of the German Revolution. The lack of a strong, ideologically mature Communist Party rooted in the masses was one of the determining causes of the set backs suffered by the German Revolution in the Kapp putsch.[55]

1. Quoted in H J Gordon, *The Reichswehr and the German Republic 1919-26* (Princeton 1957) p115.
2. Ibid, p101.
3. Heinrich Ströbel, *The German Revolution and After* (London 1923) p223; and Paul Frölich and others, *Illustrierte Geschichte der Deutschen Revolution* (Berlin 1929, reprinted Frankfurt 1970) p458.
4. H J Gordon, op cit, p57.
5. H A Turner, *Stresemann and the Politics of the Weimar Republic* (Princeton 1963) p50.
6. *Bericht über der IV Parteitag der KPD*, p20.
7. R M Watt, *The Kings Depart* (London 1973) p561.
8. Erhardt Lucas, *Märzrevolution 1920* vol 1 (Frankfurt 1974) p127.
9. Ibid, p135.
10. Ibid, p137.
11. Adolf Meinberg, *Aufstand an der Ruhr* (Frankfurt 1973) pp74-75.
12. Ibid, p94.
13. Quoted in P Frölich et al, op cit, p499.
14. Quoted in E Lucas, op cit, pp307-308.
15. See for example, M Buber-Neumann, *Kriegsschauplätze der Weltrevolution* (Stuttgart 1967) p20.
16. E Lucas, op cit, p214.
17. Quoted in E Lucas, op cit, vol 2, p67.
18. Ibid, p71.
19. A Meinberg, op cit, p97.
20. P Frölich et al, op cit, p487. Much of the detail in this section comes from the *Illustrierte Geschichte*.
21. Ibid, p468.
22. Quoted ibid, p490.
23. Ibid; and E Lucas, op cit, vol 2, p163.
24. Ibid, p163.
25. Ibid, p168.
26. P Frölich et al, op cit, p25.
27. H A Turner, op cit, p58.
28. H J Gordon, op cit, p120 onwards.
29. Order quoted in full in A Meinberg, op cit, p86.
30. Reproduced in P Frölich et al, op cit, p471.
31. Quoted ibid, p471.
32. See for example, H J Gordon, op cit, p120 onwards.
33. Special issue of *Vorwärts*, 8 March 1920.
34. Quoted in Pierre Broué, *Révolution en Allemagne* (Paris 1971) p349.
35. For further details, see Tony Cliff, *Lenin* vol 2 (London 1976) pp304-306.
36. See P Frölich et al, op cit, p441.

37. For accounts of these arguments, see E Lucas, op cit vol 2, pp103-121; P Broué, op cit, pp349-359; and P Frölich et al, *Illustrierte Geschichte*, op cit, pp470-473.
38. Quoted by all three sources above.
39. H Ströbel, op cit, p236.
40. Quoted in A Meinberg, op cit, p128.
41. P Frölich et al, op cit, p505.
42. H Ströbel, op cit, p239.
43. *Bericht über der IV Parteitag der KPD*, p55.
44. Ibid.
45. Ibid, p12.
46. Quoted in M Buber-Neumann, op cit, p28. Neither Broué nor *Illustrierte Geschichte* quote these statements, but Frölich quotes the crucial phrase about 'not lifting a finger' in *Die Internationale* (June 1920) p19, and so does Levi in *Die Kommunistische Internationale* (July 1920).
47. *Rote Fahne*, 14 March 1920, quoted in P Frölich et al, *Illustrierte Geschichte*, op cit, p468.
48. Quoted in P Frölich et al, op cit, p468.
49. Reprinted in *Die Kommunistische Internationale* (1920).
50. *Bericht über der IV Parteitag der KPD*, p48.
51. P Frölich et al, op cit, p481.
52. E Lucas, op cit, vol 2, p157.
53. *Bericht über der IV Parteitag der KPD*, p21.
54. Ibid.
55. P Frölich et al, op cit, p467.

CHAPTER 10

The March madness 1921

The history of the German Revolution until 1920 is a history of more or less spontaneous struggles, which individual revolutionary socialists could influence, but which no one could direct. By contrast after 1920 it is to a large extent the history of a single party, the Communist Party, KPD.

At the beginning of the year the KPD was pitifully small. Only in Chemnitz was it a mass force. In many of the most important cities it was a complete nullity. The initiative shown by its members outside Berlin during the Kapp days did improve matters a little. The membership grew, and the party began to sink roots in most districts. But with 78,715 claimed members it was still smaller than it had been before the split with the ultra-left. It claimed 9,200 members in the Rhineland, 17,500 in mid-Germany, 4,200 in Württemburg (Stuttgart)—but only 1,700 in Berlin and 1,850 in Thuringia.

Nor could it boast any great influence outside its own ranks, if its press was anything to go by. Its daily papers sold 58,000 copies, with an additional 17,000 copies of local weeklies—a combined sale of less than one copy per member.[1]

Throughout 1919 and the beginning of 1920 the party had had to operate illegally. Only for three weeks in December was there not a state of emergency in Berlin. But illegality could no longer explain its small size, since the KPD had been able to return to open work after the Kapp days, and its leaders boasted that it had held 3,000 meetings during the June 1920 election campaign. Its vote, like its membership, was pitiful for a revolutionary party after 18 months of mass strikes and local uprisings—a mere 500,000, with a smaller percentage of the poll than the revolutionary left received in the staid atmosphere of France in March 1978. Its influence in the trade unions seems to have been virtually nil.

The dissident Communists who had left the party did even less well. At the time of the split the leaders of the opposition to the party leadership were the Hamburg Communists Laufenberg and Wolffheim. Their criticisms of the leadership won wide support from those regarded by the KPD leaders as 'putschist' and 'impatient', not willing to wait for revolution until the majority of workers were ready. These impatient, but instinctively revolutionary elements were further convinced of the correctness of their criticisms of the KPD leaders by the events of the Kapp days. They saw a connection between the KPD leaders' abstention from the struggle in the first days with its later talk of a 'workers' government' and its insistence on holding back the Ruhr struggle once the rest of Germany had returned to work.

In this atmosphere the various local groups forced out of the KPD met at a conference in April 1920 and formed the Communist Workers Party (KAPD), with a claimed membership of 38,000. The KAPD has occasionally been represented as the first 'anti-Moscow' opposition to break with 'orthodox' Communism. This was not so. The Communist International, proclaimed only six months before the split and with as yet virtually no structure or apparatus, opposed the expulsion of the 'ultra-left' from the German party. And the founding congress of the KAPD declared itself for the 'dictatorship of the proletariat' and applied to join the International—an application which the Russian Bolsheviks thought should be accepted.

Nor is it entirely correct to describe the KAPD as 'ultra-left'. Certainly all its members shared a 'leftist' opposition to work in the unions or parliamentary elections. But on most other issues there were several distinct and contradictory currents of opinion—many of which were based, if anything, on a 'rightist' lack of confidence in the revolution.

Laufenberg and Wolffheim, on breaking with the KPD in the autumn of 1919, had developed a theory that led *away from* militant class struggle. They declared that Germany was a 'proletarian nation' and that what was needed was a 'national war of liberation' against the Allies; if the proletariat led such a struggle, the bourgeoisie would accept a 'class truce'. Their slogan became 'a national liberation war, not a class war'. The old notion of revolution through insurrection could be abandoned: the revolution could be carried through more or less peacefully in the factories through the organisation of breakaway industrial unions. Already at the KPD congress, where the split occurred, Wolffheim declared that the party did not exist to lead a fight for power, but that 'the party can be no other than a propaganda organ for the revolution and for councils'.[2]

The second main current in the KAPD got its theoretical leadership from two Dutch Communists, Pannekoek and Gorter. Pannekoek's starting point, again, was not 'ultra-left' but rather the 'rightist' view that the time for revolution in Western Europe had not yet come. This, he said, was because of the suffocating domination of bourgeois ideas over the working class. The long, slow process of building up pure, proletarian organisations—revolutionary councils—in which workers would be free of the ideological restraints of bureaucracy and of parliamentary influences had yet to be done.[3]

It was accepted, implicitly, that for the time being these councils would involve only a minority of workers. The job of the party was to help build such councils and then to 'commit suicide'. For these 'council communists', as for Laufenberg and Wolffheim, the party had a limited, propaganda role only.

A third tendency was that of the former SPD deputy, Otto Rühle. He rejected the dictatorship of the proletariat and was moving rapidly to an anarchist position, which led to his expulsion from the KAPD in November 1920.

The majority of the party's members almost certainly did not follow any of these sets of ideas. What bound them to the KAPD was an impatient revolutionary zeal, a belief that action mattered more than theory. In their different ways both Pannekoek and Laufenberg rejected armed class struggle as an immediate perspective. But their followers were often the same impetuous street fighters.

Given such internal divergences, it was not surprising that the party seems to have declined fairly quickly. The initial animators of the left, Laufenberg and Wolffheim, were allowed in at the founding congress, only to be expelled in the same year (Wolffheim then gravitated towards the Nazis). According to KPD estimates only about half the 38,000 founding members were still active members six months later.

While the Communist forces stagnated, workers fed up with the SPD streamed to the Independent Social Democrats. The USP's membership of 300,000 at the beginning of 1919 had swollen to 800,000 by Autumn 1920.

The balance between left and right within the party was also changing. In the first period of the revolution the USP right—Haase, Hilferding,

Kautsky and Bernstein—had been able to carry party congresses by more than two to one. They were open about their perspective: to merge the two Social Democrat parties again as before the war. But the bitterness of the struggle against the Freikorps and the Social Democrat led government forced the party's membership very much to the left. A powerful left opposition developed within the party, centred around the Berlin revolutionary shop stewards.

Controversy centred on two questions—the role of the workers' councils vis-a-vis parliament and the International.

At the party congress in Berlin in March 1919 (just as the week of bloodshed was beginning) the leadership sought to conciliate the left by speaking of the need for 'councils anchored in the constitution' alongside the National Assembly. For the left, Däumig opposed this, insisting that socialism could come only through workers' councils as the basis for the dictatorship of the proletariat. The balance of forces in the congress was shown by the votes for the presidency—Haase, for the right, received 159 votes, Däumig 109.

A compromise was eventually reached over the question of parliament and the councils—a form of words which recognised the councils as 'fighting organisations' created by the 'proletarian revolution', asserting that 'the Independent Social Democratic Party strives for the dictatorship of the proletariat,' but adding quickly that parliament had an important role to play.

On the International, the issue was whether it should be reconstituted on the same basis as the Second International that had fallen apart in 1914 and include those who had supported opposed sides both in the war and in the civil war since; or whether the party should affiliate to the revolutionary international that had been proclaimed by a number of delegates of the revolutionary left meeting a few weeks earlier in Moscow. At the March congress the first option was carried; but the radicalisation of the members meant that at the next congress in December 1919 the leadership was forced to opt for 'negotiations' with the Communist International.

Such formulae corresponded, at first, to the half-thought-out ideas of the workers who had just joined the party. But as time passed and the members evaluated the bloody events of 1919 and the Kapp putsch, compromise resolutions became less and less workable. A leader of the USP right wing described what happened:

The antagonism within the Independent Social Democratic Party had been very incompletely bridged over by the highly ambiguous programme, which was the fruit of a marriage between democracy and soviet dictatorship, consummated at the Leipzig conference (December 1919)... Inside the organs and the press of the party the fierce struggle for power (between the two wings) had hardly suffered any interruption, even during the Kapp putsch and the electoral campaign.[4]

The left believed that if they struggled long enough, the right wing would eventually abandon the party, as Bernstein had already done. The left were at the same time emerging as a strong force within the unions: the Berlin 'revolutionary shop stewards' around Richard Müller and Dissmann carried the day at the Metal Workers Union conference in 1919, received a third of the votes at the conference of the main national union federation, the 9 million strong ADGB, and took control of the local union federation in Berlin.

The Communists were highly critical of the left Independents. They claimed that when it came to practical struggles, all too often the left were bound hand and foot to the right. The right controlled the party apparatus, the parliamentary fraction and much of the press, and that determined how congress decisions were interpreted in practice. In the Kapp struggle, for instance, the line of the USP's national organisation was hardly different from that of the Majority Social Democrats. Many of the party's members were engaged in the armed struggle and opposed any return to work until the right wing forces were completely disarmed and purged, but the party had no *national* policy of agitating around these demands. Even in Berlin, where the left were the majority in the party, they ended up accepting a return to work before clearly defined terms had been agreed.

The party boasted of its 'federal', non-centralised structure, but this was just what the right wing wanted, for it allowed them to get a 'revolutionary' reputation without having to bear responsibility for a national programme of revolutionary agitation.

Within the Communist Party there was considerable discussion about how they should influence the Independent left wing—by friendly collaboration or by merciless criticism. But either way any such influence was limited.

One of the younger leaders of the left Independents, Geyer, when discussing the possibility of a merger, expressed their general attitude to the KPD: 'The left of the USP has no need of a fusion of parties. The USP is the revolutionary party'.[5]

The attitude of the USP left changed in the summer of 1920. Not because of any action of the KPD itself, but because of pressure from the leaders of the new Communist International, in particular the leaders of the Russian Bolshevik Party. The USP's call for negotiations over membership of the Communist International received a simple reply from Moscow: affiliation was possible only if the left took full control of the apparatus of the party and its press, expelled the right wing leaders and set about building a centralised revolutionary party. Such was the gist of the famous '21 conditions' applied to the USP and similar parties in other countries including the French and Italian Socialist parties, the Norwegian Labour Party and the British ILP.

The aim, as the Communist International made clear, was to separate the 'many good communists' inside these parties from the half-hearted, 'centrist' and reformist leaders.

Four representatives of the German Independents—two from each wing of the party—attended the Second Congress of the Communist International. The delegates from the right remained adamant in their defence of the party as it was. The delegates from the left, Däumig and Stocker, were eventually persuaded that the only course was to expel the right, merge with the KPD and join the Communist International.[6]

The issue was resolved when the delegates returned to Germany for a special congress of the party in Halle. Hilferding made the main speech for the right wing, and Zinoviev was invited from Russia to explain the position of the International. He made a brilliant, demagogic speech which won over any waverers—and the position of the left was carried by 237 votes to 156.

The right wing split away immediately, insisting that they would keep their section going under the party's old name, complete with much of its press. The left immediately negotiated terms for a merger with the Communists, and a joint congress in December founded a 'new' party, the United Communist Party of Germany (VKPD—the V was dropped within months of its foundation).

By no means the whole of the mass membership of the Independent Social Democrats went over to the new party. At least 400,000 did not—perhaps a third of these joining the new, right wing controlled USP. The rest joined neither party, waiting to see how things would develop. This still left the United Communist Party with some half a million members—ten times more than at the time of the Kapp putsch. With the new party, it seemed that the German Revolution would again be able to take great strides forward. But it was not to be.

The March Action

The workers of central Germany around Halle and Merseberg had become among the most revolutionary in Germany in 1919 and 1920—even though the miners of the area had been conservative and non-political before the war. They clashed bitterly with the Freikorps in 1919, and virtually took the area over during the Kapp putsch.

Afterwards they had kept their arms, and used their new found strength to fight off attacks on their living and working conditions. A measure of their radicalisation is that in the Prussian state elections of February 1921 this was the only area where the Communist vote (204,000) was greater than the combined vote for the two Social Democrat parties (147,000): it was the only place in the country where the Communists were visibly the majority of the working class.

In mid-March the Social Democratic head of the province, Horsing, decided the time had come to put an end to this state of affairs. He announced that he was going to send the security police into the area to deal with 'wildcat strikes, looting, robbery, terrorists and other expressions of lawlessness'.

Horsing had chosen his time well. He knew that the Easter holidays, due in ten days time, would make defensive action by the workers difficult. He also expected that the workers in the rest of Germany would not react to a 'peacekeeping operation' directed against workers of one locality—any more than they had reacted to the marches of the Freikorps in 1919 or to the crushing of the Ruhr after the Kapp putsch.

But, unlike on either of those occasions, the majority of the Communist leadership felt that now, with the huge increase in the strength of their party, they did not need to be always on the defensive. A section of the Comintern leadership more than encouraged them in this belief. It was decided to turn the relatively insignificant clashes in central Germany into an occasion for showing what the new, mass Communist Party could do. Its whole strength was to be thrown into developing from the clashes a new revolutionary—insurrectionary—offensive of the class nationally.

The party decided to press for a general strike throughout central Germany. On 18 March the Berlin party daily, *Rote Fahne*, called for workers throughout Germany to arm themselves. It made no mention of the situation in central Germany, but instead used as a pretext the refusal of the Bavarian government to disarm right wing bands. On 20 March the paper did refer to central Germany, calling on workers everywhere to come to the area's aid. Effectively, the paper indicated that anyone who did not would be a scab: 'Who is not with us is against us,' screamed the headline.

But even in central Germany itself the protest strike was not general. The workers had struck in the Mansfeld-Eisleben area so far reached by Horsing's security police. But the feeling in Halle was such that the local Communist Party leadership hesitated to call a general strike. The attempts by the national party leadership to push the struggle forward took on a note of desperation. A representative of the Party Centre, Eberlein, explained to the Halle Communists that they had to use all means 'to provoke an uprising in mid-Germany'. He even went so far as to suggest blowing up Communist offices, so that the blame would be placed on the police and make the workers angry![7]

The tactic of self-provocation was not adopted—although the story of it was much used afterwards to discredit the Communist Party. Instead the party accepted the services of Max Hoelz, the leader of a 'Red Army' in Vogtland (on the Czech border) during the Kapp days and a virtual folk hero because of his exploits in escaping from the police. Hoelz was not a member of the party—he was one of the many who had dropped out after the split with the ultra-left. He had been referred to in party publications and at conferences as a 'non-Marxist' and a 'revolutionary adventurer'.

Hoelz's most recent activities had been extremely individualistic. He tells in his memoirs how he set out 'to disquieten the authorities and terrorise the population' by blowing up law courts: he tried to blow up Falkenstein Town Hall in the Vogtland, 'to attract attention to the fact that we Communists were still alive'; he sent friends off to carry out similar acts in Dresden, Freiburg and Leipzig; finally he robbed various banks to finance the KAPD, although he himself was never a member of it.[8]

When Hoelz arrived in mid-Germany on 21 March, he admits that the mood of the workers was far from insurrectionary. At a strike committee meeting in Mansfeld 'there was no discussion of an armed insurrection... The workers thought that a general strike alone would force Horsing to withdraw'.[9] But the next evening Hoelz claims that 'the brutality of the police forced the workers to take up arms... I began to organise workers who had spontaneously formed into fighting units'.[10]

In any case, Hoelz proclaimed himself 'commander in chief of the rising', a position which he claims was accepted by both the KPD and KAPD headquarters in Berlin. Working with a local Communist official, Scheider, he succeeded in raising an armed detachment of 400 men who began guerrilla attacks on various police posts. This 'army' moved from place to place, collecting around it more unemployed miners and allegedly 'conscripting' all men between the ages of 18 and 45,[11] until it was, according to Hoelz, 2,500 strong.

They were joined by 3,000 workers who gathered in Halle and marched to meet them. At the same time the 20,000 strong Leuna works had struck, 2,000 of its workers arming themselves and taking control of the factory; but they were unable to arrive at any plan for going on to the offensive and instead sat there for a week, an isolated fortress, not able to link up with Hoelz's forces.

There are various accounts of the actions taken by Hoelz's armies. Hoelz himself, naturally, tends to play up their successes. But even he has to admit that they were not strong enough to stay in any one town more than 24 hours. Other accounts picture an operation of very limited military impact. According to the American historian Angress, who provides a detailed account of these events, 'There was little system to his burning, dynamiting and plundering',[12] the enormous potential strength of the Leuna workers was never brought to bear; and the fighting took place according to no unified plan.[13] According to Buber-Neumann, whose memories of the period have to be set off against her strong animosity to Communism when she wrote, there was a 'general confrontation with the police' with the 'blowing up of town halls, banks, railway establishments and then private houses'.[14]

It was only a matter of time before sufficient armed police were moved into action to crush the 'rising'. They caught up with the 'Red Army' at Ammendorf, defeated it in an armed confrontation, then chased its scattering groups across the fields.

The 'rising' itself was an event of little consequence. It hardly bears comparison with the bloody battles against the Freikorps or during the

Kapp days. The government did not even need to resort to the army to crush Hoelz's force, for the police sufficed. Not surprisingly workers elsewhere, who had seen the crushing of Berlin, Bremen, Bavaria and the Ruhr three times over, did not regard it as a great event.

Its significance historically lies in the fact that the Communist Party leadership completely misjudged what was happening, reacted wrongly, and nearly wrecked their newborn party. They decided that this was a great 'revolutionary', 'offensive' action. They pulled out stops that didn't exist in an attempt to get solidarity action of insurrectionary proportions—and blamed their own rank and file for 'passivity' when such action did not come.

In Hamburg there was a demonstration of a couple of thousand unemployed. They tried to seize the docks, and failed. The government took the opportunity to declare a state of emergency. The Communist Party leadership responded by calling for an all out national general strike—the day before the Easter holiday. The response was pathetic: only 200,000 strikers according to most reports; 400,000 according to a few optimists. Yet the KPD itself claimed 400,000 members. In Berlin hardly any workers struck, despite the 200,000 votes the Communists had received in elections there barely a month before. An order from the local party insisted, 'A Communist, even when in a minority among the workers, should in no circumstances proceed to work'.[15]

The class would not move. In some places party members who had more determination than sense tried to move for it. They took the unemployed to occupy factories and block workers' access to them. The majority of non-Communist workers who ignored the strike call were jeered at as 'scabs'. The only result was to turn non-Communist workers against Communists, with rows, fights and even shooting.

> The Krupp forge in Rheinhausen was the scene of fierce fights Thursday morning between Communists occupying the works and workers arriving for work. The workers finally charged the Communists with clubs in hand and thus gained entrance to their place of work by force. In the end Belgian soldiers intervened in the brawl, separated the combatants and arrested 20 Communists. The Communists later returned with reinforcements and reoccupied the forge.[16]

Instead of explaining patiently to the Social Democrat workers how their own interests lay in opposition to the interests of their leaders, the

Communist Party treated these workers as if they were identical to their leaders:

> We are telling the Independent and Social Democratic workers in all clearness: if you tolerate or just mildly protest against the White terror and lynch justice unleashed by Ebert, Severing and Horsing...then this capital crime rests not only on the heads of your leaders but on the head of every one of you... Shame and dishonour on the worker who stands apart; shame and dishonour on the worker who does not know his place.[17]

The *majority* of workers were being condemned for not jumping to the commands of the minority!

The enemies of the party gloated. The right wing rump of the USP felt this was an issue that they could easily exploit to pull towards them all those who had joined neither party after the split. They denounced the action, implied that Horsing had been right to send in the security police—and received the support of many workers who had been close to supporting the Communists until they were greeted with catcalls of 'scab'.

The consequences for the Communist Party itself were catastrophic. Its actions seemed to justify everything its enemies inside the working class said about it being 'dictatorial', 'undemocratic', 'putschist'. Within a few weeks it lost 200,000 members—about half its strength. Militants who were too intelligent to give up their jobs by striking alone as their fellow workers worked left the party rather than obey its insane instructions. And the hundreds of thousands of former USP members who had *not* joined the VKPD, found their doubts confirmed.

The state used the occasion to step up repressive measures, imprisoning hundreds of Communists—including the party chairman Brandler—and banning Communist papers. Tens of thousands of loyal Communists who had obeyed their party's order to strike by themselves were not allowed back into the factories by the management. In many districts the ties binding Communist and non-Communist workers were broken. The Communists seemed to many other workers to have proved correct the old stories about 'Bolshevik wreckers' and 'Spartakists out to cause violence'.

The party had moved into action without the class—and had nearly smashed itself to pieces.

The KPD leadership splits

The main thesis running through this book so far has been that the German Revolution was defeated because of the absence of even the nucleus of a cohesive party in November 1918. At each point afterwards, this initial lack plagued the movement, preventing any coherent direction being given to upsurges of revolutionary anger within the working class. At first sight, however, the March Action hardly seems to fit into this thesis. The mass party existed—and behaved in just as lunatic a fashion as did Ledebour and Liebknecht in January 1919, or leaders of the Ruhr Red Army at the end of March 1920.

How is the discrepancy to be explained?

Even the most powerful revolutionary movements never completely free themselves from the taint of the society that they fight. They are built with and by men and women who grew up in that society, who have bred into them many of its vices—personal vanity, petty jealousies, irrational dislikes, obsessive fears. These necessarily cloud political judgements: of the great revolutionary leaders only Lenin seemed capable of putting such personal feelings completely aside.

The problem is made a hundred times worse when revolutionary parties are involved in desperate struggles, hardly existing one day, carried forward to the verge of victory the next. Their leaders cannot afford scruples: they have to use some of the characteristic forms of authoritarian organisation developed by capitalism in order to fight capitalism. They have to demand discipline from party members; they have to be prepared to push aside those who cannot fulfil their allotted tasks, however good their intentions, however great their reputations.

The border line between an arbitrary action, motivated only by irrational personal feelings, and a necessary action is always difficult to draw in such circumstances: there is no time to debate at length. In Germany in 1920-21 the task seemed almost impossible.

A mass revolutionary party had been formed *after* the most favourable revolutionary opportunities had passed, by a policy of breaking with impatient 'ultra-left' but obviously revolutionary elements (the bulk of the support of the KAPD), and by unifying with people who were certainly moving leftwards, but had not yet proved their revolutionary credentials. Throughout this period there had been sections of workers, in one industrial district after another, who had been ready to fight. But the party had spent as much energy holding them back from suicidal adventures as in urging other sections to support them.

Inevitably the period was frustrating for both the rank and file of the party and its leadership. They faced daily taunts from the expelled 'ultra-leftists' that they were 'centrists', 'opportunists' and 'disguised social democrats'. And they asked themselves whether a merger with the Independent Social Democrats could produce a genuinely revolutionary party.

The tension was there as early as the Bavarian Soviet Republic: Paul Levi had criticised the proclamation of the Second (Communist) Council Republic as an adventure, while another member of the leadership, Paul Frölich, had wholeheartedly endorsed it.[18]

The debate flared up again after the struggle around the Kapp putsch. Everyone agreed that the initial condemnation of the general strike by the (truncated) meeting of the Party Centre had been a gross mistake. The dispute was over where responsibility for this lay. Frölich implied that the responsibility lay with Levi—even though Levi had himself, from prison, bitterly denounced the Party Centre's decisions.

Frölich's argument was that under Levi's influence the party leadership had forgotten that *action*, not propaganda, won people to revolutionary politics. Hence the abstentionism of the Party Centre at the beginning of the struggle was linked to its support for a 'workers' government' at the end. Frölich denounced the call for the Independents to join such a government as being at the level of saying, 'You are already a whore; prostitute yourself again so that we can keep our maidenhead.'

He recalled that Levi had told a meeting of the Berlin factory councils that the conditions were not ripe for the dictatorship of the proletariat. This, Frölich insisted, was nothing less than a 'pseudo-Marxism' which saw the preparation of the revolution not through action, but through 'six months of organisation work and agitation, six months of daily reading of articles full of historical knowledge and good points'. What it really reflected was 'a yearning for a breathing space' which had led to 'purely opportunistic politics'.[19]

Levi still had considerable support inside the party leadership. The party's main theoretician, Thalheimer, wrote a scathing reply (which destroyed many of the arguments Thalheimer himself was to use twelve months later). He described Frölich's article as 'a return of the infantile disease'—in other words ultra-leftism:

When Frölich says that victory comes from a succession of defeats; when he turns away from the sentence in the Spartakus programme on the need to win the majority of the working class, then he has not learnt the lessons of the Spartakus week or of Munich.[20]

Lenin, in an appendix to his famous little book, *Left Wing Communism*, seemed to agree with the tactical position taken by the German Party Centre over the question of the workers' government—although he criticised a number of the formulations in it as mistaken. He described it as:

> Basically right...a method of practical teaching...a tactic which is without doubt right... But it was wrong not to point out that such a government will not in practice break with the bourgeoisie.

But Lenin was not then regarded as the deity he later became for the Stalinised Comintern, and his words seem to have had less impact in Germany than did the judgement of Radek. The old activist in the pre-war German left and adviser to the German party leadership at the time of the great struggles of 1919 was now secretary of the half-formed Communist International in Moscow. He had been through all the experiences of the German leadership and seems to have developed the same frustration and impatience. In the July edition of the International's journal, *Die Kommunistische Internationale*, he swung his weight behind Frölich's arguments:

'Anti-putschism has led to a certain quietism: from the impossibility of conquering political power in Germany—established empirically in 1919—they have drawn the conclusion in March 1920 of the impossibility of action in general...' The executive of the International had seen 'as correct the fight against putschism in Germany', but now saw that 'doctrinaire anti-putschist propaganda has become a hindrance to the movement.' What is more, by offering 'loyal opposition' to a 'workers' government' the Centre had 'abandoned their historical mission'.[21]

Arguments had begun earlier, with an open dispute between Radek and Levi over the lessons of the short-lived Hungarian Soviet Republic of March-July 1919. Levi had made a powerful criticism of the Hungarian Communist leaders, the foremost of whom was Bela Kun, for taking power before the workers were fully ready for it. Radek replied (with clear implications for events in Germany) that the mistake had not been in taking power, but in doing so without having drawn a clear line between themselves and the 'left' Social Democrats.[22]

By the time the Second Congress of the Communist International met in Moscow in July 1920 the dispute was becoming bitter and there was open talk of a 'right wing' tendency inside the German party, led by Levi. As the German Communist Party Congress was told in November (by Ernst Meyer) it was felt in Moscow that there were two wings in the party, a left led by Meyer and Rosi Wolfstein, and a right led by Levi and Walcher. Levi had told them that this was not a political division, but a difference of 'mood'. The 'Russian comrades' had, however, seen this as a continuation of the old differences which had divided Rosa Luxemburg and Jogiches from Lenin.[23] What had begun as a political argument was clearly being clouded by old personal animosities—perhaps going back to Rosa Luxemburg's absurd pre-war vendetta against Radek.

The key Russian Communists involved in the building of the International—Zinoviev and Bukharin, as well as Radek—urged the German party to take action to prevent a drift to the right. They urged unity with the 'revolutionary leaven' of the KAPD as well as the 'centrists' of the left USP. With this perspective in mind, they wanted to accept the KAPD as part of the International. This was prevented by the protests of the whole KPD delegation ('left' as well as 'right') and the KAPD was relegated to sympathiser status.

Zinoviev and Bukharin saw all this as evidence of Levi's 'conservative' influence. The International was not, at that time, the monolith it later became. Disagreements over such issues were taken for granted, and the 'Russians' could not deal with Levi in an arbitrary manner. If they thought his approach was wrong, they had to convince the German party that this was so. So it seems that Radek was given the brief of winning over Levi's supporters inside the German party.

The task was not difficult. Nothing is more nerve-wracking for a revolutionary leader than continually holding sections of the masses back from premature action. Even a sane, experienced leader like Brandler suffered the feeling of frustration—he had, after all, come in for a lot of criticism himself because during the Kapp days he had not engaged in 'revolutionary heroics' in his 'Chemnitz fortress'. It was not difficult for him to blame other people rather than the objective situation for policies that made him unpopular. Even with the benefit of hindsight, he could still write 40 years later that he became concerned with 'tendencies in the German working class and in the KPD as well, which admittedly did not reject armed struggle, but which looked upon it with indifference'.[24]

This 'concern' could not be justified at the end of 1920 by the needs of the situation; it reflected much more a frustration at being in a situation where armed struggle was not in truth appropriate.

The great success of Levi's policy was the birth of the new Unified Communist Party through the merger with the left Independents. But this itself turned a section of the leadership against what they saw as Levi's excessive moderation. As Brandler also pointed out, on a different occasion:

> The party had grown so big that many members believed the hour of revolution had struck. People were so impressed by the sheer number of party members that they refused to consider the overwhelming strength of the enemy.[25]

But not only the old Communists were carried away. Many of the mass of members coming from the USP were even more impatient. They had broken with the old leaders because they were now convinced of the need for a mighty revolutionary party, based on revolutionary action. They felt that half a million of them in a genuine Communist Party should be able to achieve what nearly twice that number in a half hearted party could not. So they were stunned when the first public act of the unified party, in January 1921, was an 'open letter', calling for united action to the other 'workers' parties' and unions, including the SPD, which they despised, and the USP, which they had just left. The call spelt out a number of points on which it said the public statements of these parties coincided with the position of the Communists—defence of workers' living standards, the need for armed self defence against the far right terror groups, release of working class political prisoners, commercial relations with Soviet Russia. It stated:

> In proposing this basis for action, we do not hide for a minute our view that these demands cannot bring an end to the misery of the masses. The Communist Party is ready for common action with other parties supported by the working class to achieve these demands without, however, giving up its right to continue propagating among the masses the idea of the struggle for the dictatorship.

The call for united action was ignored by the leaders of the other parties. It did receive a favourable response from certain sections of the rank and file,[26] showing that it was a way of drawing these to the Communists, particularly former Independents who had joined neither party after the split. But within the Communist Party and the International it increased hostility to Levi: only an intervention by Lenin stopped the executive of the Communist International (led by Zinoviev and Bukharin) from denouncing it publicly.

All these divisions finally came to a head at the beginning of March. Levi had upset the Comintern delegates to the Congress of the Italian Socialist Party shortly before this by openly disagreeing with their tactics of splitting the party to form a new Communist Party led by the Italian ultra-left Bordiga. One of these delegates, Rakosi, then attended a meeting of the central committee of the German party and, taking advantage of all the animosities against Levi, persuaded the central committee to condemn his attitude by 28 votes to 23. What is more, in moving his resolution Rakosi indicated that there needed to be more splits—'in Italy, in France, or in Germany'. This was clearly an attack on Levi himself.

In angry response Levi and four of his supporters—including the party's co-chairman Däumig and Rosa Luxemburg's old friend Clara Zetkin—resigned from the Party Centre. The leadership was effectively left in the hands of the group that had been won over to the view that Levi had been too 'cautious'—Frölich, Brandler, Meyer and Thalheimer. In a series of letters to them, Radek urged them to destroy Levi's position in the party for good.[27]

Ominous for the later development of the party was the enormous boost given by such promptings to a much more 'left' current beginning to grow in the Berlin district. It was, interestingly, centred around Ernst Friesland who had been chiefly responsible for the abstentionist line at the beginning of the Kapp putsch (which did not prevent the 'left' blaming this on Levi, who had been in jail). But its most outspoken figures were a pair of young Communist intellectuals in their mid-twenties, neither of whom had been revolutionaries for more than three years—Ruth Fischer and Arkadi Maslow.

The final push for the March Action did not, however, come from any of the elements inside the German party who had risen up against Levi. A few days later the Hungarian Communist Bela Kun arrived in Berlin as a delegate from Moscow. There is some doubt as to whether the advice he then gave the restructured German Party Centre was his own, or was given on orders—Brandler claims that Kun spoke on instructions from Zinoviev, the president of the International.[28] But about the advice he gave there is little doubt.

Levi explained in a letter to Lenin on 29 March that Kun had met himself and Zetkin and told them:

> Russia is in a very difficult situation [there had been widespread famine leading to peasant revolts and the Kronstadt rising]. It is absolutely an absolute necessity that it is relieved by the movement in the West and for this reason the German Communist Party must go into action...
>
> The KPD has 500,000 members. With these you can bring into action 1,500,000 proletarians, which is enough to destroy the government. So it is necessary immediately to begin the struggle with the slogan 'Overthrow the government'.[29]

Kun clearly gave the same message to the new Centre. On 16-17 March at a meeting of the central committee (a bigger body than the Centre) Brandler, the party chairman in place of Levi, argued:

> The antagonism between the imperialist states has intensified, the conflicts between America and England have increased. Unless a revolution gives a different form to events we will shortly face an Anglo-American war... Domestic difficulties lie within the realm of the possible... There is a 90 percent chance that armed conflicts will occur in Upper Silesia [between German and Polish forces]. Today we are able to influence two to three million non-Communist workers willing to fight under our banner even in offensive operations. We are obliged by the present situation to intervene with concrete actions to influence matters in our direction.[30]

From this, Frölich, also for the Centre, concluded: 'Through our activity we have to make sure an eruption occurs, even if necessary by provoking the state militia'.[31]

Thus, on the basis of highly problematic predictions, the party's general strategy was to move from the defensive to the offensive.

The 'theory of the offensive'

Underlying the new turn was what came to be known as the 'theory of the offensive'. This was a doctrine which was propagated by Bukharin in Moscow and accepted to varying degrees by Zinoviev, Kun, Radek, the new German Centre and the Berlin left of Friesland, Fischer and Maslow.

The basic argument was that it was no longer necessary for the Communist Party to be passive, awaiting spontaneous developments in the class. The collapse of capitalism meant that a mass Communist party could 'awaken' the masses to decisive, offensive armed actions of a partial character. These would increase the instability of the system and drive more workers into action until the taking of power was on the agenda.

The guidelines for this 'strategy', as applied to Germany, were outlined in a letter sent to certain members of the German Centre shortly before the March Action:

> If the rift between Germany and the Entente widens, possibly leading to war, we will talk. You must do everything to mobilise the party, if only because these possibilities exist... If you don't now do everything for incessant pressure for action... you will fail at the great moment... Less emphasis on radical formulae, more on action...[32]

The letter was guarded and conditional compared with the interpretation put on it by those who read it. Frölich told the Central Committee that the new tactics required:

> ...a complete break with the past. Hitherto we were guided by the tactic, or rather, were forced to accept the tactic of biding our time until a situation conducive to action existed... Now we say: we are so strong and the situation is so pregnant with possibilities that we can force the fate of the party and the revolution.
>
> The party now has to assume the initiative, to indicate that we are no longer willing to bide our time, to wait until we are faced with accomplished facts; we intend to create those facts ourselves.[33]

The appalling consequences of the March Action did not immediately discredit this theory. Radek, who in private conceded that the Action may have been called 'too early', insisted in public four weeks later that there had to be many more such 'partial actions'. 'The development of the German Revolution will go through a hundred partial territorial actions,' he said.[34] The Party Centre insisted:

> In an epoch of profound political tension such actions, even if they end in temporary defeat, constitute the indispensible precondition for victories-to-come, and, for a revolutionary party, the only way to conquer

the masses and to bring to their consciousness the objective political situation.[35]

In fact, of course, the Action had damaged the party terribly, losing it half its members and turning away from it the hundreds of thousands of workers who had been hesitating between the two halves of the old USP. A few more such actions would have destroyed the party altogether.

The 'theory of the offensive' was not, in fact, new. In many ways it was a restatement of what the ultra-left had said early in 1919. As a theory it has also been in vogue more recently: it underlay the Guevarist view popular among many circles of revolutionaries in the late 1960s and early 1970s—expressed in the call, 'If you are a revolutionary, make a revolution.'

All these versions of the same basic position argued that somehow revolutionaries could impel workers to insurrection through armed actions taken by an active minority. They all forget that workers, even revolutionary party members, will only take revolutionary action when *they* themselves feel that a transformation of society is necessary. It is not revolutionaries who *make* revolutions; it is the mass of workers. The task of revolutionaries is to *lead* these workers, not substitute for them.

The March Action of 1921 was the biggest test of this theory ever attempted historically. The setback which followed should have been a final refutation of the theory.

Crisis in the party

The outcome of the March Action sent shock waves through both the German Communist Party and the Communist International.

The first shock in Germany itself was the departure from the party of Paul Levi, the most prominent member to oppose the Action. Levi had been the most influential leader of the party from the time of the death of Jogiches to his resignation barely a week before the Action. He was undoubtedly the ablest of its leaders. But he seems to have had considerable disdain for those who did not agree with him, and he had virtually no understanding that sincere and courageous revolutionary convictions were what led many recently converted Communists into acts of ultra-left lunacy.

Alfred Rosmer, who had no great love for Levi's enemies, described him at the time of the Second Congress of the International in Moscow:

His main aversion was the communists who had opposed him at Heidelberg [the ultra-left]. He was obsessed with them, and the conflict took on the appearance of a personal quarrel... He loathed all anarchists and syndicalists; they were elements of an 'opposition' that permanently obsessed him.[36]

Levi was infuriated by the folly of the majority of the leadership, and did not hide his anger. In a pamphlet published a few days later he denounced the Action. The pamphlet, entitled *Our road against putschism* was a brilliant denunciation of the reasoning that had led to 'the biggest Bakuninist putsch in history'. He used all his skill in rhetoric and sarcasm to hammer home the point that it was madness to launch an 'offensive' armed action while the mass of the workers were passive, and only a few weeks after the party had received less than a third of the combined SPD/USP vote in elections across two-thirds of the country.[37]

Levi insisted that far from it being easier for the mass Communist Party to bring into struggle Social Democrat workers than it had been for the minute Spartakus League of 1918-19, it was *more difficult*.

At the beginning of the German revolution the Social Democrats were everywhere on the defensive. They had the great masses behind them, but these were unorganised. Today social reformism has organised a conscious resistance against Communism, it has gone from the defensive to the offensive... The spiritual influence of the Communists on the still undecided or still reformist proletarian masses must be acquired.[38]

Instead of winning the workers, 'the Centre played with the element so beloved of Bakunin, the lumpenproletariat'. 'The unemployed were used as storm columns' against the employed workers. The result was 'a pistol shooting putsch against the bourgeoisie and four-fifths of the proletariat'.[39]

The pamphlet demolished the proponents of the 'theory of the offensive'. The trouble, however, was that it was written in a style almost calculated not to win the rank and file of the party, but simply to infuriate them. It gave the impression of sneering at their courage, at their preparedness to go on the streets to fight. Its tone was that of someone looking at the party from outside, not someone who was part of it, mistakes and all. It was all too easy for the majority of the party leadership, who had still learnt nothing from the Action, to turn party members against Levi for writing in that tone, rather than face up to his arguments. They expelled him from the party for a 'breach of discipline' without needing to reply to any one of his points.

The international row

The argument over the March Action was soon raging in Moscow as well as Berlin. For although a section of the Communist International leadership had been pushing for offensive actions, leaders such as Lenin and Trotsky had no inkling of what was being planned and said.

Levi himself pointed out in his pamphlet one of the biggest problems the Communist International faced. It was dominated by the Russian Bolshevik Party, which, with its experience of successfully taking power, had a million things to teach the other parties. But the Bolshevik Party was engrossed in defending the revolution in Russia itself. As a result:

> Russia is not in a position to use its best people as delegates [to the parties of other countries]. They occupy posts in Russia in which they are irreplaceable. As a consequence, comrades arrive in Europe each one of whom is filled with good intentions and ideas of his own, zealous for the chance to demonstrate how he 'brings off things successfully'. Thus West Europe and Germany become the testing ground for all sorts of miniature statesmen who give the impression that they want to develop their skills here... The matter takes on fatal proportions when representatives are dispatched who do not have the necessary human sensibilities.[40]

There is no doubt that this is exactly what happened when Bela Kun went to Berlin in March 1921. Kun, most leading Communists thought, had made enormous mistakes as leader of the Hungarian Soviet Republic. Then he had fallen out with Lenin over his activities in the Soviet Middle East. Now he saw a chance to redeem himself by pulling off a successful operation in Germany—if only he could overcome the resistance of the 'conservative' 'half-centrist' German leaders.

But the responsibility did not lie only with Kun. It is virtually certain that he was given the go-ahead by those in charge of the Russian party's activities in the Communist International—especially Zinoviev, president of the International. Zinoviev had worked for many years with Lenin and had learnt a certain style of work from him. He recognised that the building of revolutionary parties involves 'stick bending',[41] sudden shifts from one tactic to another, as conditions change. Unfortunately he had not learnt from Lenin how to make the objective

215 THE LOST REVOLUTION

evaluation necessary to recognise when the shift in tactics should take place. He could copy the *form* of Lenin's method, but not its content.

Nor had he learnt from Lenin how to win other Communists to such a change of tactics. Lenin would carefully and patiently argue the party into accepting the change: his collected works are full of articles reiterating again and again the same themes at each particular point in the Bolshevik Party's history. Zinoviev by contrast was a demagogue, brilliant on the public platform, but prone to bullying rather than to patient explanation. Typically, Brandler tells of him 'thumping the table' to get foreign Communists to accept a point;[42] it is difficult to imagine Lenin doing that.

Isaac Deutscher writes of Zinoviev, 'He was superb at picking Lenin's brain and acting as Lenin's loud and stormy mouthpiece; but he had no strong mind of his own'.[43] Certainly, when not acting under Lenin's direct instruction, Zinoviev was almost always wrong: he opposed the Bolshevik Revolution in October 1917 and showed neither perception nor willpower after Lenin's death.

The other weighty Bolshevik involved in regular work for the International was Bukharin. He was less prone to demagogy than Zinoviev and was a more substantial thinker. But in 1920 and 1921 he was still very much a 'left Bolshevik'. He had held his own 'theory of the offensive' in 1918 when, at the time of the Brest-Litovsk negotiations, he had argued that the Bolsheviks could conjure a Red Army out of nothing and spread the revolution by offensive action against the German troops. In 1920 the same reasoning had led him to support enthusiastically the advance of the Red Army to the edge of Warsaw, against the advice of the Commissar for War, Trotsky.[44]

Zinoviev and Bukharin, together with Radek, very much ran the Communist International until the March Action. Lenin and Trotsky would make occasional appearances at meetings of its executive, but were usually much too busy with other things. 'The executive of the Comintern was then only a modest office. Lenin was present at its meetings only two or three times: he simply had no time to come more often,' said Brandler.[45]

Looking back now, it is possible to see that these 'two or three' visits by Lenin had already led to the beginning of a different perspective for the building of West European Communist Parties than that held by Zinoviev and Bukharin. Lenin had, for instance, supported the 'workers' government' proposal in the Kapp days and the open letter to the Social Democrats in January 1921. But until the March Action he did not grasp that his perspective was fundamentally different from that held by Zinoviev and Bukharin—he went along with them for instance in pressurising the KPD to merge with the 'ultra-left' KAPD.

Soon after the March Action Lenin wrote to Levi and Clara Zetkin:

> I've read nearly nothing on the recent strikes and the insurrectionary movement. That a representative of the Executive proposed a lunatic ultra-left tactic of immediate action 'to help the Russians' I can believe without difficulty: this representative [Kun] is often too far to the left.
>
> In my view, in such cases, you should not give way but protest and take the case immediately before a full meeting of the executive.

His attitude soon hardened considerably, however. He studied the German events in detail and decided that not merely Kun, but the Comintern leadership, had committed utter folly. He wrote to Zinoviev on 18 June: 'Levi, politically, was right on many points. The theses of Thalheimer and Bela Kun are radically false'—this after Levi's expulsion from the German party had been confirmed by the International!

'It is terrible,' Lenin went on, 'what has been allowed to happen.' Dealing with the 'theory' underlying the Action, he added:

> It is insane and harmful to write that the period of propaganda is past and that of action has begun... It is necessary to fight ceaselessly and in a systematic manner to win the majority of the working class, starting inside the old trade unions.

He told Clara Zetkin—who pleaded with him for Levi—that 'Levi lost his head: but at least he had a head to lose.' The 'theory of the offensive' was nonsense:

> Can it actually be called a theory? It is an illusion, it is nothing but romanticism... We cannot afford to write poetry and to dream... We will listen more to Marx than to Thalheimer and Bela... The Russian Revolution after all continues to teach more than the German March Action.[46]

Trotsky had, independently, come to an identical view. They decided to fight together to 'throttle' the 'theory of the offensive' at the Third Congress of the International, meeting at the end of June 1921.

Strange as it may seem, Lenin and Trotsky were by no means guaranteed a majority at the Congress. This was not the Stalin period, and the delegates were free to make their own minds up over issues. Zinoviev and Bukharin were adamantly opposed to Lenin and Trotsky and attempted to win delegates individually to their standpoint before the Congress began.

But Lenin and Trotsky were helped by one thing. A section of the German leadership that had launched the March Action had already had second thoughts: Brandler had fled to Russia to avoid imprisonment and quickly changed his mind on the matter. In Moscow Lenin and Trotsky even managed to win over the 'theorist of the offensive' Thalheimer and the Berlin ultra-left Friesland.

The Congress was a political victory for the line now adopted by the two leaders of the Russian Revolution. Lenin insisted, when he spoke, that the allegedly 'rightist' political positions taken by the German party leadership until the 'left turn' in March had been correct. The open letter, calling for a united front with the other 'workers' parties' had been, he declared:

> ...an exemplary political initiative... Exemplary because it was the first action of a political method aiming to conquer the majority of the working class. Those who do not understand that in Europe, where almost all the proletariat are organised, that we have to conquer the majority of the working class—those people are lost to the Communist movement and will never learn something they have not learnt in three years of revolution.[47]

Lenin also decided that the German leaders had been right in 1920 in their hardline opposition to the ultra-left KAPD. He wrote to Zinoviev, 'I see clearly that it was a mistake on my part to have accepted the admission of the KAPD [to the International].' At the Congress itself Lenin declared it was 'to my great regret and great shame' to have heard the views put forward by the KAPD on the 'open letter'.[48]

Trotsky was just as sharp: 'It is our duty to say clearly to the German workers that we regard the philosophy of the offensive as the supreme danger, and the practical application constitutes the worst political crime'. He not only criticised the 'theory of the offensive', but began to elaborate a strategic alternative—what came to be called in the course of the following year the strategy of 'the united front'. He argued strongly that the first great revolutionary wave was over. Capitalism had succeeded, temporarily, in stabilising itself. One more big push would *not* knock it over. The time span before the spread of the revolution would be 'years' not weeks.[49]

The role of the Communist Party, said Trotsky, was to use the two or three years breathing space to win mass support among the working class. It could do this because the bourgeoisie was using its new lease of life to launch an offensive against the past gains of workers—with wage cuts, unemployment, increased repression, a lengthening of working hours, a growth of the fascist right. The Social Democrats and the trade union bureaucracies were too closely tied to the capitalists to adopt the radical forms of struggle that alone could win these defensive battles. The Communist Party had to take up the struggle around these 'partial demands' and show to the followers of social democracy that revolutionary methods alone could win even limited, defensive battles.

In the months after the Congress the argument was further developed: the only way to win over the Social Democratic workers was to follow the tactic pioneered by the German 'open letter'—offer united action to the leaders of the social democratic parties and unions. Only by addressing the leaders could the Communists address their rank and file.

If the leaders *accepted* the invitation to united action, even round partial, limited demands straight from the reformist Social Democratic programme, all well and good: their rank and file would enter into battle alongside Communists, see that the lies told them by their leaders about the Communists were false, and learn that it was the Communists, not the Social Democrat leaders, who were prepared to fight 'for every crust of bread'.

If the Social Democrat leaders *rejected* the invitation to struggle, that too could only benefit the Communists—the Social Democrat leaders would prove in practice that it was *they* who were splitting the class.

Lenin and Trotsky carried their new strategy at the Congress of the International. But in doing so they also agreed to a partial compromise designed to 'save the face' of the section of the Comintern leadership which had backed the 'lefts' in the German party. One element of this compromise was that Paul Levi remained excluded from the Party and the International.

Lenin justified this to Clara Zetkin by pointing out that the tone of Levi's attacks on the March Action were bound to turn many good Communists against him:

> Paul Levi's wholly negative criticism which indicated no sense of solidarity with the party and which exasperated the comrades more by its tone than its content, diverted attention from the most important aspects of the problem... A ruthless criticism of the March Action was necessary. What did Levi accomplish? A cruel mangling of the party.[50]

For Lenin, this left no choice but to discipline Levi although he hoped that Levi would rejoin the party after a six month spell of disciplined behaviour outside it.

This part of the compromise might have been necessary. But it was hardly satisfactory. For while Lenin was telling Zetkin that 'I appreciate Levi and his capabilities... He has proved himself in times of the worst persecution', Radek, one of the perpetrators of the 'offensive', was writing of Levi in the pages of the International's official organ as an upper class fly-by-night and coward.[51] Furthermore, the bureau of the International was issuing statements—over the signatures of Lenin and Trotsky among others—to the effect that 'Levi is a traitor... It is an abominable lie to pretend that the executive committee or its representatives provoked the March uprising'.[52]

Such statements were unlikely to be taken kindly by Levi—or, more important perhaps, by the section of the German leadership who, knowing the truth, agreed with him. Nor would they prepare the party and its sympathisers for the truth if revealed by its enemies—which eventually happened when the Social Democrat paper *Vorwärts* in November got hold of internal party documents detailing the 'provocations' in March.

The other part of the compromise was within the International itself. Joint theses for the Congress were put forward by Zinoviev and Bukharin on one side and Lenin and Trotsky on the other, after the former two had agreed to concede the future perspective. In return their backing for the German lunacy was concealed from the great majority of the Congress delegates. The transcript of the Congress gives the impression that Zinoviev, Bukharin and Radek were as critical of the March Action as Lenin and Trotsky: the debate is between *all five* and the majority of the German delegation. It was not until the late 1920s that Trotsky revealed publicly that there had been two 'factions' within the Russian leadership.

The compromise saved Zinoviev's face, while allowing Lenin and Trotsky to carry the great majority in the International for their 'new course'. It seemed a small price to abandon an inquest on the past in return for control over the future. But with the benefit of hindsight, we must ask whether they were right to compromise. By saving Zinoviev's face they left his credibility with the international Communist movement undamaged—a credibility which enabled him to lead several other parties to disastrous defeats in the succeeding four years.

The compromise did not even prevent the Comintern leadership doing yet more damage in Germany—Zinoviev and Radek continued for several months to treat those who criticised the March Action as the 'real danger'. Lenin himself had to intervene again in October with a severe reproof directed against Radek for making 'altogether false statements... that Clara Zetkin "is putting off all general action of the party until the day when the large masses will rise",' and in effect, trying 'to frighten Clara Zetkin off from the party'. Lenin insisted that there was now a grave danger of 'overdoing' the 'fight against centrism', of 'practising the sport of "banning centrists",' which could only 'save centrism, strengthen its position'.

As for Levi, Lenin agreed without hesitation that his breaches of discipline had put him right outside the party, but nevertheless felt compelled to reiterate that 'Levi is *essentially in the right* [Lenin's own emphasis] in much of his criticism of the March Action of 1921'.[53]

The German party in tatters

By December 1921 the confident, mass party of 12 months before was no more. The ill-conceived machinations of Zinoviev, Radek and Kun had not only lost nearly half its membership and driven out its most able leader, they had also created a bitter fratricidal internal atmosphere.

The result was that Levi's exit was followed by others. The repentant Berlin 'left' Friesland became president of the party after the compromise at the Third Congress of the Comintern. But once in the driving seat, he found himself taking a position essentially the same as Levi's—and was taunted by his old 'ultra-left' friends and by the Zinoviev-led group in the Comintern leadership. He was genuinely horrified when, for the first time, he learnt the truth about what had taken place in March when

Vorwärts published the documents, and moved closer to Levi's dissident Communist group. Finally, in January 1922, he was removed from the party leadership and within days was outside the party.

The loss of the second party chairman in twelve months was not calculated to strengthen the self-confidence of the membership. Doubts and disputes wracked the party from top to bottom. Other figures of standing inside the working class soon left as well—such as Däumig, Paul Neumann, Richard Müller, Otto Brass.

For a time the ex-members still regarded themselves as part of the Communist movement. But bitterness at the way they had been treated—particularly on the part of Levi and Friesland—led them to develop deep personal antipathy to the party, its leadership and much of the Comintern. Levi was soon questioning many of the positions he had fought for in his two years of leadership of the party and veering towards the left wing of social democracy. Friesland went further, and under the name Reuter became a leading Social Democrat and mayor of West Berlin.

There was a second consequence in many ways more serious even than the loss of much of the leadership. In the factional atmosphere those who flourished were those for whom intrigue and rhetoric were a substitute for political sense. The two young Berlin-based intellectuals, Ruth Fischer and Arkadi Maslow, revelled in the internal sectarianism, 'playing at the banning of centrism'. Articulate and energetic, they were able to gather around them many of the new workers who had joined the party from the Independents—despite their own lack of anything beyond the crudest grasp of Marxism.

They did so by repeating incessantly that the new, repentant party leadership was 'soft', 'centrist' and 'reformist'. The 'offensive', they argued, was the only correct Communist method. 'A party on the defensive', proclaimed Maslow, 'is a social democratic party. If it wants to be a Communist Party it must be on the offensive'.[54] Fischer's tone was similar: 'The KPD has already become...a quagmire.'

Had the KPD possessed a firm, confident political leadership, those who muttered such inanities would have either learnt better or dropped out. But in the political chaos and the factionalism created by the March Action, Fischer and Maslow were able to win the allegiance of nearly half the party.

The final consequence of the March madness was the least quantifiable but probably the most devastating in its impact.

The madness had taken possession of some of the ablest people in the party—Brandler, who had built up the most successful working class district; Thalheimer, the party's theoretician: Frölich, a talented journalist and polemicist; Ernst Meyer, its new president; Radek, its linkman with the International. Once they realised the error of their ways, they lost all confidence in their own political judgement. They would in future hesitate before deciding on action—especially on any action that would mean workers taking up arms. And in revolutionary politics, as in warfare, hesitation can mean death.

We can now see the answer to our earlier question: why did the March madness happen? Most of the party leadership lacked confidence in their own judgements after the disasters of 1919 and 1920. They looked on delegates from Russia as the ominiscient bearers of revolutionary strategy and tactics—even though merely coming from Moscow did not make a Kun, a Radek or even a Zinoviev more perceptive than the German leaders: only Lenin and Trotsky could claim that distinction—and they too were often mistaken.

Had there been a party with many years of common struggle, instead of barely a score of months, the German leaders would have been self-assured enough to send Kun (and Zinoviev if necessary) packing. The lack of even an embryo of a party had led to the defeats of 1919 and the errors of 1920; these in turn led to a lack of self-confidence that nearly wrecked the mass party once it had come into existence; and the bitter experience of the March Action further destroyed the confidence of the leadership and led to renewed disaster to come.

1.   All figures from *Bericht über der IV Parteitag der KPD*.
2.   Ibid, pp3-4.
3.   For the views of Pannekoek and Gorter, see D A Smart (ed), *Pannekoek and Gorter's Marxism* (London 1978). Unfortunately the introduction to this work by its editor is factually completely unreliable.
4.   Heinrich Ströbel, *The German Revolution and After* (London 1923) p248.
5.   Quoted in Pierre Broué, *Révolution en Allemagne* (Paris 1971) p328.
6.   For the public discussions of the congress, see *The Second Congress of the Communist International, Minutes of the Proceedings* (2 volumes, London 1977).
7.   P Broué, op cit, p481.
8.   M Hoelz, p130.

9.   Ibid, p135.

10.   Ibid, p140.

11.   M Buber-Neumann, *Kriegsschauplätze der Weltrevolution* (Stuttgart 1967) p50.

12.   Werner Angress, *Stillborn Revolution* (Princeton 1963) p149.

13.   Ibid, p151.

14.   M Buber-Neumann, op cit, p50.

15.   Quoted in Paul Levi, *Unser Weg wider den Putschismus* (Berlin 1921) p2.

16.   Quoted ibid.

17.   *Rote Fahne*, 30 March 1921, quoted ibid.

18.   The main part of the debate is translated into English in H Gruber (ed), *International Communism in the Era of Lenin* (New York 1972) p157 onwards.

19.   All quotes from *Die Internationale*, June 1920.

20.   *Die Internationale*, July 1920.

21.   *Die Kommunistiche Internationale*, July 1920.

22.   The debate is translated in H Gruber (ed), op cit, p132 onwards.

23.   *Bericht über der V Parteitag der KPD*, pp26-29.

24.   Letter to Isaac Deutscher, published in *New Left Review* 105, p75.

25.   Quoted by I Deutscher, *New Left Review* 105, p50.

26.   For details, see P Broué, op cit, p456.

27.   Translated in H Gruber (ed), op cit, p302.

28.   Letter to Deutscher, *New Left Review* 105, p68.

29.   Paul Levi, *Zwischen Spartakus und Sozialdemokratie*, p88.

30.   Quoted in H Gruber (ed), op cit, p279.

31.   Ibid.

32.   Ibid, p302.

33.   Quoted ibid, p278-279.

34.   *Soll die VKPD eine Massenpartei der Revolutionäre Aktion, oder eine Zentristische Partei der Wartens Sein?* (May 1921).

35.   *Die Internationale* 4 (1921) p126.

36.   Alfred Rosmer, *Lenin's Moscow* (London 1971) p29.

37.   Paul Levi, *Unser Weg*, op cit. Much of the pamphlet is translated in H Gruber (ed), op cit.

38.   Ibid, p17.

39.   Ibid, p37.

40.   Quoted in H Gruber (ed), op cit, p293.

41.   For what this meant to Lenin, see Tony Cliff, *Lenin* vol 1 (London 1975).

42.   *New Left Review* 105, p52.

43.   Isaac Deutscher, *The Prophet Unarmed* (New York 1965) p77.

44.   S F Cohen, *Bukharin and the Bolshevik Revolution* (London 1974) p101.

45.   Quoted in I Deutscher, *New Left Review* 105, p31.

46.   Quotes from Clara Zetkin, *Memoirs of Lenin* from H Gruber (ed), op cit, pp305-309.

47.   Speech to the Third Congress of the Comintern, in V I Lenin, *Collected Works* vol 32, p470.

48. Ibid.

49. See Trotsky's speeches to the Third Congress in *The First Five Years of the Communist International* (New York 1945) p227 onwards.

50. C Zetkin, op cit.

51. *Communist International* (Petrograd 1921).

52. *Die Kommunistische Internationale*, June 1921.

53. All quotes from *Bulletin of the Communist International*, 21 October, p63 onwards. Compare also the version in V I Lenin, *Collected Works* vol 32, p512 onwards.

54. Quoted in P Broué, op cit, p506.

CHAPTER 11

Year of crisis 1923

There have been few periods in recent German history which would have been so favourable for a socialist revolution as the summer of 1923. In the chaos of monetary devaluation all the traditional ideas of order, property and legality had disappeared... It was not only the workers who felt more clearly every day that conditions were intolerable and that the whole system must come to a terrible end. The middle class too was filled with revolutionary ferment. (*Arthur Rosenberg, a former 'left' Communist intellectual writing in the 1930s.*)[1]

The economic misery is too great in the masses... Economic misery is preparing the ground on which coups d'état and revolutions flourish. (*A report of the Prussian commissioner for internal security, early in 1923.*)[2]

One cannot deny that the mass of the working class is moving away from the old union tactics and looking for a new way. With the best will in the world, we can no longer hold the working class in check. (*A central German Social Democrat, Horsing, writing to the government in the summer of 1923.*)[3]

Germany was at the end of its powers. With ever new strikes, demonstrations, and street fights the workers protested at the hopelessness of the situation. (*A former Communist writing in the 1960s.*)[4]

A dissolution of the social order was expected by the hour. (*The minister of finance, recalling the immediate past in November 1923.*)[5]

We are now faced with the gravest crisis the Reich has yet experienced. (*General order issued by the head of the armed forces, Seeckt, in September 1923.*)[6]

The problem of making a victorious revolution stands before us. The workers are streaming in their masses to our party... The taking of power is fully achievable. (*Brandler, chairman of the German Communist Party, in* Pravda, *23 September 1923*.)[7]

1923 for the great majority of Germans was the Year of Hunger. It was the year of the greatest crisis they had known. It was the year when wages fell to less than half their 1914 value. It was the year when inflation destroyed the savings of a vast section of the middle class.

It was the year when the unity of the German state seemed at an end, with four rival powers holding different areas of the country: the French in the Rhineland and Ruhr, the extreme right in Bavaria, the extreme left in central Germany, and the official government in the north. It was the year in which both the revolutionary left and the fascist right mobilised to seize power. Yet it was also a year which ended with bourgeois democracy more or less intact.

Origins of the great crisis: inflation

The great social crisis of 1923 was made up of three closely interlinked elements. The first was unprecedented inflation, which reached its peak in the late summer. By that time prices were doubling every few hours. Stories of the period have entered social mythology far outside Germany: the queues of people carrying cardboard boxes to the bank to pack in the hundreds of currency notes needed just to buy a few necessities; the workers paid at 11am so that they could rush off to buy things before prices doubled at midday; the student who saw the price of his cup of coffee increase by 80 percent while he sat drinking it; the million-mark notes used to paper walls.

This was the confetti money of which politicians still warn us. What they do not explain, however, is *how* inflation on such a scale could take hold of one of the world's most economically powerful nations.

The inflation began in the war, when the government had enormous bills to meet. It could not meet them by taxing the workers, who were already living below the subsistence level. It did not want to meet them by taxing its friends at the top of big business. So instead it borrowed vast sums, in the expectation that it would be able to repay them from the proceeds of a quick victory. When the victory was not forthcoming, it resorted to printing more banknotes. In the years 1914-18 prices doubled.

But the policy of financing government expenditure in this way did not end with the war. It had too many advantages for big business. Prices rose 42 percent between November 1918 and July 1919, and by February 1920 were eight and a half times their pre-war level.

In later years right wing nationalist circles financed by big business laid the blame for the inflation on the reparations and the loss of territory under the Treaty of Versailles which ended the war. But this was hardly a complete explanation—for the reparations payments did not start until January 1920. Before that date came the huge price rises mentioned above—and from March 1920 to March 1921 the international value of the German mark remained stable. This then plummetted from 70 to the dollar to 270; but there followed another five month period of stability.

The 'great inflation' began in earnest in June 1922. It took 300 marks to buy a dollar in June; 8,000 six months later. The international value of the mark was halved roughly every six weeks. Prices inside Germany did not rise as fast—but they did still rise as never before. The effect on wages was already catastrophic. In 1920 groups such as miners had seen their real wages improve from about 60 percent of the 1914 figure to 90 percent. During 1922 they slumped to less than half the 1914 figure.

The renewed inflation of 1922 was not 'inevitable'. Many procapitalist economists of the time (and many since then too) argued that it could have been avoided had the German government been prepared to use its gold reserves and to introduce a viable scheme of taxation. Indeed, as much is indicated by the fact that three times government action *did* succeed in temporarily halting the downward fall in the value of money—in 1920, at the beginning of 1922, and again in March-April 1923.

But no government could maintain such policies for long: they were steadfastly opposed by the most powerful section of big business until the autumn of 1923. As two recent writers on the inflation note:

> The representatives of German industry never tired of propagating the thesis and warned of the consequence that a reversal of the downward trend of the mark would have for the export trade, for unemployment and for the German economy as a whole.[8]

The most influential industrialist was the 'king of the Ruhr', Stinnes. The head of the US state department section for Western Europe called him 'the most powerful man in Germany'.[9] Stinnes talked openly about 'the weapon of inflation'—and the sort of weapon it was can be seen by its effect on Stinnes himself.

The industrial empire that Stinnes controlled grew by leaps and bounds as prices rose from 1914 onwards. He and his fellow magnates had ready access to bank credits which they could repay months later with paper money by then worth only a fraction of the 'real' assets they had bought with it. In this way they could buy up small businesses which lacked their ties with the banks. During the war Stinnes' empire grew until he controlled mines, iron and steel plants, and a section of the electrical industry.

The renewed inflation after the war enabled him to extend this to paper making and printing, to newspapers and publishing, to shipyards and shipping lines, to hotels and property. Eventually he owned some 4,000 separate enterprises. And that was not all. His control of the export industry provided him with foreign currency, with which he was able to speculate against the mark at will and buy up no fewer than 572 enterprises abroad.

The government's policy of financing its expenditure through printing money had one further great advantage to Stinnes and his friends: they paid last year's taxes with this year's money, worth only a fraction of the original tax assessment. In effect they paid no taxes at all; in the summer of 1923 government receipts from taxes covered only 3 percent of its expenditure.

Each time a government tried to stabilise the mark, it was the big industrialists who deliberately undermined the effort. Thus in 1920 they responded to an emergency tax on property by moving funds abroad and reducing the value of the mark until the paper marks with which they paid the tax were of negligible value. In April 1923 it was a conscious decision by Stinnes to sell large quantities of marks abroad that gave the inflationary spiral a new push upwards. Stinnes and others like him 'hoped by the sabotage of taxation and an inflation that ruined the state, the people and the country, to safeguard their power and increase their flights of capital abroad'.[10]

Were there any doubt about this, they themselves proved the point. In 1920 and again in June 1923 they offered the government a deal. The Reich Association of Industrialists said it would provide a gold loan and help stop inflation if 'the other social partners also make sacrifices'—a complete scrapping of controls over prices and rents, an extension of the working day from eight to ten hours 'temporarily' (for 15 years!), the slashing of 'non-productive' wages, denationalisation of the railways, the scrapping of the industrial participation schemes, and 'legislation to defend and increase industrial capital'.

In practice this amounted to the dismantling of all the gains the German workers retained from the revolution of 1918. The industrialists as good as admitted that if legislation would not meet their demands, then they could achieve the same goal, a massive increase in profit levels, through the effect of inflation in impoverishing the mass of the population. Inflation meant that wages continually lagged behind prices, with the difference accruing to profit, even at a time when the government still seemed to be making concessions to the workers.

Inflation was a 'weapon' all right—a weapon for increasing the concentration and accumulation of capital at the expense both of the workers and of sections of the middle class.

Origins of the great crisis: the Ruhr

German capitalism and the German governments of the 1920s faced a great dilemma. They were still committed to the imperialist goals and policies that had led them to war in 1914—Stinnes, for instance, dreamt of a Germany that would be able to wipe out Poland, dominate Russia and Italy and expand industrially into southeast Europe—the policy of Ludendorff and Hindenberg in 1914-18, and later of Hitler.

But Germany had been defeated and largely disarmed. It did not have the military means to expand. French opposition, for instance, had been able to block the request of the Austrian parliament to merge with Germany in 1919. Even worse, Germany was itself the victim of foreign expansion. It had lost territory to both France and Poland, and was compelled to deliver considerable gold and goods as 'reparations' to France, Belgium and Italy, including a quarter of total German coal production.

The Social Democrat led governments of the early post-war years saw no choice but to acquiesce in these reparations. They followed what became known as 'fulfilment politics'—attempting to pay what the Allies demanded.

But the right wing bourgeois parties found it politically advantageous to adopt an attitude of extreme hostility to the Treaty of Versailles and the reparations. They were not in government and knew they could easily increase their popular support by blaming the inflation and hardship on the 'November traitors' who had 'bowed' to the 'dictates of foreign powers'.

For the 'moderate' bourgeois parties—the Democrats and the Catholic Centre Party—things were a little more difficult. The Social Democrats relied on them to help provide a stable parliamentary majority. Yet these parties did not want to bear the main responsibility for concessions to the wartime 'enemy', knowing this would lose them support to the parties further to the right.

The result was that Germany found it difficult to get a really stable government, even after the defeat of the first wave of revolution in 1919. There were repeated governmental crises as bourgeois parties tried to increase their hold on government at the expense of the Social Democrats—and then shied away from taking responsibility for implementing the terms of the Versailles Treaty. So they forced the Social Democrats out of government in the summer of 1920, only to return to a government with the participation of the Social Democrats with Wirth as premier 12 months later.

Such manoeuvres could not, however, stop the growth of an extreme right hostile to these 'moderate' parties. One by-product was the doubling of the right wing vote between 1919 and 1920. Another was the assassination by extreme right wing armed gangs of the two bourgeois politicians most associated with the 'fulfilment politics'—Erzberger in August 1921 and Rathenau in June 1922.

German big business encouraged the far right: Stinnes' paper, DAZ, had a strident right wing nationalist tone; while Thyssen boasted that he armed right wing terror groups. But they were not foolish enough to believe that German capitalism could put up complete resistance to the demands of the Allies. Stinnes, for instance, knew war was not an option. So he sought to achieve his imperialist goals by other means—by putting pressure on the Allies, in the hope that Britain and the US would fall out with France, allowing a compromise favourable to Germany. He hoped for an arrangement by which German and French business would form a joint trust on a 40:60 basis for the exploitation of the mineral resources of the Rhine-Ruhr and Alsace.

But in the summer of 1922 the Allies—especially the French—were in no mood for compromise. French capitalism, like German capitalism, still had debts left over from the war. It was under pressure to pay what it owed to the other Allied powers and to give something to the French middle classes. A new French government under Poincaré demanded its pound of flesh: if the reparations were not paid in full, then it would move troops up from the already occupied southern Rhine region to seize control of the centre of German industry, the Ruhr.

German big business was convinced that if France did any such thing, then France would suffer more than Germany. Chaos would result, disrupting supplies of German raw materials for French industry. And Britain and the US would turn against France. Meanwhile, any cost to German industry could be recouped by further inflation at the expense of the German workers and middle classes. As Stinnes put it, 'An extension of the area of French occupation is the lesser evil', compared to continued acquiesence in the demand for full reparations.[11]

By the end of 1923 the 'king of the Ruhr' had a German government which would follow his policy. The Social Democrat supported government under Wirth was replaced by the most right wing government since the war, led by Wilhelm Cuno, a member of the party Stinnes financed and belonged to, the German People's Party. Cuno was also president of the Hamburg-Amerika shipping line, which was linked to the Rockefeller interests in the United States.

The new government broke with the 'fulfilment politics', raised the slogan 'Bread first, then reparations', and dared the French to do their worst. The French reacted as they had threatened. In the third week of 1923 they took over two thirds of the Ruhr basin.

The immediate result was a feeling of national unity in Germany as at no time since August 1914. The Cuno government suddenly found itself extremely popular. Its policy was carried in the Reichstag with only 12 votes (the Communists) against. Throughout the country there were massive rallies of opposition to the French demands: half a million people demonstrated in Berlin.

The Social Democrats threw their weight behind the policy of the government from which they had just been ousted. They organised their own nationalist meetings, and when the French arrested a number of directors of Ruhr companies, *Vorwärts* insisted:

> Whether these men are friends or enemies of the workers' movements is of no importance. The workers' sense of law and humanity instinctively recognises at this moment that all these questions are not of importance.[12]

The trade union leaders met with representatives of employers and government once a fortnight to coordinate 'resistance' to the occupation. On 15 January they backed a half-hour strike of protest. In the Ruhr itself workers displayed a quite unusual solidarity with their masters. A French attempt to arrest Thyssen was met by the threat of strike action by his workers: only his own pleadings stopped the strike.

The government's official policy was 'passive resistance'. The aim was to make the occupation counter-productive for the French, making it difficult and costly for them to get their reparations and the raw materials they needed for their industries. Civil servants and police were forbidden to cooperate with the invaders, railwaymen to move goods for them, miners to work under French bayonets.

There was an overwhelming response from the workers and from government officials. The Ruhr railway network soon ground to a halt; there were spasmodic strikes as French troops entered the mines; the post and telegraph centres were shut down. Indeed, the response went beyond what the government wanted—it spread from the Ruhr proper to the Rhineland areas which had been occupied by the French with German government acquiescence for the past four years.

The French tried to deal with the resistance by making arrests and by the expulsion of recalcitrant government employees: some 100,000 expulsions in the first six months of 1923. All the railwaymen were sacked and replaced with French troops and volunteers. German customs officials were expelled, and German security police replaced with French gendarmes. Ruhr towns such as Bochum and Essen, the scene of bitter fighting between workers and German troops in 1919 and 1920, were now the scene of clashes between demonstrators and French police. By August the French had killed 121 German workers.

At first all the French efforts seemed to achieve little. They succeeded in moving only 500,000 tons of coal in January-May 1923—a mere 14 percent of the reparations due to them. Yet there were from the beginning cracks in the 'national unity' of the German resistance.

In the minds of the Ruhr industrialists and mine owners, the resistance was designed to extract concessions from France. They did not consider it worth suffering any considerable economic losses in the process. So in January their policy had been to continue coal deliveries to the French, providing there was payment in cash:

The mineowners accepted, in accord with the government, the delivery of coal against payment, at the same time as their newspapers were calling on the German people to resist the invasion.[13]

The government finally banned these deliveries for fear of popular unrest, but the owners did their utmost to keep the mining operations going, even if it meant the accumulation of vast stocks of coal. Nor did they seem to mind much if, as with the Stinnes mine at Buer, the French took daily shipments from the stocks of coal; as late as July the Krupp mines were still working at full capacity.

The fortnightly meetings of the unions and employers were used to *discourage* too many strikes of protest at French actions. Together they insisted that 'order must reign in the face of the invader'.[14] The union leaders *opposed* a call for a general strike, and the employers granted a 77.7 percent wage increase to the Ruhr miners at the beginning of February to buy their favour.

The Stinnes press preached undying hostility to the 'traitors' who collaborated with the occupation authorities. But Stinnes himself was involved in secret negotiations with French business interests and, indirectly, with the French government. Meanwhile prison sentences against industrialists such as Krupp miraculously allowed them to continue to conduct their business from their 'cells' before they were equally miraculously transferred to 'house arrest'.

It did not take the French long, under such conditions, to begin to enjoy a certain success: they got the local railway network running, persuaded the population to use it, and above all, shifted a million and a half tons of coal between May and August. As one early historian of the Weimar Republic remarked, 'The so-called passive resistance was really a fable'.[15]

This did not, however, prevent it being a very *costly* fable for most of the German people.

The government was of necessity concerned to maintain the allegiance of the workers and lower government officials of the Ruhr. Not only would 'passive resistance' collapse otherwise, but there was a strong danger that the French might encourage Rhenish separatism—and of course there was the powerful revolutionary socialist tradition too. So the German government guaranteed the salaries and removal expenses of the 100,000 people expelled by the French, promised full wages to those sacked for directly resisting the occupation and three quarters wages for those sacked because of its indirect effects. On top of this, the government did what it could to provide food for the area, so as to alleviate shortages which meant even higher inflation than in the rest of Germany.

Yet the sums paid out on these items were piffling compared with the other expenditure on 'Ruhr aid'—credits to the Ruhr coalowners and industrialists. Huge loans were given them, readily financed by the printing of money, which they used just as readily for speculation against the mark.

The 'passive resistance' that had so united the German people in January was having consequences by late April that were tearing the country apart as never before; inflation was giving way to hyperinflation; the impoverished working class was increasingly blaming Stinnes and the profiteers; the impoverished middle classes were flowing toward right wing, anti-Semitic parties financed by Stinnes and the profiteers. In the Ruhr and Rhine chauvinism had given way to growth of Communist influence on the one hand, to a certain amount of Rhenish separatism on the other. In towns and cities of central Germany there was an enormous upswing in working class militancy. In Bavaria there was an unprecedented blossoming of the fascist right.

The origins of the great crisis: the nationalist right

The inflation had a devastating effect on a whole section of the middle class—those who lived off pensions, fixed interest bonds, their accumulated savings and rents from property. Even those with jobs had usually depended on such extra sources of income to keep themselves 'respectable'. Now they suddenly found their dividend coupons and savings books were worthless. The most 'respectable' elements in German society were on the verge of starvation—the civil servants, the retired army officers, the university professors, the former policemen. People who had spent their lives carefully preserving a lifestyle that kept them a cut above the 'common herd' suddenly found themselves thrust down below it: the elderly gentlewoman would be queuing at the soup kitchen; the brigadier's daughter would consider herself lucky if she could sell her body to a foreign sailor for hard currency.

The far right parties found it only too easy to exploit this situation. In the first years of the republic they had been forced to the margins of politics. Their values were embodied in the Freikorps, but when it came to votes, the two right wing parties—the German Nationalists, an agrarian monarchist party, and the German People's Party, backed by the industrialists—received only a fifth of the votes between them. The bulk of the middle classes still identified with the bourgeois republican parties—the Democrats and the Centre Party. The militaristic far right were not even a lunatic fringe: Hitler was in Munich throughout the days of the Council Republic and played no political role at all.

Things had already begun to change by the winter of 1919-20. Nevertheless, the middle class, by and large, joined the struggle against the Kapp putsch and the right wing parties were later embarrassed by their own half-support for Kapp.

By 1922, however, disillusion with the republic had really set in. The right was growing in strength and aggressiveness. And alongside the old, conservative right there had grown a new, militant, extreme right, based on a core of former Freikorps members. These were the men who murdered Erzberger in 1921 and Rathenau in 1922—and who carried out another 351 political assassinations in four years.

Their strength was great enough by mid-1922 to worry the Social Democrat and bourgeois democratic politicians who had used the Freikorps against the left in 1919-20. In Prussia the Social Democrat interior minister Severing tried to ban the Nazis and the conservative nationalist military formation, the Stahlhelm; and after the murder of Rathenau, the Democrat prime minister of the Reich declared, 'The enemy is on the right.'

But such efforts to deal with the right were futile. For the right had two great protectors—the state authorities in Bavaria and the national command of the armed forces.

Bavaria had been a centre of right wing influence and intrigue since the smashing of the Bavarian Council Republic. It was the one place where the Kapp putsch had enjoyed lasting success, putting into power the conservative Bavarian People's Party, with an extreme right wing interior minister, Escherich. Escherich turned Bavaria into a fortress for all the far right groups in Germany. He created an armed national organisation, the Orgesch (ie Organisation Escherich) based on the 45,000 strong Bavarian Home Guard, and gathered into the state the various remnants of the Freikorps, including the Erhardt Brigade, which had led the Kapp putsch, and other armed groups that had been fighting the Poles in Upper Silesia.

The work of the Bavarian interior ministry was complemented by that of the army command in Bavaria. Through the mediation of a Captain Rohm this began to collaborate with the National Socialist Workers, or Nazi, Party that had recently grown up around the Austrian anti-Semitic demagogue Adolf Hitler.

Nationally too the armed forces were a bulwark of the right wing. The head of the army, Seeckt, saw the 100,000 troops that were allowed under the Treaty of Versailles as the possible kernel of a much bigger army at some time in the future. So he was happy to encourage the proliferation of half-secret paramilitary groups which worked in liaison with the army and which could be absorbed into it as necessary. He also maintained the position he took at the time of the Kapp putsch: 'The Reichswehr would not fire on the Reichswehr.' He might think that the extreme right were impatient and moving prematurely, but if they succeeded, good luck to them.

What this meant in practice was shown when Rathenau was assassinated in 1922. The Wirth government passed an emergency law for action against the extreme right throughout the country—but the Bavarian state government simply refused to accept it. Because Wirth knew the army would not move against Bavaria he was forced to accept a 'compromise' which represented a complete surrender before the right in Bavaria. The paramilitaries continued to parade in Nuremberg and Munich, and to receive training from the Bavarian Reichswehr—and Wirth could do nothing.

In January 1923 it was the turn of the Bavarian premier to back down in the face of the nationalist-military alliance. Worried by a growing wave of Nazi violence, he banned a series of armed demonstrations. Hitler had a word with the Bavarian army commander, Lossow, who made the Bavarian premier lift the ban. The Nazi paper noted with satisfaction after a parade of 6,000 stormtroopers, 'This was a military parade although it lacked arms.'

The collaboration nationally between the military and the far right received a further boost after the French occupation. Seeckt believed that all out armed action against the French would be lunacy. But he was quite willing to countenance small guerrilla operations by the extreme right. And he gave the go-ahead for the absorption of many of the far right groups into an underground section of the Reichswehr, the 'Black Reichswehr'. Money from industrialists was used to train nationalist volunteers from all parts of Germany for operations against the French in the Ruhr—or against the left anywhere.

These volunteers grew in number the more 'passive resistance' became a farce. Throughout the country nationalist youth demanded the chance to fight 'the invader'.

But the growth in the strength of the right was not of importance chiefly in or because of the Ruhr. The right used the opportunity to further enhance its position in Bavaria, where by the summer even the all-too-moderate Social Democratic Party was half-persecuted:

> Conditions in Munich in the summer of 1923 were fantastic. Constant rumours of a Nazi putsch circulated and reached a climax about every four weeks. During the night the city would seethe with excitement. Stormtroopers would march through the streets, would beat up people whom for some reason they disliked... In the buildings of the *Münchener Post* [the SPD paper] and the Labour Temple, the men of the Social Democratic Security Detachment, armed with some rifles, a few machine guns and a number of home-made hand grenades, stood behind barricades of huge newspaper rolls and watched the Nazi columns marching.[16]

For the Army High Command, the Nazis and kindred groups were a useful counterweight to the forces of the left. Already in January Seeckt and Cuno had toyed with the possibility of dissolving parliament and establishing a 'temporary' dictatorship. But they had been forced to abandon the idea because of the opposition of Ebert, who was still president. But the notion grew in popularity in military and big business circles as the year progressed.

In Bavaria the local right wing government was also trying to use the Nazis for its own ends—not merely to terrorise the working class, but also to prepare the ground for the formation of a right wing, clerical, authoritarian state, autonomous from Berlin.

Hitler's own perspective went beyond those of either of the pillars whose support he needed—the army and the Bavarian government. Only a few months previously, Mussolini had marched on Rome and taken office. Hitler saw Bavaria as the base within which he would gather a fascist army for the march on Berlin. But to get there, he would first have to pass through the traditional heartlands of the extreme left—the central German area of Saxony, Thuringia and Prussian Saxony.

Inflation, the Ruhr crisis, the growth of fascism and the splitting apart of the national state, these fed off each other, creating a general political and social crisis in which the fight against inflation could not be separated from the fight against the extreme right.

The working class

1922 had been a year of satisfaction for both main parties competing for influence over the German working class. The Social Democrat leaders had felt they could relax, now that the hectic years in which class collaboration had been threatened by civil war were past. In these less turbulent times the rump of the Independent Social Democracy had grown closer to them, until a merger between the two parties was possible in the autumn. This gave the new united Social Democratic Party powerful parliamentary influence—with 170 out of 466 seats in the Reichstag. What is more, it made relations with the trade union bureaucracy easier: its allegiances were no longer split between two rival social democratic parties. Even in Bavaria the Social Democrats had regained some ground from the right. And, until the close of the year, it seemed that no national government could last long without Social Democratic participation.

Characteristically, however, the obsession with what was going on at the top of society led the Social Democrats to neglect what was happening below, in the depths of the working class.

Inflation and the activities of the right wing paramilitaries were creating a new discontent. There was a series of big strikes. The murder of Rathenau produced the same sort of working class unity and determination as the Kapp putsch had two years earlier—even if this time it did not lead to armed working class offensives.

Among rank and file Social Democrats the feeling grew that their leaders were not doing enough to cope with the situation. This year of Social Democratic self-satisfaction was also a year in which the membership of the old SDP fell a little—by 47,000.[17] And only half the Independent Social Democrat membership followed their leaders into the new unified party.

The SPD leadership could not remain forever immune to this feeling of discontent among the members. Some at the top began to hesitate over the full blooded implementation of the old politics. When the Prussian Social Democrats agreed to a Prussian 'Grand Coalition' government including Stinnes' party, the German People's Party, many deputies expressed opposition. When the same idea was floated for the central government in November, the opposition was powerful enough to wreck the scheme: the parliamentary caucus threw it out by 80 votes to 48.

Because of this vote, the SPD was forced from government by its bourgeois coalition partners. But it did not end the internal divisions. The new premier, Cuno, was a notorious right winger. Yet the SPD leadership 'tolerated' his government. When the Ruhr was occupied, they rushed to back his call for 'national unity'—though nearly half the SPD parliamentary caucus wanted to reject it. In the Prussian state parliament some SPD deputies even voted with the Communists against the party line.

The Communist Party had better reason to be satisfied with 1922. It was not a year in which they could dream of fighting for power. But they did, in the course of the year, bind the most bitter wounds created by the March Action and the loss of so many leading figures.

The party leadership now pushed through with singleminded determination the 'united front' policy. The members were enjoined to make every effort to work with non-Communist workers, to fight alongside them on apparently far-from-revolutionary issues, so as to show, in Brandler's words, that the Social Democrat leaders would not fight even 'for a crust of bread'. Only the Communists would lead such struggles and only militant, Communist, tactics could win them.

The first shining example of what this policy meant came at the beginning of 1922. The government, in a half-hearted attempt to improve its finances and appease big business, refused the wage demands of the railway workers and instead demanded redundancies and an increase in the working week. The leaders of the main, Social Democratic 'free' union were prepared to acquiesce, out of loyalty to their government friends. But an independent, 'non-political' and traditionally conservative union of railway workers and officials put up resistance.

'The members of this union', a Communist Party Congress was told a year later, 'were far from revolutionary. They believed purely trade union action would beat the government's policies.'[18]

But the government considered that a political issue was at stake. It wanted to teach the working class that it must pay for restabilisation of

German capitalism. Ebert, as president of the republic, banned the strike. The Social Democrat police chief in Berlin impounded the union's strike funds. Strike leaders were arrested. Both the army and the Technische Nothilfe, the strikebreaking force set up by Noske in 1919, were used in an attempt to smash the strike.

The Communist Party was the only organised force within the working class prepared to support the strike. The 'free' union led by the Social Democrats remained adamant in its opposition to the action—even though most of its own members had stopped work.

Eventually the 'independent' union that had called the strike backed down under these combined pressures. But the Communists had been able to make the point to hundreds of thousands of workers and petty functionaries that the reformist trade unions would not even defend reforms.

As the railway strike was developing, there was a strike by municipal workers who supplied Berlin with water, gas and electricity. Again the union leaders opposed it. Again the Communists alone called for solidarity.

When 200,000 south German metal workers started what was to be a two month long strike, the union leaders were more cautious. They gave *verbal* support to the strikers. But still only the Communists joined the strikers themselves in calling on other workers for solidarity action and in opposing attempts to dilute the strike demands.

The call for united action was not confined to economic issues. There was even an attempt at an international 'united front' against the capitalist offensive. The 'International' led by the German Independents (the so-called 'Two and a Half International') persuaded both the Comintern and the revived Second International to send delegates to meet it in Berlin. Little came of the conference except acrimonious discussions—but it provided the occasion for joint KPD-USP demonstrations throughout Germany.

But the most important non-economic reason for joint action was the rise of the paramilitary right. After bloody clashes between left wing workers and the far right in Königsberg (later the Russian city of Kaliningrad) at the beginning of June, the Communist leadership warned in an open letter to the two Social Democratic parties and the unions that this was a prelude to a national thrust by the counter-revolution. There was no reply from the Social Democrats. But the Communist argument must have seemed vindicated for many workers when the far right assassinated Rathenau barely a week later.

The murder produced a huge uprising of working class anger. The Social Democrats could no longer ignore the Communist calls for unity. All over Germany their members were marching alongside Communists against the extreme right. They would tear up their party cards unless their leaders made some gesture towards unity. At an unprecedented series of joint meetings representatives of the two Social Democratic parties, the unions and the KPD negotiated over the terms of a common response to the murder. The Communists pressed for the implementation of the policy accepted in words by the Social Democrats after the Kapp putsch—a call for the purging of the Reichswehr, the disarming of the right wing paramilitaries, the freeing of working class political prisoners, and the formation of armed workers' contingents to deal with the far right.

The Social Democrats argued that the answer should lie in parliamentary action, but signed a provisional agreement for joint demonstrations. This was sufficient to keep the rank and file of the SPD happy. Then, when the immediate anger had passed and the various leaders met again to discuss what to do next, the SPD broke off negotiations with the KPD on the rather spurious grounds that militant activities by the KPD in the localities had 'forfeited' the KPD the right to be part of any agreement. The SPD put their faith in a new 'Law for the Protection of the Republic' which was rushed through parliament—although, as we have seen, this law could never be applied in Bavaria and was, in fact, being used in the rest of Germany *against the left* within a few months.

This rebuff did not prevent the Communists again and again raising the question of united action—usually linking the question of self-defence against the far right with united action against inflation, demanding the seizure of industrial property by the state and under the control of factory councils.

The KPD's appeals were addressed to the leaders of the Social Democratic organisations, but they were intended also for the ears of the SPD rank and file. The Communist organisations in the localities set about drawing these into the joint activity that the SPD leaders refused.

In the factories, the Communists argued for powerful factory councils which would ignore the limitations set by the factory council law and unite across industry to fight for better wages and conditions.

As a new bout of wage militancy began to develop towards the end of the year, a delegate meeting of Berlin factory councils called for a national meeting. They first addressed their call to the union leaders. When it was rejected, they went ahead themselves. The resulting congress was not the congress of the whole working class which had been demanded of the unions. But it was no mean achievement either—with 846 delegates, of whom 657 belonged to the KPD, 38 to the SPD and 52 non-party (quite likely those who had dropped out of the USP when it merged into the SPD). It was an important pointer to future possibilities, and it was not to be that long before the executive elected from the congress was to play an important role in initiating and uniting major struggles of the working class.

The factory councils were not conceived as restricted to a purely economic role. The aim was for them to take on embryonic political and social functions. The factory councils were urged to link up with other factory councils and working class housewives' groups to form 'Control Committees'—committees which fought price rises and speculation in the necessities of life.

Effectively, the Control Committees spread the power of the councils from the factory to the community, binding the local, rank and file organisations of the working class into a tight network capable both of fighting the effects of inflation and of drawing workers together in self-defence against the far right.

The Communist leaders claimed that these committees were built in many places in the immediate aftermath of the Rathenau assassination and led to 'bloody clashes' with the 'police or the Orgesch' in 'the Rhineland, Magdeburg, Hessen, Baden, and Pfalz. In Zwickau workers virtually took power into their hands. There were also many dead and wounded'.[19]

The 'united front' policy was much criticised within the Communist Party. A sizeable section of the membership regarded any talk of possible collaboration with the Social Democratic leaders as 'revisionist', and the details of its implementation were criticised by the Comintern leadership on occasions for 'excessive leniency' towards the SPD (after the Congress of the Three Internationals and the Rathenau campaign). Yet there is little doubt that this policy built the party up again in 1922, after the near devastation of 1921. Membership grew by 38,000. With a total of 222,000 members (among whom 26,710 were women) it was by far the biggest Communist Party in the Western world. What is more, the party exercised considerable influence outside its own ranks.

The votes won by the KPD were one indication of this. Although it still did not have anything like the vote pulling power of the old USP of 1920, it could, for instance, pick up 266,000 votes in the Saxony state elections. It had 12,014 municipal councillors, controlled 80 local councils and was the biggest party in another 70.

In the unions too the KPD tactics led to considerable growth in strength. The Communists took the leadership of the 'free' (in other words, Social Democrat) railway union in Berlin and Leipzig, of the building workers' union in Berlin and Düsseldorf, of the metal workers in Stuttgart. At the June 1922 Congress of the 'free' union federation, one delegate in eight was a Communist and on a number of issues the party's resolutions were carried—despite a considerable purge of Communists by the union bureaucracies a few months earlier.

The KPD also had a strong presence in the conferences of a number of unions—at the railwaymen's union conference a fifth of the delegates were KPD members; at the transport union a tenth; at the municipal workers' an eighth.

Finally, a small but useful addition to the party's strength came from control of some of the breakaway unions established by the 'ultra-left' two or three years earlier: the Manual and Intellectual Workers' Union, with 80,000 members in the Ruhr and Silesia, and two marine unions on the northwest coast.

There were, however, weaknesses in the party's relationship with its supporters—whether they voted for it at the polls or fought alongside in the unions. The biggest weakness seems to have been its press. The KPD was able to produce 38 local daily papers—because of Russian finance.[20] But their combined sale was only 388,600—barely one and a half copies per member. This may have had something to do with the cost. But there is little doubt it also had to do with the content: the central KPD paper, *Rote Fahne*, made few concessions to popularity—no pictures, far too few cartoons, the occasional serialised novel, but mainly page after page of long, not particularly well written, editorialising. Often the style seemed to indicate that the paper was directed *only* at the party members: the headline of a famous front page was 'To the party members', as if no one expected left Social Democrats or non-party members to be interested.

Yet such weaknesses could not alter the fact that the KPD was a more influential and powerful *revolutionary* party than any advanced industrial power has ever seen before or since. It was, of course, smaller than it had been immediately after the fusion with the USP left—but much better organised.

1.   Arthur Rosenberg, *A History of the German Republic* (London 1936) p92.
2.   Quoted in J C Favez, *La Reich devant l'Occupation Français Belge de la Ruhr en 1923* (Geneva 1969) p35.
3.   Quoted in W Ersil, *Aktionseinheit stürtzt Cuno* (Berlin 1961) p72.
4.   M Buber-Neumann, *Kriegsschauplätze der Weltrevolution* (Stuttgart 1967) p106.
5.   Quoted in Guttman and Meehan, *The Great Inflation*, p203.
6.   Quoted in H J Gordon, *The Reichswehr and the German Republic 1919-26* (Princeton 1957) p230.
7.   Quoted in M Buber-Neumann, op cit, p109.
8.   Guttman and Meehan, op cit, p36.
9.   J C Favez, op cit, p31.
10. Ibid, p25.
11. Quoted ibid, p31.
12. *Vorwärts*, 20 January 1923
13. J C Favez, op cit, p74.
14. Quoted ibid, p111.
15. A Rosenberg, op cit, p181.
16. Landauer, *European Socialism* (Berkeley 1959) p971.
17. Figures in *Bericht der Verhandlung der III (8) Parteitag der VKPD* (28 January to 1 February 1923).
18. Ibid.
19. Ibid, p30.
20. See Isaac Deutscher in *New Left Review* 105.

CHAPTER 12

The hot summer

1923 has gone down in history as a year of monetary chaos, of mass hunger, of sections of society being plunged into the abyss, of continual street disturbances.

Yet social life seemed to proceed in a peaceful and orderly manner for the first two or three months of the year. The occupation of the Ruhr by the French created an atmosphere of patriotism and social unity. Class peace reigned as rarely before in the Weimar Republic. The only strikes in the heartland of German capitalism, the Ruhr, were in defence of the great industrial magnates. The agitation over wages that had been growing in November and December seemed a distant memory as the employers doubled miners' wages. And money still retained its value in day-by-day transactions, although prices were already rising at what we would regard today as a phenomenal rate—by 20 or 30 percent a month. Indeed, the government even managed to hold the value of the mark steady in February and March.

This seeming order began to collapse in mid-April. Stinnes moved his little finger and the value of the mark slumped. It took 31,700 marks to buy a dollar on 1 May, 160,400 on 1 July and 1,103,000 on 1 August.

In the Ruhr the solid front of 'passive resistance' against 'the invader' began to crack: non-union and immigrant (usually Polish) workers began to obey French orders, and industrialists started to negotiate with the 'enemy'.

The first demonstrations against the German authorities began as rising prices slashed the value of the payments to those made unemployed by the 'passive resistance.' *Rote Fahne* on 20 April carried the headline, 'Bloodshed in the Ruhr—more dead and 35 wounded in Mülheim', after a demonstration of 'several hundred unemployed' outside the town hall had been fired on by the criminal police. There were similar demonstrations in Essen, Duisburg and Düsseldorf.

There were not so many unemployed in the rest of Germany as in the Ruhr, but their plight was much worse. In Berlin it was estimated that unemployment assistance payments were now only 25 percent of the subsistence level. The result was 'trouble' with the unemployed in Stettin, Chemnitz, Leipzig, Plauen, Zittau and Werdau. In Dresden 'spontaneously formed' Control Committees began forcing down prices.[1]

The Hundreds

The growth of the far right evoked a response from the more militant sections of workers. The Communist Party had been calling for some time for the formation of workers' defence groups usually called 'Proletarian Hundreds'. Now these began to take root—especially in the Ruhr, where the French had expelled the German security police, and in central Germany where left Social Democratic state governments tolerated them.

The committee elected from the December congress of factory councils called, in April, for 'the building of Proletarian Hundreds as an expression of the organised, struggle-ready united front in the factories.' Membership cards issued to the Hundreds in Leipzig spelt out their aims: 'To enlighten the working class as to the dangers of fascism. To guard workers' meetings and demonstrations'.[2]

Ideally the Hundreds were to be built by the decision of mass meetings in the factories. The central committee of the Communist Party called for the unemployed to be drawn into self-defence groups based upon *employed* workers: 'No special Hundreds for the unemployed... No building of party Hundreds'.[3] In this way the movement of the Hundreds was to be closely linked to the movement of factory councils and the movement of Control Committees.

It is difficult to know how effective this was in practice. No doubt the Hundreds were often KPD organisations. But in May and June in Chemnitz the big factories *did* vote to build armed factory organisations. And in Leipzig the movement was run by a committee of seven SPD members, five Communists and three non-party members. It claimed affiliations from 96 factories.[4] Membership of the Leipzig Hundreds was two fifths Communist, one fifth Social Democrat and the rest unaffiliated trade unionists. It was claimed that the majority of the members were former frontline troops.

The first recorded activity of the Hundreds was in Chemnitz on 9 March, when they acted against a fascist meeting. Two days later 4,000, including a contingent of 100 women, demonstrated in Thuringia. And on 18 March a Communist demonstration in Halle was led by 'worker troops with red flags'.[6]

The May Day parades were used as an opportunity to display the growing movement to the whole working class. Throughout the country demonstrations were led by the ordered ranks of the Hundreds. In Berlin 25,000 of these workers were said to have led a half million strong demonstration.[7] The demonstration the same day in Essen was 100,000 strong; in Halle 50,000; while in Munich a joint demonstration of all the workers' organisations was 70,000 strong, despite threats by the fascists that they would break it up.

Shortly afterwards the Hundreds were banned throughout Prussia by the interior minister, Severing. He had argued a month earlier:

> For some time the KPD has been calling for the formation of proletarian self-defence forces—not merely as a defence against the fascists and the extreme right wing organisations, to prevent nationalist meetings and to protect Communist meetings, but also as the vanguard of a Red Army.[8]

The ban did not, however, prevent the movement continuing to grow in the French-controlled Ruhr and in the central German states of Saxony and Thuringia. On 15 May 10,000 workers fought with the police guarding an 8,500 strong rally of the right wing paramilitary Stahlheim. The Hundreds grew in Saxony to the point where they could set up roadblocks to stop fascists moving from place to place. In the Ruhr the authorities were divided as to how important the Hundreds were. The official view was that Hundreds probably existed in the factories but not in the mines.[9]

In the rest of Germany efforts were made to continue building the movement underground—for instance in Halle the factory councils voted in late June 1923 to set up 'defence forces' even though these were 'illegal'.[10]

Once established, the Hundreds did not confine themselves to antifascist actions. As inflation accelerated they were naturally used by the Control Committees as a means of enforcing decisions against speculation. They were sent out from the industrial centres of central Germany to stop evictions of agricultural workers. Increasingly they took over the defence of picket lines and the spreading of strikes.

The first strike wave

The collapse of the mark from April onwards meant that the 'peace' in the factories at the beginning of the year crumbled fast. There were already strikes by 40,000 miners in Upper Silesia and by workers in central Germany in March. But that was nothing to what was to hit the whole country in May-June.

The movement began when the miners in one pit outside Dortmund, in the Ruhr, struck over wages on 16 May—rejecting as inadequate a settlement between the coal owners and the government. The miners occupied Dortmund Town Hall and sent flying pickets to nearby pits and factories, accompanied by the local Proletarian Hundreds. Clashes with the police followed, in which one miner was shot dead. But that did not stop the strike spreading to the whole Dortmund area—even though the Communist Party was taken completely by surprise and gave no lead to the movement for four days.

A local conference of the factory councils on 20 May brought together 200 delegates from 60 workplaces, and in the week that followed the strike closed all mines and most of the big factories in the core area of the Ruhr between Dortmund and Essen—although a central strike committee was not formed under Communist leadership until the end of that week. At this high point of the struggle there were 310,000 strikers, about half the miners and metal workers of the Ruhr.

The strikers repeatedly clashed with the police. On 22 May, for example, a 50,000 strong demonstration in Dortmund fought with police and three workers were killed. The next day another 50,000 strong demonstration protested at the shootings. Further fights broke out when the police tried to evict workers who had occupied mining buildings. The miners instinctively organised themselves as they had in the early post-war struggles. The marches of the Proletarian Hundreds reminded observers of the Red Armies of 1920. They took over the street markets and shops for the local Control Committees, forcing down prices.[11]

The central government was perplexed as to what to do. The French had expelled the security police from the area in an attempt to force the local authorities to end 'passive resistance' and to cooperate with the setting up of a new police force under French control. The criminal police were all that remained and these were unable to cope.

In desperation the head of the governmental authority in Düsseldorf asked for help from the 'enemy' general, Devigues, recalling that 'at the time of the Paris Commune, the German High Command gave decisive aid in crushing the rising'.[12]

Finally a half-agreement was reached by which the French allowed the local authorities in Mülheim and Essen to set up volunteer 'auxiliary police forces'. According to *Rote Fahne* there followed 'mass arrests of strikers and Communist functionaries'.[13]

The strikers began to return to work on 28 May: the Communist Party, frightened that isolated from the rest of Germany it would be smashed, recommended acceptance of a substantially improved wage offer.

But if the KPD leadership thought the anger was confined to the Ruhr, they were mistaken. In the month of June 'there broke out protest meetings and demonstrations against price rises, and a wave of big and small strikes throughout Germany'.[14]

On 7 June 30,000 coal and steel workers struck in Upper Silesia. Within two days their number had doubled, to be joined a couple of days later by a strike of tens of thousands of agricultural workers. The strikes must have been very bitter—the Communist Party claimed that it was physically broken by the intervention of the security police. But that did not stop the agitation among the agricultural workers spreading to Brandenburg, where 10,000 struck, and the heart of reaction, East Prussia, where 'spontaneous meetings' of agricultural workers were reported.[15]

There were signs of agitation everywhere: on the day the miners of Upper Silesia struck, *Rote Fahne* carried the headline: 'Seven slain in Leipzig' after police had fired on a demonstration of the SPD and the unions. And on the northwest coast, seamen struck under Communist leadership three days later.

In central Germany there was a growing struggle by the miners against pressure to make 'sacrifices' at a time when the main mining area of the country was sealed off by French troops. Inflation had cut into their wages until, as a minister of the Saxon state government admitted, 'The miners of Zwickau cannot buy bread with their wages, let alone other means of nourishment.' Throughout May and June the miners staged go-slows which slashed production. The coal owners in desperation appealed to the central government. After it had told them, 'The movement in Zwickau is against the will of the unions, which are more and more losing control of the working class,' the owners demanded a repetition of the tactics of 1919—a march of the Reichswehr into Saxony.[16]

Alongside these great movements there was a proliferation of local strikes and partial strikes. This was when inflation accelerated to a previously undreamt of rate. Prices no longer changed every quarter or every month, but every two or three days: between 29 and 31 June prices of basic necessities rose by 25 percent. Previously peaceable workers found that only direct action could protect them—whether it was a question of taking control of the street markets to stop speculation in potatoes, or white collar workers in the Berlin factories striking for 'peacetime' (in other words, pre-war) wages, as they did on 21 June.

The wave of struggle reached its peak when the Berlin metal workers voted to strike by ten to one. By 10 July 150,000 of them had stopped work and again strikers' demonstrations were clashing with the police. The struggles had ceased to be purely economic. As a recent, non-revolutionary historian has noted, by July 'the wave of workers' demands goes forward inseparably from a truly revolutionary agitation'.[17]

An even less revolutionary source is Wissell, a spokesman at the Provisional Economic Council who wrote at the beginning of June:

> A mixture of bitterness and despair rules among the great masses and among all those who are forced to go without food. This is as much the case among government officials as among social security claimants and workers. And I must say that the atmosphere is such that in the last few weeks it has frightened me and filled me with great worries for the future. I tell you quite clearly that a revolutionary and activist spirit is rising in the most quiet and most stable of the masses... It only needs a little incitement to explode everything.[18]

A mass revolutionary party had been built up in the few previous years just for this moment. Yet the 'little incitement' was not to be forthcoming.

The Social Democrats on the wane
In 1922 there had been a barely perceptible trend within the working class, moving away from social democracy and towards Communism.

By the early summer of 1923 the whole previous structure of traditional political allegiances was being shaken to its foundations.

The rapidly accelerating inflation hit the Social Democratic Party in two ways. Firstly, it drove workers again and again into strikes which the union leaders resisted and which the Social Democratic led Prussian police attacked. And secondly it destroyed the finances of the SPD and the unions. Subscriptions were valueless by the time they reached national headquarters, with the result that there was nothing to pay for the once all-powerful party apparatus and press.

A historian who lived through the period has recorded:

> In the course of 1923, the power of the SPD decreased steadily... The independent trade unions, which had always been the chief support of the Social Democrats, were in a state of complete disintegration. The inflation destroyed the value of their subscriptions. The trade unions could no longer pay their employees properly, nor give assistance to their members. The wage agreements the trade unions were accustomed to conclude with the employers became worthless when the devaluation of the currency made any wages paid out a week late worthless. Thus trade union work of the old style became unavailing... The destruction of the unions simultaneously caused the ruin of the SPD.[19]

This overstates the case a little. But the membership of the 'free' trade unions did slump—from nine million in 1922 to four million in 1924. There was a visible falling apart of the apparatus that had constrained the German working class since the war.

The old 'trade union' job of fighting for better pay now had to be done on a weekly and daily basis, by organisations close to the workers. The *local* union sections, and above all the factory councils, took on a new directing role in the struggle. And Communist militants led the way in suggesting forms of action that could win.

Already in the factory council election in Thyssen's plants in the Ruhr in mid-February, the Communist list had received more votes than that of the 'free' trade union, while a syndicalist breakaway union list got more votes than the 'non-political' and Christian unions. The unions took the lesson to heart—and postponed elections for other factories in the occupied zone.[20] But that could not destroy the strength of the Communists in the factory councils nationally. A pessimistic Communist account speaks of *five thousand* councils which the KPD could mobilise—although not all were KPD controlled.[21]

Communist estimates in June suggested that the party's activists held positions organising two and a half million trade unionists at a local level—a third of the total trade union membership at the time. In the builders' union, for example, the KPD ran 65 of the 749 local branches and were about equal in strength with the Social Democrats in 230 others; in the metal workers' union the party was in a majority in key centres such as Stuttgart, Halle, Merseberg, Jena, Suhl, Solingen and Remscheid; in Halle they won the metal workers' election by 2,000 votes to 500, and in Magdeburg, where the Social Democrats won with 4,900 votes, the Communists could still boast 2,600.[22]

Communist Party membership grew by 70,000—or about a third—and there are signs that the party's influence over much wider ranks of workers increased dramatically. There were only two electoral contests as the struggle mounted in 1923—in Oldenburg early in June and in Mecklenburg a month later. In Oldenburg the Communist vote rose from 3 percent of the SPD vote in 1920 to 25 percent; in rural Mecklenburg the progress was even more amazing, for the Communists had not bothered to stand there in 1920 and the Independents had received only 2,000 votes—now the Communists got 10,000 votes, virtually the same number as the Social Democrats.

In Mecklenburg four out of ten workers who had voted Social Democrat three years earlier now voted Communist. These figures, of course, could be untypical of the country as a whole. But they do indicate a massive movement of allegiance within the working class, even if it is conceivable that it might not have been on the same scale everywhere.

The same point is borne out by the next round of elections, after the inflation crisis was over and the left had been routed. Despite illegality, lack of organisation and especially lack of fighting spirit, at the end of 1923 and beginning of 1924 the Communist Party at least doubled its vote in industrial areas compared with 1921. In Thuringia it received four votes for every five received by the Social Democrats and even in right wing Bavaria half as many as the SPD. It is a fair assumption that since massive numbers of workers joined strikes and demonstrations in the summer of 1923, Communist support was considerably higher then.

There seems at least some justification for the claim of the historian and former 'left' Communist Rosenberg that:

The Communist Party criticised the Cuno government and the masses flocked to it... In the summer of 1923 the KPD undoubtedly had the majority of the German proletariat behind it.[23]

Even the far from over-optimistic chairman of the party, Brandler, could claim six months later that in the industrial heartlands of the country, the Communists had the edge over the Social Democrats: 'In three places [in June]—in the Ruhr, Upper Silesia and Saxony, and later in Middle Germany, we had the leadership of the working class'.[24] And again, not long afterwards he claimed, 'We had the majority of the working class behind us...'—though from the context it is not clear whether he meant in all Germany or only in 'Berlin, the Ruhr and Saxony'.[25]

Yet at the time, in June 1923, the majority of the party leadership seem to have had no inkling of the way events were changing in their favour.

Communist policy

The first couple of months of the Ruhr occupation confronted the Communist Party with certain complex political problems. The wave of nationalism influenced considerable numbers of workers, and in the Ruhr itself, both the German employers and the French troops did their utmost to win the favour of the workers. The Communist leadership had to work out a response to the occupation that enabled it to avoid identifying with either. Much of the time it coped quite well with the situation, although at least once it went off the rails in a dubious direction.

Rote Fahne raised the slogan 'Defeat Poincaré on the Ruhr and Cuno on the Spree'. (Poincaré was the French premier; the Spree is the river that runs through Berlin.) It said that *workers* in the Ruhr would want to resist exploitation by French imperialism, but that this was quite a different aim from that of the German *employers*:

> German big business is counting on forming a trust to exploit jointly German coal and French ore. But the French want the upper hand, a 60 percent share, leaving Stinnes, Krupp and Thyssen only 40 percent. They are struggling over the 10 percent. Both of them count on the sweat of German workers, who are paid in an ever depreciating currency, to be able to sell goods abroad cheaply...
>
> The German bourgeoisie want to use hunger and the ever increasing cost of living as a means of getting the impoverished masses to march

against French imperialism. It wants to kill two birds with one stone...
To struggle for the extra 10 percent and to dismantle all the barriers to
counter-revolution erected after the Rathenau murder...the Cuno government acts as an openly counter-revolutionary government.

In this situation, the proletariat must know how to fight on two
fronts... French capitalism is no better than German capitalism, and the
bayonets of the French occupation troops no less sharp than those of the
Reichswehr.

The Communist Party asks the class conscious workers of the Ruhr
to carry on the defensive struggle against the French occupation forces
with all their energy...

Only if in the whole of Germany we march as an independent force,
as a class force fighting for its own interests, can we fight the danger
that the German bourgeoisie will be strengthened by the nationalist
intoxications.[26]

This policy meant trying to widen the scale of working class resistance to the French occupation, yet opposing the armed acts of sabotage
by the right wing terror groups. While the extreme right preached a boy-
cott against the French soldiers, the Communist Party called for fraternisation. The Communist International too worked, as it had never been
able to before, to bring about practical solidarity. A meeting of European
Communist parties was held in Essen on 6 January to organise international resistance to the occupation. A wider meeting of European socialist and trade union representatives followed in Frankfurt a couple of
months later. A special extended—and widely publicised—meeting of
the executive of the International was devoted to the Ruhr question in
June. Big public meetings were held in the main cities of France, Russia
and Germany, and the Russians sent a large consignment of grain to feed
the hungry of the Ruhr.

The French Communist Party in particular had to make special
efforts to oppose the occupation carried through by its own government. French Young Communists were urged to go to the Ruhr to agitate among the occupying forces. They were billeted with the families of
German Communists and put out a variety of papers for the troops—
titled the *Conscript*, the *Barracks*, and the *Red Flag*. Bilingual posters
were pasted up:

French soldiers, workers in uniform, you have been brought to the Rhine
on the orders of your exploiters in order to put a yoke on your proletarian

German brothers, already oppressed by their own bourgeoisie... French soldiers, your place is alongside the German workers. Fraternise with the German proletariat.[27]

It is difficult to judge how effective such propaganda was. There was certainly some response: 57 French soldiers were court martialled and received jail sentences of 130 years between them. In Paris the French government raided the Communist Party headquarters and arrested a number of leading Communists, including the party secretary, Cachin.

The agitation was probably more important, however, for its effect in fighting the nationalist current among *German* workers. When, for instance, nationalist councillors suggested that Thyssen, who had been arrested by the French, should be made honorary mayor of one Ruhr town, Hamborn, the Communists killed the proposal by moving Cachin's name, since 'he had done more for the German workers'.[28] The French occupation forces banned most of the German bourgeois papers for their nationalism—but they had to ban the Communist papers such as the *Ruhr Echo* for their *internationalism*, their appeals to French troops.

The tone of the Communist Party propaganda is conveyed by headlines in the May Day edition of *Rote Fahne*: 'The defence Hundreds in the lead', 'Red flags', 'Police provocation in Halle', 'In the Ruhr fraternisation with the French soldiers', 'Long live Cachin', 'Long live the Paris Commune', 'The *Ruhr Echo* banned by the French general', 'The Munich fascists defied'.

There were complaints inside the Communist International that the French Communist effort among the Ruhr troops was insufficient, and a French revolutionary historian has claimed since that it was ineffective,[29] but it did at least lay down the guidelines for a form of internationalist agitation quite different from that which characterised the Social Democratic labour movement.

However, there was another aspect of Communist policy which caused much more controversy—and which has come under especially bitter attack from ex-Communists who left the party during the Stalin era. This was the attempt to influence the impoverished middle classes who were under nationalist and fascist influence. The party and the International set out to win some of these people over to the revolution by explaining that only workers' power and an alliance with the Russian workers' state could overcome the misery afflicting the great mass of the

German people. The Communist aim, as Brandler put it, was to separate 'the hired Pinkerton thugs' of fascism from 'those petty bourgeois who have joined the movement from genuine nationalist disappointment'.[30]

The argument was first put by Frölich in a parliamentary speech when the occupation began:

> It is said that in the hour of danger we must all come together, we must all make sacrifices... Where are the sacrifices? The coal barons have just raised their prices 50 percent... We recognise as our brothers the French comrades who have entered into battle against Poincaré...
>
> What is to be done? Karl Marx told us that when danger threatens the whole nation, it is necessary for the working class to constitute itself as the nation by taking political power. Down with this government—then alone can the German people be saved. For the constitution of the proletariat as the nation, and on this basis the saving of the nation through the ruling proletariat...[31]

The owners of the industrial trusts, it was said, were acting against the interests of the mass of the German people; they were in fact betraying the national aims they claimed to defend. It was not a long step from this to the argument that somehow there was a national interest which Communists would defend but not the great industrialists: when Stinnes was caught negotiating with the French and when the German authorities appealed for French help in crushing the Ruhr workers, the *Rote Fahne* talked of 'the government of national treachery'.

Radek made the most famous development of the argument, in a speech to the extended meeting of the executive of the International in June. Schlageter, a right wing terrorist and former Freikorps member, had become a hero throughout the right wing nationalist circles after his execution by the French. Radek used the occasion to address these circles, attempting to show that the life of their hero had been a self-contradiction that only proletarian revolution could have resolved.

Schlageter, said Radek, had been a 'wanderer into nothing'. He had joined the Freikorps to fight in the east against Soviet Russia. The people who had sent him there hoped in that way to buy the goodwill of the French. Now the French had shot Schlageter. 'He was praised by the Stinnes press. But Stinnes lived in comfort while Schlageter sacrificed his life.'

Schlageter had first gone to the Ruhr in 1920, not to fight against the French, but to fight the working class. He had done so because he believed the workers were the 'internal enemy' who had to be crushed before the external enemy could be dealt with. But now in the Ruhr it was the same workers who were resisting the French.

The workers were prepared to fight imperialism. But how could they fight French imperialism while they were disarmed? 'The majority of the German people will only be brought to fight if there is an attack on German capitalism... Freedom for the German workers is freedom for the whole people.' Schlageter had been a 'wanderer into nothing', but he could have been 'a wanderer into the future of all mankind'.[32]

The Schlageter speech was followed by an ideological offensive against the Nazis among the Nazis' own followers. Leading Communists such as Ruth Fischer debated against Nazi spokesmen in meetings of students, for example, where the Nazis were strong and the revolutionary left was very weak.

Many of those who since attacked this policy have identified it with the National Bolshevism of Laufenberg (the Hamburg 'left Communist') which Radek himself had bitterly denounced in 1919, and with the National Communism preached by the Stalinised Communist Party of the early 1930s. Both of these made considerable concessions to the Nazis' own ideology—and in the 1930s there was also a tendency to a rabid nationalist phraseology that had little to do with working class internationalism. The tone of the Communist statements of 1923 was very different.

Frölich's talk of 'the working class constituting itself as the nation' can be faulted; certainly it is sickening to read Radek's description of a Nazi as 'comrade Schlageter'. And the attempt to win the support of the impoverished middle classes by appealing to their nationalism *encouraged* a false ideology rather than fighting it—but the overall context of the Communist statements was still one of resistance to the nationalist hysteria. It was, after all, the Communist deputies who voted in the Reichstag *against* the nationalist resolutions, while the Social Democrats voted for them.

The debates with the Nazis were a marginal tactic at a time when the party was calling, day in and day out, on the Social Democrats for a united front against the Nazis. Again, this was a far cry from the policy of Laufenberg and the KPD in the early 1930s. And, perhaps most significant, it was the Nazis who called off the series of debates—because they found it was losing them members.

The Schlageter 'turn' was an error, but not the criminal lunacy that some have said.[33]

The united front

The main burden of Communist activity in the first half of 1923 continued along the lines of the previous year—the attempt through joint activity to win the support of social democratic workers. It was this emphasis which allowed the party to grow as social democracy began to show signs of disintegration.

The general call for a united front now became a call for the Social Democrats to break with the bourgeois parties and form a 'workers' government' with the Communists. This had been increasingly the national slogan since the last months of 1922—especially after the Fourth Congress of the Communist International endorsed it in December. It found a ready response among workers in the central German states of Saxony and Thuringia.

Here the Social Democrats and Communists between them enjoyed a majority of seats in the state parliaments—but the Social Democrats insisted until early in 1923 on ruling in coalition with the bourgeois parties. Then in March 1923 the left gained control of the SPD in Saxony and a new all Social Democrat government was formed under the left Social Democrat premier Zeigner. The Communists voted for this in the state parliament in return for acceptance of the formation of a workers' self-defence force, the release of political prisoners and the organisation of 'advisory' committees based on factory councils.

The national government in Berlin was increasingly perturbed in the months that followed. 'Law and order' seemed to be collapsing in central Germany as the Proletarian Hundreds demonstrated openly, the Control Committees increasingly intervened to fix prices and the factory councils developed as nowhere else, despite sabotage from the still powerful right wing inside the SPD. But for Communists and Social Democrats alike a question mark hung over the slogan calling for a 'workers' government'. Did it mean that the Communists were prepared to govern jointly with the Social Democrats?

The question had, of course, been first raised back in the hectic days after the overthrow of the Kaiser and again in the aftermath of the Kapp putsch. On both occasions participation of Communists in a government with Social Democrats had been rejected as a matter of principle. Even the more limited idea of 'loyal opposition' to a left Social Democrat government had caused bitter controversy in March 1920.

Now, however, the leaders of the KPD and some of the leaders of the Communist International found the slogan of an SPD/KPD government very attractive. It put the Social Democrat leaders on the spot in the face of their own supporters—it proved they desired a coalition with the bourgeoisie even when the parliamentary balance of forces would enable them to do otherwise.

The result was excellent for the Communists—so long as the Social Democrat leaders refused a united government. But what if they accepted? Then the Communists themselves would be trapped, forced to operate in a 'left government' with a state machine still dominated by bourgeois officials, and to take responsibility for economic conditions which could not be solved by this feeble share of government power.

The argument over participation in the Saxon government was sharply raised in discussions, both within the KPD and within the International at the time of its Fourth Congress. It cannot be said to have been satisfactorily resolved. Thalheimer tended to be passionately for united governments, on the most minimal programme, while Lenin and Trotsky tended to insist that such a government could be formed only around a programme that contained within itself the beginnings of the destruction of the bourgeois state—especially the arming of the workers and the making of the government responsible to congresses of factory councils. Zinoviev argued strongly that the 'workers' government' should be merely a synonym for the dictatorship of the proletariat.

But none of them came to terms with a quite simple point: a slogan that could cause so much confusion among experienced Communist leaders was bound to confuse the rank and file even more, whether Communist or Social Democrat. It gave the impression that the solution to all problems lay in a different government combination, not in the taking of power by workers' councils. As Brandler, a supporter of the slogan, pointed out a year later:

> [It] led to dangerous illusions in the working class, even in our own party circles, that perhaps an intense principled agitation could have overcome. People said, 'First a bourgeois coalition, then a Social Democratic government supported by the Communists, then a Social

Democratic-Communist government, and then a Communist government without any bloody battles on the way'.[34]

The party's stress on the call for a united front and a workers' government was combined, until the summer, with the feeling that the immediate revolutionary prospect was dismal and so the only serious thing to do was to win over sections of Social Democrat workers. As Radek put it at a meeting of the KPD Central Committee on 16-17 May:

> Today we are not in a position to establish the proletarian dictatorship, because the precondition is missing, the revolutionary will among the majority of proletarians.[35]

Brandler expressed the same view at the Frankfurt international conference: 'Today we face a receding revolutionary tide.'

This had been correct in 1921 and 1922. It was still partially correct in the first quarter of 1923. But by April and May 1923 it ignored what many bourgeois commentators were noticing—that the inflation and the occupation of the Ruhr had produced a profound destabilisation of society to which a working class reaction was inevitable.

The Communist leaders did not grasp this. They pursued an aggressive united front policy—building the Hundreds, the Control Committees, the factory councils, and drawing under the influence of the party many previously Social Democratic workers. But they did these things on a purely defensive basis, without preparing their party to use the positions won in the defensive struggle to go over to the offensive.

The party was taken by surprise by the May-June strike wave: as we have seen, it took it four days to intervene effectively in the Ruhr strike. This need not in itself have mattered. It is often the case that the spontaneous militancy of workers takes established leaders, even revolutionary leaders, by surprise. But even when the party had grasped that a new militancy was developing, its posture was still defensive. It seemed to be embarrassed by the militancy of the Hundreds in the Ruhr—possibly because of the influence within them of syndicalists and former members of the KAPD. And it urged an early ending of the strike, without noticing the pressure for action that was growing elsewhere in Germany.

When strikes did break out elsewhere, the party certainly did its best to encourage them. But *Rote Fahne*, for example, did not give the impression that the party leadership realised there had been a *qualitative* change in the mood of the class. Indeed, there seems to have been a lessening of party activity during the strike wave compared with the beginning of May, when there had been a series of big propaganda meetings and mass demonstrations by the party in Berlin.

In a self critical speech some months later, Radek described the course of developments:

> The Ruhr business opened up a new phase of the development of the class struggle in Germany. We said in the resolution of the Leipzig conference [in January]: this phase will end in civil war. We were right theoretically but we did not draw the practical conclusions. We should have developed the growing mass struggle from May onwards, as the failure of the Ruhr action [the 'passive resistance'] was obvious and as the elements of social decomposition grew.[36]

Even the building of the Proletarian Hundreds, a key part of the defensive, united front strategy, does not seem to have been taken too seriously by many sections of the party. Brandler later claimed, 'I had already spoken about the need to prepare for civil war at the time of the Rathenau murder. Nothing was done, especially in Berlin...'[37]

How is this lagging behind events to be explained? There is no doubt that for the whole leadership of the party and for their mentor in the International, Radek, the experience of the March Action was decisive. They lived in fear of a repetition of the adventure they had so enthused over only two years earlier. It was to the adjustment of tactics after the March Action that Radek referred, in the speech quoted above, when describing the slowness of the party's reaction in 1923. He explained that after the March Action:

> ...we said we must first gain the masses. This period lasted until the Ruhr struggle. Then we could no longer be propagandists, but had to move over to action. But we did not move quickly enough.[38]

The leadership's timidity was aggravated by another factor. There had grown within the party after the March Action a powerful opposition faction, led by Ruth Fischer and Arkadi Maslow, and dedicated to offensive tactics at all times. They denounced the leadership for 'making concessions to social democracy', for 'opportunism', for 'standing on the ground of democracy' (meaning bourgeois democracy), for 'ideological liquidationism and theoretical revisionism'. When the tactic of the united front was formulated they denounced it bitterly. Later they formally acquiesced in it—providing it was 'from below' and not 'from above'.

The opposition's overall hostility to the united front necessarily translated itself into hostility to the 'workers' government'. But criticism from such quarters was not likely to influence those who had learnt through bitter experience the need to win over the Social Democrat workers. In the same way, Fischer and Maslow could call for a seemingly aggressive response to the Ruhr crisis—yet not provide a real alternative to the complacency of the leadership.

In February and March Fischer visited the Ruhr and began to unleash there a bitter factional campaign against the leadership. She argued that the leadership had not put forward concrete demands in the first days of the occupation. They should, she said, have called for workers' control of the mines and factories, and over the necessities of life. The struggle around these demands would have led to the workers seizing the factories. At the same time the Proletarian Hundreds should have taken over where the French had expelled the security police. Then the basis would have been laid for an immediate struggle for power throughout Germany.[39]

Instead of this 'revolutionary policy' she claimed, the leadership were offering 'support for a Social Democratic minority government'—a position which Communists should adopt 'under no circumstances'.

The leadership did not have much difficulty in exposing this as verbose nonsense. In January and February both the German and French authorities were treating the workers with kid gloves—the French claiming they had come to punish the employers not the workers, the Germans offering pay rises and 100 percent unemployment pay. In such a situation the basis did not exist for building a movement over 'control of production' and 'the necessities of life'.

What is more, had such a struggle begun, it would have played into the hands of both the French and German bourgeoisies. It would have given the French authorities an excuse to seize the mines for themselves, using 'lack of order' as an excuse; and any clashes with the French troops would have been used by the German far right to develop nationalist hysteria.

Fischer, the leadership could easily point out, was simply ignoring the most elementary facts about the consciousness of workers in January and February, the 'great passivity of the workers'. In the Ruhr conditions were 'an idyll compared with the Noske and Watter days of 1919 and 1920'.[40]

The leadership succeeded in carrying the day both at the national party congress in January (by more than two to one) and at a conference of the Ruhr districts in March (by 68 votes to 55). But the opposition had a grip on important districts of the party—Berlin, the northwest coast, and half the Ruhr. What is more, their presence ensured that the whole internal life of the party was characterised by debates as if between 'the government' and the 'opposition' within a bourgeois parliament: each side felt it was compelled to oppose any suggestion by the other on principle. Political discussion between party comrades was replaced by point scoring.

Even when the International intervened to force the two sides to work together on the leading committees, nothing was solved. For neither side was capable of understanding the qualitative change in the working class struggle that occurred in the late spring. Factionalism in the party, far from producing a dialectic of discussion that could lead to an enhanced understanding of events, merely froze both sides in irrelevant postures.

The leadership regarded the opposition (rightly) as a clock which had stopped: regardless of circumstances, they would always register the same conclusions. The opposition, for all their abuse of the leadership, at crucial moments tended to adopt the same passive conclusions as the leadership: when the real struggle broke out in the Ruhr in May Fischer had nothing to say about it.

The Anti-Fascist Day

The one attempt to reverse the defensive stance of the party did not come from the so-called 'lefts' at all, but from the party chairman, Brandler. On 12 July the front page of *Rote Fahne* bore a major statement written by him, 'To the Party'. It depicted a situation of increasing crisis, in which armed struggle could not be far away: 'The Cuno government is bankrupt. The internal and the external crises have brought it to the verge of catastrophe.'

The fascists were advancing, said Brandler. Their attacks on the working class could take different forms:

The attack of the fascists need not begin with a Kapp putsch; it can begin with the imposition of military rule on Saxony and Thuringia; or with the proclamation of a separatist Rhineland-Westphalian republic. It can follow on from an attack on the wage struggles of workers.... [In any case] we are on the verge of bitter struggles. We must be entirely ready to act.

It would be necessary to draw Social Democratic and non-party workers into this action, said Brandler:

Our party must develop the combativity of its organisation until they are not surprised by the unleashing of civil war... The attack of the fascists can only be put down by opposing Red Terror to White Terror. If the armed fascists shoot on workers, we must be prepared to annihilate them. If they put up against the wall one worker in six, we must shoot one fascist in five. In the spirit of Karl Liebknecht and Rosa Luxemburg, into battle!

The same issue of *Rote Fahne* announced that a fortnight later, on 29 July, there would be a national Anti-Fascist Day of demonstrations. Clearly, this was the day on which the offensive against the right would be unleashed.

Brandler's call was taken as an indication that the Communists were abandoning their defensive posture. The great strikes had shown the scale of popular bitterness. The party seemed about to channel this into a battle for control of the streets on 29 July. The bourgeois press claimed the call was nothing less than a call for the launching of civil war. Yet it attracted support from sections of the Social Democratic workers and unaffiliated trade unionists, whose local organisations put their names to it.

What this united action could mean was shown in Frankfurt on 23 July. A joint demonstration of the KPD and SPD took over the streets of the city, closing the shops and forcing middle class passers-by to chant slogans such as, 'The exploiters to the gallows' and 'No justice without blood'.[41]

The national Social Democratic leaders were certainly forced on to the defensive. They tried to proscribe their members from joining the Proletarian Hundreds. Then SPD ministers took the initiative in banning the Anti-Fascist Day demonstrations in the states that they controlled (excepting Saxony, Thuringia and Württemberg)—an example the other states were only too willing to copy. If the Communists went ahead with their demonstrations, they would risk armed confrontation with the security police in the main cities, possibly with the army.

The bans brought to the surface the reservations of many leading Communists towards Brandler's initiative of 12 July. 'This call had a peculiar effect on the party,' Brandler told later. 'In the working masses it caused hope, but in the ranks of the party functionaries they thought, "Brandler is deranged and will make a putsch again".' He claimed that 'this was especially the case in Berlin', the centre of the 'left'.[42]

The announcement of the bans caused disarray in the leadership. Most saw it as an excuse to retreat from Brandler's 'derangement'. Brandler himself still wanted an offensive tactic. He suggested defying the ban where the balance of forces would enable the Communists to provide some sort of armed protection so that the police would avoid attacking demonstrations—in the Prussian province of Saxony, in the Ruhr, in Upper Silesia, as well as in Saxony and Thuringia. In this way the party would show that it was able to defy the authorities without running the risk of engaging in bloody street battles while the mass of the working class stood on the sidelines.

Brandler found that not only did most of the 'majority' in the leadership oppose him; he also got no real support from the 'left' opposition. The leader of the 'lefts', Ruth Fischer, was mainly concerned that her own bastion, Berlin, was not included in Brandler's scheme. When Brandler asked her if the Berlin district could provide armed protection for a demonstration, she called him an 'adventurer' and a 'fascist'.

Opposed by both the majority and the opposition, Brandler hesitated. He had made a mistake in 1921 by launching a premature action and he was not going to do so again. So he repeated his other mistake of 1921—he turned to men who were isolated from detailed knowledge of German events to decide upon a tactical question. He telegraphed Moscow for advice.

But there was no one in Moscow to give advice. Lenin was paralysed and on the verge of death. The rest of the Russian leadership, with the sole exception of Radek—who had blundered as much as Brandler in 1921—were holidaying to recover from a gruelling conference. The first farce, Brandler telegraphing Moscow, was now followed by a second, Radek telegraphing the most distant parts of Russia for the individual opinions of leaders who did not have even second hand knowledge of the political situation in Germany.

Zinoviev and Bukharin were for an offensive tactic—but Radek knew that they too had been wrong in 1921. Stalin (this was one of the first times anyone had bothered to ask his advice about international questions) insisted that the German party would have to be held back. As he explained a few days later, 'If power in Germany fell today and the Communists took hold of it, it would end in a fracas'.[43] Trotsky alone was honest enough to admit that he had not the faintest idea of the situation on the ground in Germany and could say nothing.

Radek was effectively left to choose between the contradictory positions. Fearing a 1921-style attempt to 'force the struggle', he telegraphed back to Brandler, 'The Presidium of the International advises abandoning the demonstrations'.[44]

The planned demonstrations were replaced by meetings, except in Saxony, Thuringia and Württemberg where the demonstrations had not been banned. The meetings were large: 200,000 took part in meetings in Berlin, 50,000 in Chemnitz, 30,000 in Leipzig, 25,000 at Gotha, 20,000 in Dresden, 100,000 altogether in Württemberg. But they were an anticlimax. They did not challenge the fascists or the government, except in words. The party had effectively dropped the offensive opened up by Brandler's call of 12 July. Instead of unleashing and politically directing the militancy that had been building up within the working class since mid-May, the party had returned to the defensive posture developed in 1922.

In the Communist press the call 'to arms' was replaced by advice from Radek: 'We must always keep in mind that we are still at this moment weak. We cannot yet offer a general battle.' Brandler himself now insisted at a meeting of the Central Committee of 5-6 August that what they were preparing for was 'a defensive revolutionary struggle'.

Yet the abandonment of the short-lived offensive turn by the party came only days before the workers of Berlin unleashed the most significant strike wave yet.

1.   J C Favez, *La Reich devant l'Occupation Français Belge de la Ruhr en 1923* (Geneva 1969) p224.
2.   Helmut Gast, 'Die Proletarischen Hundertschaftten als Organe der Einheitsfront im Jahre 1923' in *Zeitschrift für Geschechtwissenschaft* 1956, p442.
3.   Ibid, p445.
4.   Ibid.
5.   Ibid, p452.

6. J C Favez, op cit, p90.
7. *Rote Fahne*, 2 May 1923.
8. See H Gast, op cit, p444; and W Ersil, *Aktionseinheit stürtzt Cuno* (Berlin 1961) p94-100.
9. J C Favez, op cit, p229.
10. W Ersil, op cit, p17.
11. J C Favez, op cit, pp238-239.
12. Quoted ibid, p240.
13. *Rote Fahne*, 30 May 1923.
14. W Ersil, op cit, p109.
15. *Rote Fahne*, 21 June 1923.
16. Quotes from J C Favez, op cit, pp248-249.
17. Ibid, p222.
18. Quoted ibid, p228.
19. Arthur Rosenberg, *A History of the German Republic* (London 1936) p193.
20. J C Favez, op cit, p230.
21. Remmele in *Die Lehren der Deutschen Ereignisse*, Presidium of the Communist International, June 1924.
22. Figures and examples from Pierre Broué, *Révolution en Allemagne* (Paris 1971) pp682-683.
23. A Rosenberg, op cit, p194.
24. *Die Lehren der Deutschen Ereignisse*, op cit, pp28-29, 32.
25. Ibid, p32.
26. *Rote Fahne*, 23 January 1923.
27. Text in J C Favez, op cit, p40.
28. *Bulletin Communiste*, 8 March 1923 (Paris).
29. P Broué, op cit, p660.
30. Quoted in Werner Angress, *Stillborn Revolution* (Princeton 1963) p318.
31. The whole text is in Michaelis and Schlapper, *Ursachen und Folgen vom Deutschen Zusammenbruch 1918 bis 1945, zur Staatlichen Neuordnung Deutschlands in der Gegenwart, 5. Das Kritische Jahr 1923*, pp37-39.
32. Karl Radek, reproduced ibid, p141.
33. An important role here has been played by the completely inaccurate book by the one-time 'left Communist' leader Ruth Fischer, *Stalin and German Communism*. The stories, once circulated, have influenced many otherwise excellent works. Even Tony Cliff, in his *Lenin* vol 3, falls for some of the exaggerated stories. For a balanced account that weighs the historical evidence correctly, see E H Carr, *The Interregnum* (London 1954) pp179-185.
34. *Die Lehren der Deutschen Ereignisse*, op cit, p30.
35. Quoted in W Angress, op cit, p318.
36. *Die Lehren der Deutschen Ereignisse*, op cit, p14.
37. Ibid, p31.
38. Ibid, p16.

39. A summary of these positions is contained in *Material zu Differenzien mit der Opposition KPD* (Berlin 1923) pp17-18.

40. Ibid, p7.

41. *Rote Fahne*, 24 July 1923. Compare also W Angress, op cit, p365.

42. *Die Lehren der Deutschen Ereignisse*, op cit, p31.

43. Quoted in E H Carr, op cit, p187.

44. Ibid.

CHAPTER 13
The German October

The summer of 1923 was when inflation reached lunatic proportions. Until then money had declined in value by the week and month, but it was still possible to make some sense of it. Now it depreciated by the hour. The external value of the mark against the dollar halved about every four days in July and August. And for the first time the buying power of the mark in Germany itself began to decline more rapidly than its international value.

The mass of the population became really desperate.

> In the Berlin markets the price of potatoes, eggs and butter was changed six times a day... Barter trade widely replaced cash transactions. People had to offer their last pieces of jewellery and furniture in order to get their daily bread... The angry and desperate masses became unruly and there were riots all over Germany.[1]

A significant change began to take place in the lot of workers. There had been more or less full employment until midsummer outside the occupied areas of the Ruhr, even if the small number of unemployed did starve. But from the end of July onwards the inflationary boom petered out and many firms went to the wall: by the time they got their takings to the banks, the money was worth too little to replenish stocks. Unemployment, virtually nil at the beginning of the year, reached 6 percent in August and 23 percent in November. Vast numbers of workers were also on short time.

But at first the level of unemployment did not affect the militancy and confidence of the workers' organisations in the factories. At the end of July another wave of strikes began, similar to those in May and June, but on a much greater scale and with greater political consequences.

In Saxony a strike of 20,000 miners had broken out on 25 July. 3,000 of the strikers stormed into the headquarters of the employers' federation and ransacked it. On the same day industrialists from eleven factories in the Saxon town of Aue were forced to give in to wage demands after threats from armed demonstrations. In Schneeberg a week later the Proletarian Hundreds seized control of a great quantity of food. On 1 August workers from the factories of eight neighbouring towns besieged wage negotiations which were taking place in Aue. On 6 August it was the turn of 4,000 metal workers in Pobeln to take to the streets. The Hundreds physically dragged employers to negotiations and forced them to make concessions.

As reports to the Reich Ministry of the Interior complained, 'Force was used to make the employers negotiate, without the union leaders or the police being able to intervene'.[2] In Chemnitz 150,000 workers marched through the streets demanding the overthrow of the government.

In the first week of August the movement spread to other parts of Germany. There were big demonstrations in Stuttgart. In Stettin the dock workers struck. In Brandenburg striking agricultural workers started looting. In Magdeburg the agricultural workers struck on 9 August.

Meanwhile, in the Ruhr-Rhine area, 200,000 miners began a go-slow despite an 87 percent wage increase at the end of June. It had already been absorbed by price increases. 'Demonstrations and meetings against price rises multiplied...clashes with the police occurred after a congress of the unemployed and those with emergency employment in government workshops on 28-29 July'.[3] These cost two lives in Oberhausen.

The inflation began to create food shortages that made the inflation itself worse: the peasants would not sell footstuffs for paper money; shops closed down because owners could not afford to replenish their stocks. By the time an arbitration board awarded the Ruhr miners 90-110 percent wage rises on 2 August, its value had already been eaten away.

> In the mines and heavy industry, spirits did not calm down. Special allocations of wages were demanded. It was in vain that the central workers' organisations obtained on 9 August an increase of 245 percent... The troubles spread.[4]

This was not surprising. The price of coal quadrupled in a single day on 9 August. The cost of some basic necessities in the Ruhr rose by 20 times in the same month. In Berlin there were already sporadic strikes in the engineering factories at the beginning of August and partial strikes on the municipal railway system. *Rote Fahne* reported a strike by the white collar workers in the engineering industry. The Borsig factory struck on 9 August, then the Metro workshops. But it was the strike by the print workers the same day that brought the movement to a head.

The print strike was official—but the union leaders did not want to involve the 8,000 workers in the government print works. The Communists succeeded in bringing these out—and hit the government where it really hurt. For the printing presses which had been pouring out ever greater streams of currency notes ground to a halt. Suddenly the mighty flow of paper money needed to keep up with soaring prices stopped. The whole economy threatened to collapse.

The Communist leaders at last grasped the scale of events: they immediately began to agitate for a general strike to bring down the Cuno government and to put in its place a 'workers' government'. The huge Siemens works in Berlin followed Borsig in striking, and in turn was followed by another eleven big factories. And now the demands were not only economic, but for the overthrow of the government. The city transport services came to a complete standstill, then the water, gas and electricity workers struck.

Outside Berlin there was a complete stoppage of the Saxon mining areas[5] and the armed organisations of workers showed their strength as never before: 'the Control Committees seemed to dominate the markets'.[6] In the western regions of the country, as reports to the Ministry of the Interior told:

> Despite the unions, the general strike paralyses Solingen and hits Krefeld, Homburg, Aachen, Kleve, Opladen, Stoppenberg, etc. Unemployed and strikers are looting the countryside for food... By the dozen, complaints and appeals from employers fall on the table of the Ministry of the Interior... On the left bank of the Rhine miners partially occupy installations and chase out management... In some mines scaffolds are erected with notices, 'This is for you if you do not pay our demands within 24 hours'.[7]

On 11 August a conference of factory and pit councils for the Ruhr met in Essen and set demands for the strike in the region. As well as calling for the overthrow of the Cuno government and the formation of a workers' government, the conference demanded pre-war real wages, the six hour day in the pits and the seizure of the necessities of life for distribution by the Control Committees. In Hamburg the shipyards were paralysed, and there was shooting in the streets of Hanover, Lübeck and Neurode.

Back in Berlin the unions couldn't ignore the pressure from their members. They were impelled to give at least an impression of leading the movement. They called a special meeting with representatives of the SPD, the rump USP and the Communists on 10 August. The Communists reiterated their call for the general strike. For a time, some of the deeply reformist trade union leaders seemed to waver in this direction. They were worried they might lose all face with their members if they opposed the call; but they were equally worried that if they endorsed the call a movement would result which they would be unable to control. One of the SPD delegates was the old foe of the revolution in 1919, Otto Wels. He argued that the strike was anarchy, adventurism, chaos—and just as, he claimed, the government was pushing through an emergency economic package which would begin to improve matters. His intervention tipped the balance within the trade union leadership. The general strike was refused.

But the Communists knew that the rank and file of the unions were in no mood to listen to the warnings from their leaders. A circular was sent to all party districts:

> Information received indicates that a situation similar to that in Berlin exists throughout the country. Everywhere there are go-slows and strikes. It is necessary to draw together these movements and bring them to a head. We must try to get the local committees of the ADGB [the main union federation] to take the lead of the spontaneous movement. Where that is not possible the factory councils must direct and organise the movement.

It was precisely for such an occasion that the Communists had attempted over the previous year to build up local and national organisations of factory councils outside the control of the union bureaucracies. The committee of 15 elected at the National Conference of the Councils the previous year now came into its own. It called a meeting of delegates from the Berlin factory councils for the next day (11 August).

'The great hall was over full', recalls one of the participants:

The streets outside were packed with cars and vans that the factory councils had seized from the factories so as to have rapid transport for the workers. In the side streets were police wagons, which did not, however, intervene.[8]

There are various estimates of the numbers present. The French historian Broué gives a figure of 2,000, the Swiss historian Favez, using official documents, says that '10,000 enterprise committees were represented'[9] and the East German Ersil writes that 'there assembled about 20,000 factory committees, among them thousands of Social Democrats'.[10] Regardless of the exact numbers, one thing is clear. The apparently weak movement of factory councils of nine months before had now generated a force capable of uniting the working class independently of the trade union bureaucrats.

The meeting called for an immediate general strike with the following demands: the overthrow of the Cuno government; the formation of a workers' government; the requisitioning of the necessities of life under the control of workers' organisations; an immediate minimum wage of 60 gold pfennigs; the lifting of the ban on the Proletarian Hundreds.

The committee of 15 outlined directions for the general strike—the election of strike committees, the organisation of Control Committees and Proletarian Hundreds, the disarming by the Hundreds of fascist groups, propaganda to and fraternisation with the soldiers and police.

The police seized a special issue of *Rote Fahne* that was meant to publicise the call by the factory councils. But if the repressive action was intended to stop the movement spreading, it was ineffective. Berlin was completely paralysed by the strike.

> [It was] a capital deprived of water, gas, electricity, newspapers—dead and yet at the same time full of tension, as meetings and demonstrations multiplied.[11]

The call from Berlin gave added impetus to movements outside the capital. In Halle 1,500 workers attended a local factory council congress—339 of them delegates from the pits who voted by 320 votes to 19 for the general strike. Seventy SPD delegates were among those overwhelmingly in favour.[12] The strike was effective both in the Halle-Merseburg area and in traditionally more Social Democratic Magdeburg.

Workers marched from pit to pit and from factory to factory spreading the action.

The general strike was a little slower spreading in Saxony and Thuringia—it was not until 13-14 August that it really got under way. But it was still possible for a Dr Weigel to complain in the state parliament on the 14th of 'terror' during wage negotiations, which were 'again and again taking place in the face of local demonstrations' which 'threatened employers' leaders'—for instance in Aue, Schneeberg and Annsberg.[13]

As the strike spread throughout the country, it led to a wave of demonstrations and street clashes:

> In all the large towns the strike spread... On 12 August there were clashes between demonstrators and police in Hanover, Rotthausen, Gelsenkirchen, with 30 dead. On the 13th there were new demonstrations, more gunfire, with six dead in Wilhelmshaven, 30 in Hanover, 15 in Greisz, ten in Aachen, 20 at Zeitz, 30 at Jena, one in Breslau, four in Krefeld, four at Ratiber. In Halle and Leipzig the workers' Hundreds requisitioned livestock from the surrounding countryside and organised its distribution to workers.[14]

There have been many arguments since as to the exact scale of the movement. Historians such as Ersil, Broué and Favez tend to portray it as a huge upheaval. By contrast the American historian Angress treats it as little more than a storm in a teacup. He admits that the strike call 'received a surprisingly strong response from several occupational groups in Berlin', but claims that 'even there it never developed as a general strike'. Elsewhere he writes, 'The whole of south Germany and the Ruhr remained unaffected'.

But this is both to ignore the official documentation of the strike movement given by Favez and Ersil, and to treat the general strike in isolation from the partial strikes which preceded it, especially in the Ruhr. Certainly these were days which worried the most perceptive sections of German capitalism. Stresemann, the leader of the German National People's Party, told the British ambassador:

> He [Stresemann] was of the opinion that the Communists could not let the occasion pass... All the circumstances spoke in their favour. There would never be offered to them again such an occasion. Stresemann said,

'I am frightened of two things, an immediate Communist success and the huge nationalistic reaction it will unleash...'[15]

The general strike came when the government was, in any case, at the end of its tether. Its attempts to solve the Ruhr crisis through British pressure had just failed. It had no answer to the inflation. And now the whole working class seemed to have fallen under Communist influence. Cuno, the 'strong man' of eight months ago, with dreams of a personal dictatorship, said he now felt 'too tired' to go on.

German capitalism found reassurance, as so often before, in the attitude of social democracy. On 10 August the SPD deputies allowed Cuno to win a vote for his financial measures. By the 12th the general strike was making them change their attitude—'benevolent neutrality' could no longer keep Cuno in power. The question was now, what sort of government should replace him? The SPD leadership decided to vote against Cuno, but offered to *join* a government run by his party colleague, Stresemann—Stresemann, the spokesman for a powerful section of German employers, the head of a party dependent on Stinnes' money, became premier.

He was only too happy to have four Social Democrat ministers:

In some political circles the situation was regarded as similar to that of the fall of 1918: just as the entry of the socialists into the cabinet of Prince Max had been necessary, so the crisis of 1923 also was supposed to require the participation in the government of the strongest working class party.[16]

The decision to join the government caused a further intensification of the arguments inside the party: 53 of the 171 Social Democrats abstained in the Reichstag vote of confidence in the new government. For, as the pro Social Democrat historian Landauer writes, 'it was a humiliation to take part in a federal government with the German National People's Party.'

Nevertheless a government was stitched together that brought together all the parties separating the revolutionary left from the fascist right—with members ranging from the 'Marxist' economist and former USP leader Hilferding to those who dreamed, with Stinnes and Cuno, of a right wing dictatorship.

The lull

The immediate impact of the new government was to take the sting out of the general strike. Its main demand had been 'Down with the Cuno government'—and the Cuno government had fallen.

The demand had, of course, been coupled with the call to replace Cuno by a 'workers' government'. But implementing that demand meant dealing with an obstacle that individual groups of strikers did not believe they could remove: the Social Democrat leaders were refusing to have anything to do with a workers' government, and every worker knew that. A continued call for such a government could be a propaganda slogan, exposing the pro-capitalist inclinations of the SPD leaders, but it did not seem to any wide section of workers an immediately achievable objective to be obtained by further strike action.

At the same time it was fairly easy for the biggest individual employers to meet many of the strikers' wage demands: such was the rate of inflation that wages doubled today would be quartered in a week's time.

Finally, the financial pressures on workers to get back to their jobs were immense. The strike funds of union sections and the savings of individual workers had been made virtually valueless by the inflation. Not to get a daily wage meant starvation—unless the strike became more than a strike and led to a revolutionary seizure of foodstuffs. Long strikes were no longer physically possible for workers. The choice was a return to work or a revolution—and no one had yet made preparations for a revolution.

The general strike began to collapse in Berlin, Brandler later recorded, despite the attempts of the Communists to continue it 'for at least another 24 hours' as a strike against the new Grand Coalition.

> Although we in the Centre decided not to end the strike after three days, our radical Berlin comrades could not implement the decision, but ended the strike despite our decisions, since its inner forces were exhausted.[17]

The *Rote Fahne* of 14 August carried the front page headline 'Millions involved in struggle'. But the return to work continued in Berlin, and by mid-afternoon a special edition of the paper called for 'A united end to the strike'. 'The strike has been called off,' it added, 'Let us prepare for the next one.' The would-be 'left', Ruth Fischer, explained to a meeting of the factory councils the need for them all to return to work (which did not stop her later attacking Brandler for the decision!)

Was there no way in which the strike could have been continued?

Brandler claimed this was possible in mid-Germany and Saxony, where the strike did not start in earnest until *after* the Cuno government had fallen. But that was because it was a much more *political* strike there than in Berlin, and the workers were almost ready to go over to a revolutionary offensive. But in Berlin itself, he argued, the strike was still basically 'economic', like the May-June wave of strikes in central Germany, Silesia and the Ruhr.

> The Cuno strike was nothing more than the continuation in Berlin of the revolutionary wages struggle in the Ruhr, Saxony and Upper Silesia. But such a struggle in Berlin had a quite different significance from the Ruhr, Saxony or Upper Silesia. The strike produced the government crisis and the fall of the Cuno government. But it was only in its effects a political strike, not in the sense of setting itself conscious political goals.
>
> When the resignation of Cuno was achieved, the force of the strike was broken. No one can claim we could have led this into a struggle against the building of the Cuno government.[18]

By contrast, 'The Saxon comrades were entering not into an economic but a political strike, which signified the beginning of an armed rising.' But Berlin was not ready for this and Saxony could not go ahead alone.

Brandler's account certainly makes sense of the immediate turn of events. It does suggest that the real weakness of the movement lay in Berlin (and the northwest coast) where the united front approach had only been carried through half-heartedly by the local 'left' leaderships of the party. But it leaves open one question: would things not have been a little different if the party had moved (as Brandler himself had suggested) from the defensive to the offensive two or three weeks *before* the strike broke—if it had not retreated on the Anti-Fascist Day of demonstrations—and if it had raised a *clearer* slogan than for the 'workers' government'?

In any case, the immediate aftermath of the strike was a downturn in the level of struggle. The wages struggle in the Ruhr mines, for instance, came to a rapid end, despite the fact that an additional 50 percent on top of the miners' 245 percent wage increase did not keep up with the 2,000 percent a month price rises.[19]

Hunger and anger did not disappear. Far from it. The level of misery rose as prices began to be measured in billions and trillions of marks.

There were more reports of the looting of fields in the Ruhr region; food riots led to 13 dead in Aachen;[20] on 27-28 August the unemployed seized the town hall at Plauen; in the second week of September 13 people were killed when the Dresden police attacked a demonstration with clubs and then opened fire (although the Saxon police chief was a 'left' Social Democrat).

But these incidents did not combine to make up a national movement as on 9-13 August. Any great strike is followed by a certain, inevitable demoralisation: the exhilaration of the demonstration and the mass picket is followed by the humiliation of clocking on and obeying the foreman. This time the return to work was accompanied by a very sharp rise in unemployment as the inflationary boom turned into an inflationary slump. As the dole queues lengthened and workers began to fear for their jobs, the employers went over to the offensive. The week after the general strike there were 100,000 sackings—including many of the militants.

The forces of the state also began now to take their revenge. Two hundred strikers were arrested, the Communist press was banned, and the Prussian Interior Ministry issued edicts outlawing both the 'Committee of 15' of the national organisation of factory councils and the Greater Berlin factory councils committee. In the Ruhr the French 'enemy' lent a hand, and banned five Communist papers.

Towards revolution?

One immediate effect of the Cuno strike was to waken the international Communist movement—and the leaders of the Russian Communist Party—to what was happening in Germany. Already on 15 August Zinoviev, the president of the Comintern, was writing, 'The crisis is approaching... A new and decisive chapter is beginning in the activity of the German Communist Party and the Comintern'.[21] Trotsky, on holiday in the Crimea, summoned two of the German Communist leaders resident in Moscow, Walcher and Enderle, to see him and questioned them at length about what was happening. The Russian leaders then rushed back to Moscow and held a special Politburo meeting on 23 August. Here Trotsky outlined a view with which everyone else present (including Radek) seemed to agree.

The moment was fast approaching, he said, for a decisive struggle for power in Germany, the German October. There were only a few weeks to prepare for it, and everything must be subordinated to this preparation.

Of the Russian leaders only Stalin was less optimistic—he thought they needed to wait until spring 1924 at the earliest.[22]

A few days later the key leaders of the German party (including representatives of the 'left') were invited to Moscow to discuss the preparations for an armed rising.

The German leadership itself had already in mid-August moved from the defensive to the offensive. *Rote Fahne* published a chapter of a book on civil war, and it advised the national committee of the workers' councils to defy the government ban. Now *Rote Fahne* took up the call of the Russian leadership: on 2 September it published a Comintern appeal written by Trotsky which explained, 'Germany is moving towards revolution'.

The German party chairman, Brandler, had doubts about the insurrectionary perspective. He claimed later that Radek shared these doubts: 'Radek was convinced of the unreality of all these decisions'.[23] But Brandler was soon overawed by the arguments of Trotsky and Zinoviev: 'I did not oppose the preparations for a rising in 1923', he later wrote. 'I simply did not view the situation as acutely revolutionary yet, reckoning rather with a further sharpening. But in this affair I regarded Trotsky, Zinoviev and the other Russian leaders as more competent'.[24]

It was decided that the whole might of the International and the German party should begin the technical preparations for the insurrection. Trotsky even wanted a date to be set for it:

The Communist Party has no use for the great liberal law according to which revolutions happen but are never made and therefore cannot be fixed for a specific date. From a spectator's point of view this law is correct, but from the standpoint of the leader this is a platitude and a vulgarity... [In a] country which is passing through a profound social crisis, when the contradictions become aggravated in the extreme, when the toiling masses are in constant ferment, when the party is obviously supported by an unquestionable majority of the toilers and, in consequence, by the most active, class conscious and self sacrificing elements of the proletariat, then the task confronting the party is to fix a definite time in the immediate future...and then to concentrate every effort on the preparation for the blow, to subordinate the entire policy and organisation to the military object in view, so that this blow is dealt with maximum power.[25]

Brandler and Radek objected to the idea of a fixed day for the revolution (Trotsky had suggested the anniversary of the Russian Revolution, 7 November), but they were sufficiently persuaded by Trotsky's approach to suggest that he be sent to Germany to prepare the rising.

The suggestion was rejected. But the Comintern did move as never before in an effort to seize a revolutionary opportunity: in the later history of the Comintern only the interventions in China in the mid-1920s and Spain in the late 1930s were on a greater scale—and these were not interventions aimed, as in Germany, at promoting *proletarian* revolution.

The German party already had a secret military organisation, the M-Apparat (and also a spy organisation, the T—for Terror—Apparat). The M-Apparat had been strengthened with the help of Russian Red Army experts the year before. Now a Red Army general, Gorev, was sent to Germany to transform this into a mechanism capable of waging a civil war. He divided Germany into six politico-military commands, corresponding to the country's six military regions. These in turn were split into districts and sub-districts. At each level was a chain of command, linking up 'struggle leaders' charged with training Proletarian Hundreds and leading them into battle.

A revolutionary committee presided over the whole structure. It had at its disposal both a number of Russian officers and many Germans with experience either in the World War or the Red Armies of 1919 and 1920. Among them, for example, were Wilhelm Zaisser, later the General Gomez of the Spanish Civil War, and Albert Scheiner and Hans Kahle, respectively Major Schrindler and Colonel Hans in that war.

The core of the Red troops on the ground was to be provided by the Proletarian Hundreds. They were 60,000 strong according to Brandler;[26] 100,000 strong and mostly former frontline fighters according to the East German historian Cast.[27] There were 300 separate Hundreds in May and 800 in October.

Each Hundred was based on a factory or working class district and organised like a military battalion. The basic unit was a 'group' of 12, three groups forming a 36 man 'column', and three columns together with cyclists and a medical team forming a Hundred. Most of their strength was in Saxony and Thuringia, where they were able to operate openly: 8,000 marched through Dresden on 9 September; 5,000 through Leipzig on 16 September. They were mainly made up of Communists; but in Saxony at least there were non-Communists and Social Democrats at every level.[28]

But not only the Hundreds would have to act when the day came. The whole party was mobilised as for war, with leaders at national and local level going into hiding to avoid pre-emptive arrest. 'There was not a city in the country', wrote a French Communist who was in Germany during those weeks:

> where the Communists had not prepared for the battle with the detailed concern of men determined to give everything. There was not a day without eager work, not a night without a special task. Not a problem was neglected. I know comrades who did not sleep a full night for weeks at a time.[29]

The tone of the party press was strident enough. There were continual allusions to the struggle for power: for instance, a poem which called, 'Proudly form ranks for the final struggle—unite, be brave till victory's here'; or a headline, 'The road to the proletarian dictatorship in Germany'. The papers were banned—but appeared often enough in semi-legal editions. And their sales rose rapidly, despite the fact that sales of the rest of the daily press were slumping.

Yet even at this stage not everything was going well. Many leading figures in the party had no notion of how to connect the still vague and apparently distant goal of fighting for power with the day-to-day struggles of the class. They were holding back the workers from 'premature actions'—but did not always grasp the alternative for which they were preparing. At the end of August the party's leading theoretician, Thalheimer, was still writing:

> It is necessary to travel a long road, as much on the political as on the organisational plain, before arriving at the conditions necessary for ensuring victory for the working class.[30]

According to Ruth Fischer (an unreliable witness), major party leaders were saying:

In no circumstances must we proclaim the general strike. The bourgeoisie will discover our plans and destroy us before we have moved. On the contrary, we must calm the masses, hold back our people in the factories and the unemployed committees until the government thinks the moment of danger has passed.[31]

The result, inevitably, was a conspiratorialism more usually found in terrorist groups than in mass revolutionary parties. Meanwhile, work among the mass of workers tended to be neglected.

Brandler later claimed that while he was in Moscow—a period of a month—'there was lacking in the party a vigorous political campaign'.[32] The fact that Brandler, the ablest leader of the party, was in Moscow at this crucial time, could not have helped. Remmele, a party leader who opposed Brandler's view of most things, agreed on this:

All other party work, the mobilising of the masses, the pulling together of the factory councils, was neglected while our whole party apparatus and our functionaries worried about the problem of armaments and the organisation of armed action... So all the bridges leading to the working class were neglected.[33]

Yet the working class itself was growing more desperate than ever. Unemployment, after doubling in August, grew in the Ruhr from 110,000 at the beginning of September to 160,000 at the end of October. Alongside the unemployed were five or six million workers on short time. Prices were rising as never before (or since): the cost of living increased by 165 percent between 13 and 19 September. The average wage was estimated to be less than half the subsistence level for a family of four. In Lübeck real wages were said to be down to 15 to 20 percent of their pre-war level.[34] It took an hour's work by a miner to earn enough money to buy *one* egg.

Partial, economic strikes were now much less frequent. The level of unemployment made victimisation an all-too-likely outcome. The lockout became more common than the strike. But the bitterness could still explode on the streets. In the relatively backward province of Baden, rioting broke out in the small town of Lorrach, with looting of street markets and shops. Striking workers stormed the jail and released prisoners.

On 14 September the town was in the hands of the extreme left... In the following days strikes and violence spread to neighbouring towns, to Mülheim, Sackingen, Heidelberg, Karlsruhe... The Baden workers marched with Soviet flags towards Lorrach, where the state police intervened. The post and railway traffic was interrupted.[35]

In the occupied territories, the anger found a slightly different expression. Right wing Rhenish separatist groups attempted, with French encouragement, to develop an agitation. But Communist led workers fought against the police and the separatists, resulting in many casualties. It was Düsseldorf's 'Red Sunday' (30 September).

September saw continual strikes in central Germany—especially a big textile strike in Saxony—and a '150,000 strong strike in the occupied territories, where adjustment of wages loses all sense because of the inability to create an index fast enough'.[36]

An English resident in Germany at the time described the general atmosphere in his diary:

With a wage of 100 milliards, which is about the average paid this week, a man is faced with semi-starvation... Men are being discharged daily from the shipyards and the factories, and the state pays a most miserable dole. Men, women and children in hundreds are on the verge of starvation, and it is small wonder that the shops are plundered and Bolshevism is gaining recruits every day.[37]

In such an atmosphere there was a perceptible shift to the left among workers who remained with the Social Democrats. A new left wing emerged in the SPD which rejected the Grand Coalition and called for collaboration with the Communists. Its best known leaders were the old USP leaders Crispien and Dittmann, the Saxon premier Zeigner, and the former Communist leader, Paul Levi. But, more significantly, it commanded the allegiance of some of the best known working class leaders in places such as Zwickau and Plauen.

'This opposition', reported a Communist in October:

has begun to enjoy great successes throughout the country. It is dominant in most of central Germany. It has penetrated the old districts of the right such as Cologne and Hamburg. The leadership of the Breslau district has come out for the dictatorship of the proletariat. On 9 September the opposition won a clear majority at the general meeting of the Berlin district... The [right wing] Lipinski group has been defeated in its Leipzig citadel.[38]

The widespread and generally successful economic strikes of May–June and early August were a thing of the past in the new climate of mass unemployment, but a blind, desperate anger remained in the class, capable of being ignited by the correct spark.

Stresemann, Bavaria, Saxony

By late September the Stresemann government seemed in almost as bad a state as the Cuno government that had gone before it. Inflation was worse than ever and was now accompanied by a rapid fall in production. The central government's orders were hardly obeyed in Bavaria, where the extreme right was more firmly entrenched than ever—100,000 paramilitaries paraded in front of Ludendorff and Hitler at the beginning of the month. The government's orders were equally ignored by the left Social Democrat governments in Saxony and Thuringia. In the Ruhr and Rhine regions, 'the tension was such that only a rapid end to passive resistance appeared able to stop an explosion'.[39]

The great industrialists decided that things had finally gone too far. The 'weapon' of inflation was finally turning against them, and the 'resistance' in the Ruhr was costing too much. On 21 September Stinnes told the American ambassador, 'This is the end. The Ruhr and Rhine must capitulate.' He added that the workers would have to work longer and harder and that there was 'need for a dictator'.[40] Helferrich, head of the Reichsbank and architect of the money printing policy, now felt that 'the collapse of the mark threatened the nation with catastrophe'.

Stresemann obeyed his masters' voice on 26 September and announced the end of passive resistance. An emergency economic programme was planned which aimed to establish a stable currency. For the first time Stinnes and company cooperated with the government by agreeing to pay reparations in kind.

The decision represented a crucial turning point for the ruling class. The inflation and the occupation of the Ruhr continued, but for the first time since March there was the feeling in ruling circles that a coherent policy was being followed which could get the country out of the mess. And this self-confidence was the precondition for re-establishing an ideological hold over the classes below them.

There were still difficult problems to deal with. The industrialists demanded as the price for their collaboration in the anti-inflationary policy the abrogation of the eight hour day. The Social Democratic parliamentary fraction knew this and resisted giving emergency economic powers to the government through an Enabling Act. A minor crisis followed, which ended with the removal of Hilferding from the government. But two Social Democrat ministers remained and finally, on 15 October, the Enabling Act passed with Social Democrat support. Even Angress, who generally tends to *play down* the strength of the left within the working class in this period, admits, 'The party's rank and file by and large opposed the Enabling Act... There were numerous demonstrations against the high cost of living'.[41]

But the first major challenge to the government's decisions of 26 September came from the far right, who bitterly denounced the 'surrender to the French'. The Bavarian government immediately declared a state of emergency and appointed a leading right winger, Kahr, as 'Commissioner General'—effectively dictator—with the cry of, 'Away from Berlin'. The excuse for Kahr taking dictatorial powers was provided by a provocative Nazi meeting—but Kahr then proceeded to designate Hitler's stormtroopers as 'emergency police', to introduce certain anti-Semitic measures and to close down the Social Democratic 'security detachments'.

The national government in Berlin responded by declaring a state of emergency for the whole Reich. But Kahr in Bavaria refused to recognise this. When ordered to close down Hitler's paper for libelling Seeckt and Ebert, he rejected that too. He was joined in his rebellion by the Bavarian units of the army—the commanding general, Lossow, refused either to obey Berlin's orders or to give up his command, and his units swore allegiance to Kahr instead of to the Berlin government. Lossow mobilised the volunteer units in Bavaria and placed them under the command of Erhardt, the earlier leader of the Kapp putsch who had escaped from prison in Leipzig barely four months before and who was still a wanted man in the rest of Germany. The volunteer units were stationed along the state's northern border, directly threatening 'Red Saxony' and ready to march through to Berlin if ordered.

Meanwhile in northern Germany the far right volunteer units of the 'Black Reichswehr' started a mutiny on 1 October, seizing two important fortresses near Berlin. But the bulk of the northern army command still remembered their miscalculation at the time of the Kapp putsch: the mutineers were disarmed and their leaders held under arrest for a short time.

The attitude of the key military and governmental figures was that they disagreed with the tactics of Hitler, Ludendorff, the Bavarian government and the right wing volunteers—but believed that the disagreement should not lead to bloodshed if it could be avoided, for they had a common interest in maintaining a united front against the left. Stresemann's biographer records:

> In Stresemann's opinion, the developments in Saxony and Thuringia were far more disturbing than the dispute in Munich... He regarded the Bavarians as loyal, if misguided, Germans.[42]

Saxony and Thuringia had been thorns in the flesh of the central government for months. As early as June the coal owners had been demanding the 'pacification' of the area by the army. Throughout July, August and September the Proletarian Hundreds and the Control Committees had become more and more powerful, effectively taking over whole localities during strikes and demonstrations.

The left Social Democrat governments were not wholly in support of such revolutionary activities: they refused, for instance, to back a congress of the Hundreds in September. But they also refused to clamp down on the Control Committees and the Hundreds—partly because this would lose them support within the working class, partly because they could not do so without unleashing forces within the police and the army that they feared. Yet their unwillingness to use the local police against the workers was matched by their failure thoroughly to purge the ranks of the police: so the Saxon police, for example, could still act independently of the state government, as when they fired on a Dresden demonstration in early September, killing 13 workers.

The left ministers thought the best way to stop army intervention in the states was to promise Berlin that they themselves would keep order. Zeigner, for instance, assured the Cuno government on 8 August that his government would suppress the revolutionary movement 'with all determination' by sending police to disorderly areas;[43] but in practice such police detachments were rarely dispatched. Brandler later claimed in fact that 'the Social Democrat governments in Saxony and Thuringia were helpless in face of the Communists'.[44]

Liberal and Social Democrat historians usually refer to the Saxon premier Zeigner as 'well-intentioned' but 'unstable'.[45] They forget to add that such characterisation has been applied to a whole host of figures historically, from the Girondists in the French Revolution to Kerensky in Russia 1917, Dubcek in Czechoslovakia 1968 and Allende in Chile: all were figures who sought to compromise between rapidly polarising political forces. Their 'good intentions' consisted in knowing that full blooded reaction (whether of the royalist, Tsarist, Stalinist or CIA variety) would mean a bloodbath that could destroy their own popularity; their 'instability' consisted in an inability to take a firm stand against reaction, instead trying to achieve their ends by persuasion rather than violence. Such was Zeigner's position in the autumn of 1923.

By the beginning of October it was clear that at some point the national government was going to act against Saxony and Thuringia. The national state of emergency gave the government added powers for use against the left. Already a general, Müller, had been made special commissioner with powers in Saxony, and had used his powers to assert military jurisdiction over public meetings, publications and the right to strike. It could only be a matter of time before the state government that defied this injunction was deposed by force—whether by Erhardt's troops moving north from Bavaria, or by the troops of Seeckt and Müller moving south from Berlin.

The plan for taking power

The Communist Party spent September making military preparations for the seizure of power. But the final mechanics of the operation were not decided until the end of the month—at meetings in Moscow.

The advance of the right against Saxony and Thuringia was to provide the occasion for launching a revolutionary counter-offensive. Throughout Germany there were millions of Social Democrat supporters who saw the governments of central Germany as a positive alternative to the discredited Grand Coalition. The right's attack on these governments could galvanise such supporters into revolutionary action alongside the Communists. The Communists had to point out that the only way to defeat the attack on Saxony and Thuringia was for the workers to go over to the offensive, to build the Proletarian Hundreds, and to disarm the right wing paramilitaries, the police and the Reichswehr. And this was no longer merely a matter of propaganda. Such defensive moves had to be implemented in practice the moment the attack against Saxony and Thuringia started.

But although presented as defensive, these moves were *offensive* as well. The far right and the army units could not be disarmed except by armed attacks on them. The call for the defence of Saxony and Thuringia was necessarily the call for a massive revolutionary offensive to culminate in the establishment of a new power. The basis of this would lie in a congress of factory councils—that network of working class organisations which best represented the active section of the working class and which was closely tied to the Hundreds and the Control Committees.

The local Communist groups throughout the country were now put to preparing themselves for this. They had to draw up local operational plans—including schemes for the seizure of vital supplies, the elimination of the most dangerous local state officials, the taking over of power stations, railways and telecommunications centres. Above all they had to find supplies of arms for themselves—to locate police stations and armouries where weapons could easily be captured.

The call for a national general strike against an attack on Saxony and Thuringia would be the signal for all the local groups to put their plans into operation. In west, southwest and central Germany the revolutionaries were to take power, sending any spare units to help out in the battle for Berlin. In the occupied Ruhr local uprisings were to be avoided, for fear of premature conflicts with the French army of occupation; but the Hundreds were to march to the unoccupied areas to seize power there. As many forces as possible were then to be deployed along the Bavarian border, so as to prevent intervention from there until most of Germany was in insurgent hands.

The key role in the rising went to central Germany, with its legal force of Proletarian Hundreds. 'We thought we could use central Germany to deploy our troops, to go from the defensive to the offensive'.[46]

One final element in the plan caused dissension between Brandler and the Russian leaders: the Communists were to enter the Saxon and Thuringian governments. Not as part of any belief that a Socialist-Communist government would be better at running capitalism than any other, but in order to locate supplies of police arms, so that they could easily be seized by the workers. This, claimed Zinoviev, should help them to arm '50,000 to 60,000 men'.[47] Brandler objected:

The Saxon government was in no position to arm the workers because, since the Kapp putsch, all weapons had been taken away from Saxony, so much so that even the police were not armed.[48]

He later claimed that he had warned:

The entry of the Communists into the government would not breathe new life into the mass actions, but rather weaken them: for now the masses would expect Communists to do what they could only do themselves.[49]

If he did give this warning, then there was a strange reversal of roles: in the discussions of the previous December the German party leadership had strongly favoured Communist-Socialist governments and it was Zinoviev, Trotsky and Lenin who had been more reserved.

In any case, after 'Zinoviev banged his fist on the table' and 'Trotsky spent a whole evening' with Brandler, trying to persuade him,[50] Brandler accepted the decision. He returned from Moscow to Saxony and, as he got off the train, found from the newspapers he was already a government minister!

The decision about the bid for power was followed by a huge worldwide propaganda campaign by the Comintern. Everywhere Communist parties were told that just as in the past their first priority had been the defence of workers' Russia, now it would be defence of workers' Germany. Typically, the French Communist weekly, *Bulletin Communiste*, which had hardly mentioned Germany for months, was now turned over to extensive reportage of German events. A typical lead article ran: 'Five years after the bourgeois democratic revolution in Germany, the proletarian revolution is in sight!'[51]—unfortunately, the article appeared after the revolution was defeated.

Nowhere was the message hammered home more than in Russia itself. Newspapers, posters, meetings, demonstrations, dwelt on the theme of 'the forthcoming German Revolution'. Russia in 1923 was already a long way from the exuberant proletarian enthusiasm and democracy of 1917. The civil war had exacted an enormous price and working class democracy gave way to poverty, starvation, the closure of most of the factories, and the increasingly authoritarian rule of a party whose direct links with the workers were rapidly withering. The civil war had ended, only to give way to the 'enforced retreat' of the New Economic Policy. Mass unemployment coexisted with a new privileged layer of petty traders and bureaucrats.

By 1923, as Lenin lay paralysed and dying, bureaucratic practices had invaded the very top of the party, as the incipient Stalinist faction manoeuvred with Zinoviev and Kamenev against Trotsky.

Yet all this seems to have been forgotten for a few brief weeks of the early autumn. The advance of the German Revolution created new enthusiasm among those who had been growing cynical or bureaucratised. The inner party intrigues were replaced by a united concern to find the means to spread the revolution. In Russia itself in these weeks, we can glimpse, briefly, how its revolution could have been reborn if a revolutionary Germany had rescued it from isolation and poverty.[52]

When Brandler returned to Germany, Trotsky saw him off from the station, kissing his cheeks, the leader of one victorious revolution expressing his regard for the certain leader of another. Even Stalin enthused in a letter to Thalheimer:

> The revolution approaching in Germany is the most important international event of our time. The victory of the German Revolution will be still more important for the proletariat of Europe and America than was the Russian Revolution of six years ago. The victory of the German Revolution will transfer the centre of world revolution from Moscow to Berlin...[53]

The German October

Events now moved rapidly to a climax. The Communists had already, in September, threatened to bring down the Saxon left Social Democrat government because of its failure to purge the Saxon police, as evidenced in the shooting of demonstrators in Dresden. Now the government was reformed with three Communist ministers—Brandler, Böttcher and Heckert. Significantly, however, the Social Democrats denied the Communists the position they wanted most—the Ministry of the Interior, with its control over the police.

Zeigner introduced his new government to the state parliament on 12 October as a government of 'republican and proletarian defence'. One of its aims, he said, would be to disarm bourgeois military formations and to reinforce the Hundreds. The chairman of the KPD parliamentary group in Saxony made his party's attitude clear: 'Prepare everywhere for a general strike! Make arrangements to stop the movement of transport carrying the Reichwehr and armed gangs against the workers!'

Frölich, for the Communists, declared to the Reichstag in Berlin:

> The Socialist-Communist government is a struggle against reaction and against separatism in Bavaria and the Rhineland, against the oppressive policies of the great economic powers in Germany. That is a step towards the freeing of the proletariat in Germany.

If there was any attempt to crush Saxony, he added, '15 million German workers will rise against you'.[54]

For their part, the military authorities in Berlin stepped up their pressure against Saxony. General Müller banned the Proletarian Hundreds and 'similar organisations', giving them three days in which to surrender their arms.

The decree was openly defied. The same day, 13 October, there was a congress of the Saxon Hundreds in Chemnitz, which set up a new central committee for the movement, composed of four left Social Democrats and four Communists.[55]

The two parties held meetings throughout Saxony against the threats from the Reichswehr. They were strengthened by the announcement the same day of the foundation of a joint Socialist-Communist government in Thuringia, committed to building 'Control Committees to take control of the necessities of life' and the creation of a 'Republican Self Defence Force'.

In Leipzig the Communist Saxon minister Böttcher threw General Müller's ultimatum back in his face and called for the immediate arming of the Hundreds. The Communist Centre in Berlin called for workers to arm themselves to prepare for 'a battle to establish a government of all working people'.

The general retaliated by issuing a further decree, putting himself in charge of the Saxon police—which the police hastened to obey—and by giving Zeigner another ultimatum: he had 48 hours to disown Böttcher's words. Zeigner refused. Instead he too made a speech designed to infuriate the Berlin generals: he gave details of the secret activities of the paramilitary groups attached to the Reichswehr, the so-called 'Black Reichswehr'.

General Müller's threats against what was, after all, a legally constituted state government caused consternation within the one party in the country which really believed in the constitution—the SPD. Even hardened counter-revolutionaries such as Otto Braun and Severing claimed to be upset. There were protests within the cabinet. An assembly of union delegates in Berlin voted by 1,500 to 50 for a general strike if Saxony was touched. The SPD district leadership in Berlin opened discussions with the Communists on the possibility of forming a united Committee of Action in support of the Zeigner government. Even *Vorwärts* denounced the state of emergency—saying that it had been introduced with the pretext of fighting the right, but was being used against the left.

But for the Social Democrat leaders such protests were gestures, not to be taken too seriously. A government statement claimed that the military units were being sent to Saxony to defend the state against any advance of the right wing paramilitaries from Bavaria—and the Social Democrat leaders accepted the claim.

In the cabinet Stresemann told a different story—but one which still avoided any mention of the overthrow of the 'constitutional' government in Saxony. The troop concentrations, he insisted, were 'to intimidate radical elements and restore public order'—there was nothing in that exercise to disturb Social Democrat ministers who had themselves used the Freikorps to 'intimidate' the left.

Then on 20 October General Müller issued his final threat. The limited number of soldiers already in Saxony plastered the state with the text of a letter from him to Zeigner. Müller, this said, had been ordered to deploy military units so as 'to restore constitutional and orderly conditions in Saxony'. The next morning large contingents of troops with loaded weapons began to march across the Saxon border—although for the time being they carefully avoided clashing with workers.[56]

This was the moment of truth for the revolutionaries. They must either act now, or stand back and see the Saxon launching pad of the German Revolution disarmed and dismantled. As E H Carr has put it:

> The Reichswehr had done what Brandler had shrunk from doing. It had fixed the date on which the Communists must either act or confess their impotence.[57]

What was the mood among the German working class at this moment? Historians and revolutionaries have been debating ever since over the extent to which the majority of workers were prepared for revolutionary action. There is no doubt there was still great bitterness within the working class. The French Communist weekly, *Bulletin Communiste*, reported that between 12 and 18 October there were clashes in the streets of Hoesch, Frankfurt, Hanover, Leipzig, Bibrich, Gelsenkirchen, Düsseldorf, Cologne, Halberstadt, and shops were looted in Berlin.[58]

The left Social Democrat deputy, Toni Sender, later gave an account of events in Frankfurt that week. She described how the news of the moves against Saxony coincided with the closure of an important local factory. Much to her horror she found a meeting of the local factory councils forcing the local trade union leaders to endorse a general strike in this not particularly militant city.[59]

In Hamburg the news from Saxony coincided with a renewed bout of wages militancy. On 20 October there had been a strike in the docks, which spread to the warehouses, and, on the same day, the unemployed and the police clashed on the streets. On the 21st the dock workers voted for a general strike if there was an attack on Saxony—and the next day a meeting of union representatives from the whole city called upon the national union leaders to declare for a general strike.

During these same days there were further clashes with Rhineland separatists attempting to form an independent republic. The separatists attacked the town halls of Speier, Bonn, Koblenz, Krefeld and Gladbach. According to one historian of the Weimar Republic there were also riots with casualties in the next few days in Aachen, Berlin, Erfurt, Kassel, Harburg, Essen, Marienburg, Frankfurt, Hanover, Beuthen, Lübeck, Braunschweig and Allenstein.[60]

One measure of the anger within the working class at the attack on Saxony was its effect, a fortnight later, in forcing the ultra-respectable ministerial socialists in Berlin to quit their cabinet posts.

But whether this working class anger would translate into a willingness to fight could be tested only by revolutionary action. The point had been reached where most workers were no longer prepared to engage in struggles for limited demands or in protest strikes: apart from anything else, the level of unemployment was such that victimisation was all too easy for the employers. Only the struggle itself could now test whether the anger that had brought down the Cuno government had grown into revolutionary determination, or whether, as the then Communist International functionary Victor Serge thought, 'the unemployed are passing by swift stages from an insurgent enthusiasm into weary resignation'.[61]

The need to apply a *practical* test to the popular mood applied even more to the other strata of society. Since the 'passive resistance' had been abandoned the ruling class had regained a certain self-confidence for the first time since the spring. They now believed they could solve the reparations question, the problem of inflation and preserve national unity. But it is doubtful whether this new confidence had yet percolated down to the lower ranks of officialdom and the petty bourgeoisie, who were more impoverished than ever.

Within the middle ranks of the armed forces the surrender in the Ruhr had *increased* rather than diminished the bitterness, although it was usually the far right who benefited from this. The Communist Party had been projecting propaganda towards the ranks of the army and the civil service for months. But propaganda alone could provide no measure of the extent of any real divisions in the forces of the state—only revolutionary action could do that.

The debacle

Until 21 October the Communist leadership seemed determined on the action that alone could put to the test the balance of forces. True, General Müller's action was forcing the Communists to move earlier than they had wished. They had not been able to arm nearly as many men as they had hoped—they had only 6,000 guns as against the predicted 60,000. Nor had it been possible to call a national congress of factory councils to provide legitimacy for revolutionary action; the government ban on the national factory council movement had proved more of an impediment than had been expected. But throughout Germany there were hundreds of thousands of Communists ready to move. And it seemed likely that their lead would be followed by the huge disoriented section of social democracy.

Early in the morning of Sunday 21 October, as Müller's troops began to enter Saxony, Brandler explained the plan for the insurrection to a meeting in Chemnitz of representatives of all the Communist Party's districts. There would be agitation throughout the country for a general strike the next day, as workers returned to the factories after the weekend. On the Tuesday, against the background of the strike, the armed revolutionary units would carry through the operations they had been planning for a month and more—seizing control of police stations, barracks, communications centres, railway stations, administrative buildings.

The call for the general strike could not come from a fully representative congress of factory councils. But that need not matter. A conference of various local workers' organisations from Saxony had been jointly called some time before by Social Democrat and Communist ministers for that very day. It was due to discuss action to deal with the rapidly deteriorating economic situation—one person in seven in the state was on the edge of starvation. It would be easy to get the conference to take up the urgent matter of defence against the Reichswehr invasion and to call for a general strike.

The Proletarian Hundreds patrolled the streets of Chemnitz as the delegates arrived in the city for the conference. But they did not need to take action. Müller was playing a clever waiting game, not provoking the workers in such a way as to force the Social Democrats to react. The 498 delegates assembled without interference—among them 140 from factory councils, 120 from union branches, 79 from Control Committees, 66 from Communist Party sections, seven from the SPD. The proceedings began routinely enough. There were speeches on the economic crisis, the acute food shortages and the catastrophic growth of unemployment from the Social Democrat minister of labour, Graupe, and from two of the Communist ministers, Böttcher and Heckert. Delegates speaking from the floor were meant to keep to the same themes, but a number mentioned the Reichswehr movements which made discussions on the government's economic programme rather redundant. Then Brandler went to the rostrum.

Brandler insisted that now was the time for the workers of Saxony to call for assistance from the rest of Germany. Otherwise they would be destroyed. The only salvation lay in the immediate call for a national general strike of solidarity. He called on the Social Democrats to drop their vain hope of a peaceful settlement with Berlin. Only an immediate, unanimous vote for the general strike could save the situation.

Brandler seems to have expected the Social Democrat leaders to agree enthusiastically. Instead he was greeted with stunned silence.

Then the Social Democrat minister Graupe took the floor. The present conference, he said, could not by itself decide the response of the workers of Saxony to the army's threats. The defence of Saxony was the task of the 'Government of Republican and Proletarian Defence' and the Social Democratic-Communist majority in the state parliament. It would be quite wrong for the present conference to usurp the power of such official bodies. If a motion was put to do so, the whole Social Democratic delegation would walk out.

Brandler had got himself—and the German Revolution—into an impossible position. He had expected the left Social Democrats to agree to a project that they well knew meant civil war—even if they did not know of the secret Communist preparations. But the left Social Democrats were, for all their good intentions, still *Social Democrats*. They had boundless faith in the possibilities of compromise, and were not prepared to abandon these possibilities for a revolutionary gamble, however desperate the situation. They half believed the government's claim that the army was moving in to deal with Bavaria—and they would not abandon that belief until the army itself made continued ignorance of its real aims impossible. After all, they figured, they could not yet be *certain* that there would be no continued role for Social Democrat politicians.

The Communists took Graupe's threat as an indication that the Social Democratic rank and file would not support any revolutionary offensive, and allowed the strike resolution to be talked out. As Brandler recalled 36 years later:

> After discussions with other members of the Centre I advised against the proclamation of a general strike and in this course I received the assent of all the Centre members present, including Ruth Fischer.[62]

In this account Brandler claims that the military situation determined his decision—but other accounts make it clear that it was the refusal of the Social Democrats to fight that was decisive:

> In Chemnitz the second part of the plan was smashed—ie the common uprising of the Social Democratic and Communist masses. The proposal for the proclamation of a general strike was not put because of the opposition of the left Social Democrats... The Centre decided that the united front of the proletariat could no longer stay in existence [if the Communists went ahead alone] and in this situation because of the divided forces of the proletariat and the state of technical preparation the uprising was impossible.[63]

In any case, whatever the detailed motivation, the decision was taken there and then to abandon the general strike—and with it the German Revolution. The general strike call was replaced by the establishment of an Action Committee which would sound out the 'official movement'.

The conference had taken place—and the call which revolutionaries throughout Germany were waiting for had not been issued. The lynch-pin of the whole revolutionary strategy was gone.

An extended meeting of the Communist Centre met immediately afterwards. It decided that since the plan for the general strike had fallen through, the rising too would have to be cancelled. Emissaries were dispatched to the different parts of the country with orders to this effect.

By the time the Centre met again the next day, Müller's troops had taken over the streets of Chemnitz. Present at the meeting was Radek, who had just arrived from Moscow. He agreed with the cancellation of the rising, accepting that the party did not have enough arms in Saxony—only 600—and that with a divided class, defeat was inevitable. But he argued that the Communists could still call a defensive general strike. 'All the comrades rejected this plan'[64]—including the members of the so-called 'left'.

The German October, which had started with such hopes, was ending in nothing. The Reichswehr troops were able a few days later to remove and imprison Zeigner without any resistance. They installed a new right wing Social Democrat premier. Now the left Social Democrats did agree to a general strike. But the workers no longer thought that resistance was possible and the strike was only half-supported.

But the revolution did not quite go down without a shot being fired. The countermanding order calling off the rising never reached one city, Hamburg. In the small hours of 24 October a few hundred Communist insurgents put into effect the operation they had been planning so meticulously for weeks. They seized 12 of the 26 police stations in the suburbs and began moving towards the centre of the city. The insurgents believed at first that theirs was part of a coordinated national rising. 'In all Germany,' declared the 'Provisional Executive Committee' to 'the people of the Schiffbeck district', 'the working class is fighting for power. In the greater part of Germany power is in the hands of the workers'.[65]

But the rising lasted barely 24 hours. The mass of workers did not join as had been expected. It will never be known whether this was from a lack of revolutionary feeling (contrary to later claims, Hamburg was not a 'Red stronghold'—there were only 1,400 Communists in the city, as compared with 78,000 Social Democrat members)[66] or from a realisation that the rising was isolated and doomed. In any case, the insurgents soon dispersed in most of the suburbs, holding out only in Barmbeck.

The Hamburg rising was later mythologised by the German Communist Party—chiefly because of the role played by the future Stalinist leader Thälmann. But in fact it was several times smaller and less significant even than the March Action, and was nothing compared to the great struggles in Berlin, Munich and the Ruhr in 1919-20.

End of a chapter

The collapse in Saxony spelt an end to hopes for a revolutionary outcome to 'the year of hunger'. Not only was the most powerful base of the revolutionary left now occupied by armed troops, but more important there had been no coordinated resistance. The much-vaunted Zeigner government had abandoned office without raising a finger to defend itself. The quarter of a million strong Communist Party had abandoned the field of battle just as readily.

Throughout Germany there had been millions of starving, desperate people who had at least half hoped that the Communists would do something to provide an alternative. Instead the Communists declared themselves impotent in the face of General Müller. It seemed that nothing would ever be able to change the old order, however destructive and inhuman its workings. Those who would have acquiesced with relief in a revolutionary seizure of power, now acquiesced in the taking of virtually dictatorial powers by General Seeckt.

The French Communist Albert expressed a widespread feeling:

> In September and October and November Germany lived through a profound revolutionary experience, which is hardly known about and understood. The armed vigil was long, but the hour did not sound... A silent, almost inconceivable drama. A million revolutionaries, ready, awaiting the signal to attack: behind them the millions of the unemployed, the hungry, the desperate, a people in pain, murmuring, 'Us as well. Us as well.' The muscles of this crowd were ready, the fists already clasping the Mausers that they were going to oppose to the armoured cars of the Reichswehr. And nothing happened, except for the bloody buffoonery of Dresden, when a corporal and a few men chased from their offices the workers' ministers who had made bourgeois Germany tremble, and a few puddles of blood—60 deaths altogether—on the pavements of the industrial cities of Saxony.[67]

There is a mechanical interpretation of history according to which the outcome of events is determined in advance by the interplay of 'objective forces'. But this forgets, as Marx put it, that a 'revolution-ary idea that takes hold of the masses itself becomes a material force'. Economic development, the growth of large scale industry, spells of prosperity giving way to spells of poverty, great crises—all serve to pro-pel large numbers of men and women into new social movements. But the future of these movements depends, beyond a certain point, on their success or failure in battles with their opponents. No battle is ever won simply by a commander deciding that his troops are bigger or smaller in number than those on the other side. The psychology of the troops, their deployment in the right place at the right time, the correct allocation of armaments, all play a part. As tens of thousands of soldiers move in a confused mass from one side of the battlefield to the other and back again, even the raising of a simple standard at the right moment can make a vital difference: either tired, hard-pressed men are re-assembled and led to victory, or they are left to run, routed from the conflict. And what applies in simple battles applies even more in great social conflicts, in strikes, demonstrations, revolutions.

Whatever may or may not have been the real possibilities of victory in the German October, the banner was not raised in Saxony. And the working class, so powerful in the first weeks of August, ran for cover at the end of October. German capitalism was left unscathed, in control of the field of battle.

In political terms this meant a sharp swing to the right. On 2 November the Social Democrat ministers resigned from the central gov-ernment. They had played their part in keeping important sections of the working class quiet in the aftermath of the fall of the Cuno govern-ment and during the manoeuvres against Saxony. Now German capital-ism could manage without them. The party that had dominated the first five years of the Weimar Republic was to be excluded from office for the next five years.

In Munich Hitler thought his time had come. On 8-9 November his stormtroopers tried to force the Bavarian special commissioner, Kahr, and the head of the Bavarian army, Lossow, to join Hitler in a seizure of power as a prelude to a march on Berlin. But Lossow was satisfied with the new swing to the right in Berlin, and Kahr wanted separatism, not Hitler's National Socialism. Fascism was not yet strong enough to operate without the shield provided by the Reichswehr; and the gener-als thought they could control events without bending to the Austrian upstart. The putsch was quickly disposed of, and Hitler had to endure the indignity of six months in jail.

The German bourgeoisie now hastened to push through its solution to the crisis. The mark was stabilised by a huge credit squeeze, which caused wholesale factory closures until 28 percent of union members were unemployed and 42 percent were on short-time.[68] Meanwhile the main gain that workers still retained from the struggle of November 1918, the eight hour day, was scrapped.

The year that many had thought would finally bring the German Revolution in fact ended with the right wing parties and the military High Command in an even more powerful position than after the Freikorps marches of 1919 and 1920.

The Reich government could only assert its power through the intermediary of the Reichswehr, whose commander-in-chief, General Seeckt, was invested with extraordinary authority. Under military protection the economy was stabilised, the economic independence of the cartels brought to heel, the eight hour day abolished, and the principle of compulsory arbitration enforced.[69]

The High Command was not all powerful. It still had to adjust to changes in the balance of social forces. In particular, it still had to allow social democracy to tame an independent workers' movement in which Communists could not be prevented from playing some role. But it had regained much of the power it had enjoyed in the years of the World War.

For the time being, at least, the dream of a workers' Germany joining a workers' Russia in reshaping the world was over.

The lessons of October

The debacle in Saxony led immediately to a huge debate within the Communist International as to what had gone wrong. Unfortunately, it cannot be said to have been a clear and rational debate. It came just as increasing bureaucratisation in Russia was drowning rational discussion there. Lenin was completely incapacitated and died in January 1924. Zinoviev, Kamenev and Stalin were using the bureaucratic complacency of wide ranks of the Russian party to isolate Trotsky and destroy his popularity. Now they spread the methods they were employing in Russia to the arguments inside the International.

In the row over Germany, Brandler, Thalheimer and Radek defended the tactics of the German party with rational and generally factually based arguments, even if these were often confused and self-contradictory. But most of those who attacked them did so out of personal animosity, factional bitterness and bureaucratic intrigue, picking up and discarding arguments, even inventing facts, as it suited them.

It has not been my purpose in this book to go into the internal faction questions that arose inside the Russian party or into the history of the degeneration of the Russian Revolution. The issues are important, but they have been dealt with adequately elsewhere.[70] So I will limit myself to a couple of examples of the method of argument that followed the German defeat.

Both Zinoviev and Stalin attacked Brandler and for a year or so supported the ultra-lefts Fischer, Maslow and Thälmann against him. Yet in the summer of 1923 Stalin had been most insistent that the Germans 'must be held back', and Zinoviev had fully backed the decision not to go ahead with the general strike and the uprising. Again, Zinoviev allowed Fischer to hammer away at Brandler and Radek as being responsible for the Saxon 'workers' government'—yet, as we have seen, Brandler was against entering the government in October. Finally, the condemnation of Brandler and Radek at the Fifth Congress of the Comintern in 1924 was based upon a new, and insane, evaluation of social democracy as 'the left wing of fascism'.

The real 'lessons of October' can only be assessed by ignoring the conclusions of the debate inside the bureaucratised Comintern. But some of the *contributions* to that debate do give an insight into what went wrong.[71] Various different explanations were put forward. Indeed, such was the confusion of the debate that it was common for individuals to put forward two or more contradictory explanations in the course of a single speech.

Four main explanations were presented.

The first claimed that there had been no revolutionary situation in Germany in 1923: the majority of the working class had not supported the Communists, but had remained with social democracy. This was an important part of the argument used by the Brandler leadership to justify their retreat in Saxony:

The common mistake of the Executive [of the Comintern] and the Centre of the KPD was a false estimate of the balance of forces between the SPD and the KPD within the working class... The majority of the working class was not yet won to Communism.[72]

If after the Chemnitz conference we had gone into battle, we would have suffered a decisive defeat that would have made impossible for years any discussion over the possibility of victory for the proletariat.[73]

At the Chemnitz conference it was obvious that the workers still believed that the march of troops into Saxony was directed against Bavaria... If we had risked the fight, we Communists would have gone down to a bloody defeat... A wide section of the petty bourgeoisie had passed into the enemy camp.[74]

Clara Zetkin insisted that even the strike against Cuno had not shown any real revolutionary tendency. Instead, it revealed among the masses, 'the great lack of political maturity for revolt, for the capture of power'.[75] For Thalheimer, the defeat had causes 'of an objective nature and could not be blamed on the faults of the party'.[76]

The majority of the working class was no longer prepared to fight for the democracy of November [1918], but it was not yet ready to go into the arena for the dictatorship of workers' councils and socialism.[77]

Because of this, any action in October would have pitted pitifully small groups of armed workers against the combined forces of fascism, the army and the paramilitary police.

Such arguments have led some later historians—in particular the American, Angress—to accept the evaluation of 1923 as a non-revolutionary situation. Yet the argument can be faulted in a number of ways.

Firstly, those who put this argument in 1923 were not themselves fully convinced by it. Brandler, for instance, on a number of later occasions seemed to imply, contradicting his friend Thalheimer, that there had been revolutionary possibilities in 1923, although not in *October* 1923. At fault had not been the assessment of the year as potentially revolutionary, but the assessment of October as the time to make the offensive. This comes across clearly in his speech to the Fifth Congress of the Comintern nine months later, and also in the interview that he gave to Isaac Deutscher 25 years later:

Asked whether today he would consider the 1923 situation as revolution-ary, Brandler does not give a clear answer. From the way he describes events one has the impression that his answer would, on the whole, be affirmative. But he does not draw any final conclusion.[78]

The pessimistic evaluation made in October 1923 itself flowed from a continual obsessive fear of a rerun of the March Action. Brandler argued:

The March Action shows for us that the whole class position, the whole objective situation, was not ripe for us to defeat capitalism: the objective situation caused us to suffer a big defeat after a frontal assault... I was personally made responsible for this defeat... I think I have the character not to make the same mistake twice.[79]

But it was absurd to equate Germany in 1923, when the whole of society was wracked by a crisis, with Germany in March 1921 when the crisis was a figment of the imagination of Kun, Brandler, Radek and others.

Also, those who held this view grossly overestimated the inner cohe-sion of the forces arrayed against the left. They spoke of 'hundreds of thousands' of extreme rightist forces easily crushing a 'few thousand' armed workers, without recognising that there were still powerful ten-sions within the counter-revolutionary forces that would hinder a quick and unified response to an offensive by the left. Of course, the central government, the Reichswehr command, the Bavarian separatists and the supporters of Hitler were all enemies of the revolution. Nevertheless, within a fortnight of the debacle in Saxony they were to be fighting among themselves.

Instead of recognising this, even after Hitler was put in prison for his putsch in Bavaria, the German Communist leadership were lumping all the right wing forces together as 'fascist'. In a remarkable travesty of history, the Brandler leadership declared:

The November Revolution is delivered up to fascism. Power is in the hands of military forces determined to annihilate the organisations of the working class... While the working class saw the centre of fascism as Bavaria, it is in Berlin that fascism establishes itself in the form of the dictatorship of Seeckt.[80]

This overestimation of the forces lined up against the revolution was matched by a tendency to state *as a fact* what had actually not been proved: that the Social Democrats were still the decisive force within the working class. Only action could determine the real balance of forces by October 1923—yet the KPD leadership avoided action on the assumption that the balance of forces could not have shifted radically despite the total crisis of society.

The second explanation given for the debacle was that the date for the insurrection had been set *before* the revolutionary situation had fully matured. Even Brandler on occasions opted for this view: 'I simply did not regard the situation as acutely revolutionary yet, reckoning rather on a further sharpening'.[81] This was also implicit in the claim by Zinoviev and the Comintern leadership *after* the defeat that nothing had changed in the objective balance of forces, that 'Germany is marching towards a sharpened civil war'.[82]

History itself proved the fallacy of this argument. No further great wave of strikes or demonstrations followed. Workers were demoralised by the massive unemployment and, above all, by the feeling that the Communists had had their chance and had refused to take it.

The third explanation put forward was that the real revolutionary opportunity had been *earlier* than October, but that the Communist Party and the International had been quite unprepared for it. Virtually every Communist leader accepted part of this explanation (except Zinoviev, who dubbed it a 'sophistry'—no doubt because it implied his Comintern executive was as much at fault as the German party).

Radek claimed that in April and May neither the Executive of the Comintern nor the German party leadership drew the 'practical conclusions' from their theoretical evaluation that 'the Ruhr struggle would end in civil war'.[83] Clara Zetkin claimed that at the time of the Ruhr occupation:

> The party did not take timely cognisance of the revolutionary situation with sufficient vigour... The party did not consider the fight for partial demands as a means of recruiting, mobilising and educating the proletariat for the mass fight for power.[84]

The most extreme version of this argument holds that by October there was *no chance* of a successful insurrection. The Stresemann government had already restored confidence to the bourgeoisie by ending the passive resistance and by beginning to take measures to deal with the inflation.

The trouble with this extreme argument is that it assumes that the mass of people, even the mass of the bourgeoisie, accepted in advance that Stresemann's schemes would work. But the end of the passive resistance was not *immediately* followed by an agreement with the French: the French-backed separatist movement was still active in the Rhineland at the time of the debacle in Saxony. And the inflation continued to accelerate for another fortnight. There was little reason for people who had seen the failure of three previous governmental attempts to tackle inflation to believe that this one would work.

The fourth explanation for the defeat came from Trotsky and his followers. There is a vulgar version of the argument which is sometimes found in Trotskyist literature, and which is clearly incorrect: that there was a revolutionary situation in October that Stalin wrecked.[85] The argument falls because it ascribes to Stalin's disastrous judgements an influence inside the Comintern which he simply did not possess in 1923.

However, Trotsky's own argument is much more sophisticated. It does not depend upon accepting that success was guaranteed in October (although Trotsky certainly thought it likely). Trotsky's central argument is that the situation had become so fluid that *only* an offensive by the revolutionaries could reveal the real balance of forces:

> Only a pedant and not a revolutionist would investigate now, after the event, how far the conquest of power would have been 'assured' had there been a correct policy.[86]

But the German party had failed to respond to the sharp change in the objective situation in the course of the year:

> In the summer of 1923, the internal situation in Germany, especially in connection with the collapse of the passive resistance, assumed a catastrophic character. It became clear that the German bourgeoisie could extricate itself from this 'hopeless' situation only if the Communist Party failed to understand in due time that the position of the bourgeoisie was 'hopeless' and if the party failed to draw the necessary revolutionary conclusions.
>
> Why didn't the German Revolution lead to victory? The reasons for it are to be sought in tactics, not in the existing conditions. Here we had a classic example of a missed revolutionary situation. After all the German proletariat had gone through in recent years, it could be led to a decisive struggle only if it were convinced that this time the question would

be decisively resolved and that the Communist Party was ready for the struggle and capable of achieving the victory. But the Communist Party executed the turn very irresolutely and after a very long delay. Not only the rights, but also the lefts, despite the fact that they had fought each other very bitterly, viewed rather fatalistically the process of revolutionary development up to September-October 1923.[87]

Trotsky thought that the German party leadership had made a terrible mistake in not pressing ahead in October 1923. But this was only a final expression of the fact that they had been lagging behind events throughout the summer of that year.

The fact that *after the event* the reformists seemed to have as firm a hold as ever on the majority of the working class did not prove that the workers would not have followed the Communists into battle at the height of the social and political crisis. For the failure of the Communists to act would restore the masses to social democracy:

> A party which carries on a protracted revolutionary agitation and then, after the confidence of the masses has raised it to the top, begins to vacillate, to split hairs, to hedge and temporise—such a party paralyses the activity of the masses, sows disillusion and disintegration among them and brings ruin to the revolution; but in turn it provides itself with a ready excuse—after the debacle—that the masses were insufficiently active.[88]

Trotsky quotes at length statements from Bolsheviks—especially Zinoviev and Kamenev—who in October 1917 in Russia had used arguments against the insurrection that were similar to those used in October 1923 in Germany by Brandler and Radek. He suggests that had these arguments carried the day in 1917, then after the event they would have seemed correct:

> It is not difficult to imagine how history would have been written had the line of evading battle been carried in the central committee. The official historians would, of course, have explained that an insurrection in October 1917 would have been sheer madness; and they would have furnished the reader with awe-inspiring statistical charts of Junkers and Cossacks and shock troops and artillery deployed fan-wise, and army corps arriving from the Front. Never tested in the fire of insurrection, these forces would have seemed immeasurably more terrible than they proved in action.[89]

In fact, the revolution would have failed, not because it was impossible, but because the party had failed to act at the decisive moment. Its hesitation would have given the bourgeoisie time to move its troops and reassert a commanding grip over events. For revolutions develop to a point at which *either* the revolutionary party acts, or history falls back into its old mould:

> The strength of the revolutionary party increases only up to a certain moment, after which the process can turn into the very opposite. The hopes of the masses change into disillusionment as a result of the party's passivity, while the enemy recovers from his panic and takes advantage of the disillusionment.[90]

Trotsky stressed the need for the party to have acted in *October*. Even if the arguments of Radek and Thalheimer are accepted—that by October the crucial moment had passed and the bourgeoisie was back in control of events—Trotsky's essential diagnosis holds. From May onwards great possibilities went untested because the party remained on the defensive, and did not respond to the change in the mood of the masses and the increasing disintegration of society.

For Trotsky a certain level of conservatism within the party was inevitable. This followed from the fact that, throughout most of the lifespan of any revolutionary party, the objective possibility of seizing power just does not exist:

> The working class struggles and matures in the never-failing consciousness of the fact that the preponderance of forces lies on the side of the enemy. This preponderance manifests itself in daily life at every step. The enemy possesses wealth and state power, all the means of exerting ideological pressures and all the instruments of repression. We become habituated to the idea that the preponderance of forces is on the enemy's side; and habitual thought enters as an integral part into the entire life and activity of the revolutionary party during the preparatory epoch...
>
> The consequences entailed by this or that careless or premature act serve each time as most cruel reminders of the enemy's strength. But a moment comes when this habit of regarding the enemy as stronger becomes the main obstacle on the road to victory. Today's weakness of the bourgeoisie seems to be cloaked in the shadow of its strength of yesterday.[91]

The decision to fight for power involves not just a tactical change decided on by this or that leader of the party, but a complete transformation in the party's approach to every one of its activities. It is hardly surprising, then, that whole sections of the party try to avoid accepting the change:

> Every period in the development of the party has special features of its own and calls for specific habits and methods of work. A tactical turn implies a greater or lesser break in these habits and methods. Herein lies the direct and most immediate root of internal party friction and crises... Hence the danger arises that if the turn is too abrupt or too sudden, and if in the preceding period too many elements of inertia and conservatism have accumulated in the leading organs of the party, then the party proves itself unable to fulfil its leadership in that supreme and critical moment for which it has been preparing itself in the course of years or decades. The party is ravaged by crisis, and the movement passes the party by— and heads towards defeat.[92]

The confusion within the party has most profound effects upon the class:

> On one and the same economic foundation, with one and the same class division within society, the relation of forces undergoes change depending upon the mood of the proletarian masses, depending upon the extent to which their illusions are shattered and their political experience has grown; the extent to which the confidence of the intermediate classes and groups in the state power is shattered; and, finally, the extent to which the latter loses confidence in itself. During a revolution all these processes take place at lightning speed.[93]

If the party shows a confidence in the stability of the bourgeois state which even those in control of that state do not have, then it inadvertently helps them keep the masses under their thumb. Instead of exacerbating the internal conflicts inside the enemy camp, instead of showing the middle classes that the revolution offers a way out for them, it ends up by reassuring them that their only hope lies in the status quo.

This, Trotsky argued, was what had happened in the German October. The Communist leadership, after bringing the majority of workers and a section of the middle class to a point where they welcomed the prospect of revolutionary deliverance from the social crisis, then failed to deliver the goods. The masses lost confidence in the party, and the Social Democrats and the right wing parties were able to regain their trust.

The trends towards conservatism were inherent in any party. But this did not mean Trotsky thought nothing could be done to combat it. It could be avoided by a leadership that combined strict scientific stringency in assessing events with the ability to respond to sharp and sudden changes in the mood of the masses—the sort of response Lenin and Trotsky had been able to make in 1917. But a leadership of that sort could not be conjured out of thin air. The party had to develop leaders of that calibre through long years of struggle, selecting from among its members those who show that they grasp the interrelation between the objective situation and rapid changes in the mood of the masses. Only then would the party leadership be prepared for giant, world-shaping battles. The German October came to nothing because the German Communist Party lacked such leadership.

Such an interpretation takes the analysis of what went wrong in 1923 back to the historical assessment of the previous decade.

We have seen, in earlier chapters, how the fatal absence of even a stable nucleus for a party produced the devastating defeats of 1919 and the inability to grasp the revolutionary opportunities after the Kapp putsch of 1920. These failures produced within the party an impatience which went to its head with the March Action of 1921. That traumatic experience then prepared the ground for the debacle of 1923.

The party leadership had lost its self-confidence. Its neurotic obsession with March 1921 prevented it from responding to the changed mood of the masses in May 1923. The party was riven by internal rows, with the leadership unsure of itself, vowing never again, while the opposition still showed all the symptoms of the March madness. The party sought reassurance, not in the struggle in Germany itself, but instead by turning for tactical advice to men in Moscow who, however able (and many were no more able than the German leaders), were in no position themselves to assess how the mood of the German workers was changing from day to day.

1923 was the summation of all the problems that had plagued the German Revolution from the beginning—or, more accurately, of the repeated impact of the one major problem: the lack of the nucleus of a party in November 1918. Without such a nucleus the experience of 1918-19 could not produce a layer of militants capable of responding in a coordinated, national manner to the possibilities of 1920. And that in turn ensured a combination of foolhardiness and hesitation in 1921 and 1923.

German society produced hundreds of thousands, indeed millions, of men and women who wanted revolutionary change between 1918 and 1923. The tragedy of the German Revolution was that a party capable of harnessing and coordinating their energy did not come into existence until it was too late. History has often been compared to a locomotive— but it does not wait for revolutionaries to board it. Those who miss their time are forced, like the wandering Jew of mythology, to suffer for the rest of eternity.

1.   Guttman and Meehan, *The Great Inflation*, p31.
2.   Summary of reports given by J C Favez, *La Reich devant l'Occupation Français Belge de la Ruhr en 1923* (Geneva 1969) p291.
3.   Ibid, p291.
4.   Ibid, p295.
5.   Ibid, p293.
6.   Ibid.
7.   Ibid, pp293-294.
8.   Erich Hochler, quoted in W Ersil, *Aktionseinheit stürtzt* Cuno (Berlin 1961) p245.
9.   Pierre Broué, *Révolution en Allemagne* (Paris 1971) p713; and J C Favez, op cit, p294.
10. W Ersil, op cit, p249.
11. J C Favez, op cit, p295.
12. W Ersil, op cit, pp290-295.
13. Michaelis and Schlapper, *Ursachen und Folgen vom Deutschen Zusammenbruch 1918 bis 1945, zur Staatlichen Neuordnung Deutschlands in der Gegenwart, 5. Das Kritische Jahr 1923*, p476.
14. P Broué, op cit, p714.
15. Viscount D'Abemon, quoted in Michaelis and Schlapper, op cit, p171.
16. Landauer, *European Socialism* (Berkeley 1959) p974.
17. *Die Lehren der Deutschen Ereignisse*, Presidium of the Communist International, June 1924, p30.
18. Ibid.
19. J C Favez, op cit, p306.
20. Ibid, p308.
21. Quoted in P Broué, op cit, p718; and E H Carr, *The Interregnum* (London 1954) p201.
22. P Broué, op cit, p720.
23. *New Left Review* 105, p52.

24. Letter to Isaac Deutscher, ibid, p76.
25. L Trotsky, *The First Five Years of the Communist International* vol 2 (New York 1972) p349.
26. Quoted in P Broué, op cit, p732.
27. Helmut Gast, 'Die Proletarischen Hundertschaften als Organe der Einheitsfront im Jahre 1923' in *Zeitschrift für Geschichtwissenschaft 1956*, p452.
28. Ibid.
29. A R Albert, quoted in P Broué, op cit, p739.
30. Quoted ibid, p737.
31. Quoted ibid, p735.
32. *Die Lehren der Deutschen Ereignisse*, op cit, p34.
33. Ibid, p41.
34. *Bulletin Communiste*, 11 October and 6 November 1923.
35. J C Favez, op cit, p310.
36. Ibid.
37. Harold Fraser, quoted in Guttman and Meehan, op cit, pp75-76.
38. Heinz Neumann, in *Bulletin Communiste*, 11 October 1923.
39. J C Favez, op cit, p370.
40. Quoted in Michaelis and Schlapper, op cit, p201.
41. Werner Angress, *Stillborn Revolution* (Princeton 1963) p432.
42. H A Turner, *Stresemann and the Politics of the Weimar Republic* (Princeton 1963) p124.
43. Quoted in Raimund Wagner, *Zur Frage der Massenkämpfe in Sachsen vom Frühjahr bis zum Sommer 1923, Zeitschrift für Geschichtwissenschaft, Heft 1* (1956) p258.
44. Quoted in I Deutscher, *New Left Review* 105.
45. See for example Michaelis and Schlapper, op cit, p470.
46. Heinrich Brandler in *Die Lehren der Deutschen Ereignisse*, op cit, p20.
47. Quoted in P Broué, op cit, p755.
48. Quoted by I Deutscher, *New Left Review* 105, p51.
49. Ibid, p76.
50. Brandler, quoted by I Deutscher, ibid, pp50-51.
51. *Bulletin Communiste*, 1 November 1923.
52. For a description of the mood in Moscow, see P Broué, op cit, p722.
53. *Rote Fahne*, 10 October 1923.
54. Text in Michaelis and Schlapper, op cit, p483.
55. H Gast, op cit, p461.
56. The sequence of events leading to the entry of the troops into Saxony is described in: Michaelis and Schlapper, op cit, pp484-492; H A Turner, op cit, pp125-131; and P Broué, op cit, pp759-764.
57. E H Carr, op cit, p221.
58. *Bulletin Communiste*, 2 November 1923.
59. Toni Sender, *The Autobiography of a German Rebel* (London 1940).
60. Scheele, p73.

61. Victor Serge, *Memoirs of a Revolutionary* (London 1963) p170.
62. *New Left Review* 105, p75.
63. Karl Radek in *Die Lehren der Deutschen Ereignisse*, op cit, p6. Compare also Remmele in the same work, p42.
64. Radek, ibid, p6.
65. Text in Michaelis and Schlapper, op cit, p494.
66. *Die Lehren der Deutschen Ereignisse*, op cit, p23.
67. Quoted in P Broué, op cit, p739.
68. Figures given in Arthur Rosenberg, *A History of the German Republic* (London 1936) p219.
69. Scheele, op cit, p77.
70. See, for example: Isaac Deutscher, *The Prophet Unarmed* (New York 1965); Tony Cliff, *Lenin* vol 3 (London 1977); and Moshe Lewin, *Lenin's Last Struggle* (London 1975).
71. In particular the speeches of Radek, Brandler and Remmele in *Die Lehren der Deutschen Ereignisse*, op cit, and those of Brandler, Radek and Clara Zetkin in *The Fifth World Congress of the Communist International* (London 1924).
72. Thalheimer and Brandler in Michaelis and Schlapper, op cit, p505.
73. Brandler in 'Die Lehren der Deutschen Ereignisse', op cit, p26.
74. *Fifth Congress*, op cit, p66.
75. Ibid, p80.
76. *1923: Eine verpasste Revolution?* quoted in P Broué, op cit, p785.
77. Thalheimer and Brandler in Michaelis and Schlapper, op cit, p504.
78. I Deutscher, in *New Left Review* 105, p52.
79. *Die Lehren der Deutschen Ereignisse*, op cit, p256.
80. Theses of the KPD printed in *Bulletin Communiste*, 15 November 1923.
81. Brandler in *New Left Review* 105, p76.
82. Zinoviev in *Pravda*, 2 February 1924, quoted in Leon Trotsky, *The Third International After Lenin* (New York 1957) p100.
83. *Die Lehren der Deutschen Ereignisse*, op cit, p14.
84. *Fifth Congress*, op cit, p8.
85. See for example C L R James, *World Revolution* (London 1937) p181.
86. L Trotsky, op cit, p92.
87. Ibid, pp92-93.
88. Leon Trotsky, *The Lessons of October* (London 1971) p41.
89. Ibid, p38.
90. Ibid, p40.
91. Ibid, p36.
92. Ibid, p8.
93. Ibid, p39.

CHAPTER 14

Legacy of defeat

One assumption underlay the reactions of liberals and Social Democrats throughout the turmoil of the revolutionary years. They believed that history would flow back into safe channels, assuring an eternity of social democratic bliss—if only they could isolate and suppress the revolutionary forces. If they controlled the present they could guarantee the future. It is the same assumption that today enables social democrats somehow to retain their self-satisfied optimism as the world crisis rages around them.

In the Europe of the 1920s such a view rested on delusions of the most incredible magnitude. It assumed that the First World War was an accident of history which men of good will could have avoided. It also assumed that the economic forces connected with the war could be peacefully contained within a new era of prosperity.

It is true that for five years after 1923 Europe and America did enjoy a seeming return to the pre-war idyll of economic expansion and high profitability. But 1929 brought an economic convulsion whose effects were as terrifying as the military convulsion of 1914. The demons that had seemingly been banished in 1923 returned as, by the millions, ordinary people turned bitterly on the social democrats and liberals who promised so much and delivered so little.

The third great crisis of post-war Germany proved that those who had preserved the old order through the first two crises of 1918-20 and of 1923 had done humanity no service at all.

The most obvious symptom of this was the rebirth of Nazism at a much higher level than in 1923. In 1928 Hitler's party had received only 2.6 percent of the popular vote. In 1930 this had shot up to 18.3 percent, doubling again to 37.3 percent by July 1932. But not only votes mattered: the number of stormtroopers rose to 100,000 by 1930 and 400,000 by 1932.

Hitler could not have come to power if he had relied just upon the stormtroopers. He also depended upon the active collaboration of those forces in German society which had been given a new lease of life by Social Democrat governments in November-December 1918 and April 1920—the generals, the top government bureaucrats, the great industrialists and landed interests. These had dominated all the governments since 1923, with a brief interlude of Social Democratic rule in 1928-30. In 1930-33 their nominees, Brüning, Papen and Schleicher, sat in the Chancellory, ruling through decrees, with only occasional reference to parliament.

The generals and industrialists still had to reckon, however, with a powerful, Social Democrat led labour movement. To retain a minimum of Social Democrat compliance, they had to stop just short of an all-out onslaught on the working class. In the years 1930-32 they used the Nazis as a counter-balance to the workers' movement, retaining their own freedom to manoeuvre by allowing each to keep the other in check. But as the crisis dragged on, they found the price they had to pay for social democracy—the continued toleration of certain gains made by the workers in the past—was too high. The generals and industrialists estimated late in 1932 that ruling with a Nazi movement that would destroy the working class organisations was preferable to ruling with a Social Democratic movement that would try to buy off the workers.

The first test came in July 1932. The Social Democrat Severing still sat ensconced in the Prussian Ministry of the Interior, complete with its 80,000 strong, heavily armed police force. The president of the republic was Hindenberg—the same Hindenberg who as war-time dictator had been discredited by the collapse of the Front and then rehabilitated by Ebert's pledge of a joint effort against 'Bolshevism'.

Early in 1932 Social Democratic support had ensured Hindenberg's re-election as president. Now he repaid the Social Democrats. He agreed to the removal from office of the democratically elected, constitutionally sound right wing Social Democrat led government of Prussia, in exactly the same way as Ebert, nine years before, had agreed to the removal of the democratically elected, constitutionally sound left wing Social Democrat led government of Saxony. Severing, who had bid the Freikorps on their way as they went to terrorise workers in central Germany and the Ruhr, was now thrown out of his office by the Reichswehr that had been built from the Freikorps.

This was only the dress rehearsal. At the end of 1932 Goebbels confided to his diary the fear that the Nazis had missed their chance; they had received fewer votes than the combined SPD-KPD total in the second general election of 1932, and disillusioned stormtroopers were going over to the Communists by the thousand. The future, Goebbels wrote, 'is dark and gloomy: all prospects and hopes have completely vanished.'

But at this point the old rulers of Germany threw their weight behind Hitler. The industrialists Thyssen and Krupp met Hitler and were reassured that he would follow their interests. The former Chancellor from the 'democratic' Centre Party, Papen, negotiated with Hitler. Then Hindenberg gave the Nazis control of the government. Those who had been saved from 'socialisation' by the Social Democrats in 1919 now worked with Hitler to destroy the Social Democratic labour movement.

Yet even after Hitler was installed as Chancellor and the stormtroopers had started to 'clean up' Berlin, the Social Democrats could not believe that the ties of blood they had established with the ruling class between 1918 and 1923 had been dissolved. In the Reichstag, Social Democrat spokesmen declared that they would be a loyal opposition to what their leader, Breitscheid, called 'a lawful government'.[1] Groups of the Berlin Socialist Youth who began to work underground were expelled from the party.[2] The trade union leadership sent instructions to its members telling them to celebrate 1 May alongside the Nazis as a 'national day of labour'[3]—but this did not prevent the Nazis seizing control of trade union offices on 2 May and sending the leaders off to concentration camps. Breitscheid died by Nazi hands—and so did Hilferding, the 'Marxist' whose prestige had been so important for German capitalism in the desperate summer of 1923.

Those who had believed in capitalism with a human face, in 'the orderly march towards socialisation', in 'the anchoring of the councils in the constitution', only ensured that all Europe was subjected to a medieval barbarism armed with the monstrous devices of modern technology.

Not only in Germany did the defeat of the revolution spell catastrophe for mankind. Next to Germany lay the huge land mass of the former Tsarist empire. Those who had led the revolution there in 1917 had believed its destiny to be tied up with the destiny of the German industrial giant. The spread of the revolution from Russia to Germany was no idle dream. As we have seen, there was a brief moment in 1918 when workers' councils were the *only* power all the way from the Urals to the North Sea. There was a world movement with its Red Armies in the Ruhr as well as Siberia, Bavaria as well as the Don Basin, its councils in Turin and Bremen as well as Tsaritsyn.

But this movement was destroyed in the West—in Germany, Austria and Italy—by the influence and the policies of social democratic reformism. Instead of the European revolution rising to the rescue of the beleaguered Russian workers' republic, European social democracy gave new life and new hope to the forces that wanted to destroy that republic.

Under such conditions, the workers' democracy inside Russia could not stay alive for long. As Rosa Luxemburg wrote as early as 1918:

> Everything that happens in Russia is comprehensible and represents an inevitable chain of causes and effects, the starting point and the end term of which are: the failure of the German proletariat and the occupation of Russia by German imperialism.

There is no space here to detail what followed in Russia: the decimation of the working class as a result of the civil war and foreign intervention, the withering of workers' democracy, the bureaucratisation, the rise of a new state capitalist class, Stalinism. But it *is* necessary to repeat: the rise of the new form of exploitation and oppression was inseparable from the isolation of the revolution. Social democracy in the West begat Stalinism in the East. The blood spilt by Stalin, as much as the blood spilt by Hitler, lies also at the door of the right wing Social Democrats Ebert, Noske, Severing and Wels...and the left wing Social Democrat Hilferding.

Perhaps the mutual influence is shown most clearly by Moscow's brief Indian summer of 1923. In August and September of that year the news from Berlin briefly recreated enthusiasm for the revolution. Once again it seemed that the interaction between Germany and Russia could create a new prospect for humanity. There was a glow from the West that could evoke warmth even in the cold bureaucratic heart of a Stalin. But all too soon that warmth turned to icy disappointment. The defeat without battle in Germany produced even greater demoralisation in Moscow than in Berlin.

For the Bolshevik-turned-bureaucrat the prospect of a liberated humanity once again seemed far more distant and unreal than the enforcement of production targets and the placating of careerists; for the Russian workers, revolution was once again a distant mirage, obscured by the present reality of shortages, low wages and an increasingly authoritarian regime.

The destructive effect inside Russia fed straight back into the revolutionary movement inside Germany. The new bureaucrats in Moscow were accustomed to instant obedience to their commands: they imposed the same obedience on their followers abroad. The effects of policies pursued in particular countries came to matter less than who dictated those policies.

The very terminology of politics became corrupted. Serge tells how:

> The parties were changing their faces and even their language: a conventional jargon was settling upon our publications—we called it 'Agitprop Pidgin'. Everything was now only a matter of '100 percent approval of the correct line of the Executive' or of 'Bolshevik monolithism'.[4]

Rational discussion concerning what to do became replaced by a series of arbitrarily connected code words designed to justify decisions after the event.

The German Communist Party made numerous profound mistakes in the first five years of its existence. But at least, if we read the records of the congresses and debates of those years, we feel in the presence of human beings attempting, however blunderingly, to change history. By contrast, in the congresses and debates from 1924 onwards, what we find are backstage manoeuvres sanctified with the out of context quote and the invented 'fact'.

By the time the third great crisis hit Germany in 1929-33 the Communist Party was no longer a *positive* factor, pointing a way forward as it had in 1918-20 and 1923. Bureaucratic idiocy had transformed it into a negative factor in history. Certainly it was capable of attracting millions of votes from workers, especially unemployed workers, who saw no future in social democracy. But it could not translate that into a challenge to the hold of the Social Democrats over the organised labour movement, because of an insane, Moscow-ordained ultra-leftism that made the ultra-leftism of 1919-21 pale into insignificance. Moscow had decreed that social democracy was the same as fascism and the German Communist leaders then ignored the threat of real fascism. The KPD's own membership remained at only half the 1923 figure. Despite its five million votes, it positioned itself on the sidelines of history, refusing to challenge the Social Democrat leaders to put the words with which they beguiled their supporters to the test of a united front. While the Nazis made their way towards power, the KPD continued to talk gibberish about the danger of 'social fascism' and to lull workers to sleep with the slogan, 'After Hitler, us'.

The degeneration had come full circle. The whole world has had to pay the price.

1.   Quoted in C L R James, *World Revolution* (London 1937) p381.
2.   Braunthal, *The History of the International* vol 2, p385.
3.   Ibid, p386.
4.   Victor Serge, *Memoirs of a Revolutionary* (London 1963) p191.

Glossary

This glossary is presented in four sections: people, political organisations, key dates and events, and geographical terms. Readers should refer to the index to find where each of these is to be found in the main text.

People

BARTH, Emil (1879-1941): Social Democrat metal worker; joined USP 1917; replaced Richard Müller as leader of revolutionary shop stewards after Müller was conscripted in January 1918; member of Executive of Berlin Workers' and Soldiers' Councils and member of Council of People's Commissars November-December 1919; member of USP until it re-merged with SPD in 1922, then of SPD.

BERNSTEIN, Eduard (1850-1932): Member of SPD from 1880s; exiled in London during anti-socialist laws of 1880s, friend of Engels; developed ideas of 'revisionism' at turn of century; against war in 1914 but also against revolutionary agitation; joined USP 1917; rejoined SPD 1919.

BRANDLER, Heinrich (1881-1967): Building worker; active trade unionist from 1897; imprisoned for 'violence' in 1900; joined SPD 1901; secretary of builders' union in Chemnitz from 1914; expelled from SPD in 1915 for opposing war; activist in Spartakus League; deported from country as Austrian citizen in 1919 but returned to build the most powerful local organisation of the KPD; leader of the Chemnitz workers' council at time of Kapp putsch in 1920; president of KPD in 1921; imprisoned for part in March Action, on release member of praesidium of Communist International in Moscow for six months in 1922; general secretary of KPD 1922-23; member of 'united front' government in Saxony and involved in preparation of abortive insurrection in October 1923 but agreed to call it off, blamed for failure of insurrection; worked in Moscow until 1928, supporting Bukharin against left opposition of Trotsky; returned to Germany and expelled from KPD in 1929; opposed lunacy of Stalin's 'third period' and built KPO (Communist Party Opposition), but still supported Stalin's policies in USSR until trial of Bukharin in 1938; refugee in France after 1933; interned 1939-40; refugee in Cuba 1941-47; returned to Germany to lead small revolutionary group in Bremen until his death.

BRASS, Otto (1875-1960): Metal workers' leader in southern Ruhr; joined SPD then in 1917 USP; charged with high treason after struggle against Kapp putsch; joined KPD end of 1920; defended Levi at 3rd Congress of Comintern August 1921; expelled from KPD January 1922; rejoined USP and then SPD; arrested for underground resistance 1945; joined Socialist Unity Party of East Germany.

BUBER-NEUMANN, M: Young revolutionary of early 1920s who became wife of one of KPD leaders, Heinz Neumann; imprisoned in Russia in late 1930s, handed over to Gestapo after Hitler-Stalin pact; survived to write bitterly anti-Communist memoirs.

CRISPIEN, Artur (1875-1946): Painter-decorator, then Social Democrat journalist; supporter of Rosa Luxemburg's group at beginning of war; moved away from revolutionary left; leader of USP at its foundation; member of Council of People's Commissars November-December 1918; leader of USP right; rejoined SPD 1922; exiled in Switzerland after 1933.

CUNO, Wilhelm: Member of German National People's Party, the right wing party that stood for industrialists' interests; Chancellor during the Ruhr crisis and the inflation of 1923; forced to resign by strikes of August 1923.

DÄUMIG, Ernst (1868-1922); Of bourgeois background; joined SPD and became *Vorwärts* journalist in 1911; opposed war; founder editor of USP paper *Freiheit* 1917-18; co-opted into revolutionary shop stewards; member of Executive of Berlin Workers' and Soldiers' Councils; opposed foundation of KPD; opposed call for uprising in January 1919; leader of left USP and theoretician of the 'system of councils'; delegate to 2nd Congress of Comintern and urged USP to accept '21 conditions'; joint president of unified KPD with Levi; left KPD with Levi after March Action.

DISSMAN, Robert (1878-1926): Metal worker, holding various local union positions before war; oppositionist in SPD from 1911; joined USP; president of metal workers' union October 1919, but opposed merger of USP and KPD; remained in USP until it merged with SPD; organised left in SPD together with Levi in 1923.

DITTMANN, Wilhelm (1874-1954): SPD deputy; opposed to war; founder member of USP; sentenced to four years military imprisonment after strikes of January 1918; People's Commissar November-December 1918; opposed merger of USP with Communists; rejoined SPD in 1922; exiled after 1933.

DORRENBACH, Heinrich (1888-1919): Social Democrat union official before war; junior officer during war; injured and demobbed 1917; took command of People's Division of Marines December 1918; supported rising of January 1919 and was disavowed by the Marines; fled Berlin but was caught and murdered by Freikorps.

EBERLEIN, Hugo (1887-1944): Draughtsman, joined SPD 1906; revolutionary opponent of war in 1914; USP 1917; member of Centre of KPD at its foundation; delegate under name Max Albrecht to 1st Congress of Comintern, where he opposed foundation of International as premature; played key role in organising 'provocations' during March Action; exiled in Moscow after revelation of these; supporter of Brandler until 1924; deputy in Prussian parliament 1921-33; exiled in France, then USSR after 1933; arrested by GPU 1937; on list of German prisoners to be given to Hitler by Stalin in 1940, but died in Russian prison.

EBERT, Friedrich (1871-1925): Secretary of SPD from 1906; chairman of Council of People's Commissars in November-December 1918; collaborator with generals in organising anti-revolutionary forces in 1918-19; president of German Republic 1919-25.

EICHHORN, Emil (1863-1925): Glass worker, full-timer for SPD from 1893; joined USP 1917; took control of police HQ in Berlin, 9 November 1918; removed by Social Democrat government 5 January 1919; fled after suppression of rising; USP deputy in new Reichstag; joined KPD 1920; left with Levi 1921 but rejoined later.

EISNER, Kurt (1887-1919): Staff member *Vorwärts* 1898; removed as revisionist in 1903; at first supported war, then opposed it as pacifist; joined USP in 1917; organised network of militants in Munich; imprisoned January 1918; leader of Bavarian revolution November 1918 and prime minister of Bavaria; assassinated 21 February 1919.

FISCHER, Ruth (1895-1961): Joined Austrian Social Democrats as student 1914; first member of Austrian Communist Party on 3 November 1918; criticised as 'rightist' by other Austrian leaders in May 1919 and moved to Berlin; joint leader ultra-left opposition to German party leadership based in Berlin; made with Maslow head of KPD by Zinoviev in 1924-25; expelled from party August 1926; formed opposition group, the Leninbund; exiled after 1933 in France, Spain, Cuba and US; became vehement anti-Communist and wrote unreliable book *Stalin and German Communism*.

FRIESLAND (Reuter), Ernst (1889-1953): Teacher sacked for activities in SPD; active in pacifist league in 1914; prisoner of war in Russia, 1916, becoming KPD member and commissar in 1917; returned to Germany clandestinely December 1918; a leader of left in KPD 1920-21; moved to Lenin's position at 3rd Congress of Comintern in August 1921 and became party general secretary; formed new right opposition, expelled January 1922; rejoined SPD same year; exiled in Turkey and Scandinavia during Nazi years; after war SPD mayor of Berlin.

FRÖLICH, Paul (1894-1953): Self taught clerk then SPD journalist; on extreme left of SPD even before war; founder of 'Left Radical' anti-war paper *Arbeiterpolitik* in 1916; delegate to international anti-war conference at Kienthal, where he supported Lenin's position; delegate of International Communists to foundation congress of KPD; elected to KPD Centre; active in Bavarian revolution; supporter of 'theory of offensive' in 1920-21; deputy after 1921; expelled from KPD as 'rightist' 1928; member of Brandler's Communist Party Opposition (KPO), and then of centrist SAP; arrested 1933, freed after nine months in concentration camp; exiled in Czechoslovakia, Belgium, France and USA; returned to West Germany and joined SPD 1950. Author of biography of Rosa Luxemburg.

GORTER, Hermann (1864-1927): Dutch teacher and poet; member of Dutch socialist party from 1896; expelled from party in 1909 and helped found left socialist party; revolutionary opponent of war, helped found Dutch Communist Party in 1918; in Germany

1918-20 as leader of ultra left; helped found KAPD in 1920; criticised March Action in April 1921.

HAASE, Hugo (1863-1919): Social Democrat deputy from 1897, president of the party from 1911, head of Reichstag fraction 1912; opposed voting for war credits in 1914, but did so under discipline of parliamentary fraction; joined USP in 1917; member of Council of People's Commissars in November-December 1918; assassinated by nationalist on Reichstag steps in 1919.

HILFERDING, Rudolf (1877-1944): Marxist economist, wrote *Finance Capital* in 1910; leader of USP from 1917 and of USP right in 1918; rejoined SPD in 1922; minister of finance in Stresemann government of August 1923; minister again in Müller government of 1928-30; seized by Gestapo as he tried to escape from occupied France in 1940.

HOELZ, Max (1889-1933): Metal worker; joined USP 1918; organised unemployed in Vogtland in 1919 into guerrilla actions; joined KPD in 1919 and organised armed struggle against Kapp putsch; close to KAPD while on run; organised fighting in central Germany during March Action; sentenced to life imprisonment; released in 1928 and emigrated to Moscow; died in accident.

HOFFMANN, Johannes: Social Democratic premier of Bavaria 1919-20.

JOGICHES, Leo (1867-1919): Born in Lithuania, active in underground revolutionary movement from early age; met Rosa Luxemburg in exile in 1890, was her lover until 1906 and her close comrade for the rest of her life; founded Polish Social Democratic Party with her; active in 1905 revolution in Poland, arrested but escaped to Germany; organiser of Spartakus League during war; opposed foundation of KPD as premature, but joined it anyway; opposed uprising in January 1919; murdered by Freikorps in March 1919.

KAHR, von (1862-1934): Leader of separatist, right wing Bavarian People's Party; premier of Bavaria during Kapp putsch until September 1921; appointed special commissioner with dictatorial powers by Bavarian government October 1923; agreed to Hitler's putsch in Munich November 1923, but then changed sides after a couple of hours; among victims of Hitler's 'night of the long knives' of 1934.

KAUTSKY, Karl (1854-1940): Austrian by birth, active in SPD from period of antisocialist law (1880-90); friend and disciple of Engels; editor of SPD theoretical magazine *Die Neue Zeit*; known as 'Pope of Marxism'; seen as defender of Marxist orthodoxy before 1914; privately opposed to war in 1914, but against public agitation; joined USP in 1917; opposed attempts to carry through socialist revolution in Germany; rejoined SPD 1922.

KNIEF, Johann (1880-1919): SPD journalist in Bremen from 1905; leader of anti-war opposition in 1914; founded weekly revolutionary paper of 'Left Radicals', *Arbeiterpolitik*; opposed adhesion of Luxemburg and Liebknecht to USP; in exile in Holland 1917-18; opposed merger of Left Radicals and Spartakists to form KPD; seriously ill from beginning of 1919 and died in April of that year.

KUN, Bela (1886-1939): Hungarian white collar worker, Social Democrat from 1902, journalist and full-timer; prisoner of war in Russia, joined Bolsheviks and founded Hungarian Communist Party in 1918; led Hungarian Soviet Republic in first months of 1919; exiled in Russia, commissar with Red Army; supported ultra-left current around magazine *Kommunismus* 1920-21; sent by secretariat of Communist International to Germany early 1921, inspiring March Action; functionary of Comintern until 1937; arrested in Russia and executed without trial.

LAUFENBERG, Heinrich (1872-1932): Academic; originally in Catholic Centre Party; joined SPD and became journalist 1902; opposed war 1914; president of Hamburg workers' and soldiers' councils 1918-19; joined KPD December 1918; supporter of breakaway unions, expelled from KPD 1919; joined KAPD, and expelled from KAPD in 1920 for 'national Bolshevism'.

LEDEBOUR, Georg (1850-1947): Teacher, doctor then journalist; SPD deputy; against war but hostile to Bolsheviks and Spartakists; member of USP from 1917 and adviser to revolutionary shop stewards in Berlin; called with Liebknecht for uprising in January 1919 and tried for high treason; broke with left USP on question of affiliation to Communist International; remained in USP and then rejoined SPD in 1922; in exile after 1933.

LEGIEN, Carl (1861-1920): Head of Social Democrat union federation, the ADGB; supporter of war; worked against revolutionary left in 1918-19; called for general strike in face of Kapp putsch 1920.

LEVI, Paul (1883-1930): Banker's son; lawyer; member of SPD from 1906; revolutionary opponent of war from 1914, in contact with Bolsheviks in Switzerland; leader of Spartakists and KPD in 1918-19; close to Rosa Luxemburg in opposing January rising; leader of KPD after Luxemburg's death, taking initiative in fight against ultra-left at Heidelberg congress of 1919; president of United Communist Party in December 1920; resigned February 1921; denounced March Action in public in April 1921 and expelled from party; joined USP 1922 and then SPD; organiser of left opposition inside SPD in 1923; committed suicide 1930.

LEVIEN, Max (1885-1937): Russian Jew; Social Revolutionary during 1905 revolution; then emigrated to Switzerland and Germany; in German army 1914-18; Spartakist leader in Munich 1918-19 and president of soldiers' council; a leader of the Council Republic; fled to Austria and USSR; executed during Stalin's purges of 1930s.

LEVINÉ, Eugen (1883-1919): Russian Jew, educated in Germany; took part in 1905 revolution as member of Social Revolutionary Party; arrested, then studied in Germany again and joined SPD; joined USP then Spartakus League during war; sent to reorganise KPD in Bavaria spring 1919; leader of the Second Bavarian Council Republic; executed by Social Democratic government. Useful biography in English by his wife, Rosa Leviné-Meyer.

LIEBKNECHT, Karl (1871-1919): Son of SPD's founder, Wilhelm Liebknecht; member of party from 1900; Berlin lawyer; leader of party youth, imprisoned for anti-militarist agitation; Reichstag deputy from 1912, voted against war in October 1914; conscripted, but organised anti-war demonstration 1 May 1916; imprisoned, amnestied October 1918, took part in preparation of November Revolution; leader of Spartakists and of KPD; murdered January 1919.

LUDENDORFF, General Erich: Leader with Hindenberg of German General Staff during World War One; collaborated with Hitler in Bavaria in 1923.

LÜTTWITZ, General von (1859-1942): Monarchist general; appointed commander of military forces in Berlin January 1919 by Social Democrats; responsible for repression in Berlin March 1919; drew up plans for crushing of Bavarian Soviet Republic, April 1919; military leader of Kapp putsch March 1920.

LUXEMBURG, Rosa (1871-1919): Polish Jew; at age of 16 became revolutionary; exiled from Poland in 1889; leader of the Social Democratic Party of the kingdom of Poland and Lithuania; active in German SPD opposing first revisionism and then Kautskyism; leading revolutionary opponent of war; founder revolutionary magazine *Internationale* and Spartakus League; imprisoned for most of war; founder and leader KPD; opposed call for January rising but participated in it; murdered by Freikorps January 1919. Author of *Reform or Revolution, Mass Strike, Junius pamphlet,* and *Accumulation of Capital.* Best biography by Paul Frölich.

MASLOW, Arkadi (1893-1941): Born in Russia, but lived in Germany from 1899; won to Communism by Paul Levi and Ruth Fischer; led ultra-left in KPD, with Fischer, from 1921 onwards; made leader of KPD with Fischer by Zinoviev in 1924; imprisoned in Germany 1925-26; moved away from ultra-leftism and expelled from party in August 1926; cofounder with Fischer of Leninbund; in exile after 1933; died in car accident in Cuba in 1941.

MEHRING, Franz (1846-1919): Liberal journalist who did not join SPD until aged 40; writer of several Marxist books on history and literature and biography of Karl Marx; broke with Kautsky at same time as Rosa Luxemburg; opposed war in 1914 and founder Spartakus League; shattered by murder of Luxemburg, he died a few months afterwards.

MEYER, Ernst (1887-1930): University educated son of locomotive engineer; strongly religious at first, but won to Marxism; joined SPD in 1907; journalist on *Vorwärts* 1913; friend of Rosa Luxemburg and opponent of war in 1914; key activist for Spartakists during war; elected member of KPD Centre at party's founding congress; editor of *Rote Fahne* 1919-20; secretary of politburo and party president 1921-22; not re-elected to Centre 1923; opposed ultra-left line of Comintern 1929. Useful memoir by his wife, Rosa Leviné-Meyer, *Inside German Communism.*

MÜLLER, General Alfred: Led troops who overthrew left wing governments of Saxony and Thuringia in 1923.

MÜLLER, Hermann: Right wing Social Democrat; editor of *Vorwärts* after purge of left in October 1916; Chancellor after defeat of Kapp putsch until elections of 1920; premier in 1928.

MÜLLER, Richard (1890-?): Engineering worker in Berlin, a leader of the metal workers' opposition to the war; an organiser of revolutionary shop stewards; led strikes of June 1916, April 1917 and January 1918; conscripted, but returned to Berlin November 1918; president of Executive of Berlin Workers' and Soldiers' Councils; opposed call for rising in January 1919; led March 1919 strike in Berlin; leader of left opposition in USP and metal workers' union; joined KPD with merger at end of 1920; left with Paul Levi after March Action of 1921; abandoned all political activity.

NOSKE, Gustav (1868-1946): Right wing Social Democrat; minister of war in Social Democrat governments of December 1918-March 1920; lived in Germany under Nazis, being arrested twice in 1944-45.

PANNEKOEK, Anton (1873-1960): Leading astronomer in Holland; joined Dutch Socialist Party in 1902, formed left-wing in party in 1905 around paper *Tribune*; expelled 1909 and formed left socialist party; spent a number of years in Bremen; polemicised against Kautsky before war; returned to Holland 1914, member of 'Zimmerwald Left' (with Bolsheviks); co-founder of Dutch Communist Party in 1918; theorist of ultra-leftism in Germany; inspired KAPD in 1920; after collapse of KAPD continued to inspire small groups of 'council communists'.

RADEK, Karl (1885-1940?): Born in Austrian-occupied Poland; active in underground revolutionary movement in Poland from age of 18; played important role in revolution of 1905 in Warsaw; arrested and escaped to Germany; active in Leipzig and Bremen; in Switzerland during World War One; supported Lenin and 'Zimmerwald Left', collaborated with Bremen 'Left Radicals' around *Arbeiterpolitik*; active in Sweden for Bolsheviks 1917-18; vice-commissar for foreign affairs in Russia October 1918; clandestine mission to Germany in December 1918; imprisoned in 1919; returned to Russia as secretary of executive of Communist International; supported March Action; supported calling off of October 1923 insurrection; supported Trotsky's opposition in Russia 1924-29; expelled from CPSU and deported to Siberia 1927-29; capitulated to Stalin in 1929; apologist for Stalin until condemned at Moscow trials in 1937; died in Russian concentration camp around 1940.

RAKOSI, Matyas (1892-1971): Hungarian, student in Budapest, Germany and Britain; prisoner of First World War in Russia; returned to Hungary early 1918; people's commissar in Hungarian Soviet Republic of 1919; exiled in Russia, working for Comintern; intervention in KPD caused resignation of Paul Levi from leadership early in 1921; arrested and imprisoned in Hungary 1925-40; exiled in Russia 1940-45; secretary of Hungarian Communist Party 1944-56, effective ruler of country; resigned July 1956; resided in USSR after revolution of 1956.

RÜHLE, Otto (1874-1943): Psychology professor; SPD journalist from 1902; Reichstag deputy from 1912; joined Liebknecht in parliamentary opposition to war 1915; joined Spartakists but then left and joined Bremen Left Radicals because of opposition to staying inside SPD and USP; supporter of breakaway unions in 1919 and member of KAPD from its foundation; KAPD delegate to 2nd Comintern Congress in 1920, opposed '21 conditions' and refused to take part in Congress; expelled from KAPD November 1920 as anarchist; returned to SPD after 1923; exiled after 1933 to Mexico; helped organise Dewey Commission inquiry into Moscow trials.

SCHEIDEMANN, Philipp (1865-1937): Leading right wing Social Democrat; proclaimed republic in November 1918; in exile after 1933.

SEECKT, Hans von: Head of German armed forces 1919-26.

STINNES, Hugo: Leader of one of the great trusts that dominated the German economy; known as 'the king of the Ruhr'; accumulated huge fortune through war and inflation; financed German National People's Party of Cuno and Stresemann; went broke after end of inflation in 1924.

THÄLMANN, Ernst (1886-1944): Docker, joined SPD in 1903; leader of USP left in Hamburg 1918-20; joined united KPD end of 1920; mobilised unemployed to enforce strike during March Action of 1921; defended 'theory of offensive' against Lenin and Trotsky at 3rd Congress of Comintern; important role in Hamburg rising of October 1923; leader of party after removal of Fischer and Maslow in 1925 with Stalin's support; arrested March 1933; executed by the Nazis in August 1944 at Buchenwald.

THALHEIMER, August (1884-1948): Joined SPD 1904; party journalist from 1909; close to Radek, Rosa Luxemburg and Mehring; member of Spartakists during war; for a few days a minister in the state government in Stuttgart during revolution of 1918; fought ultra-left in 1919-20, but helped develop 'theory of the offensive' in 1921; skeptical on chances of revolution in 1923; blamed for its defeat with Brandler; in Moscow 1924-28; expelled from KDP 1929; founded Communist Party Opposition (KPO) with Brandler; exiled in France after 1933; interned 1939; exiled in Cuba from 1941.

TOLLER, Emst (1893-1939): Russian Jew; pacifist; president of Munich USP; commander of Bavarian Red Army in 1919 and leading figure in First Bavarian Council Republic; opposed Second Council Republic but stayed in Red Army; sentenced to five years in jail after its defeat; leading expressionist playwright.

WELS, Otto (1879-1939): Right wing Social Democrat; military commander of Berlin, responsible for crushing left in January-March 1919; led opposition to Hitler in Reichstag in 1933, but called for 'lawful non-violent opposition'; exiled in Paris from 1933.

ZEIGNER, Erich (1886-1961): Lawyer; joined SPD in 1919; leader of the left in Saxony where he was minister of justice in 1921; premier of Saxony in April 1923; took Communist ministers into his government October 1923; deposed by Reichswehr and imprisoned; resumed career as magistrate; purged from job in 1933; mayor of Leipzig in 1946; joined Socialist Unity Party of East Germany.

ZETKIN, Clara (1857-1933): Became Marxist at 21; in exile 1880-90; led Social Democratic women's movement before World War One; opposed war from revolutionary standpoint along with her friend Rosa Luxemburg in 1914; member of USP 1917-19; joined KPD some months after its foundation; sided with Paul Levi in arguments over Kapp putsch, but remained in party after discussions with Lenin; denounced Hitler at first meetings of Nazi-dominated Reichstag in August 1932.

Political organisations

GERMAN NATIONAL PEOPLE'S PARTY: Right wing party of big business interests, known before 1918 as National Liberal Party.

CENTRE PARTY: Catholic party of a Christian Democrat sort, strong in southern Germany.

DEMOCRATIC PARTY: Bourgeois liberal party, but a minority within the bourgeoisie.

SPD (Social Democratic Party of Germany): Often referred to as Social Democrats and after 1917 as Majority Social Democrats; only workers' party before 1917; in words Marxist, but before war increasingly reformist in practice; crushed revolutionary movements of 1919-20.

USP (Independent Social Democrats or often just Independents): Minority split from Social Democrats in 1917; opposed war but faced both ways over question of revolution; grew rapidly until nearly a million members in mid-1920; split after Halle conference in October 1920, with majority joining with Spartakists to form United Communist Party of Germany (VKPD); minority kept party alive until 1922 when it merged back into SPD.

SPARTAKUS LEAGUE: Organisation formed by Luxemburg, Zetkin, Mehring, Jogiches and others out of anti-war socialists around magazine *Internationale*; worked inside Social Democrats then inside Independent Social Democratic Party until December 1918 when it became Communist Party of Germany (Spartakist).

KPD (Communist Party of Germany): Formed December 1918 by merger of Spartakus League and smaller group of International Communists (also called Left Radicals) in December 1918; merged with left of Independent Social Democratic Party in December 1920 to form much larger United Communist Party (VKPD).

LEFT RADICALS: Revolutionary group based in Bremen which would not join Independent Social Democrat Party in 1917 and so operated separately from Spartakus League; merged with it to found Communist Party (KPD) in December 1918; at various times Left Radicals were called International Socialists of Germany, then International Communists of Germany; leaders Knief, Frölich and (indirectly) Radek.

KAPD—party formed in April 1920 by ultra-leftists driven out of KPD in August 1919; split and disappeared within two years; leaders Gorter, Pannekoek, Wolffheim, Laufenberg, Rühle.

VORWÄRTS: paper of Social Democratic Party.

FREIHEIT: paper of Independent Social Democratic Party.

ROTE FAHNE: paper of Spartakus League and then KPD; also name of paper produced by workers' councils in Hamburg at beginning of November 1918.

ADGB—main union federation, linked to Social Democratic Party.

PARTY CENTRE (*Zentrale*): Day-to-day leading body of KPD.

CONTROL COMMITTEES: Workers' committees formed to control food supplies and prices in 1923.

PROLETARIAN HUNDREDS: Organisations of workers' self defence formed in 1923.

PEOPLE'S ARMIES, REPUBLICAN SOLDIERS CORPS, SECURITY DETACHMENTS : Names given to various Social Democrat dominated armed forces in 1918-19.

HOME GUARDS: Military organisations under control of local authorities in 1919-20, usually right wing or Social Democrat controlled, occasionally under left Social Democrat influence.

FREIKORPS: Right wing, mercenary, 'volunteer' forces raised by High Command and central government in 1918-19.

REICHSWEHR: Regular army formed in 1919-20 out of minority of Freikorps.

BLACK REICHSWEHR: Secret detachments trained by Freikorps and financed by industrialists.

ORGESCH: Right wing terror groups operating from Bavaria, trained by Reichswehr and often part of the Black Reichswehr, 1922-23, founded by the Bavarian interior minister Escherich.

Key dates and events

4 AUGUST: Date of declaration of war (and collapse of social democracy) 1914.

9 NOVEMBER: Date of the 'November Revolution' of 1918 in Berlin that overthrew Kaiser.

SPARTAKUS DAYS: January 1919 fighting in Berlin after attempt at uprising supported by Liebknecht but much criticised by other Spartakist leaders.

BAVARIAN SOVIET REPUBLICS: April 1919; First 'Pseudo Council Republic' staged by anarchists, Independents and Social Democrats; Second Council Republic led by Communists.

KAPP PUTSCH: Attempt by right at military coup in March 1920.

SECOND CONGRESS (of Communist International): In fact its first real congress, July 1920.

HALLE CONGRESS (of Independent Social Democrats): Where majority decided to merge with Communist Party, October 1920.

MARCH ACTION: Abortive attempt at revolutionary offensive, March 1921.

THIRD CONGRESS (of Communist International): Congress at which Lenin and Trotsky fought ultra-left, August 1921.

FOURTH CONGRESS (of Communist International): November-December 1920 which confirmed call for united front.

OCCUPATION OF RUHR—by French and Belgian troops, January 1923.

GERMAN OCTOBER: Insurrection called off by KPD at last minute except in Hamburg, October 1923.

Geographical terms

PRUSSIA: Largest kingdom in German Empire and then largest state in republic; accounting for two-thirds of land area and stretching from Belgian border to what became Russian city Kaliningrad.

EAST PRUSSIA: Territory now partly in Russia and partly in Poland, separated from rest of Germany by Polish territory after World War One.

MID-GERMANY or CENTRAL GERMANY: Area southwest of Berlin; made up of state of Saxony, Thuringia (at first a collection of minor states and then a single state) and the Prussian province of Saxony.

RUHR: Industrial area named after River Ruhr on lower part of Rhine; also known as Rhineland-Westphalia.

RHINELAND: Area of Rhine above Cologne; under Versailles Treaty contained no German military presence; permanently occupied by British, French or Belgian troops from 1919 until mid-1920s.

DANZIG: Now Gdańsk.

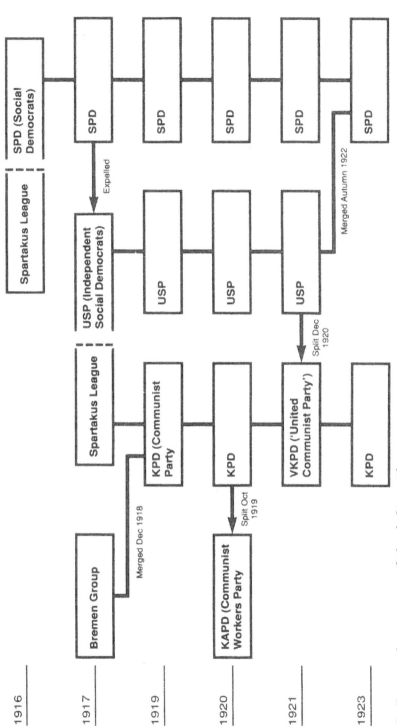

Splits amd mergers of the left parties

Index

About Haymarket Books

Haymarket Books is a radical, independent, nonprofit book publisher based in Chicago.

Our mission is to publish books, particularly new and classical works of Marxism, that contribute to struggles for social and economic justice. We strive to make our books a vibrant and organic part of social movements and the education and development of a critical, engaged, international left.

We take inspiration and courage from our namesakes, the Haymarket martyrs, who gave their lives fighting for a better world. Their 1886 struggle for the eight-hour day—which gave us May Day, the international workers' holiday—reminds workers around the world that ordinary people can organize and struggle for their own liberation. These struggles continue today across the globe—struggles against oppression, exploitation, poverty, and war.

Since our founding in 2001, Haymarket Books has published more than five hundred titles. Radically independent, we seek to drive a wedge into the risk-averse world of corporate book publishing. Our authors include Eqbal Ahmad, Arundhati Roy, Angela Y. Davis, Howard Zinn, Ian Birchall, Ahmed Shawki, Paul Le Blanc, Mike Davis, Kim Scipes, Ilan Pappé, Michael Roberts, Sharon Smith, Dave Zirin, Keeanga-Yamahtta Taylor, Nick Turse, Kim Moody, Danny Katch, Jeffery R. Webber, Paul D'Amato, Amira Hass, Sherry Wolf, Naomi Klein, and Neil Davidson. We are also the trade publishers of the acclaimed Historical Materialism Book Series, and of the Studies in Critical Social Sciences book series, as well as Dispatch Books.

Shop our full catalog online at www.haymarketbooks.org.

CPSIA information can be obtained
at www.ICGtesting.com
Printed in the USA
JSHW051448171122
33170JS00002B/2